Branding New York

This book reveals how, at the height of the 1970s fiscal crisis, a coalition of New York elites came together to brand a new image for their embattled city. By the mid-1960s, lurid media coverage of New York's troubles generated an image crisis that exacerbated economic decline. This inspired public and private sector leaders to abandon old-fashioned city boosterism and turn to the coordinated, professional, and global strategy of urban branding. From the radical chic of New York magazine to the populism of "Big Apple," and culminating with the blockbuster "I♥NY" campaign, they created a new business and tourist-friendly image for New York featuring high-end shopping, Broadway theater, and a glittering city skyline. This image challenged longstanding representations of New York as a gritty, diverse, working class city, as well as its emerging reputation as the capital of punk and hip hop. And it helped package a controversial approach to economic recovery involving harsh austerity measures, corporate subsidies, privatization, and a polarized new economy. Ultimately, the branding of New York turned the city into a powerful if contradictory symbol of urban transformation. It ignited grassroots "counter-branding" tactics, from subway graffiti to the union-led "Fear City" campaign. And it convinced tourists, corporations, and conservative politicians, that this once "ungovernable city" was now tamed and ready for consumption.

Miriam Greenberg is an Assistant Professor in Sociology at the University of California Santa Cruz and, in 2008, a visiting scholar at the Center for Urban Research and Policy at Columbia University.

Other titles in the *Cultural Spaces* series,
edited by Sharon Zukin

Branding New York

How a City in Crisis was Sold to the World

by
Miriam Greenberg

Routledge
Taylor & Francis Group

NEW YORK AND LONDON

First published 2008
by Routledge
711 Third Avenue, New York, NY 10017

Simultaneously published in the UK
by Routledge
2 Park Square, Milton Park, Abingdon, Oxon, OX14 4RN

Routledge is an imprint of the Taylor & Francis Group, an informa business

Transferred to Digital Printing 2009

© 2008 Taylor & Francis

Typeset in Minion by Keystroke, 28 High Street, Tettenhall, Wolverhampton

Library of Congress Cataloging in Publication Data
A catalog record has been requested for this book

ISBN10: 0–415–95441–X (hbk)
ISBN10: 0–415–95442–8 (pbk)
ISBN10: 0–203–93197–1 (ebk)

ISBN13: 978–0–415–95441–9 (hbk)
ISBN13: 978–0–415–95442–6 (pbk)
ISBN13: 978–0–203–93197–4 (ebk)

For
Suzanne and Peter Greenberg,
Nathaniel and Simona,
with all my love and gratitude.

All this is so vast, so impressive that a man cannot collect himself, but is lost in the marvel . . . The sacrifices which all this has cost become apparent later.

Frederic Engels, "The Great Towns," 1844

I was asking for something specific and perfect for my city,
Whereupon lo! upsprang the aboriginal name.

Now I see what there is in a name, a word, liquid, sane,
    unruly, musical, self-sufficient,
I see that the word of my city is that word from of old,
Because I see that word nested in nests of water-bays,
    Superb . . .

Walt Whitman, "Mannahatta," 1888

Contents

Illustrations

Acknowledgments

This book is a social product through and through and would have been inconceivable without the support and camaraderie of so many. While any errors are of course my own, any achievements are largely thanks to the people who have helped me along the way, over the many years of this project's gestation.

In somewhat chronological order, Elaine Abelson, Christopher Mele, and Andy Van Kleuenen introduced me to urban studies as a transplanted Californian undergraduate during tumultuous times in New York City. Following this, my colleagues and students at El Puente Academy and EPTV in Williamsburg, Brooklyn, opened my eyes to the gulf and link between dominant media representations and the lived reality in local communities. These include Hector Calderon, Zaire Estrella, Maribel Lizardo, Frances Lucerna, Joe Matunis, Monica Rivera, and many more.

I am forever indebted to the Sociology Department at the City University of New York Graduate Center for the opportunity to study and work with such amazing scholars across a range of disciplines, and so to conceive of this project. In particular, thanks to Stuart Ewen, Juan Flores, Philip Kasinitz, and Richard Maxwell for helping me make links between media, culture, and urban studies. Neil Smith and David Harvey offered many catalyzing ideas, and the fellowship at the Center for Place, Culture, and Politics enabled me to workshop early elements of the project. My deepest thanks goes to Sharon Zukin, for her creative and intellectual inspiration, sage advice, and constant encouragement in reading multiple drafts of this book.

Many people offered crucial advice along the way. I am grateful to Dennis Judd and Thomas Bender for reading an early draft of the text and giving me such insightful feedback, and to Ann Markusen for generously reading and responding to a number of chapters. I was very fortunate to work with two great editors at Routledge—Dave McBride and Steven Rutter—who patiently and expertly coached me through the editing process. Also terrific were editorial assistants Anne Horowitz and Beatrice Schraa, copy-editors Philip Parr and Belinda Wakefield and Project Managers Maggie Lindsey-Jones and Emma Wood. Thanks to Stephen Duncombe for help with statistics on New York culture industries; Alain Mariduena and Jessica Green for insights into and contacts within the New York City graffiti world; Jim O'Grady and Jonathan Bowles for their perspective on economic development policy in the 1980s; Penny Lewis, Steve Jenkins, and Joshua Freeman for sharing thoughts on New York's post-fiscal crisis environment for labor; Elsa Davidson for sensitizing me to the cultural ramifications of neoliberalism; and Suzanne Wasserman and Mike Wallace for organizing two great panels on the 1970s at the Gotham Center. I also benefited from conversations with colleagues at numerous conferences, in particular Julian Brash, Kevin Fox Gotham, Michael Spears, and Sudhir Venkatesh. Finally, many thanks to those who provided interviews, including: Clay Felker, Milton Glaser, Mary Holloway, Lady Pink, Franz Leichter, and William Stern.

Many dear friends played an integral role in my envisioning, thinking through, and completing this book. In addition to some mentioned above, I'd like to thank Stacey Abramson, Ali Bahrampour, Melissa Coss, Kristin Lawler, Jack Levinson, Stephen Lovekin, Christian Parenti, Tisha Pryor, Heather Rogers, Paula Rojas, Eric Tang, Lisa Tharpe, and the neighbors on Fillmore Place: Pam Allred, Williams Cole, Jaquie Lugo, and Meghan McDermott. I was able to strike a balance between writing and family thanks to the teachers, babysitters, and friends who helped take care of my daughter: Claudia Sermeno, Bow Sterger, Rhadika Tamang, and Leah Tedrick Moutz.

The project took shape while creating and teaching in the Critical and Visual Studies Program at Pratt Institute, and many ideas were shaped by this collective work. I wish to thank former Chair Randy Martin and current Chair Sameetah Agha, Dean Toni Oliviero, and colleagues Lisabeth During, Ann Holder, May Joseph, Amy Lesen, Paul Narkunas, and Suzanne Verderber. Janelle Farris, Brad Lander, Uzma Rizvi, Laura Wolf Powers, and Ayse Yonder helped me grasp the contemporary relevance of the work during my fellowship with the Pratt Center for Community Development. Thanks to my Pratt art, architecture and design students and colleagues who taught me so much about branding and its impact on their fields, and especially to Communications Design professors David Frisco and Michael

Kelly for their inspired design for the cover of this book. Thanks also to the Provost's Office for a faculty research grant, and to the Pratt Union for supporting faculty in myriad ways.

I was fortunate to be able to complete this book about New York City from the peaceful, invigorating remove of the Santa Cruz Mountains. And for this I wish to thank the Sociology Department at the University of California Santa Cruz for their warm welcome and intellectual community. Thanks especially to the fantastic Chair Herman Gray, as well as to those colleagues with whom I discussed the project: Ben Crow, Melanie Dupuis, William Domhoff, Wally Goldfrank, Marcia Millman, Craig Reineraman, Jenny Reardan, Gabriela Sandoval, Andrew Szasz, and Dana Takagi. I also benefited from the administrative support of Barbara Laurence and Marilyn Chapin, the research assistance of Rachel Brand, housing assistance of Diane Feldman, and the graphics expertise of Helen Cole.

I am indebted to numerous librarians and archivists who provided me access to reports and images, many of which are not typically used for academic research. These include: Barbara Beverly at the Empire State Development Corporation Archives; Rick Machung and Rose DeSorbo of ESDC's Photo Unit; Tobi Adler at the New York City Municipal Archives; Lynn Eaton at the Duke University Advertising and Marketing Archives; Mary Burke at *New York* magazine; John Lynch at the Vanderbilt Television News Archives; and Saundra Roberts at the Association for a Better New York. Many thanks to James D. Folts and the staff at the New York State Archives for a Hackman Residency that enabled me to complete much of this research. I'd also like to express my appreciation to Robert J. Freeman at the New York State Committee for Open Government for advice on using the Freedom of Information Act to access and reproduce documents produced by tax-funded public–private partnerships.

And most of all, I am grateful to my family, who sustained me before and throughout the writing of this book. Without the support, encouragement, and example of my parents, Suzanne and Peter Greenberg, I could never have even imagined myself as a scholar or writer, let alone attempted this project. I've been motivated by my indomitable grandmother Dorothy Greenberg, my siblings Sarah and Daniel Greenberg, my mother-in-law Susanna Deutsch, and my many wonderful cousins, aunts, uncles, nieces, nephews, and in-laws. I have written these pages with the beloved memory of my grandfathers Solomon Greenberg and Charlie Kirsch, grandmother Mina Kirsch, and father-in-law Henri Zvi Deutsch never far from mind.

Finally, I thank Nathaniel for his unwavering love, brilliance, humor, and childcare, and for simply never letting me give up. And to little Simona, who had no choice but to grow up with this project, it is my greatest joy that now we will have more time to explore the world together.

New York City, Capital of the 1970s

From the Standpoint
of the Out-of-Towner

In March 1971, a series of mysterious announcements began to appear in newspapers throughout the Northeastern United States. The first pictured the Statue of Liberty with a tear running down her cheek under the headline "Announcing the Beginning of the End of New York City." The next week, the same image appeared, now with the headline "On May 24, 1971, New York City Will Disappear." And, as an article in the *Daily News* revealed, come May 24 the third and final installment was to be published with the headline "Today, New York City Disappears" above an image of Miss Liberty sinking into the ocean, with "the water up to her eyeballs like something out of 'Planet of the Apes.'"[1]

As it turned out, these alarming images were nothing more than "teaser ads" for Alitalia's new non-stop service from Rome to cities like Washington, DC, and Boston. For the first time, they announced, Alitalia customers could now travel to the United States without going through New York City. According to Alitalia and the campaign's creator, Gardner Advertising, the intent was simply to run "amusing" and attention-grabbing ads. But this was not the view of New York's economic and political leaders, who launched an all-out effort to halt the campaign, and to deny publicly that "New York has sunk or is sinking or will sink into the sea."[2] First, the New York City Convention and Visitors Bureau (CVB), the city's official booster agency, sent an irate letter to the airline:

Figure P.1 Alitalia advertisement, 1971.

Courtesy Alitalia

We at the Convention and Visitors Bureau—and all businessmen who are diligently working for a better New York City—are appalled by the insulting Alitalia advertisement that has appeared in the Washington, Detroit, Philadelphia and Boston newspapers. Editors from these papers have called us to ask what the ads mean, and we are at a loss to say. What purpose can be served by the commercial exploitation of a city whose problems are certainly not going to be helped by exacerbating defeatist attitudes. And where is the rationale in tastelessly subjecting a national monument to the indignities of this advertising campaign?[3]

When this received a "flippant" response from Alitalia's CEO—who asked "how a tear on a lady of compassion" was disrespectful, and further claimed that the company was "merely seeking to relieve congestion" at John F. Kennedy Airport—the CVB ramped up its lobbying. It organized a group of prominent Italian Americans to write letters of protest, and then, with the aid of Mayor John V. Lindsay's office, got Deputy Mayor Richard Aurelio, the city's highest-ranking Italian American politician, to write his own letter appealing to the airline's sense of "ethnic" solidarity with New York City.[4]

Nevertheless, by the time these letters had been sent, the "damage" had already been done. So many readers called the *Washington Evening Star* with questions and concerns that New York City really was going to disappear that they made a news story out of it: "Some of [the reaction] was pretty far out," the paper noted, with numerous readers wondering: "Is New York going to fall into the sea like San Francisco is supposed to do?"[5] As the *Daily News* noted, the ads reflected and reinforced a prevalent fear among Americans at this time: that New York City had "deteriorated" to such a point that something terrible would happen if one were so much as to set foot there, "even if it's only long enough to change planes."[6] Alitalia, meanwhile, found a means of exploiting this popular sentiment, advising their travel agents: "So if you don't want them to see New York, tell them to see Alitalia."[7]

This anecdote about the remarkable fallout from an irreverent advertising campaign depicting a drowning Statue of Liberty is evocative of the cultural climate of New York City in the 1970s that this book will explore. That these over-the-top ads were at once so strangely believable and politically volatile reveals both the deep anxiety about New York City that they tapped into and the wider, inter-textual universe in which they emerged. They invoked the trepidation, even dread, with which the "average tourist" now boarded their New York City-bound planes, buses, and trains. And they were only the latest addition to a vivid and disturbing set of images portraying New York City as a sinking, dying metropolis, imagery that was seen repeatedly in magazines, newspapers, movies, and the TV news, and which—in combination with real events on the ground—was to help shape the public perception of the city for a generation.

Initially, as captured to comic effect in Neil Simon's 1970 hit movie *The Out of Towners*, this tableau contained the mountains of refuse left to rot during week-long garbage strikes, subways spray-painted by brazen bands of teenagers, and crafty muggers staking out airports, train stations, and hotels. By 1975, the picture had grown far more dire. After New York City suffered the largest public sector default of any municipality in US history, the visitor's mental map would have expanded to include images of catastrophic fiscal crisis—from Mayor Abe Beame going hat in hand to Washington, to Sunbelt senators cheering President Gerald Ford when he flatly refused to "bail out" the city, to the city's own policemen protesting lay-offs by handing out skull-emblazoned "Fear City" pamphlets warning tourists *"Stay away if you possibly can."* By the end of the decade, the tourist's mind would be filled with nightmarish scenes of the fateful summer of 1977, when the serial killer "Son of Sam" terrorized the populace, a city-wide blackout led to widespread looting, and a rash of fires in the South Bronx inspired the sports commentator Howard Cosell famously to exclaim during a live World Series broadcast from Yankee Stadium: "Ladies and Gentlemen, the Bronx is Burning!" Under such circumstances, it was not surprising that many travelers preferred to change planes in Boston, Philadelphia, Detroit—just about anywhere besides New York City.

As horrific as it was, however, this cultural moment was to prove remarkably brief. Come 1978, an amazing shift began to occur in the dominant representation of New York—one that would render obsolete alarmist Alitalia ads and their ilk, and provide much relief to the beleaguered leaders of the CVB. Incredibly, the mainstream media began to cover New York City's apparent *recovery*, and to do so as dramatically as they had reported the city's recent demise. In a typical article, Richard Dallos, a travel writer for the *Los Angeles Times*, noted his astonishment upon visiting New York in the summer of 1978:

> Don't look now, but that place they call The Big Apple, the one they were writing off a couple of years back, where tourist muggings got to be more prominent than Broadway shows, has staged an amazing comeback. With city fathers still crying for financial aid from Washington and many parts of the place still looking like the aftermath of a bombing raid, it can hardly be said that New York is booming. But from the standpoint of the out-of-towner, New York apparently once again is the place to visit. Getting a hotel room can be even worse than it was back before "Fun City" was renamed

"Fundless City." Broadway, which seemed on its last legs a few years ago, is having its best year ever. And nightlife generally is picking up. Somebody has even coined a new slogan—"I love New York."[8]

Dallos was only one of an increasing number of intrepid journalists covering what became a major story by the late 1970s: New York City's "amazing comeback." Instead of filth, reporters found beautifully renovated hotels; instead of poverty, they admired the spectacular views from the new five-star restaurant atop the North Tower of the World Trade Center; and, instead of a war zone, they strolled well-policed, camera-lined corridors from taxi-stands at Grand Central Terminal to the theater district in Times Square, where some truly fantastic new musicals were being staged.

As these reporters also knew, if only from reading the front pages of their own newspapers, "it can hardly be said that New York is booming." It was common knowledge that the city's unemployment rate was still among the highest in the US, that its schools and hospitals were crippled by budget cuts and lay-offs, and that entire sections of the South Bronx, their fire stations shuttered, looked like "the aftermath of a bombing raid." And it was beginning to be noticed that the city's poverty rate was surpassing that of the nation for the first time in the century—with *one in four* New Yorkers living under the federally mandated poverty level by 1982. Nonetheless, "from the standpoint of the out-of-towner," especially one safely ensconced in a Midtown hotel, New York appeared to be on the rebound. The city had become once again "the place to visit"—whether or not it was still a viable place to live and work for many of its own citizens. All the major hotels, theaters, and nightclubs were booked, even while large swaths of the city were falling under the wrecking ball. Perhaps most striking was the launch in 1977—at the height of fiscal crisis, austerity, and the "Summer of Sam"—of the city's first official marketing campaign: "I Love New York." A new and hegemonic vision of New York was being produced—one that seemed, finally, to eclipse the apocalyptic image of the city sinking into the sea that had emerged over the previous decade. It was a vision so convincing and enticing that it could be embraced by tourists, celebrated by the media, upheld as a symbol for the nation, and used to distract attention from the city's still very real and unabating problems.

From Image Crisis to Fiscal Crisis

Why begin a book about one of New York's most harrowing and trans-formative decades from the "standpoint of the out-of-towner"? Why focus on fears and fantasies fed by the media, rather than the complex lived reality of actual New Yorkers? Indeed, why talk about "average tourists" at all, rather than the era's far more interesting visitors, immigrants, and locals—the renegade painters, poets, punk-rockers, hip hop artists, graffiti writers, disco royalty, *salseros*, and adventure-seeking travelers from Japan, Brazil, and Britain—all of whom saw in 1970s New York City a cultural Mecca founded on transgression and innovation, and elevated neighborhoods like the Lower East Side and the South Bronx to legendary cultural status in this period?[9]

I begin my narrative this way not to deny this rich and complex cultural reality, but to foreground its official denial by reigning political and economic elites in a time of crisis. For, as I will argue in this book, it was in the 1970s that the standpoint of the out-of-towner and the imagination of the average tourist became overwhelming preoccupations for the established and emerging leadership of New York City. As this leadership was well aware, the dominant image of New York coming out of the 1960s was that of an "asphalt jungle" and the "ungovernable city." These stereotypes were freighted with the class and race-based prejudices of a growing right-wing anti-urbanism in the US more broadly. They referred, generally speaking, to a crime-ridden city with a bloated and corrupt public sector, dangerously militant unions and social movements, and an unruly black, Latino, and white ethnic population. And they targeted welfare state policies from the New Deal to the War on Poverty that had turned New York City into a national paradigm of "civic liberalism," earning it a reputation as a pro-labor, anti-business town.[10] Meanwhile, the city's vibrant cultural and political scene—from its long tradition of working-class popular culture, to its central role in the 1960s counter-culture, to its rising underground movements of hip hop, subway graffiti, and punk—were easily subsumed by, if not used to exemplify, these stereotypes. The city's embattled leaders in government, finance, real estate, and tourism many of whom were themselves sympathetic to anti-urban ideology in whole or in part, sought essentially to erase any aspects of local culture that might feed such stereotypes, and to frame the city's "comeback" through a tourist- and business-friendly lens, one that was almost entirely white, Manhattan-centric, and decidedly not working-class.

What was the relevance of such branding, or of representation in general, to the city's dire economic situation? Why open a book about a period of *fiscal crisis* with a discussion of public perception, media, and marketing? Compared to the litany of problems that the cash-strapped city faced—from paying sanitation workers to keeping street lights on at night—weren't such image issues relatively superficial?

I emphasize the role of media and marketing in my account because these visual forces were taking an unprecedented toll on New York's status as a national and global center, and playing an unprecedented role in official efforts at recovery. Since the late 1960s, the city's declining position was made evident by the exodus of corporations from Manhattan, the flight of middle-class residents, a rapid drop-off in tourism, and a tumbling municipal bond rating. These losses meanwhile were occurring within a constellation of broader political economic shifts linked in their own ways to questions of representation. These included deindustrialization and the rise of a global "symbolic economy," the accelerated competition between cities and regions for a share of this new economy, and the aforementioned growth of a conservative, suburban-based political movement fed a steady diet of televised urban dysfunction.[11] Local elites understood that both New York's future and their own personal fortunes were tied more than ever to the perception of the city's "climate" or "environment" for business and tourism.[12]

Against this backdrop, ubiquitous media coverage began to fuel what I will call an *image crisis*, through which negative representations in and of themselves were exacerbating the city's wider economic decline. This was particularly true of volatile, subjective indicators like real estate values, visitor attitudes, bond prices, and investor confidence. And it was particularly an issue for place-based, image-sensitive industries like real estate, tourism, and financial services that could not simply move their operations to the suburbs, and that were facing growing competition from other cities and regions around the world. So elites in the affected industries, with the aid of a growing crop of consultants and image-makers in media and marketing, began to coordinate their efforts and place increasing pressure on government to act. Through public–private partnerships, consultants' reports, high-profile magazines, city marketing, and other means, they worked to ensure that the repair of New York's interwoven image and fiscal crises would lie at the heart of any plan for "recovery"—taking precedence over competing (and arguably more important) demands like filling widening gaps in the city's budget for education, healthcare, and housing. And so, far from being minor, I will argue that media and marketing should be considered central forces in this unparalleled period of crisis and the realignment of the public sector.

But how novel was this turn to marketing in response to crisis? Was it not simply what New York City, the so-called "communications capital of the world," had always done to spur economic growth, especially in trying times?

Contrary to popular belief—produced in large part by New York's intensive use of city marketing *since* the 1970s—such marketing had never played a major role in the city's or the state's economic development program prior to this time. Gotham certainly had a venerable tradition of urban boosterism going back to the early 1800s. It was home to an array of independent impresarios and entrepreneurs from Coney Island to the "Great White Way." It created a Convention and Visitors Bureau in 1934 —one of many CVBs created in cities nationwide in this period—which would work to attract the burgeoning travel and tourism trade after World War II. But historically, New York was different from US cities like Las Vegas or New Orleans that had long been dependent on marketing themselves for tourism and business. It became the nation's industrial, commercial, and financial hub *without* the use of large-scale official marketing, and through the 1960s its political leadership continued to see promotional efforts as ancillary, if not irrelevant, to their overall strategy of economic development. If there was any concern, the city's premier broadcasting, recording, and publishing industries, left to their own devices, seemed perfectly capable of disseminating the sights and sounds of this booming metropolis to the world without city or state aid. Moreover, New York was a bastion of New Deal-style egalitarian liberalism, and largely eschewed overt public intervention on behalf of business and marketing. Thus, government and industry leaders typically assumed that the city would "sell itself," and refrained from getting actively involved in promotion. That was until the crisis of the 1970s, when a dramatic shift occurred in the attitude of both public and private sector leaders towards self-promotion.

Branding New York

In this environment, old-fashioned urban boosterism gave way to the standardized, coordinated, and far more capital-intensive practice that I will refer to as *urban branding*. As with corporate branding more broadly, this approach entailed a dual strategy that was at once visual and material, combining intensive marketing—in this case *place* marketing—with neoliberal political and economic restructuring.[13] On the marketing side, real estate and tourism executives joined economic development officials, media makers, and marketing consultants to construct and disseminate a "cleaned-up" image for the city.[14] On the restructuring side, city and state officials undertook far-reaching, pro-business economic reforms—euphemistically called "product modifications" by consultants hired at the time—that privileged certain social classes, economic sectors, and geographic regions over others.[15] Such modifications included tax cuts for corporations to build new office towers in Manhattan alongside harsh austerity measures and mass lay-offs of municipal workers. They entailed the enhancing of services and security in central financial and tourist districts alongside the elimination of services in poorer, "blighted areas" of the Bronx, Manhattan, and Brooklyn. Thus the branding of New York constituted a process of both the real and symbolic commodification of the city, and of the simultaneous production and marketing of a hegemonic, consumer- and investor-oriented vision of New York.

As with corporate branding, the representational framework of the new "New York" was tightly controlled and richly designed, transforming a simple logo and slogan into a distinct and all-encompassing universe. The origins of this framework may be traced to a series of unprecedented city-wide marketing efforts in the 1960s and 1970s. First was the World's Fair of 1964–1965, which, despite its generic, international style, was the first to coordinate coverage among New York's dominant television, film, and magazine industries and to broadcast a compelling, corporate-sponsored, "global city" image to the world. In striking contrast to this modernist vision was the one promoted by *New York* magazine, founded in 1967. In the magazine's pages, the city was artfully repackaged, warts and all, as a unique and hip place to live, work, and shop for young, social-climbing urbanites. Then, drawing inspiration from both of these precedents, came the city's first, quasi-official marketing campaign, known as "Big Apple," sponsored by the real estate-led Association for a Better New York in 1971. This campaign was to culminate in the Bicentennial celebrations of 1976, which seized upon the architectural gigantism of the newly built World Trade Center to proclaim the city's resurgence. And finally, in 1977, the New York State Department of Commerce launched the "I♥NY" campaign, combining a witty logo designed by *New York* magazine's artistic director Milton Glaser with a multimedia celebration of Broadway theater and Fifth Avenue shopping, all against the backdrop of the new downtown skyline.

None of these branded visions made reference to Gotham's famously polyglot, racially diverse, proudly working-class culture, except to extol the shopping and entertainment opportunities such culture at times provided. None had much to say about the daily struggles of citizens enduring austerity measures, lay-offs, or arson. And all steered clear of what today is seen as a cultural renaissance emerging in underground clubs, at downtown galleries, and on the walls of subway cars criss-crossing the city. These were not cultural phenomena designed to attract the corporations and tourists back to New York. To the contrary, according to consultants hired by the state, they were driving them away. And so lifestyle magazines and marketing campaigns created a cleaned-up vision, presenting New York as a safe and exciting city for the "average" white, middle-class consumer.

Symbolic Politics and Counter-Branding

Despite superficial appearances, the branding of New York had a profound and enduring effect on the social and political reality of the city. For, as distant as it was from the everyday lives of most New Yorkers, the glamorized, often utopian urban imagery produced by the World's Fair, *New York*, Big Apple, and I♥NY helped to promote and sell the city's post-industrial and neoliberal program of economic development.

The benefits of this free-market mode of development were highly unequal. Incentives to spark private sector growth were generously given at the top of the social ladder while public sector service cuts undermined standards of living at the bottom. Meanwhile, the upbeat image provided by city branding helped distract critical attention from these contradictions, selling the idea of the city's "recovery" to locals and out-of-towners alike. This was well understood by economic development officials and their private sector consultants, both of whom justified the need to spend scarce resources to mount tourism marketing campaigns by asserting that the latter were less expensive and presented a more "positive" public image than simultaneous efforts to attract corporations through tax breaks and subsidies.

Nonetheless, the introduction of branding alongside the reorientation of the public sector was a hotly contested development in this historically progressive, working-class city. The official, branded image of New York quickly became a potent political target, and ushered in a new era of symbolic politics in the city. Throughout the decade, those most affected by cutbacks, including groups as divergent as police officers facing lay-offs and Bronx teenagers armed with spray paint, developed a common oppositional tactic: to gain media attention—and a degree of power—by undermining, or *counter-branding*, the new "New York" image. Ironically, both the city's branders and counter-branders realized that their local struggles were playing out on a global stage, and adapted their political strategy accordingly.

Branding, Bloomberg, and Beyond

This all begs two final questions. How should we gauge the long-term impact of this new practice of urban branding for New York and other cities? And how should we assess the significance of such branding *today*, in the wake of the phenomenal "rebranding" of New York following the terrorist attacks of 9/11, under the media-savvy mayoralty of Michael Bloomberg, former CEO of Bloomberg L.P. and a brand marketer *par excellence*?

In short, I will argue that the city's turn to image-making in the current, post-crisis moment is a direct descendant of the marketing-led approach that was used in the 1970s. To be sure, the historic circumstances of the crisis in the post-9/11 period, and the symbolic tools used to respond to it, are qualitatively different from those in the 1970s. Nonetheless, the central, strategic role played by city marketing is largely the same—distinct only in its degree of professionalism and coordination, the greater geographic scale of its "market penetration," and the increased sums that are spent on it. And, as in the 1970s, the evidence for today's economic turnaround, and the "success" of the marketing approach, is based in the fact that real estate values are sky high, Wall Street is booming, new stores and restaurants are proliferating, and tourism numbers continue to break every previous record.

The figures are indeed mind-boggling. According to recent media coverage, partners in big firms are spending their escalating annual bonuses on $15,000 bottles of champagne and $15 million apartments; $400-a-head restaurants are booked months in advance; and the city attracted an astounding 45 million tourists in 2007, or roughly six tourists for every resident of the city. To sustain such growth, Mayor Bloomberg has argued vociferously for the importance of marketing the city as a "luxury product" to the nation and the world. He has appointed a chief marketing officer; redoubled efforts to attract major events like the Republican National Convention and the Olympics; supported the building of massive new sports stadia in downtown Brooklyn, the Bronx, and on the West Side of Manhattan; and tried to launch a bold, new slogan for the city—"New York: The World's Second Home." These efforts have not been entirely successful: for example, the city lost out to London in its Olympic bid, the West Side stadium was torpedoed by political opposition, and the new slogan was found to be offensive to many for whom New York was their *first* home. On the whole, however, this mayoral administration has normalized and institutionalized the branding approach to an unprecedented extent.

Benefits of the new economy do trickle down to some extent, and new political opportunities do emerge. Rising profits in finance, real estate, and tourism generate increased tax revenues and entry-level jobs, particularly in construction, retail, and services. Quality-of-life enhancements like improved sanitation, policing, transportation, and parks in the city center may be enjoyed by out-of-towners and resident New Yorkers alike. Many new immigrant entrepreneurs find business opportunities, particularly in outer-borough enclaves. In addition, the branded, media-saturated city provides a new degree of leverage and visibility for political groups. These include those who occupy or symbolically appropriate central urban space as part of tactical campaigns—as the mass protests at the Republican National Convention of 2004 made clear. And it also pertains to workers in key, place-based industries like tourism, security, and business services, who now may exploit their corporate employers' global networks and concern for image in their negotiations.

Yet now, as in the 1970s, urban branding conceals a highly unequal socio-economic reality. The bulk of the "rebound" is driven and enjoyed by the local elites, out-of-towners, and recent transplants. These include real estate developers and sellers; financial investors and lenders; tourists and business travelers; luxury retailers and hotels; high-profile corporate tenants; and affluent consumers from around the country and the world. And, as in the booming 1980s, and indeed during the "Gilded Age" of the late nineteenth century, the rising tide generated by this influx has not lifted all boats. This is because the benefits and success stories of the new economy have not made up for its costs. Such costs include the elimination of well-paid, union-ized jobs, the privatization of public amenities, and the near disappearance of affordable housing for average New Yorkers alongside the erosion of rent controls, welfare, and social services.

And so the 1970s in New York City should be remembered for ushering in a radical, new approach to urban economic development combining intensive media and marketing with neoliberal restructuring. As a result of this shift, the "standpoint of out-of-towner" held increasing political sway in urban affairs, and a coalition emerged among local financial and real estate elites, media and culture industries, and an entrepreneurial government to reach out more effectively to this new constituency. In the process, tourist- and business-friendly urban images and policies became dominant, and helped chip away at New York's longstanding reputation as a liberal, working-class city.

This marketing-led approach, meanwhile, provided a virtual template for how the city should respond to subsequent crises—whether following the stock market crash and recession of 1989–1992 or the recession and terrorist attacks of the early 2000s. It was also an approach that, given factors of scale and visibility, became a paradigm for cities and regions around the world. For while New York was not the first city to attempt urban branding as a strategy of growth and recovery, it ultimately became the one most heavily identified with it. And it remains, for better or worse, an international symbol of the dual power of image-making and market reforms in turning around a city's fortunes.

Like many historical shifts, the transformation of New York into a branded city has been so dramatic that it may appear natural. Indeed, one of the most important effects of branding is to naturalize, and reify, the image of its commodified object, and so to obscure the social and historical process that produced it. One of the major contributions of this book, therefore, is to uncover the specific social actors and historical forces that helped to drive the transformation of New York City in the 1970s, and made it the city we know today.

In Chapter 1, I will introduce the broader theoretical and historical framework necessary for understanding the particular case of New York City in the 1970s. This includes a brief overview of the role of media and urban boosterism in the rise of the modern city, the national and global forces driving "urban crisis" and restructuring after World War II, the rise of brand marketing as a corporate strategy, and the incorporation of branding within broader cultural and entrepreneurial strategies of urban development in the 1970s. The chapter concludes with my theory of the shift from boosterism to branding that occurred in New York in the 1970s, and served as a model for similar shifts both nationally and globally.

In Part I, "From Image Crisis to Fiscal Crisis," I address the range of visual and social forces driving the declining image of New York City in the 1960s, the contribution of this image to the city's broader financial decline, and the earliest efforts to construct a new, more marketable image for the city in the emerging global era of the 1960s through the early 1970s.

In Chapter 2, I look at the rise of image crisis through the lens of Robert Moses's New York World's Fair of 1964 and 1965. Like New York boosters before him, Moses perceived the power of city marketing and modernist aesthetics in the increasingly competitive, global arena of the 1960s. Yet the Fair was ultimately a commercial failure, and a signal of the end of both New York modernism and urban boosterism, since it was unable to compete with negative representations of the city, most of which were being produced by New York's own increasingly powerful media industries.

Chapter 3 looks at the creation of *New York* magazine in 1967, a publication that was able to craft a hip, consumer-oriented image of the city that was far more in sync with the politically charged climate of the day than Moses's modernist vision. The magazine's overt interest in the "New York power game" and its seamless combination of "new journalism" with "new advertising" were to make *New York* a dominant representation of the city in the early 1970s, and an influential means of marketing to a young, aspiring, urban middle class.

Chapter 4 looks at another important institution that arose in this period, one representing the interests of New York finance, real estate, and tourism elites at a time of "corporate exodus": the Association for a Better New York (ABNY). Launched in 1971, ABNY combined behind-the-scenes lobbying for its members with high-profile city marketing through its "Big Apple" campaign, and in the process helped construct the first brand image for New York. Ultimately, however, the group was incapable of halting (and indeed contributed to) the city's massive fiscal crisis of 1975, the causes and impact of which I discuss at the end of the chapter.

In Part II, "The Battle to Brand New York," I look at the policies of "austerity" and "planned shrinkage" imposed with the fiscal crisis of 1975, through which New York's image became a site of far wider contestation. Now, the question of who should have the power to "represent" New York became an issue not only for the new middle class and finance, insurance, and real estate elites but for city workers facing lay-offs, young people living in neighborhoods cut off from city services, and the struggling governments of the city and state.

Chapter 5 looks at the impact of the police and fire unions' "Fear City" campaign, which involved handing out fliers warning businesspeople and tourists to stay away from New York City due to the crime and arson wave that was sure to hit as a result of lay-offs. The campaign was ultimately halted, but together with other chaotic representations—including the "peak" in subway graffiti and upsurge of crime-oriented movie-making—served as a wakeup call to local elites that they had to take control of the city's image.

Thus arose the city's first official marketing campaign: a new, state-sponsored version of ABNY's Big Apple, which is discussed in Chapter 6. Together with planned shrinkage in the outer boroughs, and tied in with the Democratic National Convention and Bicentennial celebrations, Big Apple targeted scarce resources on the revitalization of the image of the city center, now symbolized by the façades of the newly completed, and largely empty, towers of the World Trade Center. But these attempts proved no match for what was to follow: the unforeseen "plagues" of the fateful "Summer of '77," the worst period yet in the New York City image crisis.

In response, official city marketing was elevated to a new scale and scope under the auspices of the State Department of Commerce, as is discussed in Chapter 7. On the advice of market consultants, this entailed making two key "pro-business product modifications" in the late 1970s: government restructuring and New York City marketing. The former involved corporate tax breaks and other neoliberal reforms. The latter involved hiring cutting-edge advertisers, and *New York* magazine's own graphic designer, to create "I♥NY," which was to become one of the most influential tourism marketing campaigns in history. Thus New York's pro-business "recovery" became a national success story, despite persistent economic problems for the poor and working class.

In conclusion, Chapter 8 explores the complex legacy of New York's fiscal crisis and its celebrated recovery. As the nation entered a period of restructuring and austerity under President Reagan in the 1980s, a newly branded New York City, purged of its reputation as a bastion of civic liberalism, was held up as a model of how other cities, and the US as a whole, should make the neoliberal shift. Meanwhile, the economic benefits of this recovery were highly uneven, going largely to new clusters of firms in finance, real estate, media, and tourism; to global corporations establishing high-profile headquarters in the city; and to the upwardly mobile middle class. This led to new problems, including growing poverty and inequality, a dearth of affordable housing, and increasing control over popular expression in public space. It also created opportunities for labor and community organizing, as well as a growing demand for new, equitable, and democratic forms of urban planning and politics. The path leading to this crossroads, I argue, was laid in the 1970s. And so it is crucial to understand this period in New York City's history as we choose our path today.

CHAPTER 1

Branding and the Neoliberal City

In order to appreciate the special significance of the branding of New York in the 1970s, it is first important to examine the broader social forces which shaped this approach, and which this approach in turn helped to transform. To do so, I will devote this introductory chapter to a theoretical and historical exploration of the interplay between media, marketing, and visual culture, on the one hand, and capitalist urbanization, on the other. First I will trace the rise of commercial media in the modern industrial city, looking in particular at the role of urban boosterism in the nineteenth century, and the growth in tourism marketing in the wake of World War II. Next, I will examine how the 1970s era of deindustrialization, fiscal crisis, and deregulation provoked the rejection of New Deal-style civic liberalism at the local and national scales, and the rise of a neoliberal, free market ideology in its place, as well as the intensification of market-based competition between cities and regions. As I will explore in the following section, this shift led most cities to turn to a new, entrepreneurial mode of economic development that combined political and economic restructuring with cultural strategies like image marketing. Because this approach was itself modeled on the private sector, I will then analyze the original development of market research and "branding" in corporate restructuring more generally in the same time period.

Finally, I will turn to the particular case of New York in the 1970s. It was then that New York's unique status as a national and global center of media and finance, as well as its reputation as a bastion of civic liberalism, set it apart from other cities undergoing similar shifts. As a result of these distinctions, New York's fiscal crisis and subsequent neoliberal, marketing-driven recovery were unmatched in scale, visibility, and symbolic weight. And so New York City will serve as a model for the theory of urban branding that I will outline here and develop in the coming chapters of this book.

Image Marketing and the Modern City

Since the late nineteenth century, with the dual rise of the industrial metropolis and modern technologies of media and spectacle, scholars have appreciated the powerful interrelationship between urbanization and representation. Walter Benjamin, for instance, saw the city as a dynamic interplay between visual phenomena and material social forces, whereby the former "expressed" and "reproduced"—rather than simply reflected or mystified—the latter.[1] From this perspective, the image and imagination of the city, and more broadly what Henri Lefebvre called "representational space," should be seen as an objective and productive social force, with real material effects, playing an integral role in shaping modern forms of production, consumption, and the collective "dreamscape."[2] This role has become only more apparent in the last thirty years, as cities have been so radically transformed by the simultaneous and interwoven rise of deregulated global capitalism and the "communications revolution."[3] And so what is needed now is a form of urban social research that combines analyses of political economy with those of the "symbolic economy," seeking to understand "the interpenetration of culture and power" in an urban context.[4]

When one looks at cities in terms of the interpenetration of cultural and material forces, a more complete picture arises of the changes cities have undergone since the 1960s. For instance, in this period, "location consultants" joined the market research field, and did as much to produce market phenomena as they did to study them. Indeed, such consultants were hired alternately by corporations looking for more profitable and desirable locales, and entrepreneurial cities and regions seeking to turn themselves into such a locale, and wanting a credible blueprint to do so.[5] This blueprint was also found in the pages of urban lifestyle magazines, which were considered required reading by powerful city leaders wanting to appeal to this new constituency on cultural terms. It was found in the plans of urban designers who began to shift their focus to questions of the imageability of urban space. And finally, it was being applied by city marketing campaigns, which sought to combine these elements and transform their city into a mirage of the perfect middle-class lifestyle.

Another important form of this interpenetration is the political and tactical use of media in the modern city. Groups with varying degrees of power have different resources with which to create, promote, and impose urban representations that serve their interests. This representational power, as I will call it, is of course not new. Dating back to the first Mesopotamian cities, dominant urban images have consistently been shaped by, and helped shape, broader political struggles. Yet with the rise of the modern "institutional matrix" of media and marketing over the last two hundred years, the potential for representational power has grown enormously.[6] On the one hand, as new media technologies have become smaller, cheaper, and more interconnected, and as mass media products have become more accessible and versatile, they have revealed a liberatory potential, giving voice to underrepresented groups, spurring creativity, expressing new forms of class consciousness and solidarity, and opening doors to civic participation. On the other hand, as mass media ownership has grown increasingly concentrated in the hands of fewer and larger corporations, and with print and broadcast media reaching ever wider audiences, the media have also revealed a formidable potential to legitimize dominant groups and to limit access to the mediated "public sphere." In this way well-connected urban groups—from the new middle class to corporate elites—have gained increasing power to promote and impose a hegemonic vision of the city that serves their interests.

Boosters and Modern City Marketing

Urban boosterism was the first instance in which modern media and marketing were used to promote and sell a particular image of the city. Boosterism was largely an American phenomenon, launched by the show-men, entrepreneurs, and chambers of commerce of frontier towns and newly industrialized cities that by the late nineteenth century were caught up in fierce competition with other cities for residents, workers, industries, and investments.[7] Beginning in this period, a contingent of urban boosters, working with local advertising agencies, newspaper publishers, and other emerging media industries created an extensive "critical infrastructure" of urban guidebooks, reviews, and press coverage, with which to promote ever more spectacular consumer spaces, from department stores to amusement parks.[8]

Generally speaking, the concern of urban boosters was to replace negative perceptions of their "product"—whether New York, Houston, or another city—with an enticing, all-encompassing, and carefully edited image of the city-in-miniature, or the "city as a whole." One of the primary sources of negative perceptions was the deep-rooted anti-urban bias that emerged in the Jeffersonian era, particularly among the country's majority rural population, its landed elites and, in the late nineteenth century, a growing suburban population.[9] City boosters' efforts to counter such bias through the selective commodification of their locale underlay their most sophisticated visual strategies. Taking advantage of new photographic and motion-picture technologies and techniques, they perfected the panoptic strategies of panoramas, city view books, and "city symphony" films. And so, entrepreneurs sold investors, pleasure-seekers, and new immigrants on exotically named cities in the swamps of Florida and the wilds of California, as well as on the rapidly expanding metropoles of the East and Midwest.[10]

Particular marketing strategies varied by locale, and by the perceived anxieties or desires of potential customers. In frontier towns boosters emphasized law and order, cleanliness, and well-managed civic life, attempting to establish the respectable "city-ness" of their nascent settlement.[11] Meanwhile, in older, more established cities, boosters seeking to attract tourism developed images of cultural sophistication and historic grandeur, often alongside new, spectacular forms of shopping and entertainment.[12] Another popular approach was to exploit the middle-class fascination with the city's poorer, ethnic quarters, and to promote a "slumming aesthetic" through voyeuristic tours of bohemian quarters, as well as more risqué sites of vice and debauchery.[13] Of course, whatever superficial treatment might be given to ghettos or elite institutions, boosters strenuously avoided reference to underlying structural inequalities, such as the poor labor or housing conditions faced by most of the working population in these industrializing cities.

As urban populations expanded in the nineteenth century, city marketing increasingly targeted the city's own residents, linking with local markets for entertainment, leisure, and consumption. Such marketing formed an essential part of the mass urban periodicals and films, which created cities-in-miniature within their montages, listings, and guides.[14] Through newspapers, serial novels, movies, and police hand-bills, readers and spectators learned to be modern urban citizens and to interpret the city made of text and image that overlay that of bricks and steel.[15] This mediated city offered a new narrative map, one which entertained as well as educated, enticed as well as disciplined, imposing a modicum of coherence and order on an unfamiliar world of constant flux.[16]

Then, in an effort to revive moribund economies in the 1930s, the practice became institutionalized and externalized to a degree through the creation of "Convention and Visitors Bureaus" (CVBs) in cities nationwide.[17] CVBs were supported jointly by local governments and private members, with the latter generally drawn from the tourism, retail, entertainment, and real estate industries. They became particularly powerful in mid-size cities and towns, for which tourism and convention business represented a significant expansion of the economic base, and a relatively easy source of new revenue.[18] For large, industrialized, port cities and financial centers like New York, they were not seen as vital to economic growth, and were relatively less powerful and less well funded.

Mid-Century Growth in Tourism and Market Research

In the post-World War II era, a number of factors—from the expanding middle class, to the globalization of the economy, to the rising popularity of jet and automobile travel—converged to propel the tourism industry into an era of massive international expansion. At the national and state levels, government increasingly felt pressure to respond to growing competition in this market. In 1961, the Kennedy administration created the United States Travel Service as the federal government's lead travel and tourism advocacy group, and the following year launched "Discover America," its marketing arm.[19] As their reports put it, drumming up tourism was not only a business opportunity, bringing "new money" into the national economy, but patriotic, keeping "American dollars" from leaving.[20] At the local level, meanwhile, tourism was part of a broad push by "urban growth machines" of the 1950s and 1960s, representing the interests of local elites in finance, insurance, and real estate (FIRE), as well as in retail, hotels, advertising, and media.[21] They joined with CVBs in an effort to grow the economic base rapidly, expand the value of local real estate, and replace blue-collar industries with those of the more profitable, less unionized service sector. And they keenly grasped the idea, as Dennis Judd has put it, "that tourism is an industry without smokestacks."[22]

This embrace of tourism was legitimated by new, quasi-statistical methods of market research. Ever since 1941, when travel agents organized their first business association, the National Association of Travel Officials (NATO), members sought to create credible data with which to demonstrate their growing importance, advance their common interests, and launch effective marketing campaigns.[23] Thus, in 1944, NATO established a research committee, and encouraged member firms that conducted tourism research to furnish results to its national center.[24] In the 1950s, this committee joined the nationwide Travel Research Association, which worked closely with the University of Michigan's Institute for Social Research, and in particular George Katona's renowned Survey Research Center, to produce classic consumer research studies that measured such things as the demographics, preferred modes of travel, and length of trips of consumers in this new market.[25]

Over the course of the 1960s, the United States Department of Commerce conducted a series of regional studies that showed the potentially revolutionary impact of increased tourism capacity on economic development and job creation in some of the nation's most impoverished regions, at little cost to the regions themselves.[26] In 1965, "Discover America" merged with NATO to create Discover America Travel Organizations, with a congressionally chartered mandate to generate more international tourism to the US via increased advertising and the coordinated application of survey data. Now, with Washington's support, thousands of market research studies were produced throughout the 1960s by every state in the union, measuring the potential consumer market for tourism, the marketability of potential tourist "attractions" and "destinations," and the potential impact of expanding tourism, recreation, and business conventions on the economy.[27] In addition to creating some of the first coordinated tourism marketing campaigns in the US, this effort made tourism marketing one of the primary ways through which American cities were represented to the world.

These tourism studies tied in with those produced by a new crop of "business location consultants." The latter were the first to employ the "science" of ranking cities, regions, and states in terms of both "tangible" benefits to business—like tax and labor policy—as well as culturally subjective "intangibles" like "lifestyle" and "quality of life." Such consultancies were hired both by corporations looking to use locational change to boost profits and worker morale, and by cities and regions seeking to appeal to these corporations and become thir desired location.[28] In line with the prescient urban design theories first advanced by Kevin Lynch in 1960, city planners transformed urban space around the criteria of "legibility," "visibility," and ultimately "imageability," in order to produce "vividly identified, powerfully structured, highly useful mental images" of entire cities.[29]

Savvy CVBs, chambers of commerce, and regions dependent upon tourism and business relocation began employing the services of professional marketing, design, and research firms. CVBs were interested in their findings because they provided supposedly hard data on how to lure tourists, business travelers, and relocating middle managers. Broader growth coalitions also found them particularly useful, as they could be cited to justify the redevelopment of the city and the restructuring of its services and tax structure to appeal to the new tourism and convention market.

Crisis, Restructuring, and the Neoliberal City

Discursive practices developed in the age of urban boosterism endured through the twentieth century. Yet the forms of capital accumulation and cultural production in which these practices were embedded changed dramatically over this time. Like their nineteenth-century mass media predecessors that arose with the modern industrial and commercial metropolis, new forms of urban media emerged in the 1960s and 1970s as panoramic navigational tools for a landscape of equally monumental flux: that of fiscal crisis and the neoliberal city.

The 1960s Urban Crisis

In the latter half of the 1960s, the First World's post-war period of prosperity and growth was coming to an end, and American urban and regional economies dependent upon Fordist systems of large-scale industry and government subsidization began to decline.[30] In addition, as the social protest movements of the 1960s, including the Civil Rights and the Anti-Vietnam War movements, gained increasing coherence and militancy, major cities across the US, Latin America, and Europe became epicenters of unrest.[31] On the one hand, urban streets and public spaces pulsed with an unprecedented sense of possibility—an international expression of people's universal "right to the city" regardless of class, color, or gender.[32] On the other, increasing factory closures, lay-offs, and rising poverty, disinvestment and "white flight" to the expanding suburbs, as well as ongoing racial discrimination and police brutality, created an equally unprecedented sense of tension in city streets.[33] Struggles for public space became violent and were met with increasingly militaristic police response. Local and state government endorsed these police tactics, and though they often took great pains to prevent media coverage, provided the media with dramatic images of violence and repression that entered wide circulation.[34]

Very quickly, a decontextualized discourse of "urban crisis" began to permeate popular culture. With the growing concentration of blacks and Latinos in American inner cities, this crisis discourse was increasingly couched in racial terms. As Robert Beauregard has shown in his analysis of media accounts of the era, this expressed a deeper concern among white Americans over the growing power of the Civil Rights Movement and desegregation more broadly.[35] Thus, as developments in media technology made scenes of urban crisis far more compelling and ubiquitous, they also evoked longstanding anti-urban and racist tropes, which were finding new justification in an era of suburbanization, integration, and mounting social unrest.[36] These old prejudices, in combination with the rise of joblessness and poverty in the inner city, allowed for the easy labeling of city dwellers as a kind of urban surplus population, and as an obsolete and dangerous rabble.

The rise of street protest, radical social movements, and instability, in combination with the rapidity of technological and cultural changes, reached such proportions that many predicted cities were on the brink of complete self-destruction, and that the age of urban existence was over.[37] For instance, in his 1970 bestseller *Future Shock*, Alvin Toffler warned of "urban man's impending loss of psycho-social orientation—and thus his ability to make thoughtful, rational decisions—because of the ever accelerating rate of growth and change of his environment." This attitude only fueled deeper anti-urbanism among what President Nixon called the "silent majority" of suburban, conservative Americans, already inclined to blame cities, young urban radicals, and costly social services for undermining the fortunes and values of the nation.

The Neoliberal Turn

The social unrest and anxiety of the urban crisis were in large part an expression of deeper economic forces, namely the shock of rapid and widespread deindustrialization in the late 1960s and early 1970s.[38] This restructuring was caused by a number of global factors—including recession, competition from newly industrialized nations, deregulation of financial markets, and the rise of new communication and transportation technologies—all of which made capital both more flexible and more inclined to seek investments outside of the industrialized West. These forces culminated in 1973 with the global oil crisis and spike in energy costs which, in combination with continuing recession and high unemployment, sent the economies of the US and much of Europe into a prolonged period of "stagflation."[39] These structural shifts were aided by a conservative, deregulatory political climate, which hastened the process of deindustrialization in older US and European cities.

Political economists have described the structural shift that ensued as one away from the rigid Fordism of the previous half century towards a more "flexible," "post-Fordist" mode of accumulation.[40] Under Fordism, capital flows were organized on a national scale, hemmed in by strong government regulation, and further contained by coordination between large national unions and manufacturers. In addition, production was oriented towards large-scale manufacturing and mass markets. Following a Keynesian logic, governments tended to believe that a large welfare state helped "prime the pump," providing needed stimulus for constant and predictable levels of consumption, production, and employment. Under post-Fordism finance and commodity capital, information, and images were increasingly free to roam across borders, enabling private industry to downsize and globalize operations in search of cheaper labor and larger markets. In the process, blue-collar jobs, which constituted the bulk of the urban workforce and were for the most part unionized and well paid, began to disappear, and were replaced by a smaller number of high- and low-end white-collar, service jobs.[41]

An ideological realignment occurred in the public sector that mirrored that of the private sector. What began as the monetarist "supply-side economics" of the early 1970s grew into the increasingly absolutist "neoliberal," free market ideology that would gain credence with the anti-government attacks of Ronald Reagan and Margaret Thatcher in the 1980s.[42] Neoliberal proponents called for an end to state regulation of the economy in general, and in particular for an end to the redistributive role of the welfare state since the 1930s that culminated with the Great Society programs of the 1960s, such as the War on Poverty and Model Cities.[43] The harsh economic climate of the 1970s, and the dislocation and disorientation that accompanied it, provided ideal conditions for the imposition of controversial neoliberal reforms like corporate tax breaks, the deregulation of the housing market, and deep cuts in public spending. Since older, industrialized cities had been the primary recipients of state aid in the previous era, as well as the base of support for the Democratic Party, they also became the primary target of such reforms. Perversely, these cities were also in the greatest of need of aid, bearing as they did the brunt of massive unemployment, an influx of new immigrants, and the flight of capital and the middle class. Ultimately, the combination of market shifts, increased need, corporate subsidies, and government retrenchment drove many cities to the brink of fiscal crisis, unable to raise funds through taxes or state aid to cover basic operating expenses.

Thus weakened by fiscal crisis and austerity, these cities became opportune testing grounds for experimental new forms of urban governance. Under pressure of creditors, bond rating agencies, and local elites, cities jettisoned their long-term "managerial" approach, geared towards sustaining the welfare state, and turned instead to short-term strategies of "entrepreneurial" development, through which urban space and resources served as a motor for rapid capital accumulation. The modernist tradition of centralized, "rational" urban planning was largely abandoned in the process.[44] "Urban growth machines" based in the local real estate and business sectors, and strongly linked to city government, pushed pro-growth, free market agendas, regardless of their social or environmental sustainability.[45] One of the key institutional bases of these machines became known as "public–private partnerships."[46] These were essentially informal, unelected bodies through which new financial and political relationships were forged between business and the public sector, including government, labor, and community groups. However, given the privileged position of the private sector, particularly under contemporary forms of uneven urban development, these partnerships were "inherently unequal," with city government, unions, and community groups playing the role, at best, of "junior partners," and, at worst, facilitating "the reallocation of public resources to fit a new agenda."[47] Indeed, through these mechanisms, the public sector faced ever growing pressure to privatize collective goods and services, as well as to adopt a new private sector discourse. The discourse was taught through a new line of glib management texts on "reinventing government," by retraining bureaucrats to embrace the "competitive spirit," and perhaps most importantly, as we shall see in New York, through the actual hiring of private sector management consultants to restructure and reform public governance, policy, and goals.[48]

One of the most important and lucrative elements of the "new agenda" which these partnerships advanced involved the privatization of the urban built environment, through creative techniques like tax breaks, subsidies, and zoning and rent deregulation. This served to accelerate the capitalist tendency towards uneven development, whereby stark inequalities in real estate prices and land rents may be exploited for future gain.[49] The consequence of this over time is the raising of rents, and the displacement of residents, in the name of "gentrifying" derelict neighborhoods that adjoin more affluent areas.[50] Thus, particularly in older, mixed-use, industrial districts and underused downtowns, one began to see the rapid displacement of both working-class jobs and residents, as witnessed most dramatically with the rise of "loft living" in SoHo in the 1970s and 1980s.[51] Over the course of the 1980s and 1990s these trends were to grow in scale and power, as downtowns in cities like New York and Los Angeles saw some of the biggest waves of real estate development in the modern period, and became "re-scaled" around globally networked, residential, and commercial zones.[52]

New Cultural Strategies of Urban Development

The public–private partnerships and growth machines mentioned above were also, from their inception, embroiled in the new institutional matrix of media, marketing, and tourism. The latter industries were based in the same cities, and for the most part shared the material interests of real estate and financial elites. But they were also particularly savvy in terms of the role that urban image played in economic competitiveness and public opinion. It is thus not surprising that prominent within the nation's first public–private partnership—the Association for a Better New York, created in 1971—advertisers, market researchers, and tourism executives sat at the same table with realtors, financiers, and government officials. In addition to lobbying for tax breaks and the elimination of rent control, they were busy planning media campaigns to market a post-industrial "fun city" and mounting surveillance cameras to encircle new tourist and business districts. In the crush of the global marketplace, and in the face of local opposition, new media and marketing tactics, and the culture workers who devised them, were understood as essential to the growth and governance of the neoliberal city.

Tourist Cities and Monopoly Rents

As David Harvey argues, entrepreneurial cities seek the same privileges and protections that accrue to monopolies in the private sector, namely the "monopoly rents" that accompany claims to "uniqueness, authenticity, particularity and specialty."[53] To establish this monopolistic privilege, cities traditionally assert claims to uniqueness and authenticity in geographic terms, an assertion that has become increasingly difficult to make as technological advances in transportation and communications render locational differences less significant. In pursuit of new sources of monopoly rent, entrepreneurial cities, like corporations, tend to turn to the "idea of culture," and to a collective form of Bourdieu's notion of "symbolic capital," to find their advantage, since "claims to uniqueness and authenticity can best be articulated as distinctive and non-replicable cultural claims."[54]

Building on urban design theories of the 1960s, city governments of the last three decades have helped finance the redevelopment of entire down-town areas as "urban entertainment destinations," replete with museums, malls, and stadia, so as to compete with other cities for new, coveted revenue sources: tourism, shopping, on-location film shoots, and new upper-income residents.[55] Such development entails the commercial "theming" of urban space, as well as increased planning of and control over circulation within the space, so as to maximize consumption and prevent loitering, graffiti, and other "quality of life offenses."[56] In addition to the built environment, the marketing of cultural and discursive elements—that is, historical narrative, collective memory, and lifestyle—plays an increasing role, as can be seen in the marketing of place names themselves.[57]

After these monopoly claims are made through the media and other cultural forms, broader urban restructuring, in particular gentrification, has tended to follow swiftly.[58] A specific form of restructuring through culture is now referred to as the "Bilbao effect," whereby spectacular buildings by celebrity architects are used to revitalize struggling post-industrial cities and put their name on the global tourist map, as Frank Gehry's dramatic Guggenheim Museum has been used in the city of Bilbao, Spain. While the new Bilbao has created a sharp upturn in the local real estate market and generated increased tax revenues, more widely spread benefits—like living-wage jobs and public services—have proven far more elusive.[59]

New "tourist city" strategies also focus intensively on media, marketing, and other cultural strategies.[60] The modern travel industry has always depended upon its ability to project seductive images to lure potential consumers out of their daily routine, and inspire them to spend discretionary income in new and unknown locations.[61] In one sense, leisure and tourism were like a range of other "lifestyle" products emerging in the 1960s, which were oriented more towards enhancing identity than fulfilling a simple need. But unlike traditional commodities, in the case of leisure and tourism marketers sell an experience and image of place. And so perhaps more than any other single industry, travel and tourism has benefited from, and participated in, the growth in place marketing services, and in particular the application of media and marketing techniques. The industry was one of the first to use psychographics and lifestyle marketing to sell locales, alongside corollary studies of consumer awareness and media consumption—known as "media coverage" studies.[62] In addition, tourist industry planners were reading "business-climate surveys" conducted by location consultancies, which specialized in ranking cities, regions, and states in terms of both "tangible" benefits to business—like tax and labor policy— and highly subjective "intangibles" like "lifestyle" and "quality of life."[63] Not only responding to broader social shifts, tourism marketing helped accelerate the twenty-six-fold explosion of world tourist travel over the last fifty years, from 25 million in 1950 to 650 million in 1999, an increase that has been especially marked in global cities like New York.[64] Along the way, the tourist industry began creating increasingly "integrated" campaigns, through which the urban destination is marketed much like any other product: that is "to represent a unique combination of product characteristics and added values, both functional and non-functional."[65]

Tourist destinations and monopoly rents have also benefited from the increased exposure cities receive, second-hand, through the commercial media that use them as a location or backdrop for shoots and other forms of merchandising. In this sense, TV shows, films, and consumer magazines provide "free" exposure, as they seek to extend their own place-based brands. Since the 1970s, this has had a heavy impact on cities, as sociologists and market researchers identified "urban lifestyle" to be central to the identity formation of the upwardly mobile, consumer-oriented "new middle class."[66] Urban backdrops in advertising and related media became an important marketing tool for corporations attempting to extend their brand among this highly lucrative demographic. By the 1980s, urban tourist agencies began to recognize this and worked increasingly with filmmakers, TV producers, and commercial location scouts to promote their destinations as possible shooting locations. Numerous cities opened film and TV broadcasting offices to facilitate location shooting, and began sending official convention and visitor bureau delegations to film festivals like Cannes, and major "locations fairs" in Los Angeles and Las Vegas. In this increasingly close relationship, "the ultimate in tourism product placement [is to] place your location in a film or TV series."[67] Cities seek to benefit *directly* from urban branding by employing new representational techniques, discursive strategies, and financial tactics. And in addition they have learned to benefit *indirectly* from secondary representations of their urban brand in the ever expanding realm of commercial mass media and popular culture.[68]

Fetish, Spectacle, Brand

In common usage, "branding" simultaneously connotes the corporate labeling of a thing, and the physical, even violent transformation and com-modification of both inanimate things and living beings. The latter meaning, associated with hot-iron brands, goes back to ancient times. The use of the verb to signify trademarking, on the other hand, is of more recent derivation. It developed with diverse methods of labeling goods and their packages as they entered into the new circuits of exchange that emerged with early forms of capitalism. With the rise of mass consumer marketing in the nineteenth century, branding was separated from the simple trademarking of products. Competitive pressures led to the creation of "brand-name" goods that further dissociated the aestheticized image of the commodity seen on the package and in ads from its origins in the factory. For consumers used to buying things produced and sold locally by people they knew personally, attaching a friendly brand name and image was intended to generate familiarity, goodwill, and trust in pre-packaged goods distributed from remote nationwide markets. This also served to distract attention from increasingly harsh systems of factory production.[69]

Through fetishization, as Marx observed in the mid-nineteenth century, the commodity, a simple product of labor, came to appear autonomous, even god-like, thus turning real social relations into the appearance of relations between things.[70] Fetishization obscures the underlying dynamic of universal exchange, disarticulating the point of production from that of circulation.[71] What is more, these products appear as desirable, even beautiful, while the exploited labor that produced them disappears from view. Branding in its current form takes this process a step further, pro-moting, in a sense, the fetishizing of the fetish: that is, the commodification of the reified image of the commodity itself. Effectively, branding not only makes the "mystical veil" which hides the social origins of the commodity that much thicker, but creates a veritable industry for the production and circulation of mystical veils, and devises methods for knitting these veils together to give the illusion of totality. This latter step, meanwhile, has been facilitated by the increasing technical and social integration of globalized networks of corporate media.

In the 1960s, the French social critic Guy Debord spoke of an entire "society of the spectacle" in which the fetishized image now drove material forces and masqueraded as the social realm.[72] Despite the linearity of this claim, it does highlight a new stage of reification that coincided with the rise of the symbolic economy over the course of the twentieth century. It is in this period that branding came into its own as a political, economic, and cultural strategy, packaging everything from soft drinks, cigarettes, and the corporations that sell them to cities, nations, political parties, and the individual self.

Branding and Brand Value

Popular usage of the term "branding" in business circles began in the 1980s, but its origins may be traced to innovations in market research and advertising that began in the 1960s. It was then that increasing competition from abroad, coupled with mounting opposition from the consumer advocacy movement at home, forced both American companies and advertisers to rethink their business plan in order to remain relevant and profitable. They were aided in doing so by the development of "psychographic" techniques of market research devised in the 1960s, and specifically by the new tools available for measuring "corporate reputation" and "consumer attitudes."[73] Integrating these with an intensive focus on design, packaging, and product placement, the notion of "branding" emerged in the 1980s and 1990s. Through business publications such as *BrandMonthly*, academic journals, and textbooks in business, communications, advertising, and design, and numerous conferences and conventions,[74] branding became a professional field. "Brand value," meanwhile, became something that could be mathematically quantified, purchased and even "repurchased," separate from the equity of the company.[75]

On one level, this greater abstraction of value was instigated by manufacturers themselves, particularly by emerging transnational corporations. The globalization and deregulation of trade in the 1970s and 1980s fed a greater demand for marketing and cost cutting. Corporations increasingly shifted their resources away from production and human resources via outsourcing and downsizing, while concentrating the bulk of their capital on building powerful global brands.[76] As Naomi Klein has put it, the goal for transnationals became "weightlessness": that is, focusing revenue and expertise on image-making while eschewing "the world of things."[77] As Nike CEO Phil Knight put it in 1994, "There is no value in making things anymore. The value is added by careful research, by innovation and by marketing."[78] This form of "value" eclipses traditional capitalist notions of supply and demand, makes quaint the idea of the "use value" of things, and, most significantly, dissociates the concept even more from its true roots in the labor process.[79] This move also helps maintain the contemporary contradiction of corporate marketing: that the increasing beauty of the brand image is accompanied by increasing exploitation at the point of production. Today, this is seen—or not seen—in the conditions of production and the status of workers in the *maquiladoras* and free trade zones of the "Global South," where the overwhelming majority of brand-name commodities are produced.[80]

The shift to branding was also driven by visionary marketing and advertising firms, who have come to think of themselves as "primary producers" of the new symbolic economy.[81] These firms became extremely successful at convincing manufacturers that while products are made in factories, "brands are made in the mind," thus requiring a new level of creative and scientific expertise to conquer this uncharted territory.[82] Arguing that brand value depended upon the quality, rather than sheer quantity, of exposure, they developed a new breed of "brand managers." Their job was to associate brand names strategically and consistently with people, places, events, ideas, etc., which were believed to resonate with the target market—and to dissociate them from those that were not, if necessary by legal means. Such "brand positioning" ultimately became as, if not more, important than the commodity being sold, as corporations struggled to have their brands "shout above the crowd" in an increasingly crowded market-place.[83] While brand positioning is targeted to appeal to a valued niche, it has also been the job of brand managers to expand this niche so as continually to increase the brand's "net value" and market share.[84] This is exemplified by global "megabrands" like Nike and Coca-Cola, recognizable in any language or culture, and with brand values worth $20 billion and $24 billion, respectively, in 1998.[85] It has also resulted in the consolidation of a few, global, vertically integrated advertising and marketing firms who design and manage such campaigns.

The Limits of Branding

Today, measurements of "corporate reputation" are still viewed as essential to the valuation of a company's stock, but are combined with ever more arcane means of quantifying the total value of the corporate brand.[86] This amorphous value extends beyond the corporation itself to everything the corporation touches, from the tangible and intangible "products" it now sells to the environments in which these products may be seen and purchased—including advertisements, feature films, live events, retail outlets, and the streets and cities in which these are all based. One should always be skeptical regarding the "effects" of branding campaigns on consumers—or advertising in general—particularly as choices are reduced in a corporate marketplace. But one cannot deny the considerable equity that those brands deemed successful have brought to corporations, the vast sums that corporations regularly spend to build such brands, nor the increased dependence of corporations on the strength of their brands in the valuation of their stock. In this sense, image has gained unprecedented prominence in economic and social life. And with the ever more sparkling illusion of the autonomous image, deeper shadows are cast on the real, human world outside.

Entering so deeply into dependence on the world of images and networks of media circulation also poses significant risks. As Stuart Hall has shown, the "encoding" and "decoding" of media signs and messages is never a simple correlation, but rather is always fraught with power. Readings may be "dominant," "negotiated," or "oppositional," depending on the social situation of producers and audiences.[87] In this sense, brands, existing now primarily as media messages, have emerged as a new site of contestation, opposition, and corporate vulnerability. On the one hand, damage can be done to brands as a result of unforeseen events that become media spectacles. On the other, damage can be done by organized anti-consumerist and anti-corporate movements that purposely subvert branded images to get media attention and send a counter-message.[88] In looking historically at what I will be calling *counter-branding* events, efforts, and movements, one sees that the bigger and more expensive the brand image that is projected by a corporation, or a city, the greater is its vulnerability to bad publicity, and the larger is the potential target for those who wish to launch a critique.[89] In this sense, the branded environment we now inhabit has also become a potential space for Situationist *detournement* on an unprecedented scale.[90]

Urban Branding

With the neoliberal shift in municipal governance, branding moved from the corporate to the urban realm. No city serves as a better case study for this phenomenon than New York. Beginning in the late 1960s, the city government and locally based corporations faced similar competitive pressures and "image crises." Separately and in concert, they devised strategies to recreate, market, and consistently manage the image of New York as a brand. In the wake of wide-scale deindustrialization, federal retrenchment, and recession, new synergies formed between city and state government, traditional city boosters based in tourism and real estate, and local marketers. The latter included management consultants, media producers, and advertising firms who were all national leaders and trend-setters in the new fields of psychographics, Pop Art, and creative advertising. They worked with their public and private sector clients to forge emotional linkages between New York and its consumers—new potential residents, investors, corporate, and tourists—so that the name of the city alone would conjure up a series of images and feelings, and with them an impression of value. In the process, the "real" material city was altered as much as possible to conform to the idealized image of the brand, facilitating its ongoing commodification. In essence, the move towards image branding may be seen as the discursive component in a broader set of material strategies employed by neoliberal cities from the 1970s until now. And New York may be seen as the capital city of this phenomenon.

Employing New York City as a model, therefore, my own theory of urban branding has three components: first, the historic shift from urban boosterism to urban branding in response to image crisis; second, the creation of public–private urban branding coalitions; and finally, the tendency for contradictions to arise, particularly once the public sector adopts urban branding as part of a broader, market-oriented strategy of economic restructuring. In the following pages, I will briefly discuss each of these components, establishing them as a theoretical framework for the remainder of this book.

From Urban Boosterism to Urban Branding

Urban branding should be distinguished from urban boosterism in a number of essential ways. While boosters were individual entrepreneurs acting independently of each other and outside formal institutional arrangements, urban branding campaigns are highly coordinated by public–private partnerships, and tied in to broader government restructuring and economic development efforts. As a result of this coordination, urban branding campaigns can maintain a *consistency of image* far beyond the eclectic urban visions crafted by boosters, using corporate brand management techniques to ensure the standardization and trademarking of logos and slogans. Urban branding campaigns operate on a *larger scale* both geographically and in terms of capital investment, as they must pay competitive rates to hire professional staff and to gain media exposure nationally and inter-nationally—as compared to the regional and erratic circulation of traditional booster campaigns.[91] And so while nineteenth-century boosterism was an ancillary form of economic development undertaken by individuals in the private sector, urban branding arose as a main engine of economic growth undertaken by partnerships between the public and private sectors, part of what might be called a *marketing-led strategy of economic development.*

Finally, though urban branding is considerably more capital intensive than urban boosterism, it is, nonetheless, far *less expensive* than the older, managerial forms of economic development (at least in the short term), and thus appears attractive to cash-strapped cities. These older methods involved "priming the pump" through infrastructure projects and public works, expanding public sector employment, and investing in collective consumption goods like education, housing, and healthcare. With leaner and meaner marketing-led development strategies, budgetary priorities shift from higher-cost social services and public employment to cheaper, more profitable, and more high-profile "campaigns." More generally, the priorities of the branded city shift from the provision of tangible use-values to the projection of intangible exchange-values, and the city itself is increasingly transformed from a real place of value and meaning for residents and workers to an abstract space for capital investment and profit-making, and a commodity for broader consumption.

Urban Branding Coalitions

Given their shared agenda, newly created economic development agencies, public–private partnerships, and global media and advertising firms work together with official city boosters to market and manage the city as a global brand. While it is useful to gauge the growing influence of a variety of media and cultural sectors over the last thirty years, looking at them in isolation weakens the sense of the larger coalition of forces that have reshaped cities' political and symbolic economies since the 1970s. To understand the new role played by media and culture industries in urban restructuring, one must understand their role in a new, coordinated strategy of economic development. This strategy represents a new kind of synergy between the public and private sectors; between services that are financial and those based in media and culture; and between local and global economic interests. The four main groups involved in this coalition include: public and quasi-public city and state agencies devoted to cultural and economic development; private commercial boosters like Convention and Visitors Bureaus that receive public subsidies; corporate-led "civic groups" and "public–private partnerships" with influence in the public sector; and global media, advertising, market consulting, and design firms hired by, and usually based in, the city.

By forming coalitions, cities use media and branding not simply to sell new urban imaginaries, but to overhaul the total image and reputation of a given city, and to impose this hegemonic vision as widely and as strategically as possible. As with the branding strategies of global corporations, this serves to obscure the reality of the city in terms of material conditions and internal class conflicts while it restructures its productive and organizational base. Meanwhile, local businesses, as well as locally based global corporations, stand to profit enormously from the increased marketing exposure. They merge their identity with that of the branded city through their own brand marketing campaigns, branded architecture, and actual products. In the interwoven realms of spectacle and political economy, urban and corporate branding support each other, and the distinction between the public and private sector becomes harder to discern.

The Contradictions of Branding

Paradoxically, increased exposure for urban locations in commercial media has exposed the city to new risks, providing as it does increased potential for controversial or negative representations which run counter to a city's marketing agenda. For cities increasingly dependent on marketing themselves for image-sensitive industries and competing for monopoly rents, negative representations can have a disproportionately bad effect on the economy. Among other things, they can lead to a decrease in the value of real estate, a decline in levels of tourism, the departure of big-name corporate headquarters, the relocation of big-budget media productions, and even downturns in the city's bond and credit ratings.

These effects are particularly intense for those large, global cities like New York in which the media corporations are themselves based, and which, as the primary stage-sets for these media corporations, receive much more attention and broader exposure than other places. These cities are also far more complex social spaces in terms of their class, race, and ethnic makeup, a complexity that commercial media, subject to the exigencies of competition and ratings, is uninterested in capturing. As New York has discovered, crimes committed on its streets are more likely to make it into national or international news broadcasts, as well as to be reenacted in the form of police dramas and films. Meanwhile, this coverage rarely captures the complexity of the events, and frequently trades in stereotypes of race and class that are associated with "crime in the city" and "street culture." While this can provide easy and profitable content for media corporations based in these cities, the cities themselves are less able to control the representation and dissemination of their urban brand.

Beyond crime coverage, the economic vulnerability to bad publicity that is faced by branded cities extends to many fronts. Particularly as cities make the move from managerialism to entrepreneurialism, and as the social safety net is worn away, a number of social problems emerge that are far more difficult to contain than street crime, and which nonetheless can easily be sensationalized and gain widespread media attention. As we shall see in the case of New York City, these include fiscal crisis, arson, mass homelessness, electric blackouts, as well as protests and other forms of civil unrest. In this sense, cities that prioritize image and investor confidence over, and at the expense of, social needs may create material conditions that exacerbate the very image crises they sought to address.

In addition, it is only a matter of time before organized groups inclined to protest and wanting media attention appropriate the branded city's most valuable symbols as a political tactic of *detournement*. This can range from groups critiquing government policies by targeting tourists with "fear city campaigns," to young people demanding recognition by covering subway cars with graffiti murals, to profit-seeking Hollywood studios wanting a cheap, dramatic backdrop for their horror movies. Thus, as we shall see, the city has emerged as a contested visual space, and a target for various forms of counter-branding—from negative representations in the mainstream media, to controversial events, to organized, media-savvy oppositional and underground tactics. However, as we shall also see, these subversive visual tactics have their limitations, and are most effective when they form part of a broader-based urban social movement.

In short, hegemonic visual strategies aided entrepreneurial city branding coalitions intent on commodifying their locales and pushing through unpopular forms of economic restructuring and austerity. They were used to "add value" to the product in the midst of tight competition with other cities, and to smooth the transition from a blue-collar economy to the "weightlessness," and joblessness, of the symbolic economy. But these strategies were not always successful. They met with opposition from disenfranchised groups—from municipal unions facing lay-offs to the residents of neighborhoods slated for demolition. They often backfired, as excluded groups realized the larger stakes involved and subverted branded images, or as the effects of austerity measures and social unrest became so severe that they stole media attention away from the campaigns. Despite these contradictions and setbacks, however, cities ultimately came to mirror the priorities of the corporate sector they sought to attract—with New York City leading the way. By the end of the 1970s, New York had successfully branded a commercialized vision of "the city as a whole," and placed it at the heart of a harsh, new political economy.

New York City: Capital of the 1970s

Throughout its 350-year history, New York City has been celebrated and vilified as an unparalleled metropolis—the city of fun and fear, of bedlam and golden dreams. To some extent, I will be joining in this tradition. For I will be arguing that, beginning in the 1970s, New York City was, for better or worse, in the vanguard. As much as Paris was the symbolic capital of the rising capitalist metropolis in the nineteenth century, New York came to epitomize the declining industrial city of the 1970s, as well as the branded, neoliberal city that was to become its successor.

New York's defining role in the 1970s was due to a number of reasons. As we have seen, many other cities throughout the US and the rest of the industrialized world suffered similar fiscal and social crises in this period. Yet, given the scale of New York's economy, level of indebtedness, and integration into global markets, its crisis dwarfed those of other cities. Many other cities were pilloried by the suburban-based conservative movement for the social unrest of the 1960s. Yet, given its long history as a racially diverse, working-class, liberal city, the "New York model" of civic liberalism under Mayor John V. Lindsay bore the brunt of this critique, and the city's decline was met with particular satisfaction in much of the country.[92] And finally, other cities could trust the media to represent them and their troubles from a distance. New York, on the other hand, was a national center of television and news media, film and theater, art and design, and marketing and PR, at a time when these industries were in the preliminary stages of corporate consolidation and global expansion.

In this broader context, as we shall see in the coming chapters, New York was to attain unmatched representational power—a power that was, as it turned out, a decidedly mixed blessing. On the one hand, it created unique opportunities for locally based marketers to brand the city. Yet, on the other, it exposed the city to an especially large risk of negative publicity. In the glare of its own spotlight, New York City emerged as the ultimate symbol of the perils of liberal governance in the traditional, egalitarian sense of the term, and of the need for a shift in course to a free market, neoliberal model for the city and the nation as a whole.

PART I

From Image Crisis to Fiscal Crisis: 1964–1974

CHAPTER 2

It's a Small World After All

Image Crisis and the End of New York City Boosterism

In that tuneful, colorful, imaginative play "Brigadoon," a village appears once every 300 years. In a very real sense the old New York of 1664 is reawakening and disappearing in 1964 in the World's Fair. Come therefore to Brigadoon on Flushing Bay and see the Renaissance of New York.

Robert Moses, 1964

It's a world of laughter, a world of tears.
It's a world of hopes, it's a world of fears.
There's so much that we share, that it's time we're aware:
It's a small world after all.

Lyrics to jingle at Disney's pavilion at
the New York World's Fair, 1964–1965

Perhaps no single event in New York's history was more freighted with ambition and symbolism than the World's Fair of 1964 and 1965 in Flushing Meadows Park, Queens. This extravagant celebration of New York's tercentenary and "world city" status was meant to serve as a "graceful exit" for the Fair's planner, Robert Moses, New York's phenomenally productive, famously cantankerous, and increasingly embattled "master builder."[1] In typical Moses fashion, the Fair was launched on a grand scale and with lavish attention paid to public relations, architectural style, and back-room maneuvering, and without much concern for public opinion, political climate, or financial cost. But adding to this potent mix was the fact that the

Fair was launched at the onset of the "communications revolution," and in a city that was arguably its global capital. Fair organizers hoped to exploit this situation, engineering an unprecedented scale of media coverage and promotions, while suffusing the Fair itself with new media technologies and forms. But the blanket media coverage the Fair received also posed a new kind of threat, creating a powerful stage for unscripted spectacles, from political protest to criticisms of Moses himself, especially once the Fair ended up millions of dollars in the red. And so, the 1964–1965 World's Fair may be seen as a pivotal moment in the battle to remake New York City's image and economy. It was through the Fair that city leaders learned their first lesson about the great potential—as well as the imitations and risks—of using media, marketing, and tourism as motors of urban development.

Moses's original vision was indeed awe-inspiring. He sought to transform Gotham into a modern "Brigadoon on Flushing Bay"—a reference to the sentimental hit musical then on Broadway, in which American tourists stumble upon an enchanted Scottish village that sleeps for three hundred years, to be awoken for just one day of family-friendly festivities. To adapt this quaint tale to brash, 1960s New York, Fair planners worked with the tourist boards of cities, states, and nations; the marketing arms of corporations like RCA, Coca-Cola, Ford, and Disney; and a formidable in-house staff of advertisers, "PR-men" and designers. Together they constructed a landscape that transcended the actual time and place, linking New York to prehistoric and magical realms, as well as to futuristic "space age" visions of travel, leisure, science, and entertainment. It was also one in which the logos and identities of US corporations, then in the process of global expansion, were prominently positioned, and associated with the prestige of New York as a global city.

A key element in the fantasy was media, the unprecedented use of which became a news story in itself. The big local broadcast networks employed new satellite technology to beam opening-night festivities to fifteen countries; RCA laid twenty-five miles of underground cables and mounted hundreds of screens to create the first closed-circuit television network within the fairground itself; and RCA and the networks worked in partnership to build microwave "dishes" to relay these signals to studios in Manhattan, and out to the nation and beyond.[2] Another factor was the influence of Walt Disney, who designed much of the fairground à la Disneyland, and created the Fair's most popular pavilion, in which spectators traveled via gondola through a miniature, "animatronic" landscape of internationally themed robots moving to the tinkling, synchronized lyrics of "It's a Small World."[3]

In a similarly fantastic fashion, Moses represented the Fair as an economic boon to the city long before its books were closed. Through films,

Figure 2.1 1964–1965 New York World's Fair poster.

Courtesy New York City Municipal Library

New York World's Fair 1964-1965

magnificent spectacle...

significant market place!

On April 22, 1964 the major World's Fair of our time will open for two years in New York City.

Exhibits by the United States, along with individual States from Hawaii to New York, and 68 foreign countries, will make this the greatest international exposition of all time.

The companies whose corporate symbols appear here have already contracted to exhibit. More exhibits are in negotiation, many under consideration. For American industry the Fair is a unique opportunity in three vital areas:

CORPORATE PRESTIGE: A world stage on which to present your company's scope and stature.

MARKETING STRATEGY: Over 70 million people will come for the sheer fun of the Fair and to see, hear, touch and sample what your company has to present.

NATIONAL IMAGE: Robert Moses, President of the New York World's Fair, calls this event an "... Olympics of Progress. Our industries must present our claim to leadership. When the Fair opens in 1964, it will be too late for excuses."

What are your plans for the World's Fair?

Figure 2.2 1964–1965 New York World's Fair marketing brochure.

Courtesy New York City Municipal Library

news conferences, and glossy magazine articles, planners tried to placate New Yorkers who still vividly remembered the city's last money-losing fair of 1939, were critical of using scarce taxpayer dollars on such a gamble, and argued instead for addressing urgent needs like housing and education.[4] To this end, Moses promised that ticket sales alone would pay back the city and investors, allowing the Fair then to generate "billions" in profits for local businesses, and tens of millions to be reinvested in the city, mostly in the form of new park space once the fairgrounds were converted to public use.[5]

Yet, in the end, the 1964–1965 World's Fair proved to be as much a liability as a bonanza of profit and publicity. As in many US cities, New York was a base for the increasingly militant Civil Rights Movement—with the 1964 uprisings in Harlem and Brooklyn arguably sparking the trend. Not only did coverage of protests and urban unrest depress tourism, it made the Fair itself appear woefully out of touch, like a wasteful spectacle just waiting to be disrupted. Recognizing this, the Coalition Of Racial Equality threatened a "stall-in" blocking traffic going to the Fair on its opening day and heckled the satellite-beamed speech of President Lyndon Johnson with shouts of "Freedom Now!"[6] From that day forward, myriad groups exploited the Fair to publicize their causes, from Cubans denouncing Fidel Castro to Israeli protests at the Jordanian Pavilion. Making matters worse, Moses's strict prohibition against a "Coney Island atmosphere"—from burlesque shows to hot-dog vendors—in favor of an aesthetic mix of "high art," corporate logos, and religious motifs—from Michelangelo to Disney to the Mormon Tabernacle Choir—was lampooned by the public and cultural critics alike.[7] Culturally and politically, the Fair backfired, looking tacky, irrelevant, even offensive in the context of the radical changes swirling just outside its gates.[8]

Then, on the Fair's last day, in an inglorious finale, crowds ransacked the fairgrounds on live TV, dismantling displays and pavilions in search of souvenirs. The lead editorial in *Time* magazine that ran the next week revealed the extent to which negative press had dogged the Fair from start to finish:

> The beginning, it has often been said, augurs the end. Certainly the axiom proved true of the New York World's Fair. It opened to disappointing crowds on a cold, rainy day in April 1964, with militant CORE picket lines all but blocking major avenues and hecklers disrupting President Johnson's send-off speech. Last week it closed with a frightening scene straight out of a Federico Fellini film fantasy. While thousands of revelers swayed to the strains of Auld Lang Syne and The Star-Spangled Banner, prim ladies in tweed suits feverishly uprooted all the chrysanthemums recently planted

for a permanent park, stuffed them into their pocketbooks or pinned them onto their hats. Tipsy men wantonly ripped signs from buildings, kicked over trash baskets, waded in the Unisphere fountain, and shinned up the 20-ft. poles near the United Nations Plaza to capture the flags. One man completely gutted a statue of King Tut near the Egyptian Pavilion, another attacked a copy of an ancient vase outside the Greek Pavilion with a hammer, while hundreds of people watched in silence. Everything from saltcellars to cameras was stolen as souvenirs.[9]

By the end of its two-year run, the Fair had attracted 51 million attendees, more than any previous World's Fair, resulting in an estimated $750 million in spending at the Fair itself and in New York City more broadly.[10] Yet, the story revealed in the press—and resonating with the public—was that these numbers fell far short of the 70 million attendees promised by Moses and upon which his estimates of $5–8 *billion* in total spending were calculated. The Fair Corporation lost $200 million to investors and lenders. There were no "millions in profits" for new schools and parks. In fact, the Fair ended up *costing* New York City taxpayers over $50 million—and this at a time of rising public debt.[11]

Ultimately, the stories of poor planning, insensitivity, and tastelessness on the part of the organizers upstaged the story of the Fair itself.[12] This led the irascible Moses to argue that the news media was biased, deceitful, and largely responsible for the Fair's problems. In one example, he used an invitation to speak before a gathering of New York publishers to vilify the news organizations they ran. Citing myriad examples of "gratuitous, sophisticated nastiness" in the *New York Times* and *Herald Tribune* and the *Reporter, Life,* and *Fortune* magazines, he showed how they used "the cutest tricks known to journalism" to "embarrass" Fair organizers and participants. And to add insult to injury, he noted, the bulk of these national opinion-makers were themselves based in New York: "All our studies indicate beyond a question that a small but influential segment of the local press, including some magazines of wide circulation which have their headquarters in the city, have been a serious handicap." Thus Moses cast the problem as one of major media corporations' victimization and betrayal of the Fair as well as their own hometown. A case in point was a cover article in *Life*—a magazine based in Manhattan, and the publisher of the official guide for the Fair—in which Moses and Walt Disney were referred to as "hopeless vulgarians." In response, Moses noted:

> We don't begrudge the Luce publications the million dollars they may make as publishers of the *Fair Guide*, which of course

emphasizes fair attractions, but we are mildly astonished at the ambivalence which at the same time pictures the fair as a bum show and New York as a dying city full of wrath and tears. How many shoulders can a publisher carry water on?[13]

However self-serving it might have been, Moses's critique was also accurate, even prescient, in its own way. New York had always been a media town, and a place in which sophisticated visual techniques were used to sell the city, but by the mid-1960s it seemed these same media—from TV and advertising to magazines and newspapers—had grown more powerful than the boosters who sought to wield them. Hometown loyalty was increasingly demanded from media corporations, much like from other expanding, New York City-based corporations in this new phase of globalization. But unlike other corporations, the media's loyalty was called into question due to the unique power of their product to enhance and sell, or damage and undermine, the image of the city on a global scale. Of particular concern was the characterization of New York as a "dying city full of wrath and tears," from which tourists, investors, and the white middle class in general should flee.

Robert Moses's critique of the bad publicity received by the World's Fair represents an early invocation of *image crisis* discourse. Through this discourse, negative representations and the media that produced them were blamed for undermining the economic viability of the city. The recognition that, as Disney put it, "it's a small world after all" was dawning on those pushing New York to transform its economy and enter the growing competition for tourism, corporate headquarters, and new investment after World War II. And so too was the challenge of marketing a city like New York—huge, chaotic, and always in the news. This challenge only increased over the course of the 1950s and 1960s, as the nation became more conservative and anti-urban and as New York's industrial base declined. Meanwhile, New York's rising status as a global media capital was becoming a double-edged sword, creating new marketing opportunities for the city while also exposing it to greater risks of negative publicity. Under such conditions, it became clear that old-fashioned urban boosterism was essentially powerless—even when it achieved the grandeur of the New York World's Fair. Indeed, the Fair may be seen as the last hurrah of New York's booster tradition and a transitional moment in the city's approach to marketing itself to the world.

In the rest of this chapter I will trace the rise of what came to be viewed by the mid-1960s as a New York image crisis. To do so I will first explore New York's historic role as a national and international media capital, and the ways in which this role was enhanced in the post-World War II period. In particular, this was due to the growth of New York-based news media, especially with the rise of television as the dominant mass medium, as well as to the dramatic return of Hollywood filmmaking to location shoots on New York City streets. Second, I will analyze the increasingly dominant representation of New York as an "asphalt jungle" over the same time period. This representation characterized New York as a city out of control—as symbolized by the degeneracy of Times Square and the rise of subway graffiti—and was rife with class- and race-based stereotypes. The way in which these two dynamics—New York as media capital and New York as asphalt jungle—intersected in the 1960s and early 1970s helped to create conditions that led to the city's fiscal crisis in the latter decade. It also laid the ground for the shift from urban boosterism to urban branding that was to come in that period.

New York as Media Capital
Throughout its now 350-year history, New York City's homegrown matrix of media and marketing industries has shaped its role as a nodal point in global capitalism. The fact that New York was the birthplace of the most important media technologies and industries of the modern period—including modern publishing, telegraphy, photography, advertising, radio, and television—accelerated its political and economic rise, and also meant that the sounds, images, and words of this city, expressing all of its diversity, style, chaos, and stark inequalities, were constantly broadcast to the world.

The origins of media in New York date back to the city's founding in the seventeenth century, when it became the printing capital of the future nation. Like the tolerant yet ruthless city in which they arose, these industries always reflected the tensions at the intersection of capitalism and democracy. On the one hand, they turned New York into a proving ground for the notions of freedom of speech and the press that were later ratified in the First Amendment of the Constitution, and a haven for radical, "free-thinking" printers, artisans, and orators.[14] On the other hand, from the earliest days of the Industrial Revolution, the telegraph monopoly held by a few New York-based corporations enabled them to control the flow of financial information and spur the international expansion of capital.[15]

So, too, the city's cultural and class complexity, from "high" to "low," was reflected in the array of its media representations. New York's status as capital of elite culture may have been unmatched, but it was never uncontested. On a daily basis, nineteenth-century "penny presses" printed literally thousands of different magazines, broadsheets, and papers, for the consumption of myriad ethnic, political, artistic, and professional communities.[16] And throughout the Gilded Era and Great Depression, the revolutionary new media of photography and film exquisitely and painfully captured New York's "sunshine and shadow"—portraying the contrasts of everyday life in the capitalist city and creating the most powerful visual critiques yet seen of the city's underlying class antagonisms.[17] This contrast was reflected further in the city's thriving culture industries—from Tin-Pan Alley to vaudeville to Broadway—which produced the very notion of popular culture consumed by the rest of the nation, and infused this culture with an unmistakable "New York sensibility." In short, throughout its history New York has been unequalled among global cities in its level of technological innovation and industrial power, and in the sheer volume, range, and influence of the sounds, images, and texts that it has produced.

The Post-war Rise of Television and Related Media

New York's role at the epicenter of global communications networks became increasingly significant following World War II. This was a period of explosion in the production and consumption of media and advertising sparked by the popular embrace of television and by American hegemony in international markets, which US television itself helped to promote. With New York's existing technical, economic, and cultural networks, its companies were uniquely positioned to take advantage of new technologies and markets, and quickly developed as the center of the new television industry, while reestablishing their historic edge in advertising, publishing, and radio. In addition, by the 1960s, New York became home to much of the cutting-edge new film, lifestyle media, and advertising that was targeted to, and consumed by, the young, urban middle class. In the post-war period, therefore, New York's representational power grew rapidly and the city's streets and sound stages became once again—for better or worse—a dominant site of representation.

The centrality of New York in the emerging television industry was clearly established in 1948, when NBC and CBS seized on newly popular broadcast technology to realize their commercial aspirations.[18] They, along with the new American Broadcasting Company (ABC), had used their muscle in the 1920s and 1930s to fight and win a court ruling allowing the bulk of radio broadcasting in the US to be controlled by the private sector, rather than by the public sector as it was in most other countries.[19] They now assumed oligopolistic dominance of this new industry and decided that its base would be in New York City.[20]

Television soon became the most important form of mass media consumption in the US and in the process began to drive the expansion, or decline, of other media.[21] Certain media—like radio and magazines—were forced to restructure their operations and formats to remain competitive. National magazines based in New York, like *Time*, *Life*, and *Look*, began to include ever more dramatic photographic essays—contributing to the rising stature of photo agencies like Magnum in the early1950s.[22] A new opportunity was created for smaller, experimental, lifestyle-oriented publications, many of which were spawned in New York in this period. But increasingly over the coming decade, magazines and newspapers lost readership as people defected to the heightened realism and immediacy of television. Meanwhile, the media industry as a whole entered the initial stages of global expansion, consolidation, and increased competition.

This caused a restructuring of media production in New York City. Most dramatic was the contrast between the "television/radio" sector and that of "printing and publishing": while the numbers of jobs and establishments in the first almost doubled in this period, those in the latter shrank by 30 percent.[23] On the other hand, there was a rapid expansion of those news and entertainment media that could work synergistically with television, as well as of international media outlets. New York-based international wire services, like the Associated Press and the United Press, saw rapid growth, passing the British Reuters and the French Agence France Press to dominate the "big four" in the news wire business.[24] They were now joined by expanding news-film distribution services, which bought stock footage from mobile television production teams, armed with new, portable, sync-sound 16-millimeter cameras. Given this infrastructure, as well as the avowed preference of foreign correspondents to work and live in New York City, a constant stream of international TV and print news agencies set up their US bureaus in Manhattan, and covered the entire nation and hemisphere "from the vantage point" of New York City.[25]

As in the "golden age" of film and radio fifty years earlier, television took advantage of New York's huge pool of theatrical writing and performing talent, and invented entirely new TV-entertainment genres like the situation comedy, drama, and the late night variety show, shooting them live on disused film and radio sound stages. In turn, these first shows of "television's golden age" were infused with what became known as a "New York sensibility."[26] On one level, this term was code for dramas and comedies that were explicitly ethnic and working class, as in *The Goldbergs* (CBS, 1949–1951; NBC, 1952–1954) and *The Honeymooners* (CBS, 1955–1956). On another level, it referred to shows charged with ironic wit and sharp social commentary, as in the historical reenactment drama *You Are There* (CBS, 1953–1954). While the former grew out of the dramatic traditions of the Yiddish Theater and vaudeville in the 1920s, the latter may be traced to the innovative theater and film work done by the leftist artists of the Popular Front of the 1930s, which was largely based in New York City.[27]

The prevalence of a New York sensibility in the early years of television reflected a few factors. First, in 1948, two-thirds of all TV sets in the nation were located in and around New York City, and since production costs were still low, and advertising sponsorships limited, this audience was the one programmers most had to please. In addition, such "heroic portrayals" of the working class in the late 1940s reflect, as Joshua Freeman points out, the fact that "Culturally, socially, and politically, blue-collar workers loomed larger at the end of the WWII than at any time before or since."[28] And last but by no means least, most of the screenwriters of these early shows were New Yorkers returned home from Hollywood, after having been "black-listed" by the House Un-American Activities Committee in the late 1940s and early 1950s.[29] As the historians Paul Buhle and Dave Wagner point out, a great number of these writers and directors found work, openly and covertly, during the "remarkable grace period" of early television drama in New York between 1949 and 1954, and brought the New York sensibility back home from Hollywood.[30] The use of television for depictions of the everyday struggles of the working class continued into the late 1950s, before largely disappearing in the 1960s.[31]

The Film Revival and Return of the New York Movie

The rise of live television and the continued strength of theater also supported the "film revival" in New York in the late 1950s and 1960s, providing training for technicians and editors, opportunities for would-be Hollywood directors, jobs for social realist documentarians, and a scene for avant-garde filmmakers.[32] The film and television world also intersected with the growing downtown movement of Pop Art and Film, and by the early 1970s with the underground press and video arts movements.

The scale of production inspired Mayor John V. Lindsay to overhaul a moribund city film agency (established in 1947) and create the Mayor's Office of Television, Broadcasting, and Film in 1966 to facilitate location shooting and permits. Then, beginning in the late 1960s, the "New York movie" returned to shooting in New York City, after some sixty years of residence on "the other coast." What started as an upsurge in the 1950s of underground films and made-for-TV movies now blossomed into a full-fledged movie industry. For the first time since D. W. Griffith had abandoned New York for Hollywood in the 1920s, and after decades of making films written by New York exiles and shot on stage-set versions of "The Lights of Broadway" and "Brownstone Brooklyn," a new generation of producers and directors were now streaming back the other way to gain access to the *real* streets, skyline, and faces of New York City.[33]

Lindsay named a director with a background in PR, advertising, and B-movie production, and a coordinator with experience navigating the city's bureaucracy. Working together, they designed what became known as the "one-stop system" for shooting films and TV programs in New York.[34] This had a revolutionary effect on the schedules and budgets of locally based productions. Before, anyone wanting to shoot in New York had to find a production manager and a local film official capable of negotiating with a Byzantine assortment of city agencies and personnel in order to obtain signatures for the myriad required permits, the number of which changed annually.[35] With impatient film directors facing tight budgets and deadlines came bribes, pay-offs, and corruption. Under the new system, this was all reduced to one permit, one schedule, and one signature from the Mayor's Office.[36] As a result of this streamlining, Lindsay is widely credited with having sparked a meteoric rise in local film production.[37] And indeed, over the course of his eight-year term, an amazing 366 movies were shot in New York, or an average of 46 films per year, as compared to only 13 features filmed in New York in 1965, the last year of Mayor Wagner's third term.[38]

Fun City

One of the leading purchasers of advertising and media that featured New York City was the expanding travel and tourism industry—including hotels, restaurants, amusement services, and real estate. The industry had been in decline since the immediate post-war period due to the rising cost of real estate and labor, and the increased competition posed by "jet-age" travel, a situation demonstrated by the closing of many of the city's largest and most venerable hotels in the early 1960s.[39] But this trend began to turn around during the 1964–1965 World's Fair, when the city's hotel occupancy reached its post-war high of 83 percent. Aiding this development, media, marketing, and tourism came together in a new way to promote New York City, and international tourists and business travelers began to take the places of the increasingly absent domestic visitors.[40] In the process, what might be considered a new economic cluster based in media, marketing, and tourism became a significant economic force in the city. By 1967, over 400,000 people were working in over 11,000 establishments in some aspect of this cluster, whether in the old media of printing, radio, and motion pictures or in the new medium of television; whether in advertising and consulting or in tourism and amusements. Such jobs now represented 14 percent of all private sector jobs in the city, almost double their size of a decade earlier.[41] And according to the Convention and Visitors Bureau (CVB), while there was "no way of measuring the effectiveness of the Bureau's promotional activities," in terms of their economic benefit to the city, the proof of such benefit was "evident" in the $1 billion of tourism spending, which, by its estimates, translated into $50 million in tax revenues for the city.[42]

Despite its increasing significance, and the mayor's role in the film revival, the tourism, media, and marketing cluster was not a high priority for the Lindsay administration in the late 1960s. Indeed, Lindsay began an effort to "phase out" the city government's allocation to the CVB, which constituted 50 percent of the Bureau's budget, arguing that private members and in-kind contributions should be sufficient for its needs. Between 1965 and 1967, the city's allocation was reduced from $350,000 to $200,000—a 42 percent cut. While additional cuts were not ultimately made—in response to intensive lobbying by powerful members of the Bureau—this reduced level of funding was to continue for the next five years.[43]

Lindsay's rationale was understandable given the budgetary priorities and realities of the time. By 1967, the city had already amassed a debt of some $200 million and was still facing complaints over unnecessary spending on the money-losing World's Fair. Any significant increase in funding for tourism and marketing, rather than fundamentals like education, sanitation, and reducing the debt, would have met with scrutiny and criticism, if not controversy—even if Lindsay had been so inclined. In this context, tourism marketing was seen as an unaffordable luxury, marginal to the city's overall economic health, and primarily a private sector responsibility.

This attitude does not necessarily jibe with common perceptions of Lindsay as a charming and telegenic politician who grasped the power of media to sell a certain image of New York. It is a perception linked to Lindsay's invention of one of New York's most enduring and advertising-friendly monikers: "Fun City." The Mayor coined the term during a live TV and radio interview in an effort to lift people's spirits at the start of the bitter, twelve-day transit strike of 1966. And to this day, Fun City evokes the youthful, modish exuberance of the city in its mid-1960s heyday, as well as the idealism and hope of the Lindsay era itself.[44]

However, far from serving as a city-marketing slogan, it should be remembered that Lindsay's wishful reference to "Fun City" met with widespread derision among weary New Yorkers of the day. Perhaps the article that did most to popularize the phrase was Dick Schaap's sardonic "What's New in Fun City?," which appeared in the *New York World Journal-Tribune* on January 7, 1966:

> Not long after the transit strike began the other day, Mayor John Lindsay went on radio and television to announce that New York is a fun city. He certainly has a wonderful sense of humor. A little while later, Lindsay cheerfully walked four miles from his hotel room to City Hall, a gesture which proved that the fun city had a fun Mayor . . . The funniest thing was that New Yorkers actually were finding humor in the absence of buses and subways. One citizen was very concerned that the pickpockets and muggers, the true New Yorkers, he called them, would get out of shape. He offered to give them a room where they could practice on each

> other for the duration of the crisis . . . The New Yorker's sense of
> humor spread out of town. In Philadelphia, nearly everyone was
> talking about the contest.[45]

Ironically, therefore, "Fun City" was turned on its head, becoming a phrase that satirized the very use of upbeat slogans in response to real urban problems and celebrated the gritty resilience and humor needed to survive New York in such times. This complex meaning has certainly changed over time. Nevertheless, the term was never used as part of any official city-marketing campaign in the late 1960s. Nor was any other. For, at the time, there was no significant political or economic support for such marketing in New York City.

Any marketing that was being done was limited and relatively unsophisticated, especially in comparison to resort destinations of the Sunbelt, like Miami and Las Vegas, cities with which New York, with its diverse economic base, had not historically felt it necessary to compete. Lindsay did maintain a modicum of support for the CVB budget, and he named a new executive vice-president, Charles Gillett, who had previously served as president of the American Society of Travel Agents. Gillett was a big believer in the need for heavily marketed, year-round tourism events, and in making permanent the massive mobilization and public–private cooperation that took place during the years of the World's Fair. In addition, he sought to continue the marketing strategy of the Fair—in other words, to challenge the New York sensibility and use television and advertising to present the city as "normal" and "American," i.e. white and middle class.

To this end, Gillett worked to revive and expand New York's "Miss Summer Festival"—a 1950s-style beauty contest, in which the winning contestant represented New York City around the world at various PR events (see Figure 2.3). Despite the "200 references in publications around the world" that were trumpeted in the CVB annual report of 1970, this low-budget, cookie-cutter campaign was spread mostly through press releases, made little use of television, had no interaction with city and state economic development agencies, and was quickly forgotten. Years of lobbying by the Bureau to increase its publicity budget and expand the city's convention facilities in competition with other cities fell on deaf ears. So innovations in media and marketing occurred in the private sector, but did not yet have a significant effect on the city's declining image and ailing economy—at least not in the direction city boosters wished.

Figure 2.3 Miss Summer Festival. From 1967 to 1970, the Convention and Visitors Bureau created a beauty pageant to promote their "New York is a Summer Festival" campaign. (a) Miss 1967 is crowned by Mayor John V. Lindsay and CVB president Preston R. Tisch. (b) Miss 1969 goes on a world tour to promote New York.

Courtesy New York City Municipal Library

(a)

(b)

New York as Asphalt Jungle

Despite the best efforts of the Mayor and the CVB, by the late 1960s any notion of "Fun City" was overshadowed by more popular and sinister New York nicknames: "the ungovernable city," "the rotten apple," and "the asphalt jungle." As a *Time* editorial of the day noted off-handedly: "Scarcely anyone today needs to be told about how awful life is in nerve-jangling New York City, which resembles a mismanaged ant heap rather than a community fit for human habitation."[46] *Fortune* magazine ran a special issue in 1971 devoted to the economic and social demise of urban America, which was filled with images of nameless black and brown people "hanging out" on the streets.[47] *Time* devoted a number of its Friday lead editorials to the subject of "crime in America" that rehashed the worst urban stereotypes.[48] Popular pundits predicted cities were on the brink of complete self-destruction, and that the age of urban existence was over.[49]

While some of these epithets stuck longer than others, each contributed to a broader subtext. Locals were reduced to insects or animals, and the city itself to a zone of degeneration beyond the pale of social control. This expressed an anti-urban bias becoming more prevalent in the country with the rising conservative political movement, and that also served as a more acceptable form of traditional American racism and classism.[50] In essence, this bias blamed American cities and their residents for their own problems. Since the problems were presented as natural to these troubled populations, they were also presented as incurable. This tautology provided a strong counter-argument for any movement seeking a political means of addressing the deeper, structural causes of urban problems—since no structural causes were shown to exist.

In what follows, I will look more closely at a few of the main sources—television drama, television news, and film—of this increasingly dominant set of images. And I will analyze a few of its main motifs—the degeneracy of Times Square, and the growing "epidemic" of graffiti on New York City subways. Such ideologically laden representations were then broadcast via the television news—in contrast to the "normal Americans" on view during the entertainment programs.[51] In addition, innovations in television technology and editing made the news a more compelling format that lent itself to visually dramatic and sensationalistic reportage. Finally, a new genre of urban horror films was becoming popular—most of which, as we shall see, were based in the imagined *demi-monde* of New York City neighborhoods.

The Fall of the "New York Sensibility"

The independent, left-leaning New York sensibility that emerged in the early 1950s was soon at odds with portrayals of the city being produced in Hollywood and broadcast through New York's big-three networks. As sales of television sets sky-rocketed in the mid-1950s, as sponsors became more vigilant, and as McCarthyite purges moved into television, a new premium was placed on programming and talent that were "normal" and "American."[52] Anyone who was too urban, working-class, or non-white Anglo-Saxon Protestant became coded as abnormal, un-American, and off limits for dramas, situation comedies, and variety shows, though they were increasingly fair game for the TV news. And so Dick Van Dyke, Ed Sullivan, and *I Love Lucy* replaced *The Honeymooners*, *The Goldbergs*, and *Playhouse 90*.

This growing conservatism and anti-urbanism was also spurred by the networks' new dependency on Madison Avenue's big advertising firms, whose strength had grown along with the rise of television, suburbanization, and the global influence of corporate America. By 1954, CBS had become the largest advertising medium in the world, and by 1957 television in general accounted for $1.5 billion in spending by advertisers.[53] This was a boon for leading advertising firms, like J. Walter Thompson and Young & Rubicam, which became the largest producers of television commercials in this period. In addition, the industry was extremely successful at responding to the rise of the youth market and counter-culture in the late 1950s and 1960s. A group of new firms—including Doyle, Dane, Bernbach; Ogilvy Mather; and Wells, Rich, Greene—launched the "creative revolution" in advertising, catering to this hard-to-reach but consumer-oriented demographic.

More than any other format, the nightly news disseminated the image of New York City as asphalt jungle to the nation. Crime in New York had always been overreported. As city officials and journalists alternately complained and boasted, "a jaywalker on Broadway gets front page billing in Topeka."[54] But such disproportionate coverage increased dramatically with the advent of verité-style television news, the growing demand of New York-based TV networks and film-news services for exciting footage to sell to affiliates, and the apparent thrill of New York crime coverage for suburban viewers. Thus, New York became a leading antagonist in what Robert Beauregard called the "nightly dramaturgy of TV news" of the 1960s and 1970s, in which graphic portrayals of urban violence became some of the most popular TV viewing of the time.[55] In addition, the new genre of television documentary provided salacious "in-depth" views of criminality in New York's ghetto neighborhoods, which were to become influential models for future inner-city cop dramas shot on location against the same backdrop.[56]

The director Sidney Lumet took a critical look at this increasingly exploitative crime coverage in his 1975 film *Dog Day Afternoon*, based on a real bank robbery and hostage-taking that happened in Brooklyn in 1972. Almost as soon as the crime occurs in the film, the bank is surrounded by flocks of news crews jockeying with the police for position—NYPD helicopters competing for air space with TV news helicopters armed with cameras. As revealed by both the film and the actual events upon which it was based, the news media were now capable of covering a crime live, as it was unfolding, even to the extent of obstructing the police. Exploiting the live coverage, Sonny, the lead bank robber in the film, turns the street in front of the bank—now filled with a crowd—into his stage, whipping his audience into a frenzy, tossing wads of five dollar bills over their heads, and leading them in chants of "Attica! Attica!"[57] When he brings out a hostage, she is so mesmerized by the media attention, that she turns down the option of escape, more excited by the fact that she is now "a celebrity." Meanwhile, the news media have gathered even more sensational background on Sonny: he is a gay Vietnam vet who is attempting to rob the bank for money to pay for his transvestite partner's sex-change operation. Now the story is so big that one network taps into the bank's phone line, diverting it from the police negotiators, to interview Sonny live on the air. Sonny cuts the interview short, declaring: "I know what this is—we're just entertainment to you! What do you got for us? Huh? Let's talk about something *you* know about!" The phone line and TV transmission simultaneously go dead.

Perhaps never before had a criminal, even a fictional one, upbraided a newscaster on live TV. In part, this development reflected the new technology that had arisen in the 1960s. Television, already the nation's primary media source, was revolutionized with the emergence of satellite transmission and smaller, more portable cameras, which created the possibility of footage that was both "live" and personal. Mobile TV crews in Vietnam were able to send home graphic, close-up coverage of a battle and its casualties, helping to create the immediacy of the first "living-room war." And at the same time, roving news crews were deployed in the streets of US cities, providing similarly graphic, documentary-style coverage of the "urban crisis."

But this coverage was not only a product of new technology. Unlike the real war in Vietnam, the US urban crisis was a nebulous phenomenon, produced both by real events on the ground and by an increasingly conservative national sentiment. Graphic coverage was required to prove the very existence of the urban crisis, as well as to boost the ratings of the news shows catering to a suburban audience excited by such coverage. Vietnam-like imagery and direct comparisons of New York to Southeast Asia were used to present the city as "America's Vietnam."[58] This was a reflection in part of the return of Vietnam veterans in this period,[59] but it also expressed a growing media obsession with urban crime and "gang warfare." While cities were enduring very real problems of crime, poverty, joblessness, and social unrest, these were used as filler by a voracious news cycle that thrived on the most sensational of such stories.

In the midst of the "nightly dramaturgy" of news coverage of urban problems in the late 1960s and early 1970s, New York City took center stage, becoming a paradigm of urban crisis.[60] This occurred despite the fact that it was one of many northern cities that experienced race riots in the 1960s and that its crime rate was consistently ranked only as average on the list of the country's twenty biggest cities.[61] Nonetheless, the national TV networks and magazines, all of which were based in Midtown Manhattan, jumped at the chance to turn a mugging in Central Park or a neighborhood bank hold-up by an out-of-work gay man into a national news story. The major foreign news agencies based in New York City followed their lead, dispatching crews to cover these same local stories for their audiences. Dramatic labor actions like the sanitation and transit strikes, and the rise of graffiti writing on the subways, became huge national and international stories, providing lurid evidence of "a city out of control." As films like *Dog Day Afternoon* demonstrated, the media circus happening at New York crime scenes in the early 1970s could now damage the city independently of the crimes themselves.

Times Square as Site of Degeneration

Since the nineteenth century, New York had served in the popular imagination as the ultimate symbol of the modern city in all its contradictions. It was a site of the greatest evolution to the highest of high culture, or of devolution to the lowest of low, and attracted visitors interested in experiencing either or both extremes of this spectrum. This continued to be true into the middle of the twentieth century, when representations of New York ranged from the working-class, polyglot "Gotham" of the radical ethnic press, to the sophisticated "New Rome" of modern art openings and high fashion, to the violent, brooding "Naked City" of film noir.[62] Yet now, with the inner city deteriorating, and with social and fiscal crises mounting, a single urban imaginary began to circulate more than others: the dystopic vision of the city as "asphalt jungle." Unlike earlier representations, and in contrast to bucolic representations of the suburbs and Sunbelt, New York City now appeared as a site of pure degeneration. In the streets of the city, people devolved to their basest nature, and the bright lights were a thin cover for the true depravity lurking right under the surface.

No single space in New York symbolized this degeneration like Times Square, long the city's primary tourist destination, red-light district, and most recognized icon. The "crossroads of the world," which had always managed to strike a balance between risqué, popular, and upscale entertainment, had grown decidedly seedier during the 1960s.[63] As the number of theaters, movie palaces, and deli-style restaurants declined for lack of business, the number of pawn shops, burlesques, and prostitutes increased to take their place. The massive, garish billboards were still a fixture, but many of the most famous and sophisticated signs—like the twenty-foot woman blowing Camel smoke rings—shut down in the early 1970s when faced with sky-rocketing energy prices. These were replaced with simpler signs for foreign brands trying to break into the US market, which were content to have their names in lights above this still famous thoroughfare, despite its deteriorating reputation.[64] But pedestrian traffic below the bright lights, and tourist activity in general, took a nose-dive. As one anonymous sightseeing guide complained in 1971: "This is the worst summer I can remember since the war. They ought to burn down those porno joints on 42nd Street and those filthy movies and Broadway would come back to its own."[65]

One of the most powerful portraits of Times Square in this period was the Oscar-winning, and X-rated, *Midnight Cowboy*, which came out in 1969.[66] The film stars John Voigt as the strapping and naive young cowboy Joe Buck, who takes the long bus-ride from his small hometown in Texas to New York in the hope of excitement and a better life. Like generations of immigrants and film characters before him, he comes to the big city an innocent rube, yet, unlike them, and in a sign that times have definitely changed for the youth of the 1960s, he seeks his fortune as a male prostitute for wealthy New York women. Quickly and tragically he finds himself no match for the utter ruthlessness of the characters he encounters, or for his own desperate loneliness. After a Park Avenue woman refuses to pay him, and the hotel manager impounds his belongings, he finds himself starving and alone, and joins the junkies, hustlers, and other male prostitutes under the XXX marquees of 42nd Street. The abandoned midnight spaces of Times Square prompt horrific visions of crumbled buildings and his own memories of abuse, as he becomes one with the dereliction of the streets around him. His only friend is the crippled swindler Ratso Rizzo, played by Dustin Hoffman, who invites him to share his meager room in a condemned building. Together they steal from Italian vegetable salesmen, hustle rich bohemians, and dream of taking the "Yellowbird Special" to the paradise of Florida. As the harsh winter comes and Ratso's health deteriorates, Joe goes back to the streets one last time, and when his "john"—an effete business-man in town for the paper sellers' convention—refuses to pay him, he is finally pushed over the edge to violence.

Needless to say, *Midnight Cowboy* did not inspire an increase in convention business, and nor did the spate of "asphalt jungle" films that were to follow in its path in the late 1960s and early 1970s. These included path-breaking urban dramas, crime thrillers, and "blaxploitation" films, like Martin Scorsese's *Mean Streets* (1973), William Friedkin's *The French Connection* (1971), and Gordon Parks Jr.'s *Superfly* (1972). Such films are now considered classics of their genres, and iconic works for a new generation of experimental directors, often referred to as the *auteurs* of the "New Hollywood."[67] Freed from the constraints of the Motion Pictures Production Code, and heavily influenced by the counter-culture of the

1960s, these films sought to achieve a heightened sense of realism, and to keep Hollywood relevant for a younger audience raised amid the growing disenchantment, alienation, and unrest of the Vietnam War and Watergate era.[68] And increasingly, the backdrop that was chosen to convey such realism was New York—much to the chagrin of the city's would-be boosters.

Subway Graffiti and a City out of Control

As negative representations from the mainstream media were undermining the city from without, another major source of New York's image crisis arose unexpectedly from within. It came in the form of a small movement of teenagers writing their names in vivid color and daring style on the walls of buildings and subway cars. It was a phenomenon simply called "writing" by its practitioners, and "graffiti" by local authorities, and it was to have a profound impact on the wider cultural movement of hip hop in New York City and globally. It was also to provoke entrenched struggles over legitimate forms of cultural expression and uses of public space that persist to this day.

The "groundwork" of writing culture had been laid in the 1960s in New York as well as in other cities such as Los Angeles and Philadelphia, but the most important, "pioneering" stage in the development of writing occurred in New York City between 1971 and 1974.[69] By most accounts, the motivation for the early writers was a mixture of youthful hubris and competition, as well as the need for self-expression, recognition, and creative escape from the bleak confines of deteriorating neighborhoods and underfunded schools. As the writer Little Soul 159 recalled of those early days, this need was linked to a cultural movement that rejected existing definitions of legal rights to public property and space:

> In the beginning it wasn't just a matter of art. It was a matter of building your self-esteem, to know that you were somebody, that you counted. There's my name, I did it, I can do something that's positive. Although obviously it was illegal for society's purposes. But for our purposes, I think it was a cultural revolution. And during a cultural revolution the rules don't apply.[70]

For these purposes, the subways were the most revolutionary exhibition space imaginable. They traversed and were seen by the entire city, rich and poor; uptown and downtown; black, white, Asian, and Latino. By the mid-1970s a, if not *the*, main objective for writers in "getting up" was to gain prestige and fame by being seen on as many subway lines and by as wide an audience as possible—a phenomenon known as "going all city."[71]

Early observers of the scene noted that these writers were pursuing the classic dream of celebrity so common in New York's commercial pop culture, whereby visibility was associated with greater fame, and fame with greater visibility.[72] The marquees of Broadway had long offered aspiring "stars" the ultimate promise of success by "getting your name in lights," which was essentially what many of these young people were seeking. And commercial advertisement in the form of billboards, signs, and posters had been using public space (the streets, subways, buses, etc.) as a medium for broadcasting the brand names of myriad products for more than a century by the time writers appeared on the urban scene and "borrowed" the same spaces to display their own names. But there was one crucial difference between writing and commercial culture. In the latter, name recognition was used as a means to an end—that is, to promote greater recognition, and consumption, of the commodified face and personality of the "star," or the commodified product behind the "brand." By contrast, for writers, whose activities were illegal and for whom survival depended on official anonymity, name recognition was an end in itself, or as Norman Mailer put it famously: "the name was the faith of graffiti."[73] New York City subways were soon filled with thousands of these names, or "tags," circulating like a flock of floating signifiers, as ubiquitous as they were inscrutable to the majority of their viewers, who were not a part of the writing subculture.

In February 1971, the *New York Times* published an article on one of the writers, TAKI 183, whose tag, written in thick black marker, was being spotted on numerous Midtown Manhattan subway lines, and sparking curiosity. As the investigative article revealed, it turned out that "TAKI" was the nickname for the writer's given name, Demetrius, and "183" the number of the street in Washington Heights where he lived. And the reason he favored the 4/5/6 lines was that his work as a foot messenger meant he was on those subways frequently. As a courier between and within New York's central business districts, TAKI had the opportunity to write his tag in places that, though less likely to be spotted by other appreciative teenagers, were more visible to the elite of the city, and in particular the media elite, who might, and did, see his work as a newsworthy story.[74]

The *Times* story about TAKI 183 revealed two things—at least to the uninitiated. One was the appropriation of the subway as a media technology to spread the message of a diverse, city-wide movement of what some considered artists, others vandals. Between 1971 and 1974, hundreds of young people were getting involved, and "the subway system proved to be a line of communication and a unifying element for all these separate movements."[75] As the historian Joe Austin puts it, the subway provided these young people, who were otherwise cut off from the city, with "an alternative public broadcast system."[76] As opposed to just tagging locally, now writers and potential writers from across the five boroughs could become aware of, and inspired by, each other's efforts.

Figure 2.4 Early subway writers.
(a) SONNY 102 at work.
(b) FLIP on a train alongside his tag, *c.* 1971.

Courtesy Flint Gennari, FineArt Fotos

(a)

(b)

The TAKI 183 article proved to writers that the subway was also a stepping stone to an even wider visibility in the mainstream media, and with it, a whole new level of "fame." Since the late 1960s, writers had understood that they were working in the midst of a broader communications revolution, in which new media forms and technologies were proliferating, and in which marketing messages were able to enter new spaces of the city. Sometimes this link was made explicit, as in the case of graffiti writer and photographer Flint Gennari, who wrote tags that were influenced by the new style of advertising copy and graphics, and often placed his work alongside actual ads. Gennari was especially influenced by the work of Peter Max, a leading figure in Pop Art and creative advertising, and someone whose work was being wrapped around city buses, and even airplanes, in this period.[77] In general, especially after TAKI's interview, it was widely accepted that dissemination in almost any form of mass media offered one of the fastest routes to fame.[78] As Austin argues, this had a direct impact on writing strategy:

> Realizing that cameras [and not just passersby] were watching and recording opened up an entirely new system of exposure. Writers immediately capitalized on this fact and utilized these watchful eyes to broadcast their own works. Writers now deliberately wrote their names in places they thought were likely to be photographed, videotaped, or filmed. Many writers during these years could boast that they had repeatedly appeared in the newspapers and on TV although these "appearances" were usually made in the background of photos and camera shots intended for other purposes.[79]

The easy notoriety that came with tagging quickly led to city-wide competition, as individual writers and writing crews sought to establish themselves and gain status as the best in terms of the quality or quantity of their tags. Of course, to engage in this competition, writers were almost invariably breaking the law—thereby achieving another form of status, and attracting more media attention, through the simple, rebellious act of escaping capture and "getting over" on the system. With far greater coverage targeted at the troubled city, these daring young writers were to gain more publicity—and caused the city bigger headaches—than they perhaps ever anticipated, as will be discussed in later chapters. For now, their rolling canvases touched an already raw nerve, and were interpreted by many in the public as creating, not responding to, the larger crises in New York City. As Joe Austin put it: "Those already inclined to blame urban crisis for the woes of the 1960's found . . . in 'graffiti' their arch nemesis—a sign of barbarians at the gates, and a nation out of control."[80]

Figure 2.5 Graffiti responds to advertising.
A tag by Flint Gennari, *c.* 1971.

The End of Hometown Loyalty

In the same speech in which he railed against magazine publishers for their slanted coverage of the World's Fair, Robert Moses offered a second interpretation of who was to blame for the image crisis: New York City itself.

> Defacers of walls and underpasses give us their fatuities for nothing, but some publishers pay for such recordings. Those who fire such broadcasts at New York get their best ammunition from our own arsenal . . . No wonder the rest of the country looks at us askance as we foul our own nest, notes our lack of local pride and loyalty and concludes that New York is not even part of the United States.[81]

It was another revealing and prescient attack from Moses, and not only because it anticipated the city's "war on graffiti" by a full decade. For here Moses articulated the mainstream critique that would be taken up by New York's own branding coalition in the 1970s: not only were the powerful local media responsible for the city's declining status in the eyes of the nation, so too were a great many of the city's citizens, who were providing them with their sensational, scurrilous content. In essence, the press was colluding with "the defacers of walls and underpasses," the protesters at the Fair, the sideshow barkers of Coney Island, and the striking sanitation workers, to shame the entire city. And in so doing they were giving the "rest of the country"— that is, upstanding, white, middle-class Americans—the understandable impression that New Yorkers were degenerate, disloyal, and deserving of their fate.

The critique Moses articulated would be incorporated within the emerging discourse of "image crisis," and used to argue that such negative representations of New York in the mainstream media could now undermine the economy of the city as a whole. The rise of this powerful discourse also signaled the end of the booster era in New York City. For as it implied, the days were gone when an ingenious impresario, or even a power broker with the stature of Robert Moses, could mount a spectacle or create an attraction that would, in and of itself, sell out-of-towners on New York. Now city marketing would have to be coordinated on a much larger scale, make more extensive use of media, and resonate with the changing sensibilities of the age if it was to have any chance of rising above the sea of negative publicity.

As with any effective discourse, invocations of image crisis contained elements of empirical truth. Negative publicity did pack a mighty punch in these volatile times. And as I have sought to show in this chapter, the potential impact of such a punch was increasing throughout the 1960s with the growing representational power of New York's own media industries.

Technologies that had been harnessed to market the city for tourism during the World's Fair were now being used to produce and disseminate an image of New York as an "asphalt jungle" and the paradigm of urban crisis on an ever wider scale. And yes, such imagery did have real material effects on everything from tourist numbers to bond prices, making the notion of an impending image crisis all the more credible.

Yet the official embrace of "image crisis" discourse was, and remains, problematic on numerous levels. First, by foregrounding image, such discourse deflects attention from the political and economic roots of crisis—whether, in this case, the mismanaged budget of the World's Fair, the uneven development of the city, or the anti-urban policies of the federal government. Second, such discourse tends to accept and reify dominant notions of "negative" versus "positive" urban imagery that are laden with cultural, racial, and class bias. And third, under cover of this discourse, powerful groups may denigrate, exclude, and even criminalize forms of cultural and political expression that are not deemed marketable, or that complicate their marketing efforts.

For all these reasons, the threat of image crisis was no easy sell in a diverse and politicized city like New York in the late 1960s and early 1970s. As we will see, new levels of coalition building, design sophistication, market research, and policing were therefore required to produce and maintain a convincingly "positive," hegemonic image, or brand, for New York City as it entered the era of fiscal crisis.

CHAPTER **3**

Style and Power

The Common Sense of New York *Magazine*

One can say that the [magazine review] belongs to the sphere of "common sense" or "good sense" because its aim is to modify average opinion in a given society by criticizing, suggesting, mocking, correcting, modernizing, and in the last analysis, by introducing new commonplaces. If well written, with verve and a certain sense of detachment (so as not to sound like a sermon), yet with sincere interest in average opinion, reviews of this type can have a wide circulation and exert a profound influence.

Antonio Gramsci, 1925[1]

Magazines create a community of interest that did not know it existed.

Clay Felker, quoting Henry Luce, 2004[2]

What role do popular culture and media play in the rise of a new class to power? This was a question that preoccupied the Italian political philosopher Antonio Gramsci, writing in the revolutionary era of the 1920s. He turned for his answer to earlier periods of bourgeois ascendancy in the late eighteenth and nineteenth centuries. In both eras, Gramsci saw that modern journalism was "the most prominent and dynamic part" of the "ideological front" of the bourgeoisie.[3] In order for members of the new class to see themselves as such and then advance their political aspirations, they depended upon a journalistic vanguard capable of articulating their particular cultural sensibility and world-view, and of projecting this as the average, natural "common sense" of the age. Of all the journalistic genres that expressed this common sense, none was more effective than the "moralizing review"—or what today we would call the lifestyle magazine. It was here that the status quo was mocked in favor of the "modern way of life," and persuasively so—with wit, detachment, and a "sincere interest in average opinion."[4]

The rise of the "new journalism" in the pages of *New York* magazine in the late 1960s represented a similar moment of a journalistic vanguard. New journalists wrote in the first person, and with a fresh, opinionated, and ironic take on standard magazine fare—the political portrait, the advice column, the restaurant review, etc.—that seemed to reflect, and helped produce, the common sense of the day. The effect was the crafting of what *New York* editor Clay Felker called "a community of interest that didn't know it existed," i.e.: a community of middle-class strivers attempting to survive and thrive in a city tumbling ever deeper into crisis. The new journalists were themselves generally of the same class background, dropped the same cultural references, and shared the same everyday concerns as their targeted readers.[5] And, in the midst of New York's shifting class hierarchy, they projected this particular lifestyle and set of concerns as those of the entire city. Those not savvy enough to understand the *New York* common sense, it was assumed, were not part of the new class, and those who aspired to be part of the new class made sure to understand it.

In this sense, *New York* magazine should also be seen as a seminal text and a key institution in the construction of a new brand image for New York City. With its intense focus on consumption and lifestyle, the magazine helped transform New York City's reputation as the apotheosis of the 1960s "urban crisis," making the city hip among a young and upwardly mobile audience, and extremely popular among advertisers and investors. While created by a group of neophyte writers and editors, the ingeniously crafted image of the city promoted by the magazine became influential among new middle classes as well as the city's more elite "movers and shakers"—from the "culturati" to the financiers. So successful was its formula that it ultimately was appropriated—in essence—by a city- and state-based branding coalition seeking to attract *New York*'s increasingly affluent audience through its own official marketing campaigns.

So I turn now to a historic and discursive analysis of *New York* in order to explore how the personalities and literary tropes that characterized the magazine's "common sense" can help us to reflect on the larger social and cultural transformation of the city in this period.

The Creation of *New York,* 1965–1967

Though launched as an independent magazine in 1967, *New York* originated in 1963 as a Sunday supplement to the *New York Herald Tribune.* Under editor Jim Bellows and publisher John Hay "Jock" Whitney, the *Tribune* was at that time trying to position itself as a "lively alternative" to the *New York Times* while distancing itself from its reputation as the paper of choice of older, Upper East Side, WASP elites.[6] Using the advertising slogan "Who says a good newspaper has to be dull?," Bellows's innovation was to reimagine the Sunday edition of the *Tribune* as a local, lifestyle-oriented break from the hard, international news of the weekly editions. This was also a response to the rising competition of television news, which was siphoning off the younger generation of newspaper readers. He conceived of the "centerpiece" of this new Sunday edition to be *New York*—a graphically innovative magazine supplement covering the local scene from a more hip, entertaining perspective.[7] Bellows understood that his targeted readers, unlike their parents' generation, were focused on the local far more than the global; on lifestyle coverage far more than heavy, socio-political reports; and on themselves, or people with whom they could identify, far more than anyone else.

In light of this, he hired Clay Felker as editor of his experimental supplement. Felker was an ambitious young reporter, originally from Missouri, with experience in both journalism and marketing, and with an abiding passion for New York City. His first job was as a reporter/advertising writer/advertising seller for various sports magazines within his father's St. Louis-based publishing house, Sporting News Co.[8] Bored by the job, he used it to travel to New York, which he considered "the imperial city of our modern civilization," seeking "to become a statistician on New York City." And so, after graduating from Duke in 1951, he returned to New York to work as a reporter for *Time* in the early 1950s, and as features editor of *Esquire* from 1957 to 1962. Felker thus witnessed first hand the heyday of the general interest magazine, its decline with the rise of TV, and the emergence of a new genre of niche publications targeted at a younger, more consumer-oriented audience. As he understood, this had everything to do with the larger shifts in US consumption patterns in the post-war era, and the 1960s, in particular: "Everybody talks about the 'social justice revolution' [of the 1960s]. That was a big revolution. But the bigger revolution was the 'consumer revolution.' Young people went off in different directions. And when they did, magazines [shifted to cover] those issues."[9]

This understanding grew in tandem with Felker's expertise in magazine marketing. At *Time/Life*, Felker was exposed to the media surveys of Alfred Politz Research, the leading firm in media market research in the 1950s.[10] The survey that Felker found most significant showed that the fastest-growing segment of the economy was the "moneyed middle class," a class with disposable income and leisure time for the first time in their family history, and in need of help in learning what to do with both.[11] By the 1960s, Felker was also familiar with the "psychographic" research of firms like Yankelovich, Skelly, and White (YSW), which tracked the "lifestyle" and "attitudinal" trends of the renegade "new youth," and the anti-corporate concerns of the burgeoning "consumer revolution." As Felker saw, general interest titles were of diminishing use to these emergent groups, while advertisers were desperate for a new format through which to tap into their minds and wallets. Finally, the main fascination of such research, according to Felker, was in corroborating what he and his young staff at *New York* knew "instinctively"—being visionary members of the "moneyed middle class," and/or the "new youth," themselves.[12]

Felker combined this instinct and marketing savvy when it came to his editorial approach. He developed his famous "two rules of journalism": first, write from a "clear point of view" rather than bland, general interest; and second, "be on the reader's side" rather than the side of marketers and elites. And he saw it as his job as editor to find talented writers and designers who could follow these rules before "getting out of their way."[13] In his trust of young writers, designers, and readers as free thinkers and sophisticated consumers, Felker is credited with shepherding the rise of "the new journalism." But it was also through new journalism that he most adroitly responded to the anti-establishment attitude of the 1960s "consumer revolution." Felker was not the first to pick up on the marketing implications of this revolution—as mentioned above, hip ad agencies like Doyle, Dale, Bernbach (DDB) and Wells, Rich, Greene were doing the same with their hip "new advertising." But Felker's, and *New York*'s, great innovation was to combine new journalism with new advertising, and by extension the psychographic research on the "new youth" upon which it was based.

Thus *New York* incorporated counter-cultural advertising within the *editorial* side of the magazine itself, making the marketing pitch all the more undetectable and palatable. Design director and illustrator Milton Glaser put it succinctly: "the great marketing theory [was that] you're getting the readers to feel loyal because they feel that the magazine has been written for them, and that they are not simply victims of a conspiracy to encourage them to buy things." This loyalty then spilled over into readers' responses to the actual advertisements. According to Glaser, a 1970s survey on "advertising believability" showed that readers believed the ads in *New York* more than in any other magazine in the US. "And the reason for it fundamentally was that they believed the information in the editorial pages . . . There was a direct transfer of feeling [to the advertisements]—the magazine was straight with the readership and so the advertising was more believable."[14]

A key element in building this trust with readers, particularly among the upwardly mobile psychographic the *Tribune* sought to attract, was finding the right journalistic talent. Drawing from his circle of contacts built up from years at *Life* and *Esquire*, Felker assembled what he called "a newsroom Camelot" of smart and fashionable young writers, artists, and designers who could speak to the aspirations of their generation. These included Jimmy Breslin and Pete Hamill, lifestyle writer Gail Sheehy, food writer Gael Greene, journalist and activist Gloria Steinem, and, perhaps most famously, Tom Wolfe, a combination of hard news reporter and *bon vivant*.[15] Their approach entailed using colorful, descriptive prose, written in the vernacular, to address pressing issues of the day.[16] Sometimes this approach took the form of first-person reportage, sometimes of writing from a "fly on the wall" perspective, but always it addressed the reader directly, without condescension, and gave them the impression of being an insider in the scene described. It also served to turn opinionated writers like Breslin, Wolfe, and Steinem into some of the first "literary stars." They became quintessential "New Yorkers," and trusted tour guides to their personal "New York."

Figure 3.1 *New York* and "new journalism."
From the cover of *New York*, February 14, 1972.

New York magazine

But to achieve this subjective transference fully, the journalists' intimate literary style merged with art director Milton Glaser's distinctive graphic design and layout. Glaser, a native New Yorker, studied art at the High School of Music and Art and Cooper Union, graduating in 1951. There he broke away from the prevailing style of Abstract Expressionism in favor of a more eclectic, accessible, and "urban" form of design.[17] After studying on a Fulbright Scholarship at the Academy of Fine Art in Bologna, Italy, in 1954 he founded Pushpin Studios with Seymour Chwast and other young illustrators, which exerted great influence on the worlds of design, Pop Art, and advertising over the next twenty years. Perhaps Glaser's greatest contribution to *New York* was in understanding the necessary synergy between text and image in the creation of a recognizable brand identity.

This graphic synergy was facilitated by the power-sharing between design and editorial upon which Glaser insisted—drawing on his experience in new advertising and the multimedia eclecticism of the art world at the time. As Thomas Frank has described, at innovative agencies like DDB, copywriters and graphic designers began to collaborate as "creative teams" in the late 1950s.[18] Now Felker and Glaser joined forces as editor and design director,[19] and maintained a complementary, if often contentious, working relationship.[20] *New York*'s balance of power between editorial content and graphic design represented a radical departure from the prevailing relationship between the two in the magazine and newspaper world at the time, which was one of strict hierarchy and separation. Both Glaser and Felker remembered that it was rare for the two sides to sit in the same room, or even work in the same building, let alone collaborate in a big, open loft as *New York* writers and designers did in their makeshift workspaces. Through the artistry and commercial savvy of Glaser, *New York* managed to create a magazine version of new advertising, in which image and design were as important as text, and through which advertising messages could be effectively hidden.

This currency between visual form and written content, and between editorial and advertising, was facilitated by Glaser's "literary" approach to graphics. As he explains it: "The most important thing about the graphics [in *New York*] were that they . . . tried to reflect powerfully and in the most easily understood way the ideas that were behind them. I'm always driven by the word. My interest is literary but my talent is visual."[21] Glaser's literary approach led him to make design distinctions between the "news" and "lifestyle" sides of the magazine. With news he felt the style should be "straightforward, somewhat rigid, not beautiful." Partially this had to do with the tight deadlines and last-minute changes needed for news, leaving "no opportunity for elaborate layout considerations." But this was also due to the need graphically to extend what Glaser termed the "directness" and "believability" of the new journalism-style news pieces—an echo of the new advertisers' call for "honesty" and "respect" for the consumer. As he said: "The illusion of unmanipulated presentation [was] the goal . . . The more beautiful a magazine is, the less believable it becomes . . . *New York*'s appeal derived from its energy, not its beauty." On the other hand, the fluffier lifestyle pieces could be more "flamboyant" in both layout and illustration, and more aesthetically aligned with actual advertising. Meanwhile, both ads and fluff gained credibility from the distinct, verité style of the news side of the magazine.

While the strategy of *New York* was hugely successful in boosting sales for the Sunday edition, this could not make up for the stagnant readership in the *Tribune*'s weekly editions, and the paper went through a financial restructuring. In an early indication of the corporate concentration within the news industry that was to occur alongside the proliferation of new niche publications, the *New York Herald Tribune* was bought out and merged into the hybrid *World Journal Tribune*. Yet, lacking sufficient readership to compete with the *New York Times*, the entire venture died in May 1967. At first, it appeared that the successful supplement would be done in by the demise of its parent paper. Then, so the story goes, Felker decided to keep it alive, at the urging of Jimmy Breslin, by buying it outright for $6,572, his severance pay from the *World Journal Tribune*, and turning it into an independent publication. But as Felker himself recounted, he also had a friend who was a top partner in Loeb Rhodes, a prominent Wall Street investment bank, and "this partner helped me raise the money . . . because he had the connections." Other well-connected friends like Gloria Steinem helped arrange meetings with investors she knew. Initial investors included corporate financiers like Edgar Bronfman of Seagrams, and their total investment was in the tens of millions of dollars.[22] All of this is to say that *New York* was never quite the small, independent start-up it was touted to be. Indeed, many within the financial community were responsive to the magazine's deft business plan and marketing potential.

After raising the requisite capital, and rehiring most of the old staff writers, Felker and publisher George Hirsch Jr. launched their new publication in November 1967. They announced the magazine would "concentrate on news about the arts, economics, and social problems for the sophisticated, intelligent reader who is not afraid of colorful, impressionistic journalism."[23] The first issue appeared on April 8, 1968.

In many ways *New York* was, from its inception, atypical as an urban lifestyle magazine. It was a weekly as opposed to a monthly; it reported on current, hard-hitting news stories; and its local articles were of interest beyond the boundaries of New York City. For this reason, the *Standard Rate and Data Service* classifies *New York* as a "news weekly," separate from its "metropolitan/regional/state" grouping.[24] And *New York* was perhaps the only urban lifestyle magazine to sell its articles to wire services and nationally syndicated presses. But by establishing early on the unique "attitude" of its city, and thus of "the publication that bears its name," *New York* became a trendsetter in the area of branding cities, and in that sense a paradigm for other urban lifestyle magazines nationwide. It is not surprising that Felker is now almost universally credited as "the founder of the modern city/regional magazine."[25]

New York's Branding Strategy: Negotiating High and Low

No one was as sensitive to the cultural nuances and contradictions of the new middle class, and as able to capitalize on these, as the original staff of *New York* magazine. While YSW struggled to quantify data on this psychographic category, Felker realized that they could be gauged through the "savviness"— that is, the education and cultural capital—of those who could, or more likely *wished they could*, appreciate the avant-garde style of the writing and bold nature of the content of the magazine. This aspirational strategy reflected and helped spark a broader movement within consumer marketing in the 1960s and 1970s, and was the model of what became a new genre of urban lifestyle magazines.[26] Rather than hyping the modernist vision of "city-as-skyline," or simply celebrating and instructing readers in the pleasures of the good life, *New York*'s branding strategy captured what the readers felt was the distinctive attitude of their iconoclastic generation, and their city, from a perspective that was both sophisticated and gritty, campy, "high" and "low."[27] The magazine's key innovation was in creating a literary and visual means of merging such "high" and "low" discourses, and doing so in such a way that New Yorkers, who felt caught between these worlds, could learn to climb into one without feeling they had to leave the other behind. As artistic director Milton Glaser put it:

> The magazine was never designed for beauty or style. It was designed for directness, clarity, impact. It was gritty, it wasn't refined, and it was never objective. It tried to be like the city itself, an odd combination between high and low, black and white, tough and soft. The truth of the matter is that the city itself is too complex to be encompassed by a single idea.[28]

In what follows I will analyze this complex, seemingly contradictory discourse. I have surveyed some one hundred issues of *New York*, looking closely at the January and June issues of every year between 1967 and 1982, and seminal articles published at other times, and extended my analysis through interviews with former editor Clay Felker and art director Milton Glaser.[29] I have thus identified three primary strategies of negotiation between high and low that produced the unique "New York lifestyle" branded by *New York*. These include: "radical chic," "the urban consumer manual," and "the New York power game."

"Radical Chic": From Critique to Celebration

One of the elements that characterized *New York* from its inception was a split personality. On the one hand, it sought to provide cutting-edge political and social analysis that cut through the old guard sterility of mainstream publications like the *New York Times*, using journalistic feature articles. On the other, it intended to distinguish itself, and attract advertisers, through consumer-oriented lifestyle reporting in shorter, eye-catching columns and listings. *New York*'s young journalists were all white and middle class; yet they journeyed into non-white, working-class neighborhoods in Queens, Brooklyn, the Bronx, and the far reaches of Manhattan to deal with issues of racism and poverty seldom featured in the mainstream press. Moreover, the magazine seemed to uphold progressive gender politics—in the types of men and women featured in its articles, the gender balance of the editorial staff, and the fact that it was one of the first mass-marketed magazines to deal explicitly with issues of feminism. Yet, at the same time, in a style reminiscent of Victorian slum literature, these representations were contained within a framework of voyeuristic pleasure-seeking in the city's colorful, working-class neighborhoods that often upheld the stereotype of the bargain-obsessed female consumer. Despite appearances, however, these two agendas were not really at odds—indeed it was one of *New York*'s innovations to show how they could support each other. *New York*'s opening issue of April 8, 1968 provides the perfect example of this synergistic dichotomy, containing some of the most politically charged reporting in mainstream magazines at that time, while also launching a number of its now famous consumer-oriented columns.

On the cover of *New York*'s first issue is a dramatic photograph of Manhattan's West Side skyline, shot from New Jersey. Taken at midday, it is drenched in a golden glow, yet storm clouds hover low in the fishbowl frame, creating a beautiful but ominous composition. Immediately *New York* makes clear that the old urban booster publication is being challenged by a magazine that will reveal a complete picture of the city, warts and all.[30] The titles of in-depth feature articles are emblazoned above the photo, authors' names listed prominently. One is Tom Wolfe's "You and Your Big Mouth" about a CCNY linguistics professor, "the Henry Higgins of New York," who can identify ethnic and class distinctions in New York accents and coach people to hide their origins.[31] Another is Gloria Steinem's "Ho Chi Minh in

New York," about a recent trip by the commander of the Viet Cong to the city.[32] And a third is Jimmy Breslin's "Life in the City of Gold," which, given its connection to the cover photo, can be taken as the cover story.[33]

In his five-page, 5000-word article, Breslin is the intrepid journalist-cum-ethnographer, taking a subway trip from Grand Central Station to the northern suburbs, along with the wealthy white stockbrokers and bankers who take this daily ride home. His main observation is that "they never look out the windows" to see the poverty, and the residents' mounting anger, as they ride over the streets of Harlem. This oversight ultimately becomes a metaphor for the plight of the city and the nation as a whole, as leaders of both are characterized as willfully ignorant of mounting race and class tensions. Breslin's is an unambiguously angry view, written in a terse, politicized tone. It is an indictment of the race and class polarization emerging in the late 1960s, with working-class jobs declining and federal retrenchment depriving the city of social programs for the poor, and with suburbanization and the rise of a new economy benefiting the wealthy commuter class. As the train picks up speed, one can almost feel the flow of resources out of the city to the suburbs.

Later in the article, Breslin goes down into the Harlem neighborhood the train passed by and does a profile of the family of a black GI killed in Vietnam. This indictment then expands to include a critique of national policy and the lack of national response to mounting urban unrest and anti-war protest. He argues the commuters are "like politicians in the White House," who never look out the window to see what's going on in the street, remaining oblivious to brewing, insurgent struggles "no different in Algeria, Newark, Detroit." This problem reaches as high as the President:

> With this going on the Report on the President's Commission on Civil Disorders, a report which stands as a major American docu-ment, came to Lyndon Johnson's desk last month. He made no comment on it. The president of the United States became another man sitting in the train and not looking out the window. And if the president does not look anymore, then the country does not look.[34]

Yet, in the same first issue in which Breslin's lengthy polemic appeared, the "slumming aesthetic" was championed in columns like "The Passionate Shopper" and "The Underground Gourmet." Filled with humorous listings and dramatic imagery, these pieces presented a combination of frugality and cultural sophistication which both congratulated the reader on his/her good taste and provided a useful guide to bargains on the urban fringe. This ironic juxtaposition presented a lifestyle manual to status-conscious penny-pinchers, and ennobled their efforts as socially worthwhile.

Figure 3.2 *New York* and the slumming aesthetic. From the cover of *New York*, February 21, 1972.

New York magazine

Such social value was established in two ways. First, this offbeat consumption was presented as a means of perpetuating old-world craftsmanship which was then at risk of being done in by the modern mass market. This was exemplified by the letter to the editor, "Mock Knishes and Ersatz Pickles," which extolled the old-fashioned fare of Guss' Pickles on the Lower East Side. Appearing as the first article on the first page alongside the paper's masthead, this letter, complete with a smiling picture of Isadore Guss himself donning glasses, cap, and apron and stirring a vat of pickles, presented itself as the emblem of everything for which the magazine stood. It began:

> I feel it is incumbent on me to dip pen in brine to bring to your attention, sir, the necessity of speaking out to preserve the pickle. That this city, beset by so many ills, should be allowing another asset to slip into oblivion prompts my protest. In this era of mass production sanctifying the ersatz, the plight of the pickle—once this city's peerless pinnacle of penny piquancy—bears an unhappy

resemblance to that of the whooping crane. Like those grotesque jarred mutants that mesmerize tourists in the less favored recesses of the complex known as the Jardin des Plantes in Paris, something said to be a pickle—usually stillborn and embalmed in one of those ubiquitous clear plastic placentas called a Twin-Pak—is being foisted off today on a forgetful public.[35]

Far from the short-sighted urban policy of the Johnson administration, this author decries the death of the pickle as the apotheosis of the city's "ills." His point is clearly tongue-in-cheek, but is nonetheless quite serious in its own way: the relentless march of mass production is rendering obsolete true New York "assets" like pickles, which are delicious, inexpensive, and connected to a wider, richer culture—in this case, that of the Jewish Lower East Side. Arguing that such simple pickles should be considered *haute cuisine*, he points out that "mavens" from "all the opulent suburbs and exurbs, from the length and breadth of the megalopolis, even from as far off as Texas, Florida, Georgia, and Tennessee" flock to Guss' for this unique delicacy. Yet, while it may be worthwhile, as well as humorous, to "speak out to preserve the pickle," one senses another goal in the author's florid prose and witty, offhand references to Paris parks. In showing his appreciation for pickles, he is also showing off his own cultural capital—and doing so in a way that would be socially acceptable for a hip audience in the late 1960s. His expertise is based in his familiarity with this earthy food as well as his privileged, well-traveled frame of reference—that is, with his easy negotiation between high and low.

Here is writing that both celebrates the working class and strives to transcend it. A variety of readers could identify with this theme. Ethnic, working-class social climbers from the Lower East Side, Brooklyn, and the Bronx could feel validated, and even a bit superior, in the idea that their birthright was so highly prized, even as they left it behind. Middle-class suburbanites could indulge their nostalgia for the old neighborhood, even as they enjoyed their safe distance from it. And upper-class slummers could find out about a new, tasty treat that they could hunt down and use to display their connection with the common people.

A second way in which *New York*'s shorter, consumer-oriented pieces presented themselves as socially worthwhile was by positioning consumption as a means of mending the rifts of a race- and class-divided city. For by venturing outside the standard supermarkets and department stores to discover esoteric products, one ended up in underserved neighborhoods in the outskirts of Manhattan or the outer boroughs that were home to poor and working-class blacks, Latinos, Asians, and ethnic whites. These were neighborhoods which were then in the process of unraveling, their resources being drained by suburban flight, their housing and infrastructure crumbling from government neglect. These were also neighborhoods which were, for the white, middle-class core readership, largely forgotten or unknown and, as such, thrillingly exotic.

This take is exemplified in Milton Glaser and Jerome Snyder's short article on East Harlem's Latin American enclosed market, "La Marqueta"—the first dispatch of what was to become the highly popular "Underground Gourmet" column. Whereas readers may have had insiders' knowledge of the ethnic Jewish food of the Lower East Side, the fare of East Harlem was another story; most Latinos were not yet moving out of the neighborhood, climbing the social ladder, and buying lifestyle magazines. Adorned with colorful photographs of the fashionably dressed actress Rita Moreno and her infant daughter buying produce, the article reads like a travel brochure to a foreign land, albeit one that is a subway stop away from the Upper East Side, New York's wealthiest census tract. In this way one gained entry into La Marqueta's mysterious world, and the possibility of connection—via shopping—to the city's colorful underclass.

When one looks closely at *New York*'s contrast of political reportage and lifestyle pieces, of Jimmy Breslin and the Underground Gourmet, one discerns a larger statement being made: namely, the same neighborhood in which poverty and the Vietnam War are feeding deepening resentment and potential violence (according to Breslin) is also a great place to go shopping for bargains (according to Glaser and Rita Moreno). While "Life in the City of Gold" seemed to call out for a political response, the shopping tour of La Marqueta appeared to shape that response through class-conscious consumerism. For though these impoverished neighborhoods had a host of serious problems, the clothes, food, and brownstone real estate they offered were cheaper and hipper than they would be on the Upper East Side. And though such "slumming" did not allow the targeted reader to mobilize politically to address these very real problems, it did provide the opportunity for a perverse kind of conspicuous consumption, enabling them to display concern for the underclass while fulfilling their desire for bargain hunting, or even social climbing.

No single article articulated *New York*'s peculiar dichotomy like Tom Wolfe's "Radical Chic: That Party at Lenny's," published in the magazine in June 1970.[36] Wolfe's piece satirized the newly arrived "culturati" and "limousine liberals" of emerging 1970s "New York Society," among whom it was in vogue to hold gala fundraisers for the most politically radical elements of the day. It seemed to critique the very tensions between the new middle class's consumer habits and political stance that the previous issues of the magazine had themselves made manifest. To Wolfe, these "radical chic" parties were another instance in the grand tradition of *nostalgie de la boue*, or "the romanticizing of primitive souls," through which the *nouveau riche* had sought to distinguish itself for some two hundred years.[37]

This trend was epitomized by Leonard and Felicia Bernstein's lavish cocktail party for the Black Panthers in 1969, which combined "Roquefort cheese morsels rolled in chopped nuts" with "white South American servants," the latter being "the cutting edge in Radical Chic," since it would have been "unimaginable" to have black maids and butlers serving the likes of Stokely Carmichael.[38] The brilliance of Wolfe's essay was its ability to capture these surreal, contradictory images and, in social scientific fashion, use them to illuminate the conceits of this new class. Here is an example from what Wolfe calls the "first big Radical Chic party, the epochal event," which inspired the many others: namely, the party that then twenty-four-year-old Assemblyman Andrew Stein gave for the striking California grape workers, during the United Farm Workers' strike led by Cesar Chavez, on his father's estate in Southhampton on June 29, 1969:

> When the fundraising began, Andrew Imutan [Cesar Chavez's undersecretary] took a microphone upon the terrace above the lawn and asked everybody to shut their eyes and pretend they were a farm worker's wife in the dusty plains of Delano, California, eating baloney sandwiches for breakfast at 3 a.m. before heading out into the fields . . . So they all stood there in their Pucci dresses, Gucci shoes, Capucci scarves, either imagining they were grape workers' wives or wondering if the goddamned wind would ever stop. The wind had come up off the ocean and it was wrecking everybody's hair. People were standing there with their hands pressed against their heads as if the place had been struck by a brain-piercing ray from the Purple Dimension.[39]

Wolfe made it clear that he was critiquing the hypocrisy of such scenes. His intimate narrative entered the minds of the party-goers, seeming to identify with the thrill they felt to be "down with the cause," but then mercilessly detailed their conspicuously displayed, obsessively hip possessions—thus coyly betraying the superficiality of their commitment.

This was not all Wolfe's narrative accomplished—for his witty insights, with details only an insider could catch, also held the opposite appeal. They allowed the average middle-class reader, who would never be invited to such an A-List event, at once to feel superior to the elite and learn how, irreverently, to emulate them. Indeed, *New York* itself was guilty of precisely this same ambivalence towards radical chic—and it was not long before critics began to observe that the concept had turned back on its inventors, and could accurately be applied to the style without substance of *New York*'s own content. By 1974, when Felker joined Taurus Communications in a move to buy out the *Village Voice*, critics jokingly described the move as "the merging of radical cheek with radical chic."[40] But by this point, Felker and most of his co-founders were not shamed by such criticism. For they now understood radical chic as part of their mission, as something that provided a vital service to style- and status-conscious readers.

From Urban Survival Guide to Urban Consumer Manual

New York was ahead of its time not only in targeting this new radical chic audience but in conceiving of the role of the urban lifestyle magazine as "service provider." In representing New York as both crisis-ridden and consumer-friendly, *New York* carved a unique niche for itself among new middle-class readers: one that aimed to assist this group both to "survive" and to shop. As *New York*'s sixth-anniversary edition proclaimed, it was this "unique mingling of information, service, and analysis that has made the magazine a survival manual for coping with the urban mechanism."[41] As the term "survival manual" implied, this service should not be fluffy or hedonistic. Rather, it should be useful in confronting the real-life issues and urban problems people of the targeted socio-economic bracket faced, while at the same time enabling residents to locate and consume the pleasures that were still to be found in the city.

In positioning itself as a "survival manual," *New York*'s approach to "service" emphasized practicality, frugality, and maintaining a sense of humor in the face of adversity. This meant letting the harried New Yorker in on simple lists, usually reduced to the "top ten," of the best bargains, information, and contacts to confront the difficulties, absurdities, and consumer pleasures of living in a recession-crunched city. A number of regular columns that were created in this vein in the early years were presented as a package, as this promotional ad indicates:

> We tell you everything you should know about everything and everyone you have to deal with to survive in this city—cabbies, cops, mayors, muggers, doormen, garagemen, repairmen, block-busters, landlords, schools, supermarkets, antiques, hustlers, doctors, restaurants . . . Every week "Underground Gourmet," "Best Bets," "Passionate Shopper," and "Urban Strategist" tell you where to go for great meals under $3.00 (and conversely, what $20 meals not to go to).[42]

The survival guide motif added an urban angle to the middle-class consumer revolution then sweeping the nation. The special year-end issue for 1970 was devoted to this topic. It was entitled "Guerilla Guide for the

Consumer: A Field Guide of Strategy and Tactics for the New York Shopper."[43] Its cover was a full-page, three-dimensional illustration of a carton, its contents listed on the sides, printed in military-style block font. Thus the entire magazine presented itself as a no-nonsense, systematic survival guide, in which consumer products were analyzed primarily for usefulness, not style.

Within the issue were a series of politically oriented articles on the "many fronts [of the] consumer battle."[44] The lead story was Steinem's interview, "Ralph Nader for President," for which the blurb read, almost apologetically: "Compared with war or racism, the consumer issue seems tame. But it's the one issue that gets *everyone* mad, and Nader is the man everyone believes."[45] Following this were articles on Nader-style consumer activism, including "The Greening of James Roche," on the attempted shareholder revolt at General Motors that year. A more local story was Breslin's "How to Fight City Hall," which detailed how "the recent victory of homeowners in the Corona section of Queens over the city's effort to condemn their property to build a high school was yet another manifestation of the power of an aroused consumership."[46] In addition to these full-length articles, the "Guerilla Guide" included dizzying lists of dilemmas apparently faced by the New York City consumer, including "a key to the mysterious coding of supermarket items, notes on vitamin C (including a comparison-shopping table), and an updated how-to-complain-and-whom-to-complain-to directory." As the handbook explained: "That old slogan, 'Let the Buyer Beware,' has outlived its usefulness. 'Beware the Buyer' is now closer to the mark as the voice of the consumer becomes audible in our land."[47]

But in the contradictory mode of "radical chic" discussed above, consumer advocacy was also a trend in itself, and afforded a new kind of distinction. One such status-conscious consumer advocate was food critic Gael Greene, who by the early 1970s had taken over the Underground Gourmet column from Milton Glaser. Rather than traipse up to La Marqueta, Greene's social contribution was in introducing a generation of young urbanites to the joys of being a "foodie." As Sharon Zukin has pointed out, she undercut the snobbery of the upper-crust restaurants, and of imperious food writers like Craig Claibourne of the *New York Times*, only so that she could make these delicacies available to the middle class.[48] Her first *New York* article, "The Menu Rap and How to Beat It," detailed the "cunning, discipline, poise, and unjellied chutzpah [it takes] to make a dent in the cost of haute dining," and then offered devious strategies of getting discount lunches in "posh restaurants."[49] This was also a "pragmatic" skill. The goal was:

> *How to eat rich though poor.* Or, more realistically, how to eat *with* the rich at austerity prices . . . Now it is no longer a matter of getting the most for the money. It is an exercise in spending the least for the

ambiance. You may not get much to eat, but you can hold down a table at "21" or The Colony for hours and even quiet a few hunger pangs.[50]

Over the course of the early 1970s the tone of *New York*'s service journalism began to shift, leaning towards the pleasure- and status-seeking strategies of Gael Greene, and away from the training guides and political critiques of Ralph Nader. This was due to three basic changes: a change in ownership of the magazine, a change in the personal concerns and ambitions of the targeted readership, and, underlying both of these, a change in New York's economic landscape. In 1977 Rupert Murdoch bought out the magazine, and hired a new editor, Edward Kosner, to tone down its editorial style, reduce the investigative reporting, and refocus its energies on "service" so as to take advantage of its loyal and increasingly affluent readers. Meanwhile, the service orientation as originally conceived was shifting towards more high-end listings. In 1980 Murdoch bought *CUE New York*, the events listings publication, for five million dollars in order to merge it with *New York* and so make the latter magazine even "more New York."[51] As they advertised it in the magazine, these listings would enhance "*New York*'s editorial mix, adding a practical element . . . [and providing] the essential service for New York readers because it enables them to enjoy the cultural opportunities that make their city the world's most rewarding."[52]

The standing introduction of the weekly "Best Bets" feature changed in 1980 from "The best of all possible things to see and do" to "The best of all possible things to *buy*, see, and do." Increasingly, the notion of service the magazine used implied consumption rather than overcoming "real problems." As Kosner observed, New York had become, "oriented more towards using, enjoying, and finding, than surviving." By the 1980s, he said, the "urban survival manual" had become the "urban consumer manual."[53]

This role was widely remarked upon, and derided, in the mainstream press. *Time* referred to *New York* as a "manual" for those concerned with "avenue-smart urban-survival one-upmanship."[54] What we have been provided in *New York*, as media industry correspondent David Shaw put it, is "a combination of social consciousness and handy how-to manual for the credit-card cultural consumer."[55] *New York* was setting the pace, for better or for worse, for the style of urban lifestyle magazines to come. It introduced many magazine branding tactics, including special advertising inserts that copied the design of the magazine, "special issues" that tailored editorial content to advertising-friendly themes, and "Best of New York" listings that linked reviews with the magazine's top advertisers. And, as *New York* and its readers became more influential players in the city over the 1970s, its branding strategy would become a model for New York as a whole.

Figure 3.3 *New York* and "service journalism." From *The Passionate Shopper Guidebook* written by the editors of *New York* in 1972.

New York magazine

Shopping the city for price and quality

NEW YORK Guidebook $2.95

THE PASSIONATE SHOPPER

animals
armoires
art supplies
back packs
band saws
banjos
bicycles
bikinis
bottle stoppers
box turtles
brass beds
bread
cacti
candles
car parts
cellos
cheese
coffee & tea
croissants
drums
eels
fabrics
firewood
flowers
graphics
greengrocers
guidebooks
hammocks
handmade cigars
hardware
hats
health foods

kids' clothes
kitchenware
kites
lumberyards
meats
murphy beds
music boxes
orchids
penny candy
pet fish
pillow stuffing
pipes
plants
puzzles
quiet
rare books
records
roll-top desks
seashells
shoes
snow peas
spices
terrariums
tools
toys
umbrellas
vitamins
wallpaper
wicker
wines
and much more

"The Power Game": From Spectators to Players

The economic restructuring and impending crisis of the late 1960s and early 1970s led to a profound shift in traditional power arrangements in the city and the nation—presenting both new opportunities and new challenges for the young, aspiring middle class. Not surprisingly, the "most important service" *New York* said it offered its readers by 1969 was how to grasp, and ultimately play, New York's so-called "Power Game." This was a topic with which, by their own admission, the editor and writers of *New York* were obsessed. Except for 1976, every New Year's issue from 1969 through 1978 featured a cover article on the theme of power, along with a list of the "top ten most powerful men in New York." Meanwhile, a range of articles throughout the year were geared towards dissecting the shifting workings of power in all its cultural, economic, and political guises. As such, the idea and image of the "power game" as a metaphor for the city constituted a key element of the New York brand produced by the magazine.

A fascinating compilation of the early articles on power was made by Clay Felker in 1969 under the title *The Power Game: From the Pages of* New York *Magazine*. The book's impetus is explained in its introduction:

> For years my favorite dinner conversation when I was with knowledgeable New Yorkers was a variation of the old ten-best game: name the ten men who run New York City. I soon found that The Power Game was not only popular but increasingly complex and confusing. Everyone had (and has) differing lists according to his degree of personal sophistication or point of view from the particular social and economic pyramid he occupies. This is to say, it came down to a question of how power is defined . . . Power of course is more than a game. The real reason it fascinates . . . is that power is the name we give that mysterious force which shapes our lives in the city. The thrust of this book is identical with the force that brought *New York* magazine into being. We live in an urban civilization and unless we understand it we will be overwhelmed by the scale and complexity of its problems.[56]

Initially, *New York*'s writers and targeted readers—new middle-class, white professionals—were most interested in the possibility that there would be an opening for them in this "increasingly complex and confusing" power structure. Indeed, *New York* initially wrote about the political and economic shifts that were happening as if in an effort to speed the process, rattling the foundations to make space for their own arrival. One such shift that they wrote about extensively was the sectoral shift from blue- to white-collar jobs, and in particular the growth in importance of the "communications" industries. In addition to creating opportunities for new media ventures like *New York*—that is, the power to define *itself* as part of this new form of power—Felker advised all those interested in achieving power in New York to consider the importance of the emerging media field:

> Definitions of power change . . . New York is not a political capital in the way that other imperial cities of the past—such as Athens, Rome, Paris, or London—were . . . It is the communications capital of America and the world. In New York it isn't military might that matters but the power of ideas.[57]

This theme was reiterated by Tom Wolfe in "Radical Chic," when he noted that culture and media savviness played as much of a part in class succession as did larger economic shifts. Wolfe, a Southern WASP from a genteel background, was fascinated in particular with the swift ascent of white ethnic New Yorkers—the Jews, Italians, and Irish—to the position of tastemaker in the media industry, and in "New Society."

> By the 1960s yet another new industry had begun to dominate New York life, namely communications—the media. At the same time erstwhile "minorities" of the first quarter of the century had begun to come into their own, Jews, especially but also Catholics, were eminent in the media and in Culture. So by 1965—as in 1935, as in 1926, as in 1883, as in 1866, as in 1820—New York had two societies, "Old New York" and "New Society." In every era, "Old New York" has taken a horrified look at "New Society" and expressed the devout conviction that a genuine aristocracy, good blood, good bone—themselves—was being defiled by a horde of rank climbers . . . In the 1960s this quaint belief was magnified by the fact that many members of the "New Society," for the first time, were not Protestant . . .
>
> Today . . . the Social Register's annual shuffle, in which errant socialites, e.g., John Jacob Astor, are dropped from the Good Book, hardly rates a yawn. The fact is that "Old New York"—except for those members who also figure in "New Society," e.g., Nelson Rockefeller, John Hay Whitney, Mrs. Wyatt Cooper—is no longer good copy, and without publicity it has never been easy to rank as a fashionable person in New York City . . . The press in New York has tended to favor New Society in every period, and to take it seriously if only because it provides "news."[58]

Thus, as Wolfe seems to imply, the change that *New York*'s own journalists sought to hasten was the one that would place them in the most influential position possible. If "the press" provides the publicity that elevates a new class, this new class was now increasingly filling the ranks of the press, and other forms of media and communication. Essentially, *New York* writers had discovered a great advantage: they were able to write about themselves and their associates, define themselves as the new power in town, and then call this "news."

But reporting from inside the world of the new "culturati" was only half of what *New York* did in the early power game articles. It also identified those in "Old New York" whom it believed still exerted power—if only in refusing to get out of the way. These articles served as a kind of primer on the entrenched New York elites among the elder white male bankers, elected officials, establishment media, and union bosses. Though excluded from this lofty group, *New York* writers, editors, and illustrators wielded a new kind of power through their ability to name and caricature its members.

In an analysis of *New York*'s "Top Ten Most Powerful People in New York" lists between 1967 and 1973, the movers and shakers identified by the magazine fit into neat and predictable rank orders. They were dominated by the Rockefeller brothers, David (the CEO of Chase Manhattan) and Nelson (the Governor); by Mayor John V. Lindsay and other rising stars in the state Democratic and Republican parties; by the leaders of the city's most powerful unions and labor groups, District Council 37 and the Central Labor Council; and by the *New York Times*. Generally speaking, one's connection to government—local, state, and federal—was the key to success and power. By 1973, over half the magazine was filled with in-depth articles about the power players in different fields, public and private, legal and illegal, and how they got to where they were through government connections.[59] One saw little change over this period, except for the fact that, by 1972, Nelson Rockefelier occupied *three* top slots, as opposed to just one. This was in recognition of his different roles as, first, a Rockefeller, a "blender and distributor of money and ideas"; second, "Nixon's man in town," the successor to John Mitchell as the surrogate heir of federal power; and, third, "The conquering hero [and] all-powerful governor manipulating his political friends and punishing his political enemies."[60]

The theme of established white male power bridging the elite worlds of government, finance, labor, and media was carried through in the illustrations on the magazine covers and accompanying the lead articles. In looking at the covers from 1970 to 1973, we see illustrations dominated by simple visual metaphors for this power. In 1970, Milton Glaser's cartoon entitled "The New York Power Pantheon" pictures ten white men in suits standing on a cloud from which descends an enormous lightning bolt.[61] The following year, a white man's fist, raised in power salute, is dressed up in a suit and tie, with a cigar clenched in the curled fingers.[62] In 1972, the year of Nelson Rockefeller's triple listing, Paul Davis's illustration shows a single white male hand dressed in a star-spangled sleeve, with Lower Manhattan clutched in the palm.[63] And finally, by 1973, the headline "Who Holds the Power in New York?" is accompanied by Davis's image of a thunderbolt clutched in a white, male, cufflinked fist, surrounded by the words "Politics, Labor, Crime, Business, Real Estate, Finance, The Arts, Communications."[64]

With the Watergate scandal, oil embargo, recession, and fiscal crisis of the mid-1970s, the image of an uncontested old guard was abruptly replaced by images of, and articles on, struggle, intrigue, and instability. The neat, predictable "Top Ten Most Powerful Men in New York" lists were rendered

(a)   (b)

Figure 3.4 *New York* and the "power game."
From the covers of *New York*. (a) October 14, 1968. (b) January 3, 1972.
New York magazine

obsolete, thus revealing their obsessive and naive—to say nothing of sexist and racist—focus on powerful, individual, white males, rather than more complex social forces. The turning point in this regard was 1974. Milton Glaser's cover illustration of January 14 that year shows two paunchy, mean-looking white men with horns on their heads butting each other like rams, with the headline "Battling for Control of the City: Winners and Losers in the Power Game."[65] Robert Daley's cover story on the top ten is scattered and incoherent, listing the following: 1) Richard Nixon, 2) Special Prosecutor's Office, 3) Big Oil, 4) Arab Oil, 5) Arab Money Managers, 6) the *New York Times*, 7) Nelson Rockefeller and Malcolm Wilson, 8) Abraham Beame, 9) "The Stickup Man," 10) Big Labor, Big Real Estate, Big Banking, Big Business.[66] Daley explains, almost sheepishly:

> A year ago it seemed so easy. We knew most of the men who led us, and power seemed secure in their hands. But an astonishing number are gone now—some of them headed for jail. The power is still there, all around us. But in too many cases it now exists in places we had not been required to consider before, and with no individual man's name attached.[67]

And so, following 1973, we see the simple top ten format erode ever further. Aside from hold-outs from labor, banking, and government, the lists now had to include a range of new players in finance, real estate, law, PR, and media who were then filling the ranks of public–private partnerships, agencies of the city's "crisis regime," and criminal rings. As Nicholas Pileggi saw it in 1974, the city was dominated by "predatory underwriters, political manipulators, and mob loan sharks."[68] The magazine had to contend with the fact that power and governance were increasingly opaque, and that the most important deals were made behind closed doors. An issue from January 1975 again set the tone. It included two top ten lists, one for "Visible Power" and the other for "Invisible Power." The cover shows a mummy unraveling the bandage around its empty head with its own white hand, and the headline: "The Ten Most Powerful Men in New York and Ten Invisible Powers You Better Know About."[69]

Clearly unscientific, *New York*'s power game lists were as much about name-dropping as they were serious analyses of the workings of power in New York—indeed, a cursory perusal of the lists shows how many of the bold-faced names are completely forgotten today. Nonetheless, they serve to document power as understood, and as sought, by the magazine's aspiring writers and readers, and as such they are very revealing. They can also be seen as the political underpinnings of the new journalism's fixation on the cultural vicissitudes of "high" and "low." The lesson seemed to be: cultural capital was important, but it had to be combined with an analysis of the many forms of power now operating in the city—if your goal was to be a player in the power game.

The *New York* Legacy

New York crafted a formula encompassing both high and low—whether in the realm of "radical chic," the "urban consumer manual," or the "power game." And in doing so the magazine attracted exactly the kind of readership editor Clay Felker envisioned. As commentators at the time described them, *New York* readers were "young strivers and achievers who are committed to living in the city . . . [and] . . . although they are comfortable, are anxious about the challenges, complexities, and frustrations of contemporary urban existence."[70] Circulation in the first five years rose from 50,000 to 335,000 at an average increase of 63 percent a year, with increases in subscription as well as single-copy sales. Advertisers soon took notice: by its sixth year, advertising revenue had reached $7 million.[71]

Many of the original writers, on the other hand, made very public displays of disgust over what they considered to be the selling out of the political and literary principles of the magazine. In 1971, Jimmy Breslin, one of the star writers, left the magazine, claiming it had become "too dilettantish":

> If I see one more issue with a bleeping maid on the cover and one more story about the people who have trouble getting maids, I wouldn't even read it. For Christ's sake look at the times in which we live. I think people have more on their minds than that . . . I left *New York* because it caused me to become gagged by perfume and disheartened by character collapse . . . [I foresee] a new flourishing of boutique journalism—all frivolity and no more serious journalism.[72]

Similarly, Gloria Steinem, Susan Brownmiller, and others who had been writing on the burgeoning feminist movement for *New York* found themselves increasingly marginalized by the editorial slant, and quit in order to start *Ms.* magazine in 1973. In her history of *Ms.*, Mary Thom curtly noted of Felker, in reference to his attitude towards feminism: "he was a good enough journalist to recognize a hot story."[73] As Steinem added, he was only willing to publish positive articles about feminist issues or events if he could then run a negative one—by another female reporter like Julie Baumgold or Gail Sheehy—beside it. "That's really why I gradually stopped writing for *New York*," Steinem recalled. "It was just too painful to be only able to do it in the context of two women fighting."[74] In addition to this patronizing attitude, Steinem and other feminists decried the fact that *New York*, for all its avant-garde lifestyle focus and design, reified the gender bias of magazines like *Ladies Home Journal* and the other "seven sisters," with content about food, home, romance, and fashion meant to appeal to female readers—while the articles about finance, technology, and the "power game" featured, and were targeted at, men.[75]

When asked, Milton Glaser acknowledged the potential contradiction between the magazine's progressive politics and its emphasis on consumerism and social climbing—a contradiction felt among young middle-class progressives more broadly coming out of the 1960s:

> There wasn't a sense that the way to achieve social justice was by overthrowing the system. Rather there was a sense that there were benefits to being a part of the system, and that you could achieve social justice and economic affluence and so on through the existing system. Things were much more optimistic then—about what the possibilities for capitalism were . . . We didn't see an essential conflict between ideas of materialism and consumerism and social justice and political activity. We thought that you could

have it all. I suppose that was a paradox that we never thought about. The idea that you could take advantage of capitalism in terms of affluence and having things, eating well, and still protect the rights of minorities and women, and so on. That these two things could be simultaneously pursued . . . Our point of view was full of contradictions. Such is the nature of life. We did know that the magazine had to be bought by people who had enough money to buy things that advertisers were interested in selling. That's for sure. We had to make the magazine an attractive buy for an ad agency basically because they had to feel that the readers were sufficiently affluent to put an ad for an expensive stereo system in the thing. We always understood that.[76]

Felker was even more blunt about what he saw as the pro-establishment orientation of the magazine, and dismissive of the critiques of writers like Breslin and Steinem:

You have to remember the people Milton Glaser and I picked reflected us. We didn't pick them because they agreed with us, but they did have the same attitude. It was like directing an orchestra; we had to find harmony. Jimmy Breslin had a different view. He had to write more about East New York. "That's where the battle is." And I would say, "Jimmy, we're not writing for those people." He had a very developed social conscience. Not that I don't, but my view is that you reach the movers and shakers and that's how you accomplish what I wanted to accomplish. Not by fighting for the homeless or something like that. Not that I don't have sympathy, but that's not who I'm aiming at . . . I want to talk to people that interest me. Not to social consciousness. I want to talk to the people who are going to make things run.[77]

Felker's magazine did ultimately reach the people that interested him, and regardless of high turnover among its "celebrity writers," it remained a hot property. The magazine had found and cultivated its niche, and done so despite—or because of—the ideological contradictions between its seemingly radical content and fundamentally conservative, consumer-oriented slant. As Tom Wolfe joked in reference to the stylish but apolitical guests at the Bernsteins' party for the Black Panthers—in what could be a description of the magazine's conflicted readers and staffers—it was politically incorrect to get too political:

This is, after all, a period of great confusion among *culterati* and liberal intellectuals generally, and one in which a decisive display of conviction and self-confidence can be overwhelming. Radical Chic, after all, is only radical in style; in its heart it is part of Society and its traditions. Politics, like Rock, Pop and Camp, has its uses; but to put one's whole status on the line for *nostalgie de la boue* in any of its forms would be unprincipled.[78]

In the end, however, the commercial success of Felker's strategy brought about his own demise as editor, and, some would say, of the magazine itself. In the early 1970s, Felker sought to expand *New York* into a national magazine while purchasing other magazines, and so joined with Taurus Communications, publishers of *The Voice*, to create New York Magazine Co. In so doing, he handed over a third of the stock to the new corporate parent. Increasing pressure was exerted by advertisers to give free space in editorials along with paid ads, and to increase the proportion of "fluff" to actual city reporting. Felker was in no position to resist.

Jimmy Breslin was prescient about the troubled future of "serious journalism." The example of *New York*'s success, combined with broader political-economic changes shaping both urban and corporate America, launched the urban lifestyle genre into a new phase of restructuring in the 1970s. *New York* became a model for how to package cultural capital for the new middle class, how to merge advertising and editorial content seamlessly, and thus how to market the city effectively as a brand in this new era.[79]

CHAPTER 4

Selling the City in Crisis

Corporate Exodus and the Big Apple Campaign

Perhaps the most detrimental effect of the corporate exodus is its impact on New York City's image as the business capital of the nation. While the impacts on employment, taxes, and general business in the City are important, they generally reduce these bases by only a small percentage and thus are not by themselves essentially crippling. The weakening of the City's business image, however, strikes directly at the heart of its existence.

Wolfgang Quante, 1976[1]

We were already losing the ball when the credit rating of the City slipped and the public image went south with it. The rest of the world seemed to look upon New York as an urban jungle inhabited by surly, beleaguered natives . . . On *Johnny Carson* every night you would hear jokes about muggings in Central Park. Well, we couldn't move our buildings across the bridges. Our assets are in New York. So I decided to create a civic group.

Lewis Rudin, founder of the Association
for a Better New York, 2002[2]

In February 1971, then New York City Comptroller Abraham Beame issued a public statement reprimanding the major credit-rating agencies Dun and Bradstreet, Moody's, and Standard & Poor's for not lifting the city's bond rating for five years, after their first downgrade to "high risk" in 1966.[3]

Beame was especially upset because New York City's rate was significantly lower than that of New York State and its essentially bankrupt Urban Development Corporation, despite the fact that the city was not in such dire straights—yet.[4] This was indeed a serious matter for Beame and his employer, Mayor John V. Lindsay. With a lowered rating, New York City had to pay higher interest rates for borrowing money through municipal bond sales—huge sums that cities require to maintain vital public infrastructure.[5] In January 1970 the city paid a record 7.31 percent interest in selling $176.8 million of bonds, while in January 1971 it paid just under 7 percent on $239.9 million—its two most costly financings ever. From Beame and Lindsay's perspective, the agencies' ratings, and their effects, were patently unjust. Not only were the bonds "completely secure [and] backed by the full faith and credit of New York City," but as a result of being kept at high risk the city faced the threat of being unable to cover its most basic and vital operations, was forced to borrow more, and was falling ever deeper into debt.[6]

The complaint did not receive its desired response. Rather, within a week, a highly unusual reply arrived on Beame's desk, and in the newsroom of the *New York Times*: a report from Harries W. Brenton, vice-president of Standard & Poor's. In it Brenton bluntly enumerated the reasons for New York City's rating freeze and elevated interest rate, laying the blame squarely at the feet of the city. First were the "standard reasons": a new round of pay increases for municipal employees, a budget deficit of $300 million, the likelihood of a $1 billion deficit in the coming year, and "spiraling" municipal service costs. But then (as if the aforementioned were not enough) came the two "real reasons" for New York's special treatment: the massive volume of bonds the city must sell, in combination with "the bad publicity the city continually receives because of crime, strikes, welfare, etc." This fatal mix, Brenton concluded, put New York City in a rating category that "stands by itself."[7]

Eliciting the headline in the *Times* "Publicity is Said to Bar Better Credit for City," the report made embarrassingly public something that many in New York government and business had been discussing quietly since the financial troubles of the World's Fair in the mid-1960s—that the city's deteriorating image in the media was having a real and damaging effect on its economic prospects. Applying notions of "reputational capital" that had only recently been developed for the private sector, a range of marketing consultants began treating New York City like an aging corporation losing its competitive edge. Perceptions of the city as an "asphalt jungle" were to be blamed not simply for its plummeting municipal bond ratings but for a veritable chain reaction of economic troubles that gave credit agencies even more cause for alarm. These included the "exodus" of corporate headquarters from Manhattan, the sharp drop-off in tourist numbers, and the declining popularity of the city as a residence for the middle class.

This image-driven dynamic was to inspire the creation of a new kind of political entity in New York City and the nation: the public–private partnership. On the very same day of the above headline in the *Times*, a related article appeared on the paper's front page announcing the creation of a powerful new "civic organization" whose primary goal was to take on this scourge of bad publicity and "establish a positive image for New York."[8] Called the Association for a Better New York (ABNY), the group was formed by "a core of real estate men who have a direct interest in keeping the city economically healthy." It was led by the charismatic Lewis "Lew" Rudin, CEO of Rudin Management, Rexford E. Tomkins, president of the Real Estate Board of New York, and Alton Marshall, president of the Rockefeller Center, former chief of staff to Governor Rockefeller, and "one of the most important men in state government."[9]

From its start, the association spoke of two goals. The first was to promote the city in the media as a business-friendly town. Initially this included media events like "Operation Clean Sweep," in which Midtown employees cleaned the streets in front of their own buildings, as well as the creation of a brochure on the business advantages of the city, which, as Tomkins put, it was "the kind of basic promotional tool that New York had never had."[10] But on the other hand, as Tomkins hastened to add, these PR efforts did not mean the association would simply be an old-fashioned "booster club." Rather, "what we're trying to do is get a 'business presence' in [addressing] New York problems." In other words, in addition to its pro-bono publicity, ABNY's second goal was a new level of influence in government decision-making, particularly in regards to issues of concern to the real estate industry and corporate sector. Mayor John V. Lindsay was supportive of this plan, saying that he was particularly pleased that ABNY was "establishing a continuous dialogue between city government and New York's corporate tenants."[11]

In what follows, I will explore more fully the conditions that led to the creation of this new kind of public–private partnership: namely, the "exodus" of corporate headquarters from Manhattan, the plummeting numbers of New York City tourists, and the *image crisis* to which both problems were linked. I will then turn to the rise of ABNY itself, exploring its "two-pronged" approach combining high-profile city marketing with behind-the-scenes government lobbying. As we shall see, this approach established important precedents such as the creation of year-round, city-wide promotions like the "Big Apple" campaign, as well as the support of policies, incentives, and forms of shared governance that were beneficial to ABNY members in real estate, tourism, and finance.

The Corporate Exodus

Representations of New York as the "asphalt jungle" came at a particularly bad time for the city's elites and new middle class. The real value of New York City's bonds, credit rating, and real estate was declining rapidly in the late 1960s, due primarily to years of profligate borrowing practices, and the debt-financed development of millions of square feet of high-end office space on a scale far greater than the market could bear. Now this bad financial situation was worsened by increasingly negative representations of New York in the mainstream media. This conjunction was particularly devastating in this era of mounting inter-urban competition, deindustrialization, and the city's growing dependence on flexible service industries.

New York was hemorrhaging manufacturing and commercial jobs, the bedrock of its working- and middle-class communities, losing an astounding 600,000 jobs between 1965 and 1973, with an average of 100,000 jobs lost every year from 1970 to 1975. But in addition to these "smokestack industries"—and of far greater concern to the members of the CVB and the FIRE elites—tens of corporations with headquarters in Manhattan were abandoning New York. When combined with the increasing rate of corporate mergers in the period of restructuring, by 1974 New York City had a net loss of between seventy-six and eighty-eight of the nation's most important corporate headquarters, as well as tens of smaller firms, and with them tens of thousands of high-end service jobs.[12] The gain to New York's local suburbs was massive—between 1968 and 1974, they tripled their share of Fortune 500 companies while New York lost 30 percent of its share. But in addition, as part of a national redistribution of corporate headquarters, New York State, in line with its Eastern and Midwestern counterparts, lost approximately 20 percent of its headquarters, the majority from New York City, while the Sunbelt of the South and West gained 100 percent more headquarters over the same six-year period.[13]

These corporate move-outs were not an entirely new phenomenon. Most firms were moving to the suburbs of New York's Westchester County, Connecticut, and New Jersey, as they had in earlier "waves of relocation" in 1910, 1920, and 1946–1953, and so commentators initially saw the moves as simply another such wave. Also like the earlier waves, they were a response to "pull factors" which were created by New York City's own regional planning practices over the previous half century, which had made the local suburbs more accessible through the construction of improved regional public transportation, and a vast new highway system. These were constructed by public authorities under the direction of master planner Robert Moses, who explicitly mapped rail lines and highways to tear through working- and middle-class neighborhoods in the South Bronx, Upper Manhattan, and Brooklyn. His rational, white-collar vision of New York

City—and that endorsed in the 1960s by then Governor Nelson Rockefeller and Mayors Robert Wagner and John Lindsay—conformed to Le Corbusier's ideal of the radiant city: a massive, symbolic downtown, dominated by office towers and centers for arts and culture, surrounded by rings of residential suburbs, all connected via arterial highways for the use of commuters and urban tourists.[14] But what Moses and his supporters did not anticipate was that the highways intended to bring commuting office workers into the city would be used instead to get them out, once corporations had the will and means to vacate urban skyscrapers for suburban office parks.

Yet, despite these similarities, as the economist Wolfgang Quante warned in 1972 and again in 1974, the current move-out wave was far more damaging than any New York City had seen before. Earlier relocations had involved a handful of mostly small firms, and had "started with a flash, peaked rapidly, and then quickly faded" after no more than two years. In addition, the traditional, suburban "pulls" had always been counter-balanced by the incomparable advantages of doing business in the headquarters complex of Manhattan: that is, the greater efficiencies, opportunities, and communications provided by agglomeration, and the unparalleled "executive ambiance" of a city devoted not to a particular industry, but to offices *per se*.[15] In contrast, the current wave involved hundreds of moves, from small firms to Fortune 500 companies, and after seven years it showed no sign of abating. And, amazingly to many observers, New York's unrivaled position as headquarters capital proved incapable of stopping it.

The immense scale of the wave was due in large part to the intensification of the old pull factors luring corporations out of town. Now there were the tax incentives, bucolic corporate campuses, and aggressive ad campaigns being launched by economic development agencies in neighboring states and the New York suburbs. The Connecticut Department of Commerce, for instance, put out blunt ads showing subway tokens in the grass over the question "Turnstile or Life-style?" and a larger state-wide campaign proclaiming "So Much, So Near."[16] And then there was the famous allure of the Sunbelt. As major beneficiaries of government largesse during and after World War II, these regions had become famous not only for their sunny climes, sporty lifestyles, and vast highways, but for their heavy security, segregated neighborhoods, low taxes, relative lack of labor unions, and conservative, pro-business politics.[17] These features proved to be particularly powerful lures in the early phase of the move-outs between 1967 and 1970.

But as early as 1970, a new dynamic had begun, as stronger "pulls" were combined with monumental new "pushes," namely the deteriorating image and reputation of New York City itself. As Quante observed, this was the result of a vicious cycle of imagery. He argued, "perhaps *the* most detrimental effect of [New York's] corporate exodus," even greater than its effect in terms of lost jobs, taxes, and business services, was "its impact on New York City's image as the business capital of the nation."[18] The losses in employment, taxes, and general business, while significant, represented only a small percentage of the overall base, and thus "are not by themselves essentially crippling." On the other hand, "The weakening of the City's business image . . . strikes directly at the heart of its existence." As he explained:

> New York's reputation as a business center has always been and remains its major attraction and selling point, the one bright area in the current sea of problems. The importance of the City's image can be seen not only from the sheer size of its business community but from the extent of the private investment that has occurred in the Manhattan Central Business District over the past few decades.
>
> Bad publicity is the first major image problem brought on by the current headquarter relocations. The extensive press coverage of many of the moves and the reasons given by the departing corporations have tended to focus attention on the City's problem areas and away from its good points. This has been extremely detrimental to the City's interests [i.e., bond ratings] and the bad publicity, if it did not actually trigger additional departures, may well have started many executives thinking about the possibilities.[19]

Quante was arguing two things: that unnuanced "press coverage" of fleeing corporations and their new locations was essentially "bad publicity"; and that this publicity set off a downward spiral of economic decline. His first point was echoed at the time by a range of New Yorkers concerned with the fate of the headquarters complex. For instance, the urban sociologist William H. Whyte noted that across mainstream media—from the "news reporting" on TV documentaries and in magazines, to crass Sunbelt marketing campaigns and brochures for new office parks—one found the same dramatically contrasting images of New York as "hell on earth" and the suburbs as "Arcadia."[20] Telephoto shots of traffic-snarled streets and dingy offices, and close-ups on somber, white businessmen rushing out of packed, racially diverse subway cars, would be juxtaposed with awe-inspiring low angles of modernist, fortress-like "corporate campuses," long, slow pans of their lush, green lawns, and comfortable wide shots of young, white employees in shirtsleeves taking leisurely walks to their private cars. These stereotypes were then reinforced through the highly questionable survey techniques of location consultants, like the Fantus Company, which used skewed formulas to prove not only New York's "tangible" disadvantages—like strong labor laws and long commutes for average (suburbanite) workers—but the "intangible" disadvantages of its "environment" for business. Whyte's deconstruction of this innocuous term indicates the extent to which media and market research were reproducing the old, racially inflected, anti-urban discourse, and serving as a veritable advertisement for corporate relocation.

> It is the intangibles, executives say, that are the key. "Environment" is the umbrella term. Shorn of euphemism, here is what it means: (1) New York City is a bad place—crime, dirt, blacks, Puerto Ricans, etc. (2) Even if it isn't, Americans think it is a bad place and so they don't want to be transferred here. (3) To hold and attract people a company has to offer a better setting. Thus Union Carbide concluded after a two-year study: "The long-term quality-of-life needs of our headquarters employees" were the overriding factors.[21]

The prevalence and power of such bad publicity led to Quante's second point: that images in and of themselves were now causing real financial damage to New York City. Such imagery was pushing additional CEOs to consider abandoning the city—whether out of choice or facing pressure from employees. Once these move-outs reached a critical mass, this could then undermine the agglomeration effect that attracted corporations to New York City in the first place, especially once the big names in one's industry began to leave. Thus, for instance, Johnny Carson's highly publicized move from Rockefeller Center in 1972 to NBC's West Coast Studios in Burbank could result in an industry-wide shift, "a realignment of American pop culture from East Coast to West Coast, from Broadway to Hollywood," and hundreds of New York's TV and movie directors, producers, actors, and technicians followed in his path.[22] And of perhaps even graver concern, the repeated representation of such move-outs, and of a sunbronzed Carson sitting by his swimming pool in Malibu, began to affect New York's already declining bond ratings, and thus the overall value of its financial and real estate markets.[23] This in turn created additional pressure for more companies to leave, and so on, in a vicious cycle of bad publicity, disinvestment, and corporate flight.

From the perspective of leaders in the FIRE, tourism, and media industries, an important (if not *the* most important) reason for New York's economic decline in this period was the deterioration of the city's image. First, as mentioned, they bemoaned the relentless media coverage of the fleeing corporations, and the features on their luxurious new office parks, studios, and residences in Greenwich, Burbank, and suburban Atlanta. But their media-focused critique of the city's decline did not end there; rather, they saw these representations as part of a larger, spiraling, image crisis. Leaving aside the impact of global pressures like recession and deindustrialization, and avoiding mention of the city's increasing rates of joblessness and poverty, New York's elites expressed their concern in terms of the media's increasingly negative coverage of local crime, disorder, and the "quality of life" in the city as a whole.

Mainstream media often conveyed this deteriorating quality of life through cutaways to graffiti on the city's subways, imagery that was emerging as a kind of visual shorthand for a city out of control. By 1973 such imagery was to become even more prevalent. It was then that graffiti writers shifted to using aerosol-spray paint, a medium that could cover a larger surface area more quickly, colorfully, and permanently than the markers they used previously. This made it possible for the first time to "bomb" the sides of subway cars with elaborate "masterpieces" without getting caught. With the rise of bombing, or "piecing," came even greater competition, and the rapid proliferation of new writing styles. Innovations included new script and calligraphic styles, as well as tag embellishments like stars, arrows, and cartoon characters. And in addition to new tag styles came innovations in tag scale, as writers started to use wider spray-paint nozzles and more colors, and take more time and care. These provided more space in the interior and background of letters to "enhance the name" further and create dramatic 3-D effects and other distinctive design elements. As we shall see, piecing was soon extended to works spanning the entire height of a subway car, called "top to bottoms," and by 1975 to entire sides of cars, called "the mural whole car."[24] As the size and artistry of pieces grew, so too did their visibility to the beehive of media outlets emerging in New York City and looking for graphic images of the local scene, and signifiers for rising crime.

Not surprisingly, according to surveys conducted by the CVB beginning in 1973, the crime factor was viewed as "the major deterrent" to prospective visitors to New York City, particularly domestic tourists and business travelers.[25] Psychographic studies by marketing consultants found crime consistently high among the "top of the mind" associations held by CEOs and businessmen when asked about their image of New York City—with other common associations including "dirtiness," "graffiti," "traffic," and "lack of a work ethic."[26] Similar findings were produced through basic survey data culled by location consultancies.[27] Dominant media representations were only one part of such associations, joined as all such "decodings" are to existing stereotypes, and to the social position of the viewer—in this case, the actual experiences businessmen and tourists likely had walking the anxious Midtown streets of an increasingly class- and race-

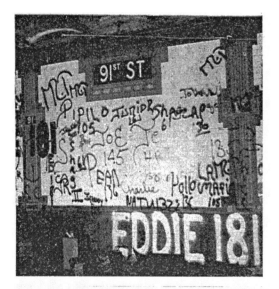

Figure 4.1 Aerosol epidemic. Writers' technology of choice changed from markers to spray paint by 1973, enabling graffiti to cover the entire side of subway cars. From articles in the *New York Times.*
(a) February 11, 1972.
(b) January 26, 1973.

New York Times

These graffiti were scribbled on a wall in an abandoned subway station at 91st Street on the Broadway-Seventh Avenue line. Since there is no access to this station from street, culprits must have walked to 91st Street through tunnel from a nearby station.

Subway Graffiti Here Called Epidemic (a)

Fight Against Subway Graffiti Progresses From Frying Pan to Fire

An example of the "grand design" graffiti sprawls over a large part of a subway car, including door windows, on a Brooklyn-bound Lexington Avenue IRT train at Grand Central Station. (b)

divided city, in which garbage strikes and muggings really did happen.[28] Nonetheless, these media-obsessed elites were onto something. First, mainstream representations of life in New York City were increasingly coded as "negative." And second, in the current climate of financial instability and inter-urban competition, these negative portrayals were having a devastating effect on the city's economic prospects—especially for their own industries.

Tourism Tumbles

After New York's record tourism numbers of the 1964–1965 World's Fair, and to the great chagrin of the CVB, the city's tourism industry soon fell into a severe slump. As the downturn continued unabated into 1972, it could no longer be passed off as a temporary trend, but had become part of a full-fledged recession. Between 1967 and 1972, tourism revenues, establishments, and employment figures had all dropped by 15 percent. And according to the CVB, tourist numbers were down 500,000 from their all-time high in 1969 of 16.5 million, while hotel occupancy rates had fallen over ten percentage points, from 75.4 percent in 1969 to 64.3 percent in 1972. In three or four short years, the fortunes of this once powerful industry had tumbled in New York City.[29]

Part of the problem clearly lay in the "corporate exodus." In addition to its impact on the FIRE sector, corporate flight was devastating for New York City tourism, since it undercut its ability to lure business travelers to the city. Foreign visitors to New York were on the rise, particularly from the UK and Japan, but this was not enough to compensate for the overall loss from business travel, which was emerging as the most lucrative piece of the tourism economy nationally.[30] Meanwhile, New York was already at a major disadvantage in attracting this segment on a number of grounds: it did not have a good convention center; its hotel tax was among the highest in the country; and the discounts and travel packages it could provide business travelers were less than those of cities with better-funded CVBs.

What New York had long depended upon to overcome this disadvantage, as Wolfgang Quante points out, was its "executive ambiance"—the perception of the city as an unequaled site of deal-making, networking, and entertainment.[31] But now, with so many New York City-based corporate giants racing each other out of town, and so many new downtown office towers standing empty, the city's reputation as a place to schmooze in hotel lobbies was also evaporating.

Meanwhile, there was an imbalance emerging in the cluster of industries devoted to representing the city—that is, tourism, media, and marketing (see Figures 4.2 and 4.3). The strength of the tourism industry was declining rapidly, and at a rate similar or greater to that of the private sector overall—

losing 14 percent of its establishments and 8 percent of its employment in nine years. In terms of revenues, the losses of leading industries within the sector—that is, hotels and motels, and amusements and recreation—was equally steep, at 17 percent and 11 percent, respectively. And yet, the same was not true for media and marketing, which was generally growing at a healthy pace in the same period. One significant exception was printing and publishing, which laid off 15 percent or over 18,000 of its workers, and shut down 12 percent of its shops, as part of its decades-long contraction caused by new technologies, foreign competition, and the real estate industry's successful effort to deindustrialize Lower Manhattan, where most of the industry was based. But otherwise, television, radio, and news services added 24 percent more jobs and 41 percent more firms, while market consulting and PR added 23 percent more workers, 16 percent more establishments, and gained 6 percent in receipts. This would have been substantial growth in any period, but the fact that it was occurring at a time of recession and decline in almost every other sector indicated that something else was happening. In the case of the media, this was the continued strength and expansion of the industry nationally and internationally, from which New York, as broadcasting center, was benefiting. And in the case of marketing and PR, this was the fact that struggling industries of all kinds were buying their services as a means to survive the downturn and gain a competitive edge.

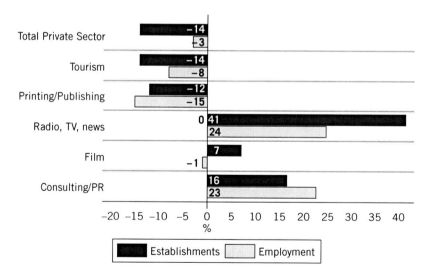

Figure 4.2 Percentage change in employment and establishments in tourism, media, and marketing in New York City, 1963–1972.

Source: US Department of Commerce, Bureau of Census, 1963, 1972, and 1977.

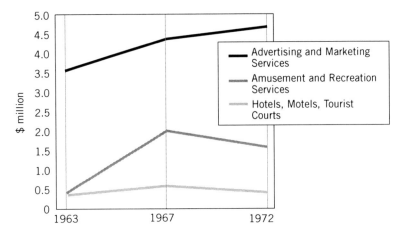

Figure 4.3 Changing revenue of tourism and marketing in New York City, 1963–1972.

Source: US Department of Commerce, Census of Manufacturers, 1963, 1967, 1972, and 1977 (revenues listed as receipts).

It seemed only natural to the members of the CVB that media and marketing, emerging as some of the city's most powerful industries, would be able to solve their problems much as they were doing for other industries. To do this, however, they could not just emulate the struggling car and cigarette companies, and market individual products—such as their hotels, theaters, or office buildings—since they were dependent on the image of the city as a whole. For this scale of marketing, they assumed the state government, and in particular the Department of Commerce (DOC), would assist them, as states were doing for cities elsewhere in the country, particularly in the Sunbelt. Charles Gillett, the new executive vice-president of the CVB, had long called on them to lend public support to sustained marketing campaigns, and not just the temporary city marketing that the Discover America Travel Organization (DATO) had provided.

But the DOC was in no position to lend such support. This was primarily because of the department's outmoded, retention-oriented approach to economic development, which had changed little since its inception in 1934. When it came to attracting new industries—namely the growing service sector—the overall "philosophy" of the DOC was that "other businesses [would] locate, on their own, in a manufacturing based economy to provide retail, wholesale, finance, and other essential services."[32] By the late 1960s and early 1970s, the state's fortunes were declining rapidly, as it was able neither to retain existing manufacturing nor to attract new business.[33] As for the DOC's approach to marketing the state for tourism, such appeals were criticized as antiquated, unsupported by market research, and disconnected from broader economic development efforts.[34]

Making matters worse was a historically poor relationship between the state agency and New York City, and what "down-staters" perceived as a bias in Albany.[35] Indeed, according to critiques and recommendations found in repeated annual audits of the New York State Comptroller's Office between 1969 and 1974, the DOC was doing little of significance in New York City to staunch the outflow of corporate headquarters, industry, and jobs, or to increase tourism. As a result, it was suggested that the department begin coordinating its operations with New York City agencies like the Economic Development Administration (EDA) and the CVB, and improve its use of research, marketing, and media. While the DOC was ill prepared and disinclined to act on these recommendations, impatient private sector leaders in New York City were already making plans to take the lead on them.

Enlightened Self-interest: The Birth of the Association for a Better New York

By the early 1970s, the influential realtors, hoteliers, and corporate leaders on the board of the New York City CVB were growing increasingly irate. Just as their massive, gleaming office towers and hotels were being completed in downtown and Midtown Manhattan, corporations began fleeing the city in droves, and tourists were staying away in ever-rising numbers. So far as they were concerned, this was due almost entirely to the city's image crisis— namely, its growing reputation as a pro-labor city unfriendly to business, and as an "urban jungle" unable to control its unruly "natives." This should have been a clear enough problem to address—especially in light of the new tools that had been unveiled at the DATO "Pow Wow" in New York the previous year to sell cities and regions like never before. Yet the city and state governments, in the CVB and the DOC, were not acting decisively, or at all, to adopt these tools to counter negative perceptions.

Therefore, some CVB members got together to organize their own "civic group" simply called the Association for a Better New York (ABNY), to take on the task, as former executive director Mary Holloway put it, of "cleaning up the image of New York City."[36] The CVB member who played the leading role in this image clean-up was Lewis (Lew) Rudin, CEO of Rudin Management. In 1967, at the age of only forty, he and his elder brother Jack had taken over the helm of one of the most powerful family-run real estate empires in New York City. The Rudins owned eight office buildings in the city, mainly in Midtown and on the West Side of Manhattan, as well as some five thousand residential apartments, all of which the firm both built and managed. His father, Samuel Rudin, a Russian Jew who had come to the US in the early 1920s, had built the company from the ground up, following the simple principle that he should "build wherever the

Rockefellers owned."[37] Thus, in the early 1970s, he and his sons were as concerned as the Rockefellers were with the worsening fate of the downtown real estate market in particular, and of the city more broadly. As Holloway put it bluntly: "when people didn't sign leases, [the Rudins] got alarmed."[38]

There was, however, a major difference between father and son in their approach to remedying this problem. The elder Rudin believed the family could weather the storm by keeping their heads down and focusing more intently on running the business; Lew argued they had to do something completely different—to get more involved in high-profile politicking and marketing on behalf of New York City. As Holloway recalled, he justified this move as simply being in the family's "enlightened self-interest." Lew Rudin saw the fate of Rudin Management as pegged directly to that of the city, and thus insisted the family business could not afford to stand by and watch the city fall apart. This was due to the nature of the real estate business. Unlike the holdings of other, more footloose corporations, Lew Rudin said, "We couldn't move our buildings across the bridges."[39] And if corporations and the upper middle class, who were their main tenants, did not feel safe walking to the subway at night, there was no way these buildings, or their business, had any hope of survival. Making matters worse, the Rudins, along with other major real estate families like the Rockefellers and the Tischs, had borrowed heavily and invested the bulk of their assets in the building boom of the late 1960s and early 1970s. They stood to lose millions of dollars very quickly if they could not rent out these new units.

The Creation of a Public–Private Partnership

In 1971, Lew Rudin decided to create and run ABNY, in partnership with a few high-powered associates in the New York real estate and hotel world, and under the guidance of a man with great experience in both the public and private sectors—Alton Marshall. Marshall had originally come to New York from Michigan to do graduate work in public administration at Syracuse University. Afterward he worked under Governor Thomas Dewey, and then for three terms under Governor Nelson Rockefeller, ultimately as chief of staff. It was in this role that he first met Lew Rudin, when Rudin came to Albany in 1970 as the youngest member of a real estate industry delegation lobbying against a proposal for commercial rent control. As Marshall recalls:

> [Real estate owners] were afraid the State was going to impose commercial rent control, because the owners had been increasing rent considerably and that was affecting our business community, [who were] considering that when they moved out [of New York City]. So this delegation of gray beards came from the real estate industry to Albany and the one I remember was a tall, kind of

skinny, fuzzy haired young man in the group. And that was Lew Rudin, representing Rudin Management. The Governor was late to the meeting and had to go on to another meeting, and during the course he sat down with them and got the essence of the meeting. "I have to go," he said, "but Al will be here, and whatever Al says, goes." And so when the Governor walked out I had heard all I wanted to hear, and I said to the group, "there won't be any commercial rent control." Well, Lew never could get over that, the thought that anyone could sit there and say it with such certainty. That this was the way it was going to be. He was always very impressed about that.[40]

Soon after this meeting, Marshall came down to New York City, at the behest of Nelson Rockefeller and the Rockefeller Family Fund, to run both the Rockefeller Group and Rockefeller Center, Inc., thus instantly becoming a very important player in New York City real estate. His combination of a background in public administration, high-level contacts in government and real estate, and an ability, as Rudin had witnessed, to "cut through red tape" and circumvent the legislature in order to get things done for the real estate industry had indeed greatly impressed Rudin. As soon as ABNY was created in 1971, Marshall was named its vice-president.

As Marshall and Rudin envisioned it, ABNY would do more than any existing city and state organizations, or private sector lobbying groups, to advocate for those like them, with "sunk investments" in New York City. It was to form a new kind of "public–private partnership"—more enlightened about current marketing and financial practices than out-of-touch government agencies like the DOC, unencumbered by government bureaucracy and procedures, and more coordinated than individual, private sector lobbying firms. It worked proactively to organize the corporate executives—primarily those in real estate, but also key players in banking, retail, tourism, and advertising—to develop a coherent agenda for the city, and then to seek a role that was equal if not greater than that of the government in pursuing this agenda.[41] To do this, it used invitation-only ABNY meetings to position itself as an "adjunct" to the Lindsay, Rockefeller, and even Ford administrations, and to shape policies according to the agenda of ABNY's private sector constituents.[42]

Such privileged access led some to suspect that ABNY's efforts were not simple acts of "enlightened self-interest" and a reflection of the greater "responsibility" they were willing to assume on behalf of their beleaguered city. Rather, critics accused Rudin of using ABNY as a ploy for patronage, and to "hide his own and his fellow builders' high rise greed."[43] This view gained traction as policies enacted by the City Planning Commission and

Economic Development Agency in the early 1970s provided zoning variances, tax exemptions, and other incentives for the building of high-density, luxury residential towers, and for the tearing down of low- and middle-income and subsidized housing. All of these high-rises were built by ABNY members in the name of "providing badly needed housing for [corporate] executives" on the East and West sides of Midtown.[44] At the same time, they resulted in displacing, often through evictions, tens of thousands of low- and middle-income residents.[45]

In addition, an exhaustive research project conducted by a group within the Social Services Employees Union showed that "well-connected landlords and realtors" fared better at winning assessment reductions worth millions of dollars than did landlords of otherwise equivalent buildings.[46] They found by far the greatest discrepancies in the number and size of the reductions were granted to the Rudin Management Corporation, which added up to savings to the firm of some $32.3 million between 1970 and 1975. The study concluded there was "a connection between the Rudins' political contributions, connections, and influence and the many reductions in assessments which the politically appointed tax commissioners have granted them."[47] Despite the evidence presented to the press, the case was not investigated further. Perhaps this is best understood in Rudin's incensed response to the accusations: "If the city is to survive, they damned well better consider encouraging new construction. If they want to discourage the Rudins and others we'll go elsewhere."[48] This was presumably not a risk the city was willing to take at this time.

Aside from such perks, perhaps the greatest advantage ABNY provided its members was in the subtler art of social networking. An important bond shared by Lew Rudin and many of his ABNY associates was their marginal status in the upper echelons of New York deal-making circles due to their ethnic and class backgrounds. Rudin, along with Robert Tisch of Loews Hotels, Alan Tishman of Tishman Realty, and Irving Schneider of Helmsley Spear, had all inherited businesses founded by very ambitious Jewish immigrant fathers who, within a single generation, used savvy investments and other means to launch their families into the ranks of the New York elite.[49] As such they represented a *nouveau riche* class within the established, WASP world of New York finance and real estate. This old world was dominated by families like the Rockefellers, Pratts, and Dewinters, whose fortunes went back three or four generations, and who were sheltered financially to a great extent by their large, diversified holdings outside of New York City. These families already had their lobbying and networking organizations, including the Regional Plan Association and Chamber of Commerce, the boards of the Metropolitan Museum of Art and Carnegie Hall, and their exclusive social clubs, fraternities, and churches. These organizations were not especially hospitable to Rudin and his friends, whom they saw as "too Jewish,"[50] nor were they necessarily sympathetic to their vision for New York City. Indeed, these families, and the people with whom they socialized, were among those only too happy to move out as the city declined, in favor of their palatial estates, country clubs, and more secluded office space in the suburbs.[51]

Thus ABNY also served as a social-climbing vehicle for the young, non-WASP, aspiring elite. In addition to advancing the business interests of its members, it provided a new form of cultural capital for the young guard of the real estate world, much like the radical chic parties did for the *culturati*, as described by Tom Wolfe in the pages of *New York* magazine. While a far cry from the *nostalgie de la boue* of Leonard Bernstein and his clique, ABNY events also elevated a stratum of *arrivistes*—albeit one far wealthier—by creating a new foothold for them among the upper classes. And like the editors of *New York*, ABNY members understood that their position in the increasingly competitive and unstable economy of the 1970s depended to an ever-greater extent on a new combination of influence peddling, cultural capital, and media image—or what the magazine called "playing the New York power game."

The Power Breakfast

To this end, ABNY adopted a "two-pronged approach": behind-the-scenes networking, lobbying, and socializing on the one hand; and the very public use of media and marketing on the other.[52] The first "prong" involved providing members with unprecedented private access to public officials and other power brokers at the local, state, and federal levels. Standard ABNY membership dues cost $25,000 a year,[53] and bought invitations to "VIP" or "power breakfasts" at the Waldorf Astoria, the Plaza, and other major New York hotels (all owned by ABNY members), where a few hundred of the select could hear speeches given by movers and shakers in government and business, and then personally meet with them afterwards. On the "history" page of ABNY's website, Rudin explains the "advocacy group's" beginnings in terms of these breakfast meetings, saying simply: "We had to change our ways, become user friendly. We decided to bring people here to meet and speak to New Yorkers."[54]

This, of course, greatly benefited the invited VIPs. First, they were paid thousands of dollars to speak—which, for government officials, skirted campaign finance laws, since the money was not paid as a direct campaign contribution. Second, they gained access to important players in New York City, represented by ABNY's membership—what Rudin called "a cross section of the 300 most important New York entities."[55] And finally, they got a great "photo-op" with big-name New Yorkers, since the city's—and the nation's—most important news organizations, like ABC News and the *New York Times*, would invariably cover the speeches they gave at the breakfasts (while politely avoiding coverage of the schmoozing afterwards). As Mary Holloway recalls, this offered a new way for federal government officials to gain media exposure.

> In the beginning, no one in DC could care less [about ABNY breakfasts]. So they would get Senator Whosie Whatsie to come, and there they would meet the best of New York. People in the news who could make news in a ballroom for breakfast. Everybody in city and state government would be there. People didn't realize how important media attention was. But that all changed very quickly.

In turn, doing a favor for the invited officials provided ABNY members with a mechanism to push for the pro-business policies they cared about: tax abatements, the elimination of rent control, the building of a major convention center, and "quality-of-life" initiatives. As Holloway puts it, political influence worked because these events "merged the social aspect of things with foundations and fundraising." And, she adds, this was of greatest benefit to Rudin himself, who, as president of ABNY, was the one directly giving money to the speakers: "[Rudin] would give thousands [of dollars] to a politician—therefore he had access, locally and nationally."[56] As Rudin's history of ABNY on the official website concludes unabashedly: "In addition to creating public forums for policy decisions through these breakfasts and meetings, ABNY has been influential in helping to shape policy behind the scenes."[57]

One of the public figures ABNY's breakfast meeting attendees courted most assiduously in their early years was John V. Lindsay, who was then serving his second, embattled term as New York City Mayor. Throughout the late 1960s, the CVB had aggressively lobbied the city and state governments to build a new convention center in Manhattan, without which they claimed the city "stood to lose $100 million a year in tourism-related business," based on CVB estimates produced for the 1969 DATO International Pow Wow.[58] This message was reiterated at ABNY's first-ever breakfast meeting, in February 1971, at which Lindsay was the keynote speaker. Soon thereafter, in March 1971, Lindsay issued a statement which reproduced the ABNY and CVB statistics, claiming that the travel industry brought in sixteen million visitors annually, and adding: "They spend some $1.5 billion, which generates approximately $50 million in tax revenues, creates thousands of jobs, and adds greatly to the reputation and lustre of New York."[59]

The Mayor then announced the creation of a new Office of Travel Industry Assistance which would offer "promotional, ceremonial, and technical assistance to the travel and hotel industry." This would exist within the Department of Public Events and give the industry "a one-stop, direct link with this administration [and] the added strength and resources of the city government in their efforts to promote New York and . . . assure that tourists who visit the city have an enjoyable stay." It was to be financed from the existing budgets of the Public Events Department, the EDA, and the Mayor's Office "so that no new expense to the city will be required."[60] Despite the fact that the Office of Travel Industry Assistance was to be a short-lived, under-funded, and largely ineffectual body, and although it was not the convention center ABNY members had been fighting for, the Mayor's action showed the new influence the real estate and tourism industry was gaining over both the city's economic development policy and its rhetoric, through ABNY's style of public–private partnership.

The "Big Apple" Campaign

Alongside ABNY's breakfast meetings, which raised traditional lobbying to a higher and more effective level, the second "prong" in the ABNY approach involved the New York elite in an altogether new activity: coordinated city marketing and PR campaigns. ABNY sought to use their network in media, marketing, and PR to change the perception of New York from "asphalt jungle" to the greatest city on earth, via its "Big Apple" campaign. There is considerable debate as to the true origins of this nickname for New York—with the prevailing view that the term was invented by a jockey in the 1920s who wanted his horse to think that if he was victorious in New York, he could win "the big apple."[61] Whatever the truth, going back to its origins as a Native American settlement, the island of Manhattan and lands sur-rounding it have had innumerable sobriquets and superlatives, indeed more than any other city in the country, according to a compendium of such popular place names.[62] It was only once the CVB and ABNY chose the "Big Apple" for their campaign, and applied their considerable representational power to marketing the city as such, that this name became elevated above all the others.

Alluding to New York's hucksters of old, Mary Holloway called this element of the operation "smoke and mirrors," while Alton Marshall referred to it as "selling snake oil." And certainly much of ABNY's Big Apple campaign drew on old-fashioned marketing techniques—such as calling everything about New York the "biggest," the "best," or, if possible, both. Marshall described the general message of the campaign:

> We had to convince people that New York City is a hell of a town. And it's a town you want to stay in. It has more of everything. It has

bigger of everything. We have the greatest medical facilities in the world in New York City. Why shouldn't your employees have that available to them? We have the greatest financial center of the world. And so on . . . We were going to convince, reconvince in some cases, the people. It has the best transportation system in the world. Even when people were complaining about the traffic jams and this and that. We can still sell the biggest and the best. We didn't have the best, maybe, educational system, but we had the biggest. And if necessary we can sell it as the biggest.[63]

Just as significantly, Rudin understood that simply producing positive messages about New York was not enough to counter all the negative ones. Along with people like Clay Felker, and with the help of some major figures in the New York advertising world, Rudin anticipated the growing importance of targeted, "lifestyle" marketing, and made use of two key principles then emerging in the industry. First, he understood that messages should be derived from professional market research, leading ABNY to commission a professional study to understand what "quality-of-life" elements would keep companies in New York City. Second, he saw that the distribution and placement of the messages had to be strategically coordinated so they would be pervasive and strong enough to combat negative messages on their own turf and scale—in the increasingly powerful media outlets of lifestyle magazines, national newspapers, and television.

The first location for ABNY's messages was to be in the so-called "Mobil position" of the *New York Times*—the lower right-hand corner of the editorial page—so named because that was where Mobil Oil had placed its editorial-style ads since the 1950s. Once a week, in 1971–1972, ABNY bought this space for ads that focused on the retention and recruitment of corporate headquarters in New York City, using testimonials from local corporations who had chosen to stay. ABNY would purchase the space for the standard rate of approximately $20,000, then resell it to a sponsoring corporation at a reduced rate of $10,000. Each spot would then be underwritten by a local corporation that had not moved out of New York—such as Bristol Meyers—whose name would appear at the base of the ad.

In the beginning, the ad copy was created by Sam Norman from the public relations firm of Norman, Craig & Kummell. As Mary Holloway says, his ads had a straightforward tone that ranged from "New York—what a city!" and listed elements unattainable outside New York to "To hell with people who wanted to leave!" Ultimately, however, Norman, with the help of Rudin's salesmanship, recruited New York City's biggest ad firms, whose CEOs were by now members of ABNY, to donate their time and ideas to the campaign.[64] As Marshall recalled:

If you are a top executive of a corporation with headquarters in New York— and can't answer "yes" to all these questions, we'd like to take you to lunch.

a) Have you seen the great new Avon Products' headquarters building on 57th Street?

b) Have you noticed the streets and gutters are getting cleaner?

c) Talked about how Norton Simon, Inc. relocated in New York from Fullerton, California?

d) Do you know that the number of good-to-excellent air days is mounting steadily?

e) Have you checked and found New York office rents are now competitive with both suburbs and major U. S. cities?

f) Have you read about the great new retail, business residential complex that's being built on 51st and Fifth?

g) Or seen the Clean-Up miracle that the task force in the Garment Center has done?

h) And realize that a similar task force is undertaking the same job in Times Square?

i) And that other special task forces are being formed in every business district throughout the city?

j) Have you considered the difference the Anti-Crime Section of the Police Department makes to safety?

k) Did you examine the plans for Battery Park City?

l) Or Waterside?

m) If you have concerns about New York, have you discussed them with anyone from A.B.N.Y.?

n) Do you know who and what A.B.N.Y. is?

The Association for a better New York is made up of business, industrial, financial and civic leaders each of whom is contributing time and effort to improve New York's quality of life and business environment. For a year now we have been organizing, developing, and supporting specific programs for better transportation, more housing, street clean-up, increased police protection and a federal revenue sharing plan. We have also underwritten a major study in preparing a recommendation to help alleviate the drug addiction problem.

There is evidence of real growth and change taking place right now in New York. Would you like one of our members to tell you the hard facts and discuss with you the exciting plans for the future?

As you learn more about us and some of the exciting results we have participated in implementing, you too, may want to join in working for a Better New York.

Better New York maintains its own association offices and Executive Director and staff. The names of our Board of Directors are listed below. We invite you to choose any one or more who you feel can talk most helpfully to you: Then put in a call to tell William D. Swan, Jr., Executive Director—Better New York, 1270 Avenue of the Americas, New York, N.Y. (212) 581-4014.

He will arrange the meeting; lunch, dinner, breakfast —or in your office, if you prefer. We're looking forward to it.

ASSOCIATION FOR A
better new york
WHERE THE CORPORATE ACTION IS

BOARD OF DIRECTORS

Chairman, Lewis Rudin   Rudin Management Co. Inc.

Sandford Abelson	J. G. Hatt & Co., Inc.	Robert Kaufman	William Kaufman Organization	Fergus Reid III	Roosevelt and Son, Inc.
Clifford Barr	Uris Buildings Corporation	Kenneth D. Laub	Kenneth D. Laub & Co., Inc.	Irving Schneider	Helmsley-Spear, Inc.
Charles Benenson	Benenson Realty Company	Sylvan Lawrence	Sylvan Lawrence Co. Inc.	Richard W. Seeler	Cross & Brown Company
Jerome Cohen	Williams & Co., Inc.	David J. Mahoney	Norton Simon, Inc.	Arnold Steinberg	Steinberg & Pokoik
Robin Farkas	Alexanders, Inc.	Peter Malkin	Wien, Lane & Malkin	Edward Sulzberger	Sulzberger Rolfe, Inc.
Zachary Fisher	Fisher Brothers	Alton G. Marshall	Rockefeller Center, Inc.	Preston Robert Tisch	Loew's Corporation
Bertram French	Cushman & Wakefield, Inc.	Jon Minskes	Uris Buildings Corporation	Alan V. Tishman	Tishman Realty & Constr. Co., Inc.
John Goodman	Downtown Lower Man. Ass'n.	Jerome Minskoff	Sam Minskoff & Sons	Rexford E. Tompkins	Brown, Harris, Stevens, Inc.
Aaron Gural	Newmark & Co. Real Estate, Inc.	Norman B. Norman	Norman, Craig & Kummel, Inc.	Harold Treanor	Cox, Treanor & Shaughnessy

Figure 4.4 Association for a Better New York advertisement.
Run in the "Mobil position" of the *New York Times*, February 7, 1972.

Courtesy Association for a Better New York

In our snake-oil sales department we had Norman, who repre-sented the public relations firms and advertising firms on our board. So one time . . . we actually got the heads of fourteen of the largest advertising firms in the city to a luncheon. And Lew went into one of his sales pitches, and we got them to cooperate with us [in] giving us free time and free effort in running a whole series of ads to build up New York City. And I recall we had a real knock-down drag-out fight, [with them asking] why the hell should they do something for the city? And in a burst of probably too much enthusiasm, we said, "Look, you wouldn't exist in the form you are now if you were working in Cancikey, Illinois. If your headquarters was in Illinois you wouldn't be B & O. There's no question you'd be some tiny little local advertising firm. You're big and you've got the jobs you've got because you're in New York and New York is big. And New York makes you and you make New York. So you've got to pay back New York for what it's done for you." And we got fabulous support from that group that otherwise felt that it was so independent that it didn't need New York.[65]

Through this new form of private sector political organizing, ABNY was now challenging the lack of hometown loyalty among business leaders and the media that had been bemoaned by Robert Moses a decade earlier. The group helped New York's corporate elites to recognize their common class interests in the face of fiscal crisis, and to act on them. In the case of the meeting recalled above, the result was that New York's own top-tier advertising and PR agencies—including, notably, Howard Rubenstein and Associates—offered their services at reduced rates, and gave New York its first professional, coordinated, year-round marketing campaign. Under the expert guidance of these Madison Avenue firms, Rudin got together with other ABNY members to hold high-profile Big Apple media events that were covered by local and often national news. Responding to the survey data on why companies chose to leave the city, most of these PR events were designed to combat the two main problems cited: "grime and crime." Mean-while, by showing what the private sector could do when it was organized, this PR was also effective in promoting ABNY members as good corporate citizens, and in advancing the neoliberal idea that the corporate sector was a necessary player in addressing major social problems formerly under the sole jurisdiction of the state.

When it came to grime, ABNY was very creative. Through the "Apple Polishing Corp.," they enlisted legions of corporate employees up and down Fifth Avenue, Broadway, and Lexington, to sweep in front of their own buildings. This allowed ABNY to claim that 29.6 miles of sidewalk were being swept every morning by "corporations who cared about New York."[66]

Another time—as Victor Gotbaum, head of the District Council 37 public employees' union, remembered—Rudin and Tisch met at 5 a.m. with city sanitation workers and gave them a pep talk and spiffy new uniforms before they went out on their shift.[67] Similarly, to challenge a pervasive notion among CEOs that taxicab seats were dirty, Rudin, Tisch, and other ABNY CEOs spent one evening at the Taxi and Limousine Commission's headquarters, personally hand washing the back seats of cabs.[68]

ABNY was perhaps even more influential when it came to crime. They helped fill the gaps in funding for the police, and ensured that policing and surveillance were expanded for the Midtown Manhattan financial district and Times Square. The group met with the chiefs of the police department, and in a very public ceremony presented them with bulletproof vests for the entire police force, paid for by ABNY members. Through "Operation Interlock" they purchased a private radio frequency from the Federal Communications Committee and a transmitter in Midtown, got walkie-talkies for thousands of doormen, and so gained direct access to the police beyond the standard "911" line. And in a campaign which had perhaps the most far-reaching impact, they financed the first 24-hour closed-circuit television cameras for police to use to monitor Times Square. According to the *New York Times*, this was "the first time television has been extensively used to monitor city streets," and it signaled a new era in police tactics, as well as in the privatization and militarization of urban public space.[69]

But most famously, ABNY produced tens of thousands of golden apple lapel pins and cloth stickers, and handed them out all over the city wherever businesspeople congregated—at taxi stands at JFK, at the Four Seasons restaurant, on the steps of City Hall, and, during the evening commuting hour, at Grand Central Terminal. In addition, they tried to get the apple image placed prominently on the clothes of TV personalities, to give it wider circulation.

Big Apple was therefore the first attempt to create a coordinated brand logo for New York City. As a *New York Times* account from 1975 relates:

> Three years ago the bureau began passing out small Big Apple lapel stickers and, according to officials, they have become something of a worldwide craze . . . Tom Snyder, the New Yorker—he came here a few months ago from Los Angeles—wears a Big Apple on his Channel 4 news show. Alan King, the comedian, Dave DeBusschere, the basketball figure; and Lewis Rudin and Preston Robert Tisch, the real estate and hotel executives, all have joined the Big Apple corps of city boosters and pass out the little stickers. Mr. Rudin, who is chairman of the Association for a Better New York, has given away about 4,000 cloth Big Apple stickers, in the three-quarter-inch version that sells for 10 cents a sticker.[70]

Crime-Monitoring TV Goes On in Times Sq.

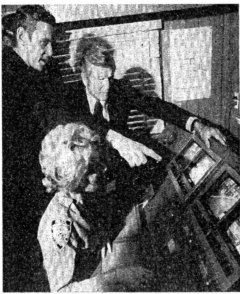

Police Officer John Lazar explaining to Mayor Lindsay the areas being observed by TV cameras as he pointed to a blank of monitoring screens in a trailer in the area.

TV camera, on top of pole at 44th Street and Broadway. has a motor that allows it to scan the area.

Figure 4.5 ABNY's image clean-up: Times Square surveillance.
With financing collected by the Association for a Better New York, New York erected the nation's first twenty-four-hour surveillance cameras in Times Square in September 1973, as part of a wider "crackdown on crime" in the area.

New York Times

Taking on TV

One of the most ambitious of ABNY's image clean-up efforts was their attempt to pressure major New York-based television stations into censoring comedy routines on their late night talk shows. As Mary Holloway recalls, Rudin would often lament, "How can we change the image of New York when Johnny Carson's opening monologue every night is about people getting mugged in Central Park?"[71] So he decided to take action by going to the station heads themselves, in an effort to get them to censor these monologues in the interest of New York's economic well-being. As Marshall remembers it:

> In those days the comedians, most of whom worked on New York [TV] stations, were having a heyday making fun of New York City and putting it down . . . [So] Lew said, "Why don't you and I just go around and visit the heads of all the TV stations . . . and see if we can convince these people they're doing New York City an injustice when they criticize and put it down?" And I remember out of that I think we had ten or fifteen meetings. We would take our time off of our regular work and go see these people. We'd say, "Well, comedy was one thing, but why does it always have to be a comedy that puts New York City in a bad light?" Because this was going out all over the country. And maybe CEOs who were considering coming to New York could have been influenced. And the CEOs that were in New York could use that as general fodder for them to move out of the city. I can remember Lew's often heated discussions with the heads of these broadcasting groups, many of whom he knew. And he would come down with a real wallop and say, "You just can't do this to the city. We've got to find a way for them to get their humor from somewhere else. Or at least for someone to say something positive about the city."[72]

We may never know to what extent Rudin's pressure paid off in terms of a decrease in Central Park mugging jokes or an increase in upbeat New York anecdotes in the opening monologues of TV hosts. But, according to Holloway, in 1973 Mayor Lindsay himself, who was by now a member of ABNY's board, convened a meeting at City Hall with prominent comedians and network heads, asking them to stop "spreading the bad word about New York City."[73] In addition, he worked to expand the Mayor's Office of TV, Broadcasting and Film in an effort to assist and encourage a more diverse range of representations of the city.[74] One of the ways that ABNY could help with this new office was in expediting clearances and security for location shooting since, as Rudin understood, "one of the most important things producers needed was access to real estate for shoots."[75]

This indicates that ABNY was attempting to regulate mainstream media coverage of New York City through television and film. Given the times, of course, this was to prove impossible. These network executives may have been based in New York, but since the late 1950s they had been more concerned with what suburbia considered "normal" and entertaining than with what New Yorkers considered offensive or unprofitable. Regardless of how well New York's economy was doing, they still were getting lots of business from the rest of the country, as demonstrated by the unfettered growth of their industry in this period. And, as noted above, by the end of 1972 *The Tonight Show with Johnny Carson* had left for the West Coast, taking with it the last vestiges of live TV programming shot on sound stages in New York City. Now the most damaging thing for New York's image was not Johnny Carson making mugging jokes, but Johnny Carson giving poolside interviews to Barbara Walters and joking about the boredom of his idyllic new lifestyle.

Legacies of the ABNY Era

Despite the naiveté of its image-policing efforts, ABNY's overall, two-pronged approach was quite successful in its own way. VIP breakfast meetings were effective forums for back-room deal-making for the players involved, while Big Apple events in which CEOs cleaned up the city alongside sanitation workers, policemen, and the hoi polloi were effective PR. The best evidence for this success, as we shall see in coming chapters, is in the influence ABNY continued to wield through the years of the fiscal crisis. Not only did Rudin and other ABNY members gain coveted seats at the table of the "crisis regime," their dream of combining intensive city marketing with neoliberal restructuring was realized once full-fledged city branding was taken up as official policy by city and state agencies.

Another legacy of the era was Lew Rudin-style leadership itself—whether in his role as behind-the-scenes power-broker or as the jolly face of the Big Apple campaign. This style was to earn Rudin the moniker of "Mr. New York," and to inspire the city to change the name of the plaza at 52nd Street and Park Avenue to "Lew Rudin Way," as this was where Rudin would walk from his office to the Four Seasons restaurant, "his cafeteria," networking all the way.[76] Rudin was very proud of his status as a quasi-statesman. Alton Marshall characterized Rudin's perception of himself, paraphrasing Rudyard Kipling: "[Rudin loved the fact that] he could walk amongst kings, but never lose the common touch."[77] In this sense, the leaders of ABNY, like those of *New York* magazine, were able to exploit notions of the "common" New York experience, lifestyle, and image in order to advance the narrower interests of their social class, and of their industries. As Marshall put it: "That's why we formed ABNY—[out of a] desire inherent in Lew to try to do something to improve the lot of the city, and thus the lot of its economy, and thus the lot of the real estate people in the city."[78]

This conflation of the interests of real estate and tourism with those of the city as a whole in a time of crisis is the final, troubling legacy of the ABNY era. The limitations of the vision were apparent on April 18, 1974 at the annual board meeting of the CVB, a lavish affair at the 21 Club, at which Charles Gillett was named the new president of the organization. Preston Robert Tisch, the CVB's president and ABNY co-founder, announced: "New York has had a lot of image problems in recent years, but we've fought our way back. Our image has changed—or been restored—to that of a city unmatched in the variety of its tourist attractions." The dubious barometer of the change to which he referred was the hotel occupancy rate, which had crept up from 64.3 percent in 1972 to 66.1 percent in 1973. Though he did not mention the fact that this was still significantly lower than the generally accepted break-even point for large hotels in New York City (70–75 percent), he did emphasize that it was "considerably higher" than the national hotel occupancy rate (which actually stood at 66 percent).[79] He was trying to be optimistic, optimism being the key element in selling snake oil.

The New York City Fiscal Crisis of 1975–1976

No amount of marketing could change the facts on the ground. Irrespective of whether ABNY's image clean-up helped restore a degree of confidence among New York's tourists, CEOs, and bond agencies, the budget shortfall was worsening. Furthermore, the professional activities of ABNY's own members, as well as others among the city's financial and real estate elites, played a major role in exacerbating the problem. In the minds of the city's potential investors, tourists, and creditors, the financial problems that resulted reversed any improvement to the city's reputation that might have accrued from the Big Apple campaign.

The Onset of the Crisis

The fundamental cause of the city's fiscal crisis of the 1970s, along with those occurring in cities and states throughout the industrialized world at the same time, was and continues to be a matter of major political debate. Leftist sociological analysts of the day like James O'Connor and Giovanni Arrighi understood such crises through a structural lens—that is, as a predictable "articulation" of the growing struggle between elite class interests and the state under capitalism.[80] This view contrasted with the explanation offered by right-leaning academics and editorial-page writers, who focused on the "public largesse" dispersed by overly generous governments in response to the excessive demands of unionized labor, the poor, and people of color.[81] In the middle were liberals, critical of federal government retrenchment on the one hand, while blaming irresponsible social spending on the other.[82]

In the New York City case, conservative and liberal critics have been the dominant voices in this debate, seizing upon the issue of excessive expenditures for the poor, people of color, and union workers over the course of the

1960s. In a series of cautionary tales including *Lesson's of the Lindsay–Wagner Years*, *The Streets Were Paved with Gold*, and *The Cost of Good Intentions*, as well as the more recent retrospective *The Ungovernable City*, scholars and journalists have blamed the crisis on the city's overly generous social programs and pensions for city workers at a time when the state and federal government were retrenching and tax revenues were shrinking.[83] Generally underlying this argument is an indictment of the growing power of the city's public sector unions and welfare rights movements, who had gained significant political and economic ground over the previous decade. As we shall see, this view became the consensus among those who were charged with overhauling the city's budget and policy in the wake of the crisis.

Public expenditures did indeed grow over the course of the 1960s. As discussed above, New York had been the municipal testing ground for the New Deal and Great Society programs of the previous half century, as well as the heavily unionized manufacturing and commercial hub of the post-World War II boom.[84] The period of the Lindsay mayoralty from 1966 to 1974 was arguably one of the high points in New York's liberal tradition, seeing a marked increase in public spending on welfare, housing, and education, as well as a dramatic rise in labor activism and power, particularly among public sector unions.[85] Meanwhile, over the course of the 1950s and 1960s, the city welcomed hundreds of thousands of African American migrants from the South as well as immigrants from Puerto Rico—the latter through the federal government's "Operation Bootstrap" program, which provided free, one-way tickets to JFK Airport, along with a promise of good jobs and a better life. Tragically, the industrial and commercial economy these newcomers were looking to enter was fast disappearing, as were the social programs and services that might have cushioned their transition.[86] With revenue from the federal government shrinking and demands on the city's purse rising, the finances of this traditionally liberal city were being squeezed as never before.

However, it does not appear that New York's relatively generous social spending and union contracts were solely, or even primarily, to blame for this financial squeeze. Many cities faced similar combinations of deindustrialization, federal retrenchment, and growing welfare demands, but did not go into default. Rather, as critics on the left have contended, New York's extreme budget shortfall was also due to the city's increasing use of "corporate welfare" to placate members of its finance and real estate sectors—many of whom were ABNY members—and of short-sighted borrowing strategies to fund these misguided expenditures.[87] The latter took the form, primarily, of tax abatements for large real estate firms and outright subsidies of commercial property development through mortgage underwriting.

As we have seen, increasing corporate flight led ABNY members, and FIRE elites more broadly, to pressure the city to convince big owners, renters, and financiers to stay by providing them with incentives that the state DOC was unwilling to provide.[88] This drive to provide corporate incentives helps explain the very poorly planned development strategy led by Rockefeller and Lindsay to shore up New York's real estate market. First they formed "local development corporations" (LDCs), which enabled private companies to establish financial partnerships with government outside normal channels of public oversight.[89] They then borrowed billions of dollars in the short-term money market to enable these LDCs to get long-term mortgages, in order to finance the greatest office tower development in the city's history. Over 66 million square feet were built between 1967 and 1973, more than double any similar period between 1960 and 1992.[90]

Most of this development occurred in Manhattan's downtown—in particular with the construction of the World Trade Center's 10 million square feet of office space. This downtown development involved the purposeful deindustrialization of New York's still thriving port district, the elimination of some 30,000 blue-collar jobs, and the overall transformation of a historically mixed-use district into a global financial center. And, with the conversion in zoning from industrial to grade A commercial real estate, it served to raise real estate prices in the district up to a thousandfold. Yet, as the building boom progressed, mortgage money dried up, as did the market for high-end rentals. This led major financial and real estate interests, including the Rockefellers and the Rudins, to lobby the city to continue subsidizing more development via mortgage underwriting and actual rental of the new office space by government agencies.[91]

Though New York made up only 3 percent of the country's population, during the late 1960s and early 1970s it borrowed nearly half of all the money secured for short-term purposes by US cities.[92] This money was used not only to cover the city government's operating expenses, already an extremely problematic practice, but to make *mortgage payments*. The latter was a highly unorthodox, and risky, use of short-term loans—which explains why New York was alone among US cities in borrowing for this purpose. Not only did it contravene generally accepted accounting procedures by borrowing money to pay mortgages, it was doing so in the amount of $3 billion, equivalent to one-quarter of the city's entire budget, half of its debt, and over three times its total budget deficit.

Meanwhile, the property tax levy shrunk as a portion of total tax revenue from the mid-1960s to the mid-1970s, despite the enormous increase in office and luxury construction. By 1976, 40 percent of all real estate was tax-exempt, up from 28 percent in the 1950s, costing the city tens of millions of dollars annually. This was largely due to lobbying efforts by ABNY and several politically connected real estate firms, who managed to convince the tax commission to lower assessments on an annual basis, despite state law. According to labor scholar Kim Moody, citing a 1980 New York University study, even a "modest increase [in assessment] could have averted the Fiscal Crisis."[93]

So it was that between 1966 and 1974 the city ran up massive amounts of short- and long-term debt, depleted its tax revenue, and created a huge budget shortfall, as it borrowed to pay operating expenses, maintain social spending, *and* make mortgage payments. Incoming Mayor Abe Beame (the city's comptroller under Lindsay) made only modest efforts to rectify this situation.[94] Meanwhile, the flight of investors from the city's money markets, which began with the high-profile freezing of New York's bond rating in the early 1970s, was accelerating. This led a consortium of banks to anticipate default and sell off all New York City bonds in early 1975.[95] They then refused Mayor Beame's efforts to underwrite future city bonds, placing the bond market completely off limits to the city between 1974 and 1976.

Meanwhile, the city's 1974–1975 fiscal-year budget reached $11.9 billion, second only in size to that of the federal government, and its deficit ballooned to $726 million.[96] Without money even to pay off interest on its debt, the city was pushed near default. In a last-ditch effort, Beame, accompanied by bankers David Rockefeller and Ellmore Patterson, and realtor Lew Rudin, traveled to Washington, DC, to appeal to President Gerald Ford and Secretary of the Treasury William Simon to provide the city with short-term loans. Ford and Simon argued that any federal assistance would "merely postpone" the inevitable collapse of the city's finances, and its need to face up to its fiscal problems through budget slashing, and flatly turned them down.[97] In June 1975, the city was unable to honor $792 million in maturing securities and, in all but legal terms, declared bankruptcy.

The Crisis Regime

Once the fiscal crisis emerged full blown in the summer of 1975, New York's new governor, Hugh Carey, fearing for the entire state's access to credit, took over the city's affairs. He immediately turned to Wall Street financiers, CEOs, and realtors, who long had been clamoring for a greater voice in governance. Together they created new supra-governmental bodies with enormous control over the city's budget, contracts, and policy.

The first such official body was the Municipal Assistance Corporation, known as "the Big MAC." Drawing on advice from a group of prominent bankers and executives, Governor Carey devised the MAC as a temporary financial institution that could overcome bureaucratic hurdles to provide the city with cash to pay off its debt and meet operating expenses.[98] The MAC was authorized by the state legislature in early June 1975 to sell up to

$3 billion in bonds, using the proceeds to retire city notes. To defray risk faced by buyers, the MAC board was given control over city sales and stock transfer taxes. If the board felt the city was not taking sufficient or appropriate steps towards reforming its budgetary practices, they could refuse to lend to the city, and hold these vital tax proceeds in arrears.[95] At a time of fiscal crisis, this obviously gave the MAC and its board overwhelming leverage over city affairs. However, this power was contingent upon the MAC being able to sell off the city's bonds, a task which was by no means easy.

Over the course of the summer and fall of 1975, Mayor Beame followed the MAC directives to the letter, imposing austerity measures on the city, which forced deep cuts in wages and services and undermined gains made by municipal workers and the working class more broadly over the previous two decades.[100] This led to numerous protests, culminating with 10,000 angry members of DC 37, the city's largest public sector union, holding a mass lunchtime rally in front of Citibank's downtown headquarters. While terrifying Felix Rohatyn (one of Governor Carey's chief consultants) and Citibank CEO Walter Wriston, the rally did nothing to turn the tide of austerity. To the contrary, soon thereafter leaders of the biggest city unions —DC 37's Victor Gotbaum, the UFT's Albert Shanker, and the sanitation workers' John deLury—having made a grand display of their rank-and-file support, joined with the MAC in its project. By August, the MAC had drafted a financial plan that included a wage freeze, lay-offs, a transit fare hike, the imposition of tuition at the City University, limits on rent control, and cuts in welfare benefits—with Gotbaum going against his own membership to marshal it through.[101] Many of these cuts saved the city little money, but served as a powerful form of "political symbolism," letting organized labor and the working class know in no uncertain terms that their days of major influence were over.[102]

To ensure that cutbacks were put into effect, the Emergency Financial Control Board (EFCB) was created. Here elected officials had a nominal majority, but they were subject to veto power by the three so-called "public" bank and corporate representatives, including: Rohatyn, from Lazard Freres; William Ellinghouse, CEO of New York Telephone; and David Margolis, CEO of Colt Industries.[103] This group gained control over city revenue, had a mandate to develop a financial plan for the city, was empowered to reject city spending and labor contracts, and was even authorized to remove the Mayor and other officials if they defied EFCB policies. At the last minute Governor Carey reached out for labor support, making the calculation that this would aid in getting the bill that created the EFCB passed by a Democratic legislature.[104]

Yet, despite all the concessions and cutbacks, by early fall it was clear that nothing the MAC or EFCB could do would prevent default. Again, an influential group went to Washington for aid.[105] But while commending their leadership, Treasury Secretary Simon opposed any "city bailout" and supported the city's default. By early September, Ford had the Treasury Department develop a plan that essentially anticipated the city's bankruptcy, enabling the federal government to compensate the major banks while voiding union contracts and overhauling the local governance structure.[106] Ford then let it be known he was "prepared to veto any bill that has as its purpose a Federal bailout of New York City to prevent default." The following day, the *Daily News* ran its blunt and basically accurate headline: "FORD TO CITY: DROP DEAD."

The New Balance of Power

At that point there was a shift, now famous in city lore, to using the public sector unions' own pension funds to "save the city" by buying its unsellable bonds for $2.5 billion over a 2.5-year period. The effort to convince the unions to donate their pensions had begun during the failed negotiations with the federal government in spring 1975, but at that time most union members saw bankruptcy as preferable to such an action. By the fall, however, the unions had endured major lay-offs and had much less leverage. In addition, the possibility of a general strike, their major weapon, was vetoed by Gotbaum and Shanker. Finally, Jack Bigel, the labor lawyer in charge of union pension funds, threatened that if the unions refused, the city would default, contracts would become null and void, and labor would be hindered in future negotiations because the public would blame them for the bankruptcy. The unions consented, and the immediate crisis was averted. The federal government, convinced the city had finally learned its lesson, matched the unions' contribution with $2.3 billion in "seasonal loans."[107]

In striking this historic deal, an enormous burden was placed on the shoulders of city unions. As Bigel himself admitted twenty years later: "We shot craps with the assets of 350,000 pension fund members." Meanwhile, this risk was in no way shared by the private sector financiers who had proposed the deal in the first place, and who themselves refused to buy the city's devalued bonds. Thus city unions were put in the politically compromised position of being the creditors to their employers in city management.[108] Joshua Freeman offers the following, trenchant analysis of this new bind:

> City workers, having won through hard battle a massive accumu-
> lation of capital to ensure secure lives in their old ages, now saw that
> money being used to allow some of the world's richest institutions

to disinvest from New York City. By the spring of 1978, the six major New York banks had less than 1% of their assets in city paper, while the city pension funds had 38% of their assets so invested ... Though periodic crises arose over the next several years, in a wild season of capitalist creativity the banks, state government, and financial community had found a way to retrieve the money investors had lent to New York City, in the process stripping the city government, the municipal labor movement, and working-class New Yorkers of much of the power they had accumulated over the previous three decades. The result could be seen on every street corner and in every institution of working-class New York.[109]

And so union leaders, working with the corporate boards of the crisis regime, forced their members to reverse political course, bringing to a sudden end the post-war tradition of public sector labor activism and influence. This process paved the road for a neoliberal era of accommodation with city management, or what became known as a "corporatist" labor strategy. It also enshrined the role of unelected bodies like the MAC and EFCB, in which no more than a dozen private sector leaders were charged with overhauling the city's finances. These groups were in many ways more powerful than the ABNY-style partnership, creating what both critics and participants have referred to as a "permanent" or "shadow government" of the city's elites.[110] Nonetheless, following that metaphor, ABNY positioned itself as a kind of populist, media-friendly legislature to the MAC and EFCB's more secretive executive branch. Together, these groups fought for policies that were pro-business and anti-welfare state, and echoed each other's demands for belt-tightening by the public sector and unions.[111] Meanwhile, they both also ignored or denied the notion that corporate welfare was at all to blame for the city's troubles, and so naturally did not include their own sector in their calls for sacrifice. As we shall see, this effort at total control over the terms of the city's "recovery" was to provoke new kinds of social unrest and resistance, and in turn spark a New York City image crisis the likes of which had never been seen before.

PART II

The Battle to Brand
New York: 1975–1985

CHAPTER **5**

Welcome to Fear City

> The best advice we can give you is this: Until things change, *stay away from New York City if you possibly can.*
>
> Committee for Public Safety,
> "Welcome to Fear City" pamphlet, 1975

On Wednesday, June 4, 1975, at the nadir of the New York fiscal crisis, Mayor Abe Beame announced a radical plan to regain the city's financial footing and appease its creditors. In the name of austerity, he would terminate the contracts of some 50,000 city workers, the single largest lay-off in New York City history, by July 1. By all accounts, this would deal a major blow to the city's powerful municipal unions and to their ability to provide public services city-wide. Many unions immediately began strategizing how to fight the lay-offs, including the city's twenty-four police and fire unions and their newly formed coalition, the Committee for Public Safety (CPS). With an anger they believed reflected that of their 80,000 members and the city as a whole, the CPS proposed one of the most controversial tactics ever employed by organized labor in New York: the "Welcome to Fear City" media campaign.

Designed with the aid of a PR consultant, and announced at a press conference on June 9, Fear City was "a publicity drive to arouse public opinion against the proposed layoffs." By "public," the CPS meant not only local residents, but that other influential constituency concerned with public safety in New York: tourists and other out-of-towners. To this end, they printed one million four-page pamphlets emblazoned with a shrouded skull and entitled, "Welcome to Fear City—A Survival Guide for Visitors to the City of New York."[1] The pamphlet detailed the wave of crime, arson, and violence that would overtake the city in the wake of the proposed budget cuts, and was to be handed out to visitors at the city's major airports, bus and train terminals, and Midtown hotels, beginning on June 13, 1975, by off-duty police officers and firemen. The threatened campaign would be stopped only if the Beame administration reversed its lay-off plans. If necessary it would continue through the summer of 1976 when the city planned to host the Democratic National Convention and the United States Bicentennial as part of a massive push to revive its moribund tourism industry and attract positive media attention. From the CPS's perspective, the cost of the lay-offs to their members, and the danger they would pose to city residents and visitors, was far worse than the symbolic damage it would undoubtedly cause to these events.

The introductory paragraph of the guide set the grim tone of the campaign. It advised visitors: "By the time you read this, the number of public safety personnel available to protect residents and visitors may already have been still further reduced. Under those circumstances, the best advice we can give you is this: *Until things change, stay away from New York City if you possibly can . . .* The incidence of crime and violence in New York City is shockingly high."[2] Then the leaflet gave a list of urgent cautions, including:

- Stay off the streets after 6 PM. Even in Midtown Manhattan, muggings and occasional murders are on the increase during the early evening hours . . . If you walk in Midtown at about 7:30 PM you will observe that the streets are nearly deserted.
- Do not walk. If you must leave your hotel after 6 PM . . . summon a radio taxi by telephone or ask the hotel doorman to call a taxi while you remain in the hotel lobby . . . The same procedure should be followed when leaving a theater or restaurant in the evening.
- Avoid public transportation . . . you should never ride the subway for any reason whatsoever. In Midtown Manhattan you may, at only slight risk, ride the buses during daylight hours.
- Do not leave valuables in your hotel room and do not deposit them in the hotel vault. Hotel robberies have become virtually uncontrollable.
- Be aware of fire hazards . . . You may have to evacuate quarters without assistance if a fire should occur . . . Try to avoid buildings that are not completely fireproof.[3]

What made Fear City so powerful—perhaps more so than the unions themselves ever imagined—was the tactical way it exploited and subverted the increasingly organized methods for branding the image of New York City that marketers had been developing since the late 1960s. Just like the media initiatives of *New York* magazine, the Association for a Better New York, and the Convention and Visitors Bureau, the unions used the campaign to craft a unified, memorable, and resonant brand, or what might be called a *counter-brand*, for New York City in a time of fiscal crisis. In so doing, they targeted the same "psychographic" audience of their erstwhile competitors: the middle- and upper-class residents, business travelers, tourists, and corporate executives whose decisions about whether to live, visit, or keep their headquarters in the city were shaped by their image of it and its "quality of life." Fear City drew on many of the same, time-tested tactics used by the city's boosters, but aimed for opposite effect.

Like *New York* magazine, the unions developed their brand by combining a simple and powerful visual symbol, in this case a shrouded skull, with wry and alarming prose: "In Midtown Manhattan you may, *at only slight risk*, ride the buses during daylight hours."[4] They backed this up with crime and arson statistics, and put this all in the compelling, user-friendly format of a "survival guide." They thus provided their audience with a putative "service," showing them that they were "on their side," just like the bargain-hunting reviewers of the lifestyle magazine. And like the Big Apple drive created by ABNY and the CVB, Fear City was a centrally organized campaign involving ingenious PR stunts designed to draw maximum media attention—albeit negative. Hundreds of off-duty police officers and firemen brazenly handing out fliers warning visitors to stay away from their city would have made news anywhere, at any time. But the fact that the CPS was doing this in the media capital of the world, and at a time when the city's fiscal troubles and crime statistics were already drawing international coverage, ensured a far greater impact. The *coup de grâce* was timing the campaign to occur in the months leading up to New York's Bicentennial celebrations, and just as the city was making its bid, in competition with other cities, to host the Democratic National Convention. Never before had New York's public and private sector leaders been so obsessed with promoting an image of the city as safe for travel, tourism, and investment, and never before had the city been so vulnerable to a media campaign like Fear City.

And so, predictably, Fear City was immediately seized upon by the local, national, and international press, lambasted by government officials and business leaders, and turned into a huge, embarrassing media spectacle. Setting the stage, the *New York Times* issued its editorial, "Unions vs. New York," which denounced the "irresponsibility" of the unions' campaign and

The New York Times/Don Hogan Charles

Mayor Beame announcing that he would seek to bar distribution of "Fear City" booklet

Figure 5.1 City Hall confronts the Fear City campaign.
Mayor Beame displays the offending pamphlet at a news conference.
Courtesy of the New York City Municipal Archives

the "foolishness" of their demands, and argued the combination of the two was sufficient "to destroy this still vibrant city."[5] The Beame administration responded with a hastily organized media event of its own. At a City Hall news conference on the afternoon of Thursday, June 12, the Mayor, flanked by his commissioners of police, fire, and transit, said the Fear City campaign was "untrue . . . and seeks to undermine the economy of the city," denounced the unions' "brass knuckled tactics" as "an act of rank disloyalty," and cited FBI crime statistics that ranked New York only sixteenth among the twenty largest American cities.[6]

The administration then mounted a last-minute drive to block the campaign. After receiving orders from Beame to "take whatever legal means are necessary to see to it that the scandalous 'Fear City' literature is not distributed,"[7] the city's Corporation Counsel tracked down two New York Supreme Court justices—one at a restaurant, the other in bed—and got them to sign restraining orders preventing the unions from distributing the pamphlets until Monday, June 16.[8] To get around the sticky issue of the unions' right to free speech, the city crafted an argument drawing on two lofty legal precedents. One was the "Holmes doctrine" that the right to free speech could be abridged if the speech presented a "clear and present danger," such as a person yelling, "Fire!" in a crowded theater. The other was a New York State precedent that required proof of the potential for "immediate and irreparable injury, loss, or damage" as a result of the banned speech.[9] Thus, the city argued that the Fear City pamphlet, in and of itself, presented "a clear and present danger to the welfare of the city," that it would "cause irreparable harm to [the city's] mercantile interests, tourist trade, and economy," and finally that it would "induce fear, panic, and disruption of public services."[10] Furthermore, the pamphleteers would "harass" visitors and residents, "many of whom are foreigners and don't speak English."[11] The restraining orders led to a bizarre spectacle on Friday, June 13, when only "a handful" of leaflets were passed out at Kennedy International Airport "to airport employees and newsmen," while the CPS leaders "were kept in a fenced off area outside the international arrivals building by the Port Authority police."[12]

What followed was a flurry of battles in the courts and the press. The following day, lawyers for the unions appealed to the State Supreme Court, decrying these attacks on their right to freedom of expression. Finding that "the plaintiff's leaflet, although intemperate, is probably entitled to protection as an exercise of free speech," Judge Orrin G. Judd wrote an ambivalent decision that permitted rank-and-file members to distribute the fliers but left the city free to serve summonses on them if they did. This equivocation led to public outcry by a host of First Amendment lawyers. Declaring that "the First Amendment has been temporarily suspended in New York," Barbara Shack of the New York chapter of the ACLU offered her support to the pamphleteers—while ironically noting the unusual opportunity this provided the ACLU to file a lawsuit *on behalf of* the NYPD. Famous First Amendment attorney Floyd Abrams was astounded by the reach of the city's case, and what it indicated about the life-and-death importance they now seemed to ascribe to the tourist industry:

> It certainly would be surprising to me that New York City is so vulnerable that the speech of its employees is akin to yelling fire in a theater . . . It would be an enormous expansion of the doctrine of clear and present danger not to allow city employees to speak even if the effect is to have fewer tourists. We're ready to risk a lot more than that to protect freedom of speech.[13]

It seemed the CPS was winning. By June 16, the State Supreme Court finally lifted all limitations on pamphlet distribution, ruling that not to do so would deny union members "the right to reasonable dissemination of opinion," and violate their constitutional rights.[14] The vast majority of the membership of the public safety unions had continued to support the Fear City tactic, even when their leaders were issued restraining orders.[15] Other municipal unions embraced the campaign, too, devising spin-off slogans like the teachers' "Stupid City" and the sanitation workers' "Stink City" that they used to draw media attention to the elimination of *their* jobs.[16]

And yet, the following day, Fear City was suspended. On June 17, four high-powered members of ABNY, including Lew Rudin himself, met with the leaders of the CPS the night before the Fear City pamphlets were scheduled to be distributed, and tried to convince them to stop a campaign which would destroy the Big Apple image they had been carefully constructing since 1971. The unions believed they had a commitment from ABNY to negotiate on their behalf with the Mayor, and agreed to postpone the resumption of the campaign, "to give Mr. Rudin's group and other business leaders a chance to speak out publicly against the layoffs."[17] Yet when they said as much to the press, Rudin quickly called his own news conference at which he "denied flatly that his group had promised to intercede with Mayor Beame."[18] As the *Times* described it, "The Association for a Better New York, whose goal is to preserve New York's position as the country's business and financial capital, wasted no time yesterday in rebuffing the CPS call for help in the anti-layoff drive."[19] Perhaps ABNY's reversal was due to their not wanting to appear to have undue influence on City Hall, or be sympathetic to the unions' militant tactics.[20] Or maybe ABNY simply lied to the CPS as a stalling tactic. Whatever the reason, the CPS was left stranded: "Yesterday, Mr. McFeeley said he was 'unable to believe' that the Association for a Better New York was unwilling to honor what he understood to be a commitment to support the 24 unions in their contention that no public-safety officers should be dismissed in the budget crisis."[21] Without further explanation, the powerful Fear City campaign was aborted after a single week, with no more than a handful of pamphlets distributed.

The speed, scale, and legal reach of the Fear City backlash revealed the extent to which the leadership in New York had become—or felt themselves to be—profoundly dependent upon the city's good reputation as a tourism and business capital, and vulnerable to effective attacks against it. It also revealed the new priorities that had emerged with the fiscal crisis, such that the preservation of New York's *image*—as a safe place for corporations to do business and out-of-towners to visit—had become more important than maintaining public sector salaries and services for existing city residents, to say nothing of freedom of speech.

The incident also exposed the potential reach of well-planned counterbranding tactics in a time of crisis, and in a media hotspot like New York. For indeed, this brief PR stunt by a small group of labor leaders, in combination with the massive budget cuts that inspired it, generated "worldwide publicity" and wreaked havoc on efforts to reconstruct the New York image. The mess was left to the city's image custodians—the CVB—to clean up. Its president, Charles Gillett, tried to remain upbeat, claiming tourists were still "flocking" to New York in the weeks following Fear City. But even he had to admit such "adverse publicity might work against the bureau's effort to change the city's image." As he complained:

> Our campaign has been to make people think of New York City as the Big Apple, not the asphalt jungle . . . Good things happen here but there's no question that the Fear-City campaign did terrible damage. News of that was carried around the world. In Germany, there were front-page headlines that read, "New York Police Warn Visitors Not to Come to New York." It's a black eye for the city, and we're hoping it will be resolved.[22]

Meanwhile, the CVB, ABNY, and the Beame administration refused to enter into a public debate about the wisdom of the service cuts and lay-offs themselves. This is notable, since it was also these massive cuts—not just the lurid fliers that publicized them—that terrified so many potential tourists and business travelers. Rather than defend or even address the new priorities of the crisis budget, the CVB spent hundreds of thousands of dollars creating a new, multimedia Big Apple presentation and taking it on the road to four European capitals in its own international campaign to "counter 'Fear City.'"[23] Charles Gillett explained the impetus and importance of the tour:

> A businessman called us from Hamburg earlier this week to ask if it was safe to bring his family to New York . . . What we're worried about is the people who haven't called, but may just change their minds about coming here on the basis of a very distorted picture that's been given wide circulation . . . We expect to hear the worst, but we think we can answer the "Fear City" publicity. We'll cite the true comparative crime statistics showing that the city is far down on the list and not a place of danger for visitors.

In response to the question of whether "the dire predictions of decreased services voiced by city administrators and commissioners in the last few weeks of the budget crisis would have an inhibiting effect on tourism," Gillett said simply: "Those comments don't get broadcast outside New York . . . But Fear City—that went to the whole world."[24] This partial response reveals two things: the perceived power of simple campaigns like Fear City to communicate news of New York effectively to a global audience; and the myopic view of local leaders that extreme budget cuts carried little negative consequence so long as news of them did not leak out to the wider public.

Ultimately, the crisis regime's cuts to the police and fire departments *almost* went through as planned on July 1, 1975. While the absolute numbers of lay-offs remained the same, their geographic distribution did not. As we shall see, rather than the "city-wide austerity" promised by Beame, police and fire precincts located in the financial districts and middle-class neighborhoods from Lower Manhattan to Midtown to the Upper East and West sides were to be relatively unaffected, while the bulk of lay-offs and police and fire station closures were to be borne by residents in poor and working-class districts—from the Lower East Side and Harlem, to the boroughs of Brooklyn and the Bronx. So while it is little remembered today, the Fear City campaign of June 1975 had a lasting impact—if not the one hoped for by the CPS. For all it failed to accomplish, Fear City taught the leaders of the crisis regime a lesson they never forgot: it is fine to lay off public safety workers as long as you do it away from the financial centers, tourist destinations, and media hot-spots of the urban core.

Planned Shrinkage as an Economic and Visual Strategy

Following the Fear City debacle, public officials turned quickly to the management of the city's devastated finances and reputation, and in doing so were guided by a new approach to urban governance and economic development called "planned shrinkage." This approach was formulated in 1976 by Roger Starr, head of the New York City Housing and Development Administration (HDA), implemented under different titles by the crisis regime, and in its emphasis on individual responsibility and free-market solutions served to articulate the emerging, neoliberal philosophy of the city leadership.[25]

Starr placed the blame for New York's fiscal imbalance squarely on the backs of over-indulged New York residents, arguing that "the central fact of New York's financial crisis is that the city government does not have enough wealth to sustain the city at the level to which its citizens have become accustomed." And so he called for not only cutting city services, but for doing so in a way that would radically reorient New York's tradition of civic liberalism. Rather than cutting services uniformly city-wide, Starr argued the city should reduce services only in its neediest districts—a move that has been called "selective scarcity."[26] Applying Darwinian reasoning to the logic of capital, he argued that just as corporations were eliminating unprofitable plants, the city should shift services and resources from poor neighborhoods that were already "dying" to those that were better off and most likely to survive. This process of "urban triage," as he called it, would also, finally, do the necessary job of changing the more progressive "role of the city" that had existed since the Industrial Revolution of the nineteenth century:

> [We must] stop the Puerto Ricans and rural blacks from living in the city. [We must] reverse the role of the city . . . It can no longer be the place of opportunity . . . Our urban system is based on the theory of taking the peasant and turning him into an industrial worker. Now there are no industrial jobs. Why not keep him a peasant?[27]

According to the principles of planned shrinkage, the transformation of the city's scale, economic base, demographic mix, and fundamental social policy priorities were all necessary to restoring fiscal health. First, the logic went, the poorest residents needed to be driven out of their neighborhoods, thus "shrinking" the population demanding services, and making their abandoned properties available for more profitable purposes. Then, the city's scarce resources could be concentrated on the relatively affluent areas where the tax base was stronger, and which were easier to maintain. Thus, the impact of the fiscal crisis would be socially and spatially planned, its heaviest burden shifted to outlying areas of Manhattan and the boroughs, as well as to mostly poor and working-class communities, disproportionately made up of people of color. Meanwhile, resources would be targeted towards the upkeep and security of the central business districts, tourist destinations, and white, upper-middle-class enclaves of Manhattan—precisely those areas whose reputations were most affected by the Fear City campaign and the broader image crisis. As for those who would not or could not leave, Starr called for the city government to aid in "population transfers" of entire neighborhoods, particularly of poor blacks and Latinos, out of New York City.

In so ruthlessly targeting particular communities, planned shrinkage revealed its dual economic and visual logic. First, like most policy-makers of the time, Starr argued that the root cause of New York's deficit and subsequent fiscal crisis lay in the city's excessive social welfare and public sector burden, rather than in the corporate welfare and debt-fuelled real estate boom of the previous decade.[28] Second, he worked on the prevailing assumption that the declining image of the city and its financial strength in the minds of investors, tourists, and the business community was playing a key role in exacerbating the crisis. In this sense, eliminating what were seen as the most troubled neighborhoods and populations, while cleaning up the financial districts and better-off areas, served both a pragmatic and a symbolic purpose: providing a far more orderly picture of New York for front pages and television screens.

One of the main policy initiatives through which planned shrinkage was applied was the "Blighted Areas Plan" of Felix Rohatyn and the MAC.[29] According to this plan, a zoning category of "blight" was created whereby "visual signs of decay" could be used to designate residential and commercial areas eligible for redevelopment. This extended the principles of 1930s-era slum clearance carried out by municipal governments, and 1960s-era urban renewal carried out under federally financed Title I grants. But now power was assigned to the private sector to determine which areas were to be cleared and "renewed," and for what purpose. At the same time, new quasi-public urban development agencies that were created by the city's newly formed Office of Economic Development (OED) focused their subsidies and tax incentives on Manhattan's central business districts. This centralized approach was encouraged by large banks and investment houses—including those, like Rohatyn's Lazard Freres and the Rockefellers' Chase Manhattan, which had long placed their hopes for the city's resurgence on the ability to attract more white-collar, service sector employers to the empty towers of the downtown and Midtown business districts.

Blight designations, in turn, provided greater incentive for these and other banks to "red-line" poorer, mixed-use neighborhoods—undercutting their credit rating and then stopping loans—thereby making it difficult if not impossible for residents or businesses to invest or maintain their properties in these communities.[30] Thus, in a prime example of what David Harvey and others have termed the "spatial fix" for capitalist crises, the bankers, realtors, and CEOs of the MAC's board deemed the poorest neighborhoods of Manhattan, the Bronx, and Brooklyn eligible to be "blacktopped," their remaining populations "removed," and their land rezoned for industrial or commercial use, so as to attract new business and investment to the city.[31]

The efforts of Starr and the MAC met with immediate and widespread protest.[32] Particularly vocal was a group of city planners led by Ronald Shiffman, director of the Pratt Institute Center for Community and Environmental Development, which issued a statement labeling Starr's plans "genocidal" and called for his immediate dismissal.[33] Chanting, "Roger Starr must go," and carrying signs reading "Antihuman," the planners' group joined a cross-section of community leaders to demonstrate at a Regional Plan Association meeting where Starr was speaking, thus preventing the meeting and "highlight[ing] some of the volatile realities underlying the massive housing problems that the panel had been seeking to discuss with academic detachment."[34] The plan also met with "a great outpouring of disgust and outrage" in the black and Latino communities that were primarily targeted for shrinkage, and moved the City Council's Minority Caucus to decry it as "genocidal, racist, inhuman, and irresponsible." They were aghast that "instead of promoting, rehabilitating, and saving these neighborhoods from decline [Starr] would leave them to die in their own prime and accelerate their death."[35] This sentiment, and the call for Starr's ouster, was reiterated by New York State Congressmen Herman Badillo and Charles Rangel, who made the link between the Blighted Areas Plan and planned shrinkage, seeing both as "promoting the interests of bankers over those of the people." To Rangel, Rohatyn's and Starr's version of economic development was evidence of America's "third-world policy coming home":

> It amounts to an attempt to deport blacks and Puerto Ricans from the regions that are vital to the commerce and transportation of our city . . . We cannot get away from the fact that if the cities were not inhabited by people of color, the planners would have the ingenious creativity to think of other approaches to the problem.[36]

Planned shrinkage was the most draconian of the crisis regime's proposals, and drew so much criticism that Starr was forced to step down from his post.[37] Not surprisingly, city officials never used the terms "planned shrinkage" or "population transfer" in official documents or speeches. But any critique of Starr and his ideas by the city's power brokers proved to be skin-deep and short-lived. Immediately upon leaving public office in September 1976, Starr was named Henry Luce Professor of Urban Values at New York University, assigned to the editorial board of the *New York Times*, and given a special award by the Regional Plan Association. Meanwhile, the city government and its financial overseers were busy implementing almost everything Starr's proposal entailed—albeit now using innocuous terms like "blight clearance" and "urban renewal." Services were curtailed throughout most of the outer boroughs, but not in the more affluent areas of Manhattan. The city HDA, under its new leadership, ceased all building of new public housing, lessened its support of existing housing, and sold off vast stretches of publicly held land that it decided it could no longer maintain.[38] Investment of public and private economic development monies into these abandoned neighborhoods was also brought to a halt. While stopping short of actual population transfers, massive displacement from under-served areas did indeed result, and the shrinkage of the city's population—already occurring since the late 1960s—accelerated dramatically.

In the end, the implementation of planned shrinkage and the Blighted Areas Plan caused graver problems than those they were intended to solve. The combination of service cuts and financial disinvestment with ongoing job loss and inflation led to a vicious spiral in which landlords could no longer afford the upkeep of their buildings, renters could no longer afford to rent them, and properties were simply abandoned *en masse*. According to one study: of 200,000 housing units abandoned between 1967 and 1977,

130,000 occurred between 1975 and 1977.[39] Many landlords also realized the perverse fact that they could make more money by burning down their buildings and collecting the insurance than by maintaining them. This desperate calculation led to a massive wave of arson throughout the poorest districts of the Bronx, the Lower East Side, and Brooklyn, an "epidemic" exacerbated by the closing of fire-houses and the slowing of response times in targeted neighborhoods.[40] The fires were met with a city-wide crime wave, one which went all but unchecked outside the city center. As *Daily News* crime reporter Michael Daly recalled of that time:

> The level of violence was so terrible, you thought you were covering a war . . . It was the one time up in the Bronx that anybody who pled guilty to murder got zero to three. It was the era of what the police called "misdemeanor homicides." And if you weren't killed in Manhattan below 125th Street, it really didn't count.[41]

Ultimately, while planned shrinkage did help accelerate a demographic shift in New York, it was one that (at least in the short term) was the opposite of what Starr had envisioned. Most of the approximately 1 million New Yorkers who vacated the city between 1970 and 1980 were working- or middle-class whites who relocated to the expanding suburbs of Westchester County, Connecticut, and New Jersey—*not* the mostly poor and working-class blacks and Latinos targeted by these policies.[42] Instead, the latter were disproportionately among those who chose or had no option but to stay behind in deteriorating, unhealthy, and unsafe neighborhoods. The doomsday warnings of the Fear City campaign seemed to have been borne out, if only for the city's poorest districts.

As in the city's crack-down on Fear City, the desired impact of this geographically explicit policy was never solely economic, but also visual. It was meant to narrow the frame within which the broader public, as well as New York's own residents, might imagine New York City. Those living, working, and visiting within what Dennis Judd would later call the "tourist bubble" of downtown and Midtown Manhattan should feel a sense of belonging and legitimacy in an area that was cleaner, safer, and better cared for by city workers.[43] Meanwhile, those living in poorer neighborhoods uptown, on the Lower East Side, and in the outer boroughs very quickly got the message that they existed outside of this unified vision. For many communities this created a new and profound sense of abandonment, isolation, and alienation within their own city.[44] But in addition, for many living and growing up in these communities, or coming as voyeurs to these devastated landscapes, planned shrinkage was to spark a powerful new creative vision.

The Abandoned Movie Set

If the city's plan to counter Fear City and the broader image crisis was to push New York's "problem populations" away from the city center and impose a hegemonic image of a white-collar capital in their stead, it was to prove woefully naive. These under-served areas were to provide what actor John Leguiziamo later called "apocalyptic yet fecund" ground for entirely new forms of artistic creation and cultural innovation.[45] This included independent, neighborhood-based movements, in particular the birth of the youth movements of punk and hip hop. It also included the dramatic return of movies produced in Hollywood and shot on location in New York City. So the New York of the 1970s witnessed an amazing phenomenon: despite the hardships of those times, or because of them, the city was to see a veritable explosion in local cultural production, and enter one of the most experimental and dynamic periods in its history. In so doing, New York was to create the conditions for a far more extensive and significant counter-brand than that of the limited Fear City campaign.

Much of this cultural renaissance can be attributed to the clusters of artists and creative industries that flourished amid New York's crumbling urban infrastructure and slack job market. For an unanticipated consequence of these harsh conditions was the emergence of many of the key elements that fuel artistic innovation—including an abundance of affordable space, an excess of free time, and an urgent pleasure in camaraderie. When the *New York Times* conducted interviews for its 2005 New Year's edition asking local luminaries to name what they considered the "golden age" of New York City, a remarkable number of the artists interviewed cited the 1970s.[46] Most of them, like the performance artist Laurie Anderson, nostalgically recalled the cheap rents and collective spirit to be found in neighborhoods like SoHo and the Lower East Side, through which the famous "downtown arts scene" was born.

> It was a tremendously exciting time, dangerous and fun and fantastic. We helped each other all the time on our projects—I could ask someone to light a dance performance, or help paint my ceiling. That's something I'd never think of doing now. In downtown New York, there was still a little bit left of the commune spirit. I was aware we were making a scene, "we" being Gordon Matta-Clark, Philip Glass, Trisha Brown, Richard Serra, Tina Gerard, a mix of musicians, artists, performers. There was great music and everyone was broke. We all lived in cheap lofts, near each other, and we were all building stuff.[47]

Similarly, the punk impresario Legs McNeil remembered how the depopulation of the city provided a fertile terrain for those who remained, inspiring visionary young people to assume new identities and styles, invent new artistic scenes, and imagine themselves as stars in their own New York movie:

> New York was very open, and you could kind of imagine yourself in these great scenarios. It really was kind of abandoned . . . and [felt] like a big movie set. And you could just go in and imagine yourself as "rap guy" or "punk guy." There was a lot of imagining yourself where you wanted to be. Because nobody else wanted to be there. It was like they'd abandoned this movie set, and you could just, you know, go crazy. It was great.[48]

Subway Writing Hits Its Peak

Nowhere was this sense of abandonment more complete than in the Bronx, the borough that had suffered most from the deindustrialization and white flight of "urban renewal" in the 1960s—catalyzed by Robert Moses's building of the Cross Bronx Expressway—and the epicenter of the city's planned shrinkage policies in the mid-1970s.[49] The Bronx alone lost over 300,000 people between 1967 and 1977, or 30 percent of the city's total, and by 1980 had passed counties in rural Mississippi to become the poorest congressional district in the United States.[50] But amid its extreme hardships, the Bronx's creative uprising in the 1970s was unlike any in the city or the nation. It included interventions by established artists and arts collectives, many from other parts of the city and the world, who took up residency in the Bronx and launched a new generation of street photography, popular dance and theater, and public art.[51] Above all, however, the 1970s-era Bronx is remembered as the time and place that gave birth to hip hop.

Hip hop as an art form and a cultural movement was based in four essential elements. The first three involved music and dance—including the instrumental element of "DJ-ing" on turntables; the dance element of "breakdancing"; and the oral and spoken-word element of "MC-ing" or "rapping," as well as the simulation of electronic beats through "beat-boxing." The graphic and visual style of graffiti or aerosol art was the fourth element, a practice that was started by subway writers of the early 1970s, as we saw in Part I. In the early days of 1973–1977, these four elements traditionally came together in spontaneous block parties, competitions, and ciphers (improvisational circles), helping to solidify what MC Africa Bambaataa, founder of the seminal hip hop collective Zulu Nation, calls the fifth element of hip hop: "knowledge" of the underlying principles of the culture, like peace, love, unity, and having a good time.[52]

To sociologist Juan Flores, such hip hop events were "moments of freedom," becoming opportunities to transcend the drudgery of both joblessness and the nine to five, and to infuse everyday life with spontaneity, rhythm, and even poetry, if only temporarily.[53] And, as innovated by mostly African Americans and first- and second-generation Puerto Rican and Jamaican young people, hip hop music and dance also presented a unique opportunity for the fusion of a new Afro-diasporic cultural form—linking, for instance, call-and-response verbal battles; the rhythms and improvisation of jazz, funk, and reggae; the syncopation of *bomba y plena*; and setting them all to electronic break beats and scratching on vinyl.[54]

Emerging as it did in the Bronx of the 1970s, this powerful new expression of freedom and cultural hybridity was to serve as "its own form of urban renewal"—taking the place of the arts programs eliminated from public schools, and bringing life to the dilapidated parks, streets, subways, and housing projects of the neighborhoods hit hardest by fiscal crisis.[55] As cultural theorist Tricia Rose puts it, hip hop was inextricable from its urban setting, based as it was on "appropriating and alchemically transforming resources found amidst the urban detritus."[56] These resources included new techniques of mixing and dubbing via boom boxes, turntables, and pre-recorded music; pirated energy from streetlights; any potential public space that could be "borrowed" for a street party; the sides of subway cars and (often stolen) spray paint; as well as the body, the voice, and language itself.[57]

Yet a key issue also separated the four elements of hip hop. While the music and dance-based elements were the temporal expression of this new movement, through graffiti, or "writing," hip hop entered the visual space of the city to a far greater extent. In this way, graffiti helped politicize the urban context shared by all four elements of hip hop, and specifically the deteriorating and offensive conditions of the inner-city neighborhoods in which hip hop's young creators were growing up. Of course, all hip hop, lacking other means, developed through the appropriation of public space. But for MCs, DJs, and break-dancers this involved local, temporary spaces—turning stoops, streets, rooftops, rec-rooms, basketball courts, and school cafeterias into impromptu dancehalls, music studios, and community events. Unless "brave"' downtown music producers were prepared to trek out to these isolated neighborhoods, there was little chance the wider public would find out about their work—this being a good decade before rap videos would appear on MTV.[58] Thus, at least in the 1970s, graffiti was distinct among hip hop's elements due to the far greater scale and duration of its impact on the physical city, and of its carefully cultivated image.

In 1975, this impact exploded. As we saw in Chapter 2, graffiti had its "pioneering stage" between 1971 and 1974. In the fiscal crisis years of 1975 to 1977, the creative destruction inherent within the practice hit its "peak."[59] It was in this period that this relatively small, underground phenomenon became a city-wide movement, with thousands of practitioners, a new level of artistic talent, and a scale of work that now regularly encompassed entire sides of subway cars. As @149st. puts it in their unofficial history:

> All the standards had been set and a new school was about to reap the benefits of the artistic foundations established by prior generations and a city in the midst of a fiscal crisis. New York City was broke and therefore the transit system was poorly maintained. This led to the heaviest bombing in history ... At this time bombing and style began to further distinguish themselves. Whole cars became standard practice rather than an event.[60]

With planned shrinkage, and the infrastructure of their neighborhoods literally crumbling around them, graffiti writing became both an easier and more urgently meaningful practice for young people. It was easier, quite simply, because far fewer police and transportation authority officials were guarding the train yards. And it was more meaningful in a physical environment that told young people that their fate and that of their communities were unimportant to the powers that be. For many of the mostly teenage and disproportionately male writers, "the art of getting up" was about being rebellious, free, and proving their bravado and skill in competition with other writers.[61] But in addition, many were responding critically and creatively to a harsh, alienating environment direly in need of beautification, forcing the rest of the city to recognize their existence, and read their names, whether they liked it or not.

The evolution of hip hop culture in the South Bronx, and in particular the rise of writing on the sides of subway cars, proved that despite the efforts of the city to cut off the Bronx from the rest of New York, the will of its young people to forge symbolic links between uptown and downtown was indomitable. And it led to the phenomenal rise of a new artistic center in the heart of this "bombed-out" zone. After witnessing the rise of hip hop in his devastated home borough, Marshall Berman argued that despite the "misery and anguish" of this time, or because of it, "the Bronx became more culturally creative than it had ever been in its life."[62] He cited a story by Grace Paley from this period, in which a character visiting the Bronx observes: "The block is burning down on one side of the street, and the kids are trying to build something on the other."[63] Berman saw this too with every visit to his old neighborhood: "In the midst of dying, [the Bronx] was going through rebirth."[64]

This sentiment is echoed by myriad artists to this day—not least by a great many writers who were inspired by this original movement. As Lady Pink, one of the most important writers and muralists of the 1980s, remembered:

> In the late 1970s and early 1980s, New York was in chaos. There was no money. Everything was going to pieces. *And the only hint of life and energy and spirit was on the colorful trains coming out of the Bronx and Brooklyn . . .* New York was being crushed. And the young people just would not die.[65]

Alongside rappers, DJs, and break-dancers, graffiti writers of this period went on to tour, perform, and exhibit in major art venues across the country and the world, and to create a style that to this day is one of the dominant (and hugely profitable) forces in the worlds of art, design, fashion, and global youth culture.[66] This despite the fact that, aside from a handful of downtown gallery owners, New York's own cultural elite either turned their backs on or helped criminalize this home-grown cultural movement.[67] Even so, the fact that the subway writers were at once artists and subversives, and that their work implicated the property relations underlying the harsh urban conditions in which it was created, gave them unique status—for better and for worse—within hip hop and the wider worlds of art, politics, and law enforcement.

For while this symbolic seizure of space may have been widely appreciated, this was certainly not the dominant view in the city at the time. To a range of critics—including the official stewards of the crisis regime, the Metropolitan Transit Authority, influential publications like the *New York Times* and *New York* magazine, as well as many transit riders—graffiti was the ultimate symbol of a city out of control, run by teenagers, in which property rights could not be protected.[68] It was also, ironically, the reification of the Fear City image of New York crafted by police and fire unions. Indeed, as argued by city officials of the day, the practice became the paradigmatic example of a new category of "lifestyle crimes"—that is, minor property and street crimes that marred the visual order of the city and would, if left unchecked, inspire general lawlessness.[69] This legal designation was a precursor to the influential "broken windows" theory of urban crime developed by the Manhattan Institute in the coming decade, a theory that would legitimate the elevation of graffiti from a misdemeanor to a felony offense. In this sense, the 1970s anti-graffiti crusade helped inspire an ideological shift, as postmodern as it was reactionary, that located the source of criminal activity in the imagery and disorder at the city surface, rather than in structural and systemic social problems like poverty and unemployment.

So, to paraphrase Grace Paley, for local leaders of the day, the graffiti murals being spray-painted on one side of the street were just as damaging to New York City as the crumbling buildings on the other. Indeed, both sides of the street were seen as part of a vicious image cycle, the one feeding into the other, with both driving the city further down into chaos. As we shall see, this had a lot to do with the fact that graffiti translated so beautifully to the screen, and that the screen was becoming a dominant and hotly contested site for would-be branders of New York in this period.

The Return of the "New York Movie"

As discussed in Chapter 2, Mayor Lindsay created the Mayor's Office of Film, Theater, and Broadcasting (MOFTB) in 1966 in order to streamline the process of making media in New York City. In so doing, he helped spark a renaissance of filmmaking in the city during the late 1960s, with an average of forty-six films shot annually between between 1966 and 1974, over three times the rate during the Wagner administration. Remarkably, this accelerated rate continued into the Beame administration: in 1975, at the height of the fiscal crisis, forty-six films were again shot in New York.[70] With estimated revenue from the movie industry reaching $40–50 million a year, the MOFTB became one of the key agencies in Beame's newly created Office of Economic Development (OED).

The city's new, one-stop filmmaking office certainly helped to attract directors to New York, but it did not account for all of the huge increase in local production. New York's unionized film crews were still able to demand high wages, slow down shooting schedules, and drive up costs, relative to other cities. What really pushed New York over the top as Hollywood's location of choice was its image—now being formed in the mind of the national audience—as the capital of urban crisis. The documentary-style coverage of the city's notorious financial and social problems in newspapers, magazines, and the nightly news whetted America's demand to see "realistic" movies, particularly crime dramas, shot on location in New York's streets. This helped motivate intrepid Hollywood movie people to abandon their stage-set version of New York and make the trip out to the city itself. As Steve Kesten, assistant director on the movie *Marathon Man*, shot in Manhattan in 1975, explained:

> New York is the greatest back lot in the world. It's being sold down the pike because Hollywood people are scared to death to come here. It's strange turf. New York may be more expensive, day by day, but New York movies are big hits. Eight million people live in New York, 180 million people read about New York. It's always in the headlines, whether it's the muggings or the arts.[71]

And yet, like the OED in which it was housed, the MOFTB still saw its role as buffing up the city's image in the eyes of the rest of the country. As *New York* magazine reporter Ellen Stern enthused in 1975, the devoted MOFTB would go overboard to "work miracles" for filmmakers, often at the personal urging of the Mayor himself, so as to ensure that the real city conformed to the improved image a director had in mind, and to "make the city look better for the cameras."[72] The only exception, according to the city agency liaison, was back in 1966, when a scene in *The Out-of-Towners* required Jack Lemmon's character to encounter a garbage strike and the Sanitation Department had to place garbage on the street. But otherwise, he said, "we won't allow anything to be done that will destroy our image."[73]

It seems that either the MOFTB was not being completely honest, or the agency was extremely naive about what film crews were really doing in the streets of New York. As early as 1974, well-known subway writers recalled the thrill of being hired by the set designers of *The Taking of Pelham One Two Three* to cover a previously pristine train with tags, as well as the indignity of seeing fake and inartful graffiti festooning train cars in *Death Wish*, which came out the same year.[74] And certainly if the piles of garbage in the streets had been cleaned up in the latter film, there would have been far less to motivate Charles Bronson's descent into vigilantism. In general, films about New York in this period were twisting Lindsay's "Fun City" into a playground of purely sadistic pleasures. As the *New York Times* film critic Vincent Canby wrote in late 1974:

> [In today's movies] New York has become a metaphor for what looks like the last days of American civilization . . . It's run by fools. Its citizens are at the mercy of its criminals . . . The air is foul. The traffic is impossible. Services are diminishing and the morale is such that ordering a cup of coffee in a diner can turn into a request for a fat lip.[75]

Other critics sought to differentiate between the quality of the movies being made, arguing that the work of certain *auteurs*—John Schlesinger, Gordon Parks, Sidney Lumet, Woody Allen, Mike Nichols, and Martin Scorsese—signaled the long-awaited return of the "New York movie." For the New York-based journalist Mark Jacobson, Scorsese's semi-autobiographical *Mean Streets* (1973) was a sign that "the New York movie would finally come home in one hellish masterpiece." After getting his hopes up that the industry would be revived after the era of New York underground film in the 1950s and 1960s, only to be disappointed time and again by the "dreck" of the late 1960s and early 1970s, Jacobson found in *Mean Streets* a true cause for celebration.[76] Despite, or because of, the raw bravura of its characters and its numerous technical flaws—scenes shot with "grade Z documentary footage . . . left out in the sun too long" and sound so bad that "lots of time you can't even hear De Niro go into tirades"—the movie felt authentically and beautifully New York.

> Raging like an oily Kong on the tenement tops of Little Italy, De Niro sprayed bullets into the New York night and threatened to shoot out the lights of the Empire State Building . . . [This] is the Quintessential New York Movie. It's the story of the guys you hang out with and the city you live in; the kind of stuff that when you're doing it somebody says, "Hey man, this would make a good movie." It's immediate, jagged, energetic almost to the point of entropy; full of raunch, crazy dialogue, and with a big stiff one for you if you don't like it. But underneath there's soul and poetry too. It's like New York.[77]

Jacobson's definition of a good New York movie was very similar to the notion of the gritty social realism, poetic rhythm, ironic wit, and leftist undertone of the "New York sensibility" as cultivated by the Cultural Front of the 1930s and 1940s. After being besieged by the McCarthyite purges of the late 1940s and 1950s, this sensibility returned surreptitiously to New York with the blacklisted TV writers of the 1950s—but never again gained the national prominence of this earlier period. Now there was hope that good, authentic New York movies would be made again, thanks to the presence of a few gutsy directors as well as a range of local institutions. New York University's film school, Scorsese's alma mater, had its largest enrollment yet in 1975. A new generation of daring, idiosyncratic actors was coming out of the High School of Music and Art, and the method-acting school "The Group" was graduating stars like Al Pacino and Robert De Niro, who were "completely and compellingly New York."[78] Since the early 1960s, locally based freelancers—from cinematographers, to sound mixers, to film editors—were considered the best film craftspeople in the business.[79] As New York-based producer Ed Lynch reasoned: "There's every reason to think we can start a movie version of Off-Off Broadway; in fact, you might call it Off-Off Hollywood."[80]

But despite all the crews and money streaming in, the prospects for the return of a New York movie were complicated, at best. With the notable exception of Allen,[81] almost all of the home-grown talent was moving to LA, including Nichols and even Scorsese, the man whom Jacobson credited with bringing "the New York movie home after sixty years of wandering in the desert." By the late 1970s, these directors, and their complex and critical take on the "asphalt jungle" drama, had been replaced by B-movie directors like

John Carpenter, Michael Winner, and William Lustig, who were only too happy to play up the worst New York stereotypes for thrills and laughs. They created a new genre of what I call *New York exploitation movies*, which was to grow into one of the biggest and most lucrative segments of the US film industry in the 1980s, and spawn New York film subgenres with cult followings, like vigilante action, slasher, and horror.

The first major New York exploitation film, and the one that was to set the mold for those to follow, was Michael Winner's *Death Wish* of 1974, which became a major commercial success, earned a cult-like following, and spawned four sequels over a twenty-year period.[82] In the film, the liberal architect Paul Kersey, played by Charles Bronson, sees his family life and his faith in humanity destroyed when local thugs murder his wife and rape his daughter. After a business trip to Arizona during which a wealthy client offers Kersey target practice at his gun club and a front-row seat at a mock-gun battle in a reconstructed Old West frontier town, Kersey returns to New York City a changed man, and with a gift of a .32-caliber revolver in his luggage. Discovering that the overwhelmed New York police force won't even follow up the crimes committed against his family, Kersey takes the law into his own hands, going out on nightly raids to gun down criminals and single-handedly bringing the city's crime rate down by 50 percent. As film critic Roger Ebert wrote at the time, this is "a New York City in the grip of a reign of terror," in which "literally every shadow holds a mugger; every subway train harbors a killer; the park is a breeding ground for crime."[83] Against this backdrop, Kersey becomes a folk hero, and the film became "propaganda for private gun ownership and a call to vigilante justice."[84]

With a lone, heroic white man forced to fight bands of dark-skinned villains against a barren, lawless backdrop, *Death Wish* owed far more to Hollywood Westerns than it did to the vaunted "New York sensibility." For now that the Western hinterlands had been suburbanized, the over-populated inner-city became Hollywood's new, hostile frontier. As in the old Western, geography was destiny. New York City itself was main character and primary antagonist, a malevolent force that, as the years and sequels went by, drove its depraved inhabitants to commit ever bloodier crimes, with the local authorities always pathetically powerless to stop them.

"Asphalt jungle" films like *Midnight Cowboy* and *Mean Streets*, depicting as they did the complex human struggles of their characters, were more artistically sophisticated than those belonging to the "New York exploitation" genre. Nonetheless, the two genres shared a similarly ambivalent moral and political sensibility. This can be seen clearly with Scorsese's critically acclaimed *Taxi Driver*, which came out in 1975 and starred Robert De Niro as the New York cabbie turned avenging killer Travis Bickle. Like Kersey, Bickle taught the audience that the individual had to be prepared to

Figure 5.2 Charles Bronson, the "New York vigilante."
A promotional still from Michael Winner's *Death Wish*, 1974.

Motion Pictures Vault

degenerate to the level of animal-like urban natives if he were ever to "stand up" to them and if anything resembling justice were to be served. As Bickle screams into the dark, grease-slicked streets from his taxi-cab before he goes out to seek vengeance:

> All the animals come out at night—whores, skunk, pussies, buggers, queens, fairies, dopers, junkies, sick, venal. Someday a real rain will come and wash all this scum off the streets . . . Listen you fuckers, you screwheads. Here is a man who would not take it anymore. A man who stood up against the scum, the cunts, the dogs, the filth, the shit. Here is a man who stood up.[85]

Critics read great pathos into De Niro's performance of paranoia and his final turn to vigilantism. As a Vietnam veteran returning to a city falling apart, and as a young man who fails at every job and relationship he attempts, Travis Bickle's character may be seen as a metaphor for the increasing anxieties of the era.[86] But from the perspective of tourists, conventioneers, and the city marketers who were trying to attract them, the *Taxi Driver* message was not so nuanced. Rather, it formed part of an

Figure 5.3 Robert De Niro standing up to the asphalt jungle.
Publicity poster for Martin Scorsese's *Taxi Driver*, 1975.

Motion Pictures Vault

increasingly universal set of representations typified by films like *Death Wish*, which offered viewers the pleasurable fantasy of killing off the bad guys along with the degenerate city that bred them. In this way, both critically acclaimed urban dramas and B-movie slashers became metaphors for New York's seemingly inevitable demise.

By 1976, New York exploitation films had almost completely replaced the more complex urban dramas and crime thrillers of the late 1960s and early 1970s. Now, and for the coming decade, it seemed Gotham was impossible to film unless it involved excessive amounts of blood, gore, and righteous vengeance. Roger Starr's cold, organic metaphors for the surplus inhabitants of these "dead zones" had finally attained a human face.[87] Meanwhile, to New York's real inhabitants, and especially to those interested in making

Table 5.1 "Asphalt jungle" films, 1967–1976.

Title	Director	Date	Genre
The Incident	Larry Peerce	1967	Crime Thriller
Midnight Cowboy	John Schlesinger	1969	Urban Drama
Joe	John G. Avildsen	1970	Urban Drama
Desperate Characters	Frank D. Gilroy	1971	Urban Drama
The French Connection	William Friedkin	1971	Crime Thriller
Panic in Needle Park	Jerry Schatzberg	1971	Urban Drama
Across 110th Street	Barry Shear	1972	Blaxploitation
Superfly	Gordon Parks	1972	Blaxploitation
Black Caesar	Larry Cohen	1973	Blaxploitation
Hell up in Harlem	Larry Cohen	1973	Blaxploitation
Mean Streets	Martin Scorsese	1973	Urban Drama
Death Wish	Michael Winner	1974	Vigilante Action
Law and Disorder	Ivan Passer	1974	Crime Thriller
The Seven-ups	Phil D'Antoni	1974	Crime Thriller
The Taking of Pelham One Two Three	Joseph Sargeant	1974	Crime Thriller
Dog Day Afternoon	Sidney Lumet	1975	Urban Drama
King Kong	John Guillermin	1975	Horror
The Prisoner of Second Avenue	Melvin Frank	1975	Urban Drama
Taxi Driver	Martin Scorsese	1976	Urban Drama

Note
The late 1960s was a turning point in the representation of New York City on film. A new genre of "asphalt jungle" films emerged, depicting New York as the embodiment of the nation's "urban crisis." This was seen in three primary subgenres: action-packed "crime thrillers," bleak "urban dramas," and over-the-top "blaxploitation" films.

serious films, these representations seemed only to reinforce their sense of alienation from the rest of the country. As Jacobson lamented:

> Perhaps the most visceral issue of all these days, with the specter of default and the maddening indifference of the hick government, is that a lot of people in the Big Apple are beginning to get rather militant about the city they love. Suddenly films like "Death Wish" and crud like "Kojak" are beginning to get people mad. [Cinematographer] Arthur Ornitz, who worked on "Death Wish" and then refused to see it, says, "It was an evil film. The New York Western has got to go." It's about time the media freaks in this city stood up and decided to take our image into our own hands.[88]

Table 5.2 "New York exploitation" films, 1976–1993.

Title	Director	Date	Genre
The Assault on Precinct 13	John Carpenter	1976	Vigilante Action
Driller Killer	Abel Ferrara	1979	Slasher
The Warriors	Walter Hill	1979	Vigilante Action
The Exterminator	John Glickenhaus	1980	Slasher
Maniac	William Lustig	1980	Slasher
Escape from New York	John Carpenter	1981	Vigilante Action
Fort Apache, The Bronx	Daniel Petrie	1981	Vigilante Action
Wolfen	Michael Wadleigh	1981	Horror
Death Wish II	Michael Winner	1982	Vigilante Action
Ms. 45	Abel Ferrara	1982	Slasher
The Winged Serpent	Larry Cohen	1982	Horror
Vigilante	William Lustig	1982	Vigilante Action
C.H.U.D.	Douglas Cheek	1984	Horror
Exterminator 2	Mark Buntzman	1984	Slasher
Fear City	Abel Ferrara	1984	Vigilante Action
Death Wish III	Michael Winner	1985	Vigilante Action
Death Wish IV: The Crackdown	J. Lee Thompson	1987	Vigilante Action
Manic Cop	William Lustig	1988	Slasher
Manic Cop 2	William Lustig	1990	Slasher
Manic Cop 3: Badge of Silence	William Lustig	1993	Slasher

Note
During the fiscal crisis era of 1974–1976, increasingly violent, racist, B-movies took over, giving rise to the "New York exploitation" film. Primary subgenres shifted to: "vigilante action," based on Hollywood Westerns, pornographically bloody "slashers," and animalistic, science-fiction-based "horror" movies. This genre continued to be the dominant filmic representation of New York into the early 1990s.

Of course, appropriating the image of one's own city is easier said than done. As in the 1920s, New York's independent producers and directors were once again up against the big guns of Hollywood, albeit this time on their own turf. Now, however, they faced the ultimate, ironic indignity: rather than the New York movie coming home from Hollywood, the Hollywood version of New York was taking over the city.

Conclusion: The Legacy of Fear City

It was to be a long war of attrition. Throughout 1976 and 1977, New York residents and activist groups held almost weekly demonstrations to keep city services and, consequently, some of the harshest aspects of planned shrinkage were scaled back. In 1978, city unions continued to mount labor actions, won wage gains that partially recouped lost ground, and ended the Emergency Financial Control Board's ability to block collective bargaining agreements. Nonetheless, the ideological terrain of the city and nation was shifting inexorably to the right. As historian Joshua Freeman points out, in the aftermath of the fiscal crisis,

> working class new Yorkers remained on the defensive, forced to justify every service and benefit in a discourse that accepted governmental solvency as the highest social goal and left unchallenged the notion that there were insufficient economic resources available to undertake even the most obviously needed and beneficial government programs.[89]

Meanwhile, the city went on the offensive in its efforts to respond to the needs, concerns, and political orientation of investors, out-of-towners, and the federal government.

In retrospect, it might seem strange that the city bent over backwards to entice Hollywood filmmakers to make apocalyptic blockbusters like *Death Wish*, while reacting with such vehemence to low-budget, home-grown movements like Fear City and subway graffiti. But the choice reflected the contradictory nature of the city's new economic priorities: that is, its push to attract high-end services like media back to the city, and at the same time to protect the image of Manhattan as a business and tourist center. This image was violated when Fear City campaigners began handing out fliers at Grand Central Station, and when spray-painted murals traveled by subway through the heart of the city. It was also violated by characters playing murderous, subway-riding vigilantes like Paul Kersey in films that played to tens of millions around the world. Yet Charles Bronson was never criticized or censored by the crisis regime, let alone arrested for yelling, "Fire!" in a crowded theater (like Fear City pamphleteers) or for committing a "quality-of-life" offense (like subway writers). Rather, he and his ilk were celebrated by local leaders as lures in a hot sector that the city was courting—and perhaps even as heroes shooting the bad guys to boot.

As we shall see, in the aftermath of Fear City the crisis regime would ramp up efforts to assert control over the central space and symbolic capital of New York City, and to sell the city's favorable "climate" for business and tourism. This would be felt in the restructuring of city governance and finance—as seen in the imposition of selective scarcity, the tightening of police surveillance, and the invention of a host of new incentives for investment in the urban core. And it would also result in the launch of the city's first official, centrally managed branding campaigns: an updated version of "Big Apple" and the entirely new "I♥NY." These campaigns placed a bright spotlight on those aspects of New York culture that, according to market research, visitors in town for business or pleasure most wanted to consume: the musical theater of Broadway and the newly built towers of the World Trade Center. Meanwhile, they cast a long shadow over rising home-grown movements like punk and hip hop, as well as over the harsh reality of planned shrinkage and lay-offs in the city's crisis-torn neighborhoods.

CHAPTER 6

From Big Apple to the Summer of Sam

There is a growing pride in the city on the part of New Yorkers . . .
Boosterism is no longer an epithet to the city's officials, civic
leaders, union heads and neighborhood groups. The tourists have
taught them that the city is "The Big Apple," maybe even "Fun
City," once again.

> Charles Gillett, president of the CVB, 1976

Don't you know the crime rate is going up, up, up, up, up?
To live in this town you must be tough, tough, tough, tough, tough!
You got rats on the West Side, bed bugs uptown
What a mess—this town's in tatters . . . I've been shattered

Uh-huh, this town's full of money grabbers
Go ahead, bite the Big Apple, don't mind the maggots, huh
Shadoobie, my brain's been battered . . . This town is shattered

> Rolling Stones, "Shattered," 1977
> (Lyrics by Mick Jagger and Keith Richards)

The year between the summers of 1976 and 1977 offers a unique window on
New York City's official turn to branding itself in response to crisis, and the
contradictions inherent within this approach. Leading the effort was the
public–private relaunch of the Big Apple campaign. As we saw in Chapter 4,
Big Apple was initiated in 1971 by the Association for a Better New York

(ABNY) and the Convention and Visitors Bureau (CVB) to stem the tide of corporate move-outs and declining tourism. It was retired in 1974 with the onset of fiscal crisis, and given its seemingly final burial in 1975 by the police and fire unions' internationally publicized Fear City campaign, as we saw in Chapter 5. But now this ambitious PR effort first conceived by local realtors and hoteliers was to be embraced by city government and turned into a large-scale, summer-long campaign, strategically linked to two national media events that were coming to town: New York City's celebration of the US Bicentennial, and its hosting of the 1976 Democratic National Convention. The new Big Apple was to shy away from contemporary images of New York, drawing instead on mythic, transhistorical representations of the city as a national and global capital. The big photo-op was "Operation Sail," in which regattas of colonial-era tall-ships and modern luxury liners cruised New York Harbor past the Statue of Liberty and a downtown skyline crowned by the newly completed World Trade Center. This visual montage of New York's glorious past and triumphant future would serve, it was hoped, to blot out the ongoing, present-day horrors of the crisis. It would also present New York City, and particularly its downtown financial district, as a family-friendly tourist destination and attractive site for investment, conventions, and corporate headquarters location.

The upsurge of tourism that accompanied the early days of Big Apple—to say nothing of similar growth enjoyed by a number of New York's rival cities—taught local leaders some important lessons. First, even in the midst of crisis, recession, and austerity, tourists could and should be convinced to come to New York. Second, tourist dollars were one of the most easily attainable sources of new revenue for this cash-strapped city and, according to new industry-sponsored market research, had a profound "multiplier effect" throughout the local economy. And third, the relatively modest public expenditure tourism required was an easy political sell—even at a time of deep cuts in every other area of public spending. Whereas boosterism was historically considered outside of, if not beneath, the realm of New York City government, now it was seized upon as an essential, almost magical strategy of fiscal recovery. And the Mayor's new Office of Economic Development was deployed to institutionalize and professionalize its role.

And yet, come 1977, the dream of the shiny Big Apple was shattered, as the Rolling Stones famously put it, by the festering reality of crime, maggots, and "still surviving on the streets." For it was in 1977 that a tragic series of natural, social, and image crises transformed the geography of the city against a backdrop of escalating unemployment, lay-offs, and austerity. These included arctic temperatures followed by New York's hottest summer on record, the "Son of Sam" murder spree, garbage strikes, and a twenty-five-hour electrical blackout leading to widespread looting and arson in parts of Brooklyn, Manhattan, and the South Bronx. All of these events proved to be captivating media spectacles, gaining front-page headlines and lead TV coverage nationally and internationally. Collectively they served as a counter-hegemonic visual force, undermining the symbolic capital shored up by the Big Apple campaign, and providing the nation with its para-digmatic representation of the decline of urban America.

The terrible events of the summer of 1977 also exposed the two troubling contradictions underlying the city's new approach to economic develop-ment. First, increased spending on marketing and other business incentives alongside the imposition of harsh austerity measures was ineffective at redressing the city's deepening poverty, inequality, and social tensions. Indeed, by placing budgetary priority on attracting future economic growth and catering to out-of-towners at a time of urgent local needs, additional social problems—from hospital closures and homelessness to arson and crime—were generated or left unchecked. This in turn led to a second contradiction: the media coverage of these spectacular problems entered into wider circulation than the city's own upbeat campaigns, thus sabo-taging marketing efforts and exacerbating rather than solving the city's initial image crisis.

In this chapter, I will trace three developments that brought New York to this point of contradiction: the rise of a public–private branding coalition led by ABNY and the CVB; the embrace by City Hall of a tourism-based and marketing-led model of economic development; and the spectacles of catastrophe in the summer of 1977 that did so much to damage the city's new, would-be brand. As we shall see in Chapter 7, these events were to lay the groundwork for the more powerful, state-centralized branding coalition that would produce the I❤NY campaign in 1977. But first it is important to trace the primary agents, formative stages, and visual strategies of city branding that came together in the year between Big Apple and the Summer of Sam.

Damage Control: The Emergence of a Branding Coalition

As the right-wing animus towards New York grew over the course of the 1970s, culminating with the Ford administration's infamous refusal to "bail out" New York at the height of its fiscal crisis, those in the city's business elite found themselves in a quandary. On the one hand, they loathed the anti-New York rhetoric for the damage it did to local image-sensitive industries like tourism, banking, and real estate in which they were based. On the other, they agreed with the basic premise of the critique: that blame for the crisis lay on the shoulders of New Yorkers—that is, on the city's overly generous social welfare policy, excessive union contracts, and high taxes—

and certainly not with their own practices of receiving billions of dollars in "corporate welfare" via mortgage underwriting, tax breaks, zoning variances, and other subsidies in the late 1960s and early 1970s. The alliances they struck and reforms they helped push through at the city level very much reflected this new dilemma.

The Political Dilemma for New York Business

It may be argued that local realtors and financiers of the era of fiscal crisis came to see their ideological allies in the Republican White House more so than in the Democratic City Hall or state capital. Taking a position that would soon be identified as "neoliberal," they joined the chorus behind President Ford that called for New York's crisis to serve as a national object lesson on the effects of bloated government bureaucracy, corrupt labor unions, and overly generous welfare laws. In response, their lobby called not for the state to be eliminated, or even shrunk, but rather for it to be realigned. Rather than playing its mid-century "managerial" role, balancing the demands of business with those of organized labor and the public sector, the main role of government now should be "entrepreneurial," serving above all to improve the "climate" for business growth.[1] This entailed everything from enacting major tax reforms to enhancing the image of the city and state in global markets.

Nowhere was this growing allegiance between local elites and Washington, DC, more explicit than with the very public "friendship" between realtor and ABNY founder Lewis Rudin and President Gerald Ford, which was "cemented" when Ford was invited to speak at a heavily symbolic ABNY breakfast held at Manhattan's Federal Hall in 1976 as part of the city's Bicentennial celebrations.[2] From then on, Ford acknowledged, "Lew was recognized as a great friend of mine," and whenever he visited the city, Rudin would act as his unofficial host, putting him up in an apartment in one of his own buildings.[3] Similarly, Chase Manhattan CEO David Rockefeller credits Ford's approach during the fiscal crisis with inspiring him and his cohort to create their own public–private partnership, the New York City Partnership (NYCP), in 1979. "In retrospect," he mused, "the best thing that happened to New York may have been the famous 1975 Daily News headline, 'Ford to City: Drop Dead!' That really got our adrenaline going."[4]

And yet, while local business leaders may have quietly supported Ford's tough stance on New York, they did not and could not abide the accompanying attacks on the city's image. These "asphalt jungle" characterizations implicitly blamed the crisis on average New Yorkers, framing them within the racist and classist language of "welfare queens" and "crooked union bosses," and helped scare off tourists, investors, corporate tenants, and other valuable sources of revenue. This was a major threat to firms that had sunk investments in the city, from real estate to utilities, as well as those in finance and financial services that depended on the networking advantages brought about by physical proximity of global centers like Wall Street and Midtown. They were in no position to follow their corporate colleagues in other, more flexible sectors and abandon the city when the going got rough. Rudin, for one, often reiterated the issue that prompted the formation of ABNY back in 1971—that his company was still unable to "move our buildings over the river," or south of the border, or simply to shift to telecommunications for their deal-making. And so, even if these businessmen bought the national line on lazy, morally challenged, good-for-nothing New Yorkers, they could not afford this portrayal to be broadcast to the nation, giving the entire city a bad name.

Broadly speaking, when it came to the image of the city, the fiscally conservative ideology of the crisis regime was trumped by their local, place-based interests. Indeed, when it came to marketing the city to transform this image, their staunch support of austerity was loosened considerably, if not reversed. As we shall see, while the regime supported the drastic decrease in public spending for city workers, welfare, and services, they supported a dramatic *increase* in public spending at both the city and state levels when it came to confronting the image crisis.[5] As we saw with planned shrinkage in Chapter 5, the crisis regime increasingly embraced a strategy of "selective scarcity," whereby image and investor confidence were prioritized over public city functions, and the future needs of potential visitors and investors were prioritized over the immediate needs of city residents. The emerging crisis-era branding coalition was crucially influential in making this shift.

City Government Restructures Itself for Marketing

Responding to the lobbying efforts of ABNY and the CVB, as well as the stringent mandate of the MAC, the EFCB, and the Ford administration, Mayor Beame and the Department of City Planning (DCP) devised a new plan for economic development in 1976. In the report, entitled "Economic Recovery: New York City's Program for 1977–1981,"[6] the city spelled out two substantive shifts which were to be undertaken in its approach to economic development. One was the creation of a new "Office of Economic Development" (OED)—the first city-wide administrative division devoted entirely to generating new income for the city through its dealings with the private sector. In creating this new office, akin in its mission to the state's DOC, Beame and the DCP merged previously separate departments like Cultural Affairs, Public Events, and Budget and Finance under one roof. This office was then placed under the jurisdiction of a new "Deputy Mayor for Economic Development," whose position of authority was second only to that of the Mayor himself. The main effects of this restructuring were to streamline different aspects of what had traditionally been called "business services" under the rubric of "economic development" and then to assign economic development a much higher priority in City Hall. Most importantly for the business community, this included the increased provision of "incentives"—like tax breaks and zoning variances—to aid corporate location and retention, and enshrined the principle of "shredding red tape," that is the elimination of bureaucratic hurdles for the private sector in their dealings with the city.[7]

The second shift in the city's approach to economic development, which was to be carried out by the new OED, was what Beame called in his report "the marketing of the city."[8] Citing the "paradoxical" fact that, unlike so many other cities in the country, "the home of the world's largest, most energetic communications and marketing industries should beat its own drum so seldom and so softly," the report announced the establishment of "a comprehensive marketing program" funded by city, state, and private business. This foray into an area previously considered unnecessary was defended as now incumbent on the city in an era of stiff inter-urban competition. As a point of comparison the report states:

> Philadelphia, for example, last year launched a three-year marketing program to attract new businesses supported by $1.2 million in private subscriptions from fifty companies and $495,000 in funds provided by the Philadelphia Industrial Development Corporation, a quasi-public agency. In recent months, the "New Philadelphians" have written to many New York firms inviting them to come on down.[9]

The proposed marketing program had three goals: to "convey New York's advantages as a place to do business and to stress the City's positive attitude toward business"; to "encourage companies to locate in the City and to stay and expand here"; and to "attract more tourists and conventions."[10] The report then went to great lengths to legitimize this major new expenditure in the midst of belt-tightening in every other arena of public funding, particularly given that it was going into an area in which many people assumed government had no necessary role:

> Until recently, New Yorkers tended to assume that business would take care of itself and that the City's size and natural strengths would function as an automatic magnet. Many leading business groups paid little attention to events outside their own industries. The financial crisis in particular has changed many of these

attitudes—spurring the City's determination to become a self-promoter and enlisting the loyalties of local businessmen.[11]

The "local businessmen" to whom Beame's report referred were the CEOs of New York City-based finance, real estate, and tourism-related corporations, such as the members of the CVB and ABNY, and their "loyalties" entailed considerable sunk investments in the city's economic base. Thus, this policy meant in practice that the marketing efforts of these public–private entities were to be increasingly subsidized through city funds. This commitment was acted upon almost immediately. While the city had reduced its contribution to the CVB by $200,000 in 1975, this money was restored in 1976, and increased in early 1977 to $500,000 for the remainder of the city's five-year economic recovery plan in order to fund "stepped up promotional and marketing activities."[12] Once this "public contribution" was combined with the $600,000 contribution provided by the CVB's private members, the tourism marketing agency was suddenly flush with over a million dollars in funds, more than double its budget of the early 1970s.

Upscaling Big Apple

With new help from the OED and recharged private sector donors, ABNY and the CVB turned their sights on two major events taking place in New York City in the summer of 1976 for their branding effort. The first was New York's celebration of the national Bicentennial on July 4, for which ABNY and the Bicentennial Committee had chosen Operation Sail as the main event. This would bring a massive regatta of thousands of historic ships down the Hudson, into New York Harbor, and past the new Lower Manhattan skyline, creating a dramatic image of the modern, festive port of New York that would be broadcast nationwide. The second event was the Democratic National Convention, at which Jimmy Carter was to be nominated for the presidency. This would be held at Madison Square Garden, and also televised live to the nation, providing three days of free publicity for the city at the height of the presidential campaign season. Both of these mega events, meanwhile, were linked to a new version of the Big Apple campaign, which was upscaled from a local booster drive to a branding campaign of national and global dimensions.

Many New York City residents and neighbors were thrilled at the prospect of a carnivalesque break from the doldrums of crisis and a chance to participate in historic, nationwide celebrations. Hence the "Bicentennial fever" that swept the tri-state area in the weeks leading up to the big July 4th

FINAL

DAILY 🔲 NEWS

NEW YORK'S PICTURE NEWSPAPER ®

15¢

Vol. 58. No. 8   New York, N.Y. 10017, Monday, July 5, 1976*   Mostly sunny, 61-80. Details p. 13

6 MILLION VIEW
OPERATION SAIL

It's Happy, Safe 4th For City

Raise a Schooner To Miss Liberty

The First Lady of the world — the Statue of Liberty — welcomes the Chilean schooner Esmeralda into New York Harbor during the parade of the Tall Ships of Operation Sail yesterday. Thousands jammed vantage points on Liberty Island while flotilla of pleasure crafts filled upper bay. Six million lined New York and New Jersey shores. President Ford viewed procession from host aircraft carrier Forrestal.

---

12 Pages on Op Sail

*Stories Begin on Page 3;
6 Pages of Photos in Centerfold*

Figure 6.1 Operation Sail and the US Bicentennial.

Courtesy *New York Daily News*

weekend, and that led to unexpectedly massive crowds lining the route of Operation Sail on both sides of the Hudson.[13]

This may help explain the daring effort to join in the festivities on the part of a crew of graffiti writers named CAINE, MAD 103, and FLAME ONE, an effort still legendary in the local writing community. Equipped only with spray-paint and sketchbooks, the writers occupied a train yard in Queens on the night of July 3 and covered an entire fleet of cars on the 7 Flushing to Manhattan line—ten feet high and longer than two football fields—with aerosol recreations of the earliest designs of the US flag. According to graffiti historian Joe Austin, their plan was for the train "to fly through the shared public spaces of New York City on the morning of the nation's 200th birthday like a patriotic streamer." But the "Freedom Train," as it became known, was never to be seen—except by a handful of MTA workers and transit police, who promptly pulled the cars out of service, destroyed the paintings, and arrested the writers in their homes the next day.[14] As Austin puts it,

> [The MTA] steadfastly refused to be upstaged by what they felt was vandalism—no matter the work's patriotic appeal—and they would not risk the public's mistaking the Freedom Train as part of the officially sanctioned celebration ... CAINE, MAD 103 and FLAME ONE's gift was refused. In that refusal their "place" in the city was made clear.[15]

And in their seizure of the Freedom Train, the city's underlying economic agenda was also revealed. First and foremost, the branding coalition saw the summer of 1976 as an opportunity to remind the nation that New York was still a tourist destination and business capital. Charles Gillett expressed their main concern: "out-of-towners have wondered if the water will be turned off while they are here, if the buses and subways will stop running and if they will be hit by sudden tax and cost increases."[16] And so, through the coalition's efforts, New York would be recast as a safe destination for families, national delegates, and business travelers, as opposed to a lawless Fear City ruled by teenage graffiti writers. It would appear as a patriotic destination for lovers of colonial-era America and national party politics, as opposed to a separatist hold-out run by blacks, Latinos, and second-generation white ethnics. And finally, through an intensive focus on the Lower Manhattan skyline, the city would regain its image as a center of global finance—as opposed to the nation's worst example of fiscal irresponsibility.

Bicentennial Patriotism Meets the New World Trade Center

As a key element in this effort, city branders seized upon the newly completed towers of the World Trade Center (WTC) as the logo for a globally resurgent New York. This was a symbolically strategic move on many levels. It elevated the image of the Twin Towers, and of the downtown financial district more generally, in the midst of fiscal crisis and corporate move-outs, both of which were closely associated with Wall Street itself. In so doing, it also provided the city as a whole with a modern new skyline that eclipsed that of Midtown, centered on the Empire State Building, with which the old, bankrupt city was now universally associated. And finally, it contrasted this resplendent new downtown skyline with an invocation of the city's role in the American Revolution of 1776, and the founding of the nation, thus creating a montage of the city's glorious past and triumphant future, deftly leapfrogging over the troubles still lingering from its more recent history.

To achieve this montage, it was not only necessary temporarily to expand the ranks of the transit police to ensure that graffiti played no part in official festivities. The campaign also needed to change the prevailing public perception of the towers themselves, which was that they were inextricably linked to, and partially to blame for, the ongoing ordeal of the crisis. The WTC had been completed five years behind schedule, close to a billion dollars over budget, and was the centerpiece of a costly, publicly subsidized, and highly controversial scheme to build up the downtown real estate market. As a result, when the recession hit in the early 1970s, the bulk of the towers' expensive new office space was empty, and the city was pushed closer to the brink of fiscal insolvency. The gleaming modernist towers created the most jarring contrast imaginable to the day-to-day reality of deteriorating public infrastructure, drastic service cuts, and widespread joblessness endured by New Yorkers during the crisis. They seemed to many a symbol not of the city's resurgence, but of its widening class divide and irresponsible, self-serving leadership.

Edward Sorel captured this surreal contrast in a spoof in *New York* magazine, which ingeniously associated the "asphalt jungle" stereotype with New York's rich bankers and politicians, rather than with its poor and working classes.[17] Asking the question "With New York on the brink, can epic recapturings of its decline and fall be far behind?," Sorel designed mock-movie posters for future flics like "Metropolis of the Damned," "The Garbage also Rises," and, for a grand finale, "The Towering Insanity . . . starring David Rockefeller," in which the CEO's mammoth head looms with a maniacal grin over the teetering towers. The promo reads:

> Here at last is a truly original screenplay—a disaster movie in which the horror comes from watching not the destruction but the *erection* of a skyscraper. You guessed it, it's the incredible story of the World Trade Center! Action packed machinations that will leave you breathless! Mile high spectacle with suspense on every floor!

> David Rockefeller gives his usual suave performance as a banker
> who builds the city's tallest building only to discover no one wants
> to rent floor space in it. But—clever plot—his brother turns out to
> be the Governor, and all ends happily when hundreds of state
> agencies are moved in and the bank cleans up. A heartwarming
> morality play just in time for the holiday season.[18]

The image clean-up project of the Big Apple campaign in 1976 was aimed
not only at the seedy streets of Times Square but at the disgraced towers of
the WTC. To play on the epithet often ascribed to the latter, the campaign's
job was to transform the city's "white elephant" into its "white knight." This
was to involve a masterful separation of the interior of the buildings, still
largely empty and losing money, from their gleaming exterior, presented
now as a symbol of resurgence.

Lifestyle Media Enter the Fray

To accomplish this separation, the WTC was marketed as a site of spectacle
and visual entertainment. It was presented not simply as a utilitarian
structure in which business happened—or did not happen—but as an
awesome, architectural wonder to view from the outside, as well as to enter,
climb, and use to view the rest of the city. Unable to find paying tenants, the
WTC focused on getting tourists to visit the new observation decks—in
competition with Midtown's more famous Empire State Building. In
1975–1976, at the onset of the fiscal crisis, the Port Authority paid $225,000
to an ad agency to create a marketing campaign that turned the World Trade
Center's roof into a vehicle for transcending economic woe:

> "Come up to the top of the world" a Trade Center promotion says
> immodestly. "The world's highest observation platform" . . . "You
> can't be down when you're up" goes the slogan, with its unmis-
> takable reference to the local fiscal blahs. The slogan has been used
> on television and radio, and on municipal buses.[19]

Along with the observation decks, the WTC offered its views through a
remarkable new restaurant, Windows on the World, built in the top five
floors of the North Tower and opened to the public in May 1976. In addition
to being one of the city's most lavish and expensive eateries at that time, it
was the world's highest, and offered some of the most spectacular views of
any metropolis that had ever been seen from inside a building. As its name
asserted, its purpose was not simply to be a restaurant, but to position New
York City, and its downtown financial district, visually and symbolically as
a global center. According to its creator Joe Baum, the entrepreneur and

Figure 6.2 The Big Apple rises above Lower Manhattan, 1976.
Following the fiscal crisis, the newly completed Twin Towers were seized upon as a symbol of a
financially stable New York City.

Courtesy New York City Municipal Library

president of Inhilco, a subsidiary of Hilton International, the two goals for Windows were for it "to become an instant landmark, a place that people from all over the world would come to see" and to "re-establish a neighbor-hood" in the downtown area.[20]

The promotion of the World Trade Center and its new restaurant as a must-see tourist destination was given a major boost by ABNY and the CVB. They arranged PR events in the restaurant in early 1976, before it was officially opened to the public. These included a number of private Opera-tion Sail parties, at which assorted VIPs appeared on TV and in magazine and newspaper articles, wining and dining hundreds of feet above the city and its troubles, looking down like Olympian gods on the Bicentennial festivities. For the first time in years, audiences around the world were offered dramatic overhead shots of New York Harbor, the Statue of Liberty,

Caption: *Concierge Joseph Scialom (sixth from right) and 297 others make up the staff that runs the Windows on the World.*

The Most Spectacular Restaurant in the World

Figure 6.3 The symbolism of Windows on the World.
The lavish, sky-high spectacle of a restaurant was embraced by the media as evidence of New York's resurgence and unrivaled city status. From *New York*, May 31, 1976.

New York Magazine

and the island of Manhattan in place of close-ups of crime-ridden streets and graffiti-covered subway cars. From this vantage point, the burning buildings of the Bronx, even Harlem, were too distant to be captured in the frame.

Soon enough, Windows on the World became a *cause célèbre* for the local news and lifestyle media, and a sign that the fate of the city was, at least for its upper ranks, turning the corner. From all the cover stories and special issues devoted to the new hot-spot, it seemed like the press had gone too long without covering New York's once-famed "Society" scene. This would explain why the *New York Times'* metropolitan reporter, Fred Ferretti, previously of the fiscal crisis beat, wrote a gushing, 2,000-word piece soon after the restaurant's opening. In it he marveled at its array of spaces for "exclusive socializing," while touting it as the city's next great tourist icon. In the game of inter-urban competition, this kind of publicity could go a long way:

> Seattle has its Space Needle, San Francisco has its Top of the Mark, and now New York has its Windows. And from them the city is spread out before one in breath-taking fashion. To sit in the main dining room as dusk descends and the city begins to turn on its lights in a visual extravaganza. To wander through its many levels and its five restaurants can transmit the feeling of being aboard a vast opulent airplane or in the dining salon of the largest liner afloat.[21]

The article went on breathlessly to proclaim over fifty names—not in bold type, but impossible to miss—of the luminaries able to skip the two-week waiting list to get a table. Interestingly, many of these famous patrons had recently appeared as political adversaries. But now Congresswoman Bella Abzug and UFT president Albert Shanker were dining at tables across the room from Governor Hugh Carey and President "Jack" Ford. Even Theodore Kheel, the labor mediator (and inveterate critic of the wastefulness of the WTC), was won over: "He has had his disagreements with the PA [Port Authority] but nevertheless has reserved wine bin No. 1 and says he is grateful indeed for its existence." But the guest list was not limited to the same old local names of whom New Yorkers had grown weary—now they were joined by "the most talked-about" media celebrities, politicians, and even royalty from around the world, who came to town especially to visit this new marvel:

> To the 18 private suites have come Cary Grant, Henry Kissinger, Senator Jacob Javits, the King and Queen of Spain, the Queen of Denmark, the Prime Minister of Japan, Stephen Smith and an

assortment of Kennedy and Lawford children, Princess Grace and Prince Rainier of Monaco, Lee Radziwill, the Crown Prince of Norway and Earl Blackwell. Most, like the actress Dina Merrill and the actor Cliff Robertson, came for private Operation Sail parties, but, entranced by the spectacular 360-degree view of New York—and on clear days New Jersey, Pennsylvania and Connecticut as well—they have returned to dine privately.[22]

One of the most lavish media promotions of Windows on the World was done in an issue of *New York* magazine devoted to the restaurant's grand opening.[23] The magazine's interest in the event was twofold. Milton Glaser, *New York*'s artistic director, had been hired by Joe Baum to design the interior of the space, along with his newly formed design firm, WBMG, and so this article offered an opportunity for cross-promotion. In addition, the opening of this exciting, new, "high society" location tied in perfectly with *New York*'s greater purpose: to show New York City in the best possible light. And in 1976, there was arguably nothing to be more positive about in New York than the World Trade Center's fancy new restaurant. Glaser recalled:

It was absolutely true [that] the WTC was a symbol of resurgence, and so the opening of Windows on the World was one of the events that turned the corner of the image of New York, which the magazine was related to. It was one of the greatest restaurants in the world, the most ambitious and biggest. And it happened when the city was in terrible shape, and people were moving out of the city, and people were not investing in the life of the city. And suddenly this extraordinary place opens with a tremendous amount of money invested in it, tremendous ambition. [It was] saying, "Look, we are the greatest, and we're going to open the greatest restaurant." [This] had a very meaningful effect on life in the city. Because more than anything else it was a visible representation that showed that people trusted the success of the city. And the opening of a commercial enterprise with millions of dollars behind it, with the presumption that the city is going to be here for a while, [showed that] people are going to eat, drink, [that the restaurant will] attract tourists from all over the world. So, I really think that that was one of the signals to the city itself, and to all of us who were here, that it wasn't time to move out. That the city still had things to offer that no place on earth could offer. This kind of gesture had enormous symbolic meaning . . . [It was] a signal that "We're still a great place."[24]

In saying "all of us who were here," Glaser is referring to a particular group—including his circle of friends and colleagues, those in the creative and culture industries, and *New York*'s aspiring, middle-class readers. Much like the magazine's original reviews that taught "how to eat rich though poor," here was an opportunity for members of this group to imagine themselves among the elite, even if they could afford to eat there only once a year. But Glaser is also indicating an interesting change: many in this group were now in a position to enter these shifting upper ranks. This was a moment of the formation of a new cross-class subjectivity, in which Windows on the World, a brash symbol of extravagance and exclusivity, was equated with the city's "greatness" by those in both the middle and upper classes who survived the crash and could keep moving up the ladder. Any nostalgia for the old working-class culture once celebrated by New York was left behind in the pre-fiscal crisis era. The remarkable upsurge of underground youth movements like punk and hip hop, meanwhile, was pushed further out of sight by the gleaming façade of the towers.

And so, by the summer of 1976, the various elements of a branding coalition and strategy were coming together. The CVB and ABNY used the towers and their crowning restaurant alongside aerial views of Operation Sail on official tourism posters, pamphlets, and guides. In a two-page ad that ran in *New York*'s inside cover for a year, a sparkling WTC rises above the Brooklyn Bridge at night, as newly elected Mayor Ed Koch and Loews Corporation CEO Preston Robert Tisch remind tourists: "You'll find the Big Apple to your taste whether you're here for pleasure, for business, for a convention, or for a shopping trip."[25] A range of city marketers had come together around a common vision of New York—one based entirely in consumption, reflecting above all the desires of visitors, the business community, and an aspiring middle class.

The Magic Industry

In its press releases, the CVB called 1976 a "splendid," "excellent," and "glowing" year, and a source of growing pride for the city.[26] And, indeed, many of the statistics bore out their claims (see Table 6.1).According to a special report, "The New York City Visitors Industry," produced by Mayor Beame's office in conjunction with Victor Marrero, chairman of the City Planning Commission (CPC), the newly recognized industry welcomed 16.5 million visitors in 1976, up 500,000 from the annual figures of the previous five years.[27] Hotel occupancy rates were at 73 percent, up from the 65 percent of the previous year, and finally passing the 70 percent mark for the first time since 1969, when the record of 75.4 percent was set. The city held 834 conventions, the most since the World's Fair of 1964–1965. It seemed New

Table 6.1 Changes in the New York City travel and tourism sector, 1969–1976.

Date	Hotel Occupancy Rate (%)	Conventions	Number of Visitors (million)	Visitor Spending ($ billion)
1969	75.4	829	16.5	1.5
1971	64.3	815	16.0	0.4
1973	66.1	813	16.0	0.4
1975	65.0	N/A	N/A	N/A
1976	73.0	834	16.5	1.5

Source: Statistics as cited in the CVB, Annual Report, 1969; articles from the *New York Times*, 1969–1976; Office of John V. Lindsay, Press Release 114–71; Auletta, *The Streets Were Paved with Gold*, 6; Beame and Marrero, *New York's Visitors Industry*. N/A: not available.

York had finally put the blight of fiscal crisis and Fear City behind it, replacing them with a shiny Big Apple.

Some argued this upsurge was a fluke—the result of a good season for the Yankees, one-time national events, or a weak dollar attracting tourists from Europe and Japan. Gillett argued that the bulk of the credit for the windfall should go to the CVB itself, and that the city's successes were the "cumulative effect of hard work and hard selling, day in day out, year in and year out." In particular, he credited the Big Apple campaign, begun four and a half years previously, which had finally "taken firm root and is now blossoming." The summer's Bicentennial and Democratic National Convention, in combination with a long-term professional marketing campaign, had "put a new gloss on the Big Apple." Finally, this upsurge represented a turnaround in the city's view of the economic value of tourism in response to lobbying from the CVB and ABNY: "the growth in tourism seems to be the dividend on more than a decade of investment in a campaign to challenge the city's attitude from relative indifference to tourism to an active quest for conventions and vacationers by stressing the city's manifold appeals."[28]

The Unanswered Question of Tourism Impact

Despite the unquestionable growth in tourist numbers and spending, considerable questions remained in 1976—as they would in subsequent years—about the overall impact of tourism on the wider economy, and the primary beneficiaries of this growth. Booster groups like the CVB assured the public and the press of their industry's universal benefit. As a long-time member and former president of the Discover America Travel Organization (DATO), the leading association for the national travel industry, Gillett was armed with its market research, and in particular its multiplier effect of tourist spending, devised in the 1960s. According to the latter, every dollar spent by a tourist turned over *three times* in the local economy and returned to the city and state in the form of taxable revenues. This formula allowed the CVB to put out an astounding new estimate: with tourism spending measured at $1.5 billion, tourism was now estimated to bring in *$4.5 billion* to the New York City economy, or roughly 25 percent of the city's total revenue. And many in the industry called this a *conservative* estimate, arguing for a multiplier of four, five, or even seven times. Either way, travel and tourism was now believed to be the second-largest private sector industry in the city.[29]

Yet, if "impact" were measured in old-fashioned terms of employment and income generated, rather than this new calculation of revenue from consumption, the tourism industry was far lower down the list of the city's major industries—consistently ranking seventh out of the eight major sectors between 1967 and 1982 (see Appendix, Table A.1). In addition, while the growth in tourism receipts over the course of the decade was significant, it coincided with an equally significant *decline* in the number of jobs and establishments in the industry. According to census figures for hotels, amusements, and marketing, between 1967 and 1977, while all three were making large-scale lay-offs and two were closing establishments, all three saw their revenues rise. In hotels, the number of establishments declined by a third and the number of employees by almost half. In marketing, the number of establishments declined by 5 percent, and the number of employees by nearly a quarter. The only sector with growth in either of these measures was amusements, which saw an increase in small establishments (those with fewer than five employees). Meanwhile, the receipts in all three of these sectors grew markedly over the same time period—with a jump of 34.3 percent in tourism, 32 percent in amusements, and 18 percent in marketing (see Table 6.2, and for additional data Appendix, Table A.2).[30]

These figures indicate that during the crisis, tourism industry consolidation boosted revenues and profits, even while tens of thousands of people were laid off and hundreds of establishments closed. This would be consistent with the luxury hotel trend that began in the mid-1970s, through which large chains that catered to business and international clients, and enjoyed higher profit margins, began displacing small, local hotels that employed more people. Although new jobs were generated—for example, in services catering to high-end hotels—there was a net loss when measured against the jobs displaced. Far from sparking a broad-based economic resurgence, the "boom" in tourism appears mainly to have brought profits to a narrow class, while more people lost jobs than gained them.

Thus, it became clear that growing profits in the tourism industry were not shared by average workers. The same was true in the economy as a whole.

Table 6.2 Changes in tourism and marketing in New York City, 1967–1977 (revenue vs. employment and establishments).

Industry	Revenue ($)			% Change 1967–1977		
	1967	1972	1977	Revenue ($)	Establishments	Employed
Hotels, Motels, Tourist Courts	534,269	443,807	717,300	+34.3	–31	–47
Amusements and Recreation Services with Motion Pictures	1,875,308	1,664,275	2,475,900	+32.0	+14	–16
Advertising and Marketing Services	4,372,794	4,622,986	5,148,360	+18.0	–5	–22

Source: US Department of Commerce, Bureau of Census, 1967, 1972, and 1977.

While it could always be argued that the situation would have been worse in the absence of these growing sectors, no significantly positive impact can be shown on jobs or new establishments, despite the purported multiplier effect that propelled tourism into being the second-largest industry. Rather, this was an economy that continued its meteoric decline, from manufacturing to retail to banking. This may explain why the Municipal Assistance Corporation (MAC), comprised mainly of bankers, and charged with financial oversight of the city, was largely indifferent towards the marketing-led approach. According to the MAC annual report of 1976, every other major industry in the city was still either showing no growth or was in decline, indicating to them that tourism marketing was necessary but not sufficient to turn around the situation.[31] As the MAC chairman Felix Rohatyn cautioned in that report:

> Despite the buoyancy of spirit in the City following Operation Sail and the Democratic Convention, and despite some lessening in the rates of decline of certain local economic indicators, the overall drain of the City economy goes on, and the corporate exodus continues. Consequently, in order to continue providing the broad range of municipal services which is necessary or desirable, the City tax base must be strengthened and the overall economy of New York City must be stimulated.[32]

As we will see in the next chapter, creative new forms of stimulus and incentives for business were soon to be devised. But for those like Gillett and Rudin who were primarily concerned with the fate of tourism and real estate, it remained the case that levels of employment and payroll were less significant indictors of economic health than visitor spending, hotel occupancy rates, convention bookings, and average rents—all of which they saw increasing.[33] Gillett acknowledged that the Bicentennial celebrations and the Democratic Convention had not necessarily added much in terms of jobs, and indeed that a range of factors beyond the city's control may have been responsible for growth in tourism to New York. Nonetheless, he argued, these events "did put a new gloss on the Big Apple," while "the city's improved image undoubtedly helped" make this possible.[34] As far as Gillett and a growing number of city leaders were concerned, this combination of tourism and marketing was an essential part of the economic development package, whatever other pro-business measures might also be needed. It generated revenue while costing the public sector little to maintain, and helped to repair the damage to New York's national and international reputation.

City Hall Embraces the Big Apple

In response to the perceived strength and impact of tourism, New York City began bolstering its efforts in this new area, as indicated in the "Visitor's Industry" report from the Mayor's Office and CPC. By integrating data from a local survey conducted in 1974 with findings from the 1972 US Department of Commerce National Travel Survey, "a portrait of New York visitors began to emerge." This portrait included two main types of visitors: commercial visitors in town for business and/or conventions; and recreational visitors, or "tourists." Within these categories, conventioneers and international tourists spent the most on lodging and high-end shopping. It was incumbent on both the city and the state, the report argued, to appreciate the economic impact of these travelers, and do more to attract them.[35]

The report repeated the old refrain that New York City already had a great advantage in terms of its well-known cultural attractions. For both categories of travelers, business and international leisure, New York was still

> the unrivaled American center of cultural affairs . . . Visitors are drawn to attractions such as the City's superior museums and theaters, concerts, plays and art galleries. The Empire State Building, Rockefeller Center, and many fine restaurants, sophisticated department stores and boutiques and the sheer spectacle and excitement of the city serve as a magnet for throngs of visitors . . . Millions of visitors also come here for conventions and other business affairs.[36]

But the report went a step further, arguing that New York's existing attractions might not be enough in the current climate of fierce inter-urban competition to attract the increasingly lucrative categories of business and foreign travel:

> New York City strongly attracts visitors who make the greatest contribution to the economic base. However, as other cities grow in size and diversify their economies, they will offer increasingly more interesting opportunities for business and business related travel. While the total volume and value of business visitors' trade is in large measure dependent on the level of local economic activity and private sector "mix," additional commercial visits can be induced through deliberate strategies and programs.[37]

The deliberate strategies and programs recommended involved augmenting, improving, and subsidizing public–private efforts at marketing and promotion. To address this, the city promised to expand the operations of its local

Figure 6.4 Mayor Beame and the Big Apple campaign.
(a) Mayor Beame joins leaders of the city's cultural institutions and tourism industry to launch the city's first official marketing campaign: Big Apple. (b) Beame with Lewis Rudin behind him, affixes a taxi sticker that reads "The Big Apple Says . . . The Nicest People in the World Visit With Us."

CVB, which it saw "[comparing] unfavorably to other major cities."[38] In this way, it was hoped, the geographic scale and temporal scope of Big Apple could be extended after big one-off events like the Democratic Convention and Bicentennial left town.

It was true, as Gillett asserted, that a new image of the city had been successfully projected, and tourism numbers were up significantly. And it was also the case, as the OED report showed, that New York City stood to benefit from an increase in business travel and foreign tourism. But neither could prove the ripple effect of these visitor dollars on the rest of the city's economy, nor deny that unemployment and poverty rates in the city were still growing rapidly despite the "tourism upsurge."

Boosters would argue that any decline in jobs and earnings would undoubtedly have been worse without the new tourism dollars, and without the "hard work and hard selling" of the CVB.[39] Others—from journalists and traditionalists in city government to union members and hard-nosed bankers like Felix Rohatyn—countered that the tourism growth was a temporary fix at best, and not the place to look for the long-term solution to the city's problems.[40] Nonetheless, the debate over the city's new economic development strategy was tepid at best, and, like the Freedom Train, never surfaced in prime-time media coverage. Organized resistance in the period as carried out by neighborhood groups, unions, and welfare-rights advocates was increasingly atomized, targeting particular budget cuts, agencies, and policies rather than something as vast and opaque as the city's overall shift in economic priorities. So arose a contradictory state of affairs: the city intensified its focus on attracting tourism and business while cutting back on social programs and public services, even as the conditions of everyday life were rapidly deteriorating for the majority of New Yorkers.

Contradiction and Backlash

Despite the lack of broad-based political resistance, however, the city's new orientation did generate a powerful backlash. As we saw in Chapter 5, it was not difficult in a media capital like New York City for a range of relatively small groups—from police and fire unions to teenagers from the Bronx—to devise headline-grabbing campaigns to sabotage city marketing efforts. But in addition to such consciously oppositional tactics, spontaneous uprisings and events now posed as great a threat to hegemonic images of the Big Apple. This was due in large part to the indeterminate nature of media codes themselves, which, once they enter into circulation, as Stuart Hall reminds us, are inevitably altered by the social and historical context in which audiences decode them.[41] In this sense, the significance of the Big Apple campaign changed radically over the year-long period between the summers of 1976 and 1977. It was a period of perhaps *the* most negative media coverage, and some of the most trying events, in New York City history. As a result, the marketing extravaganza of the summer of 1976 was to be reduced to distant memory, wiped away by the spectacle of mayhem that was to come.

The Summer of Sam

The problems that began mounting in early 1977 became so horrific and all-encompassing that they seemed to many observers, and to the news media in particular, like a series of divine plagues, taking on the biblical proportions of apocalypse. First, there was the freakish weather: a long winter of the coldest temperatures in over forty years followed by the hottest summer temperatures ever recorded for New York City, climbing to 104 degrees by July 21, with the brutal heat continuing into September. This intolerable weather then served as backdrop, and accelerant, to a string of harrowing events that provided visual fodder for national and international news.

The first story that began grabbing headlines in early 1977 was the revelation that a serial killer armed with a hunting rifle was on the loose in the Bronx, and had already killed three people and injured five. When it became clear that he took aim at lone women and courting couples, panic spread—nightclubs and restaurants were deserted as people insured they were home before dark. The hysteria mounted in April when the murderer revealed himself through a note left for the police after a double homicide. This was soon leaked to the media, and the public learned that the killer called himself "Son of Sam" and believed he was following the orders of demons, as revealed through the barking of a dog named Harvey. The story grew more terrifying throughout June and July, as the murderous attacks continued and remained unsolved, even with a squad of 200 detectives and hundreds of other police officers on the case, making it "the largest manhunt in the history of New York."[42] This led many communities in the Bronx and Queens, where the killings had taken place, to mount their own vigilante patrols, inevitably resulting in ever more fear and suspicion, particularly towards blacks and Latinos who ventured into white neighborhoods at night. The killer was finally caught on August 10, 1977, and turned out to be David Berkowitz, a pudgy, white postal worker with a maniacal grin. All told, Berkowitz had killed six people and seriously injured seven more, and he gave the New York summer of 1977 its lasting moniker, "Summer of Sam."[43]

The impact of the Summer of Sam on the image of New York City was enduring. News headlines reading, "City Held Hostage by Own Fear" and "Demonic Stalker on the Loose" brought back memories of the Fear City campaign and horror-movie images of New York that the Big Apple boosters had tried so hard to erase. But, amazingly, the summer of 1977 had even more devastating events in store.

The Blackout

At approximately 9:30 p.m. on Wednesday, July 13, 1977, at the height of New York's heatwave, another natural disaster struck the city: four separate lightning bolts hit key electrical supply lines north of the city, causing a chain reaction that led to a massive blackout throughout the New York region, affecting more than 9 million people. It was not the biggest blackout the city had seen—that had occurred in November 1965, when power went down for 25 million people throughout the Northeast. But the blackout of 1977 was certainly the most devastating economically, socially, and in terms of the city's image. The 1965 blackout lasted only a few hours, and occurred on a cool winter night, during a period of relative prosperity and calm in New York City. As such, it caused relatively few problems despite its wide range. The 1977 blackout, on the other hand, continued over 25 hours of the hottest days in the city's history, during a period in which the city was still in a state of deep economic and social crisis. It was, as we have seen, a time of sky-rocketing unemployment, particularly among the working class and people of color, and of the physical deterioration of inner-city neighborhoods throughout the Bronx, Brooklyn, and Manhattan due to drastic service cuts, housing abandonment, and arson. And so, while

Figure 6.5 The Lower Manhattan skyline during the blackout of 1977.
Aside from images of looting, shots of the darkened Twin Towers were among the most heavily circulated representations of the blackout.

New York Daily News

in most parts of the city the vast majority of residents of all backgrounds pulled together and endured the disruption with little incident, in the neighborhoods hardest hit by the fiscal crisis, this single, cataclysmic event sparked chaos, setting off what became known as the "blackout riots," characterized by widespread looting, arson, and general lawlessness.

Though these so-called "riots" never turned violent—many described the mood of the looters as "festive," and something akin to "Christmas in July"—they caused deep and enduring wounds. First, there was the immediate cost in terms of damage to businesses, property, and lost tax revenue. With 2,000 businesses sacked and looted, in addition to the general, city-wide loss of revenue from the power outage, immediate costs of the blackout were estimated at a billion dollars.[44] Long-term financial costs can be measured in decades, with many of the lost stores and houses abandoned or burned down that night still unreconstructed to this day.[45] Then there was the broader social cost: 3,776 people were arrested in a single night, while more seeds of distrust and division were sown throughout the city, both within communities, between those who participated in the riots and those who did not, and between communities in which the riots occurred and those that were relatively peaceful.

Last, but by no means least, the blackout also cost the city dearly in terms of its image in the eyes of the world, as New York's trauma became, once again, the world's leading news story. It earned front-page headlines for days to come in major international newspapers, with the emphasis consistently placed on the chaos of the riots, as a sampling of headlines reveals: in the *Los Angeles Times* it was "City's Pride in Itself Goes Dim in the Blackout"; in Tokyo's *Mainichi Shimbun*, "Panic Grips New York"; in West Germany's *Bild Zeitung*, "New York's Bloodiest Night"; and in London's *Daily Express*, "The Naked City."[46] Similarly, the spectacular visuals of this racially charged "urban warfare" earned top-billing on local, national, and international TV news programs (once New York wire services were back up and running), with mobile camera crews racing police to the scenes of looting so they could film the worst before anybody was arrested. In addition, "special color editions" of the two major US news weeklies, *Time* and *Newsweek*, were devoted to the story, and filled with startling, often harrowing images.

Race, Riots, and Acts of God

The language and imagery used to describe New York's blackout across these media evoked the worst of the anti-urban, often racist prejudices that the city and its boosters had long been battling. In what follows I will briefly analyze such representations of the blackout using the special report from *Newsweek*, entitled "Heart of Darkness," and the special report from *Time*, entitled "Night of Terror."

A recurring theme in the coverage portrayed the blackout as a form of quasi-divine punishment. The very first explanation for it, given by Consolidated Edison engineers, doubtlessly eager to avert blame, was that the multiple lightning strikes were "an act of God." Conservative *Newsweek* columnist George F. Will jumped on this in his analysis of why, in attempting to understand this and other recurring New York calamities, people generally "resorted to theology, not physics":

> Few things are as stimulating as other people's calamities observed from a safe distance. So people relish Edward Gibbon's "Decline and Fall of the Roman Empire" and New York City's perils, technological as well as financial. Much of the nation thinks, not without reason, that the city is sunk in darkness, even at high noon, and that the blackout was a sign of disapproval from above, a foretaste of fire and brimstone and pillars of salt.[47]

Here New York City is cast simultaneously as a decadent and doomed imperial city, a modern-day Sodom or Gomorrah, or even a hell on earth, depending on which of the mixed metaphors—Roman Empire, pillar of salt, or fire and brimstone—one chooses. Thus, in witnessing this latest disaster to befall the city, people around the country may be excused if they find themselves gloating from afar, and laughing at the irony of literal and symbolic darkness finally being joined. The City of Darkness having been brought low appeared to have a certain Manichean reasonableness, even divine justice, to many in the rightward-tilting country.

The same tone of moral judgment and satisfaction pervades much of the *Newsweek* issue, as it does *Time*'s lead article, "Heart of Darkness." *Newsweek*'s coverage of the blackout opens with a two-page photo-spread of an almost undetectable skyline of Manhattan by night, illuminated only by scattered pinpoints of light, and shot from atop the World Trade Center. The montage of this skyline with the following text served as a death-blow to Big Apple's most important symbol, and the city's most opulent icon, Windows on the World:

> One hundred seven stories high over Manhattan, a group of diners at the World Trade Center's skyscraping restaurant, Windows on the World, downed their digestifs, took a last glance at the stunning lightshow below, and crowded into a waiting down elevator. The doors slid shut. The elevator didn't budge. Somebody stabbed irritably at the button. Nothing happened. Somebody else got the doors open and the passengers free. "The elevator's out," one of them huffily informed a white-jacketed captain. The captain

shrugged towards the nightscape outside, gone suddenly inky black. "So's New York," he replied.[48]

While much of the coverage made fun of the misfortune of high and mighty New Yorkers stranded in skyscrapers, the rest sensationalized the criminality of what is taken to be the rest of the city's population: those black and Latino "ghetto-dwellers" who participated in "the riots" down below. The articles were suffused with classically racist tropes. They used animal metaphors to dehumanize looters, as in "a band of youths swooped in like vultures,"[49] and "[they came] across Bushwick Avenue like buffalo."[50] They drew on metaphors of disease and sexual depravity, as in "plague of violence" to describe the spread of the looting between different inner-city neighborhoods, "fever" to describe the mob mentality that possessed everyone in the streets, and an "orgy of looting" to describe the pleasure perpetrators took in their acts.[51] They conjured up images of terrorism and urban warfare, describing crowds of looters as "marauders," questioning whether there might be a "white back-lash," and quoting one man, a Vietnam War veteran guarding a children's store, who associated the mangled white mannequins on the floor of the store with "the dead people I saw in Nam without legs and arms."[52] And they constantly invoked the "blackness" and "darkness" taking over the city, terms that were historically linked in the Eurocentric imagination to fear, dirt, ignorance, and racial inferiority. Such significations were associated interchangeably with the blackout, the night, the law of the jungle, and New York's takeover by the black and Latino population, as in the following opening passage of *Time*'s "Heart of Darkness":

> There was a throaty mass scream when the lights went out, and then a little festival of blackness—bonfires in the streets, a blast of soul and salsa, a torchlight parade down under Broadway. But within minutes, the night was alight with fires, the pavement alive with looters, the music drowned out by the whooping sirens and shattering glass. The pillage ran until dawn, unchecked and unabashed. "Being that the lights are out and niggers are going hungry," a black kid boasted, "we're going to take what we want—and what we want is what we need."[53]

Ultimately, both *Time* and *Newsweek* interwove these associations to make an argument about the national symbolism of New York's blackout of 1977 in contrast to that of 1965. In essence: the current event represented all that had gone wrong with New York, and indeed "urban America," over the intervening decade, beginning with the urban unrest of the 1960s. Barring a dramatic turnaround akin to divine intervention, New York and other US cities were doomed to continue to lose not only their electric power but their political, economic, and cultural power as well. Thus, *Newsweek* made the point that the blackout "underscored once again the fragility of urban America in the last quarter of the twentieth century—a state of dependence so total that a burst of lightning could shut down the nation's largest city as surely and nearly as completely as a neutron bomb."[54]

Both articles floated different theories as to the cause of this breakdown in social control. Was it due to frustration over the increasing gap in income and rising unemployment, which the articles acknowledged had reached 40 percent among "inner-city blacks," as opposed to 20 percent in 1965? Both authors shot down this hypothesis as outmoded "sixties jargon," arguing instead that the root problems were not structural or systemic, but "social psychological," and specifically "behavioral." Thus, both the rising unemployment *and* the riots were the result of a moral and psychological malaise afflicting the black and Latino communities, and the inability of the dominant, white forces of society to crack down. As Ernest Dichter, a behavioral psychologist cited in "Night of Terror," put it: "It was just like *Lord of the Flies.* People resort to savage behavior when the brakes of civilization fail." And according to "futurist" Herman Kahn, any attempt at social analysis of such criminal acts would only perpetuate the problem:

> They have no idea of what moral standards are. This suppressed rage idea is crap. This kind of reasoning will make the same thing happen again ... Respect for law and authority has declined; thieves often go unpunished; crime and violence stalk the slums ... The explanation that leans on real and perceived deprivation goes only so far ... There was an element of glee, perhaps of revenge, of a mob gone wild.[55]

The Impact on New York's Image "Cannot Be Tallied"

In the annals of anti-urban literature, the historic moment of the blackout riots served an invaluable purpose. It crystallized conservatives' vision of the city in a single, searing image of asphalt jungle. It legitimized their repudiation of two decades of research on the sociological roots of the inner city. It advanced their argument against federal block grants and the broader war on poverty. And, as packaged in the nation's leading magazines and TV news programs, themselves published and broadcast out of New York City, it made their position all the more credible. Thus, for New York City's public–private leaders, who had staked so much on marketing the city, this moment left them facing their worst image crisis yet. The one possible consolation for them was that, as the media continued to fixate on the outbursts and destroyed neighborhoods of these poor people, they never claimed that the city and its policies were at all responsible for their plight. To the contrary, the media helped pathologize the poor more effectively than Roger Starr himself could have done.

By the weekend, Mayor Beame had announced that the Small Business Administration had declared the city a "disaster area," making affected merchants eligible for long-term, low-interest loans, in the hope that some might be persuaded to rebuild. But, of course, this depressing designation only fueled more debate over "how much the city might suffer from this latest blow to its reputation."[56] The section of *Newsweek*'s special edition entitled "Impact" ended with a rehashing of this debate.[57] Predictably, those in the crisis regime downplayed the blackout's long-term consequences. Citibank chairman and the MAC board member Walter Wriston insisted it constituted a "one-shot loss to the city" in terms of lost sales and taxes, adding, "We'll all be playing catch-up ball for the next few days, but we will recover." Raymond Horton, Columbia University professor and director of the Temporary Commission on City Finances, agreed: "We should be careful not to overreact . . . It ain't good, but it ain't the end of the world." A similar, measured appraisal was politely offered by one of the city's key competitors, Gerald Sanderson, executive vice-president of the Chicago Convention and Tourism Bureau. "I'm sure there are a lot of people in New York now that are a little unhappy about being there . . . but I don't think there will be a switch of conventions out of New York any more than a snowstorm here would affect us."[58]

But this optimism was not shared by Peter Lauer, president of Lauer and Holbrook, a Chicago-based executive recruiting and placement firm—a firm that arguably had the best insight into the question of businesspeople's perception of New York. In the final paragraph of *Newsweek*'s lead story, Lauer stated flatly: "We already were handling too many resumes from people who said they'd go anyplace in the country except New York. This blackout and looting will only strengthen that feeling."[59] Following his verdict, the *Newsweek* article provided this final, sober opinion: "The eventual price may not be all that high, but even so it will be one that battered New York can ill-afford to pay."[60] A similar conclusion was reached by the anonymous author of *Time*'s "Night of Terror":

> Most of [the direct economic cost] could be made up later, when banks, brokerages, and other businesses reopened. But the far more important price cannot be tallied. What had the city lost in terms of morale and image? Deputy Mayor Osborn Elliott, in charge of keeping old jobs in the city and bringing in new ones, announced the blackout at least had not caused a group of oil suppliers from Houston and New Orleans to drop consideration of moving some

of their offices to the city. But how many businessmen thought of moving out? How many will become more difficult to sell on moving in? At best, Elliott's job has been a holding action, and last week's crisis, he said with great understatement, "doesn't help."[61]

Enduring Contradictions

By the end of the summer of 1977, the Big Apple campaign must have seemed like a surreal hallucination. So much energy and resources were spent in 1976 to transform New York into a historically transcendent, Bicentennial city, and in so doing to erase images associated with the city's deep and ongoing crisis. Yet when the dystopian imagery resurfaced during the long, hot summer that followed, it was to prove far more powerful and captivating to the sought-after national and international audiences.

This was like the Freudian "return of the repressed," in which untreated trauma metamorphoses into destructive behavior. It was also the result of two intersecting contradictions inherent within this marketing-led, neoliberal mode of economic development. The first was due to the interruption of material neglect. As the city focused on polishing its image and generating new revenue, it did so at the expense of jobs, public services, and housing, thus allowing poverty and dislocation to surge. Under such conditions, some residents took desperate, destructive, and ultimately self-destructive measures—like the looting of business corridors in their own neighborhoods—which made for an unprecedented media spectacle. This then undermined the original image campaign and led to the second contradiction, one based in the unpredictable nature of media circulation itself. Now the city had to live with an extremely unfortunate visual contrast: the transcendent euphoria of Big Apple versus the apocalyptic depths of the Summer of Sam. This created a nightmarish pastiche of an apple that was burning, bullet pierced, and rotten.[62] And, whether recognized as such or not, it also created a unique opportunity for New York leaders to rethink their current course. Should they continue in this risky, polarizing, marketing-led approach, or focus on the harder, long-term job of addressing the social and economic needs of its looted and crisis-torn neighborhoods?

As we shall see, they chose the former option. In the face of all-out image crisis, the CVB's president Charles Gillett called for a centralized and sustained plan for marketing the city. As he put it: "what is needed now *more than ever* is solid, day-in day-out professional promotion."[63] Meanwhile, the CVB's prognosis intersected perfectly with that of state economic development agencies. The latter believed that the city's recovery was linked to the ability of its hoteliers, realtors, and financiers to maintain the monopoly rents afforded them by their unique New York location. If they could not alter the material space of New York City just yet, they could still transform the media space it inhabited, and the urban imaginary circulating in the minds of the city's potential consumers, investors, and creditors. The main challenge they would face was how to do so on a much wider scale, and in such a way as to eclipse the troubles mounting just outside the frame.

CHAPTER 7

Purging New York through I♥NY

Virtually all experts and CEO(s) agree . . . New York, historically, never had to accommodate [or] compete for business. *It clearly must do so now* . . . In symbolic terms the fiscal crisis stood for all that is wrong with New York. [It] created a sense of insecurity that curtails investment . . . According to key experts and CEOs . . . the fiscal crisis can and should be addressed in marketing strategy—[as in] New York is "purging" itself and changing ways.[1]

> Yankelovich, Skelly, and White, Inc., 1977

According to legend, the "inspiration" for I♥NY came at a luncheon in the Union Carbide headquarters in Midtown Manhattan in 1977, during which the company announced plans to move to Danbury, Connecticut. In attendance was John Doyle, the new deputy commissioner for the New York State Department of Commerce (DOC), who was struck by the explanation the company gave for the move: "They said they were leaving New York because they could not get anyone to visit, let alone work here." It was then that Doyle had his epiphany: "If tourists want to visit [New York City], you can get middle managers who want to live there."[2] By focusing on tourism marketing, in other words, he could also enhance New York's image as a place to work and make a profit. Doyle abruptly called a halt to all tourism spending and used the money to finance the state's first professional market research instead. This, he hoped, would "prove" to the legislature that the state had failed to realize some $16 billion in revenue between 1967 and

1976, by his estimate, due to the fact that "vacationers and businesspeople alike" were deterred from New York City because of negative perceptions.[3] There was some debate in the legislature over whether tourism and marketing should become priorities for the state, especially in a time of austerity. But given the argument presented by the DOC—that tourism was a way to make a "fast buck," with no major investments or apparent political downsides—the legislature quickly approved the new spending.[4]

The legend of I♥NY's conception points to the ascendancy of a new mode of urban economic development that tied pro-business restructuring to tourism marketing. This approach, as we have seen in the preceding chapters, was a decade in coming. Between the mid-1960s and mid-1970s, a consensus was forming among local elites that New York City needed to start branding a business- and tourist-friendly image of itself if it was to survive. The push began with Robert Moses' intensive use of media at the 1964–1965 World's Fair. It took a hip and creative turn with the launch of *New York* magazine in 1967. It was professionalized by the Association for a Better New York in 1971 through back-room lobbying and the high-profile Big Apple campaign. And in the midst of the fiscal crisis of 1975–1976, the marketing-led approach was finally endorsed by city government under Mayor Abe Beame. Yet all of these efforts proved to be temporary fixes at best. By the end of the devastating summer of 1977—replete with blackout, riots, arson, and a murderous rampage—it was clear to many, not least transnational companies like Union Carbide, that the attempt to cast New York as "Fun City" had been an unmitigated failure.

Nonetheless, to the intrepid branding coalition that emerged in this period, such failure had nothing to do with the contradiction of luring tourists and businessmen while the city tumbled into crisis. To the contrary, the problem with previous campaigns had been that they had not gone far enough—whether due to limitations in market reach, amount of media coverage, or degree of political and financial backing. Big Apple, the largest attempt thus far, was still only a summer-long campaign launched by city-based business groups and dependent on one-time events like the Democratic Convention and the Bicentennial to gain national attention. Yet the city faced national and international competition year-round, and was courting visitors who were more likely to see coverage from the summer of 1977 than positive spin from the summer of 1976.

Thus, in geographic terms, the local branding effort "jumped scale," and was taken over by the New York State DOC, which helped launch and finance I♥NY, the city's first international, year-round marketing campaign.[5] Also distinct from previous city marketing, the new effort was based entirely on professional market research, like that of Yankelovich, Skelly, and White, Inc. (YSW), that emphasized the need to "purge New York" once and for all of the "negative associations" long held by businesspeople and tourists, and exacerbated by the fiscal crisis.

The purging was to entail a dual agenda—one visual, the other policy-oriented. First, with television and print campaigns designed by the cutting-edge ad firm Wells, Rich, Greene (WRG), and logo designed by *New York* magazine's ingenious artistic director Milton Glaser, I❤NY was to present New York City as a hip cultural capital and thriving financial center—rather than a crisis-ridden, strike-infested, industrial-age city. The DOC then continued to use images and data generated by the campaign to advance its second agenda: lobbying the legislature to spend tens of millions more dollars on marketing for tourism, as well as to increase dramatically a range of pro-business reforms—including sixty different tax cuts—at a time of austerity.

And so emerged the contradiction between image and reality that was to underlie New York's approach to economic development for the next generation. In effect, the branding coalition took a two-pronged approach similar to that developed by ABNY in the era of corporate move-outs five years earlier. Changes in economic development policy that reoriented the public sector towards the needs of business and tourism would happen behind the scenes. Meanwhile, high-profile marketing campaigns would provide positive, populist, and ubiquitous imagery. Such imagery served to sell the *new* New York to both internal and external audiences while obscuring the city's ongoing social and economic crises, thereby distracting the public from this radical shift in priorities.

The Formation of a State-wide Branding Coalition

In 1977, under newly elected Democratic governor Hugh Carey, New York State played an active role in coordinating the branding of New York City. In so doing, the Carey administration played a far more active role than any previous governor, Republican or Democrat, in forging ties between the public and private sectors and in changing the culture of what had been a Keynesian, managerial state government that eschewed overt marketing.[6] To accomplish this shift, the state DOC was first restructured to focus on an "entrepreneurial" mode of economic development under the leadership of young administrators with backgrounds in the private sector. Next, the retooled agency hired private "psychographic" market researchers and cultural producers in media and advertising, enabling it to overcome legislative opposition and launch I❤NY.

Restructuring for Tourism Marketing

As we saw in Chapter 6, New York City restructured its economic development operations between 1975 and 1976 under the auspices of a new Office of Economic Development (OED) in an effort to bring about two major reforms: a dramatic change in the tax structure of the city and state, and increased emphasis on marketing New York City.[7] Following this, in late 1976 and 1977, New York State's DOC underwent a remarkably similar process of restructuring. Since its inception in 1934, the DOC had been a wide-ranging department, comprising eight offices and twenty smaller divisions, most concerned with supporting upstate industry and agriculture, which provided the bulk of jobs in the state. Now the DOC was transformed along functional lines into two cabinet-level divisions: the Office of Economic Development, devoted to "corporate interests," "red-tape cutting," and the promotion of international commerce, particularly in New York City;[8] and the Office of Economic Planning, Marketing, and Tourism, which was devoted to those activities in addition to market research to support tourism, so as "to understand and promote this vastly underdeveloped industry."[9]

These strategic changes entailed, broadly speaking, a shift in the DOC's priorities away from favoring economic sectors based in manufacturing and agriculture and towards retaining and attracting new, more flexible and image-sensitive services largely based in New York City—particularly in finance, real estate, tourism, and the culture industries. Given the DOC's lack of expertise in these areas, Governor Carey appointed two new officials with backgrounds in finance and marketing. The first, Commissioner John Dyson, had worked on Wall Street; the second, Deputy Commissioner Bill Doyle, had been the marketing manager at Chase Manhattan Bank.

Dyson and Doyle understood the role of economic development from the perspective of the private sector, and as such acted as any self-respecting corporate executive faced with a budget crisis would have, but as no DOC commissioner had done before. They spent their entire tourism budget of $400,000 to hire two leading market research firms—Consumer Behavior, Inc. (CBI) and YSW—to assess the state's marketing potential in the areas of corporate retention and tourism, and from this research to produce studies to guide the agency.[10] These studies, based exclusively on interviews with businesspeople and tourists, were to have an enormous impact in redirecting the state's tax policies and economic development strategies.

From Psychographics to the New Advertising
Psychographics, a field of market research that applied statistical methods to the study of social attitudes and trends, was instrumental in fueling the efforts of post-war corporate America to sell an exploding amount of consumer goods and services to the emerging "baby boom" generation.[11] CBI, one of the first psychographic firms, was created out of the University of Chicago-based Committee for Research on Consumer Attitudes and

Behavior in the 1950s, and pioneered the application of behavioral psychology to the problems of business.[12] YSW, established in the mid-1960s, was a pioneer in packaging psychographic survey data, and ultimately became the most influential marketing consultancy of the 1970s.[13] They designed survey tools that measured "intangible" social psychological shifts and related these to consumption habits, thus providing clients with, as YSW put it, "the only logical foundation for building sound business strategies . . . in times of change."[14] Whereas market research traditionally focused on the habits of middle-class housewives, these psychographic studies cast their net much wider, studying and constructing whole new demographic segments—most importantly, the "new youth."[15]

As the first market researchers to measure the public *image* and *reputation* of corporations and their products, psychographic firms like YSW and CBI may also be considered key antecedents to the rise of "branding" and "brand management" in the 1980s. Important innovations included YSW's Corporate Priorities Survey, which measured the reputation of a company for its "affected publics"—including consumers, salespeople, employees, stock holders, and government regulators—so as to show how "a company lives within society." Through this device and a subsequent "corporate reputation index," published regularly in *Fortune* magazine, YSW turned "intangibles" like public image into a quantifiable asset that could be listed alongside a company's financial statements. This could then impact a company's stock price, its desirability to employees, and the marketability of its products.[16] Today, such measurements are viewed as essential to the valuation of a company, its stock, and its "brand."

Once an image problem was revealed to a company via these market surveys, the logical place to turn was WRG, one of the hippest firms in the field of "new advertising," positioning itself against old-guard ad companies by employing the sensibility of the counter-culture to appeal to the new youth. But in addition to responding to cultural shifts among consumers as documented by the psychographic researchers, firms like WRG were sharply attuned to what might simply be called the desperation of their own corporate clients. Many of the older companies, struggling to survive in the increasingly competitive and fast-changing marketplace, were grasping at whatever marketing fingerhold they could find. In so doing they were vulnerable to pitches by young, confident companies like WRG that could package themselves as representing the psychographic these firms needed to reach, and about which the firms knew next to nothing. In explaining why, for instance, the American Manufacturing Company (the most staid of Detroit's car companies) would "allow a group of Young Turks to tell them what to do," in marketing a new line of "Rebel" cars to the youth market, Mary Wells Lawrence of WRG explained:

> Clients who came to us at a time when they had problems ganging on them, stupefying arrays of hard decisions to make and businesses that were in danger of disintegrating—those clients were experiencing the long dark night of the soul and they simply had to trust advisors who were reputed to be winners. There was something convincing about the adrenaline coming out of the pores of WRG and the sureness we had.[17]

The main thing WRG, and many of the other new advertising firms, offered their clients was the promise of rejuvenation through the transformation of their entire image, or "look." The very hiring of the ad agency, which itself embodied the desired "look," became an essential part of this process. A successful ad campaign would often garner as much media buzz for the cutting-edge agency that created it as it did for the product itself. In this sense the client company was seeking to associate itself with the brand identity of the agency, hoping it would lend symbolic capital to its own products.[18]

New York State, with "problems ganging on them" like any old company trying to stay alive in the new economy, was one of those clients that "simply had to trust" this approach, and desperately needed the hip new look that WRG could provide. As Governor Carey said, in an interview on the role played by John Dyson in the "I Love New York" campaign, "Only John would have the audacity and the temerity to approach Mary Wells Lawrence of Wells, Rich, and Greene."[19] Here was an ad agency and a CEO that were believed to be so hip, sexy, and aligned with their rebellious generation that even a state official had to have "audacity and temerity" simply to approach them, let alone hire them and pay them millions of dollars for the privilege.

Amplifying the Voices of Business and Tourism

From Dyson and Doyle's perspective, and in consultation with WRG, what New York City and State now needed to jump-start economic development was professional market research that could help direct the strategy of the advertising campaign. Hopefully, this could also help them convince a skeptical, old-fashioned, managerial legislature to pay for the campaign, and support their larger entrepreneurial agenda. So, between 1976 and 1977, in an unprecedented move, the DOC used its entire budget to hire CBI and YSW, and to gather what Dyson called "highly regarded" data.

CBI conducted the state's first "in-depth market survey" on tourism.[20] Results revealed that "consumers" had profoundly mixed feelings about New York City, and next to no knowledge of New York State. On the one hand, New York City was seen as a "difficult," "expensive," and "dangerous" place to visit. Yet, on the other, Broadway theater and "nightlife" were some of the most popular tourist attractions in the entire country. Thus, CBI proposed that the DOC create a new marketing approach that emphasized theater, Times Square attractions, and the lights of Broadway, and deemphasized other images of the city, including images of "crime," "traffic," and the "outer boroughs." As for New York State, CBI's research indicated that, although its "potential vacation market was great," New York was perceived as "having minimal appeal as a tourist attraction and the public was not aware of the State's substantial tourism resources." Thus, CBI proposed that the state's marketing try both to show off the most spectacular natural resources in the state and, as much as possible, to link travel to New York City, a known commodity, to the rest of the state.[21]

The YSW study, meanwhile, focused on corporate retention, and the "market-based strategies" New York should take both to reverse corporate flight and to encourage new corporations to relocate to the state.[22] This multi-volume report, it should be noted, was thousands of pages longer than the CBI study, and unlike that single-volume survey, was to be conducted annually over the coming decade. But similar to the CBI report, the sources from which YSW drew its data were extremely narrow and targeted: a survey of the state's 2,000 largest firms, interviews with anonymous "experts and CEOs," and a small selection of other "outside data."[23]

The report opens by providing a detailed "business development plan" for the state, beginning with a definition of "economic development" as based in private business and tourism.[24] It then devotes a large section to what the business community sees as "opportunities [to] stabilize and reverse the crisis," which it also refers to as "New York's changing attitude towards business."[25] New Yorkers, it is claimed, traditionally viewed business as "lofty" and "exploitative," and thus expected "business and businessmen . . . to finance government spending."[26] The crisis, however, changed all that. Now, "it is . . . politically acceptable to be pro business" and "cooperation among government, management and labor are apparent and growing." But problems remain: "[The] danger of inaction appears great . . . If expectations and hopes are unfulfilled, the last chance is lost. [There will be a] renewal and acceleration of former trends and losses." To prevent this, it was necessary for the state to make certain "pro business product modifications." Suggestions for what these should be comprised the bulk of the report.[27] The first modifications would be in "marketing strategy." According to "key experts and CEOs," in order to send the message that New York was serious about attracting business, it must address its faults: namely, "the fiscal crisis can and should be addressed in marketing strategy—[as in] *New York is 'purging' itself and changing [its] ways.*"[28] This was followed by a special focus on marketing New York City, presumably the first and foremost place in need of "purging." The report stressed the need to emphasize the "positive product attributes" of the city—in particular its position as a financial center and tourist destination—and to downplay its "negative attributes"—in particular its long history as a "liberal" and working-class city, its high ratio of unionized workers, and its devastated areas (the South Bronx is explicitly mentioned here). The marketing strategy YSW then proposed included three "major themes": New York's attitude towards business is changing; the cost of doing business is or can be competitive; and management's career and leisure-time goals can both be fulfilled in New York City.[29]

The second set of modifications involved actual political-economic restructuring—changes in laws, tax codes, bureaucratic arrangements, budgetary priorities, and urban development plans in order to make New York more business friendly. Some of these changes were very specific. The "highest priority attention" should be given to lowering personal income tax. "Unemployment benefits to strikers and maternity benefits" were considered "particularly onerous," and their "elimination should be strongly considered." And it was advised that all marketing activities be "packaged" in a single agency so that "government–business relations may be simplified and accelerated," and "the features/benefits of the product can be communicated."[30]

Other changes proposed were more general, such as reshaping the "work ethic [and] discipline of non-workers." Elsewhere in the report "non-workers" was used to refer to welfare recipients, while welfare payments were called "overly generous." This appears to be an indirect way of recommending that existing New York State welfare laws be weakened, so as to induce welfare recipients economically and ideologically to work.[31]

Interpreting the Reports

Most likely, the CBI and YSW reports did not teach the targeted reader in the state legislature much s/he did not already know about negative perceptions of New York City. Rather, the novelty and power of the reports were in the authoritative way they marshaled this data, and in the market-oriented discourse they employed. More than anything, they read like training manuals in the proper language and strategy of entrepreneurial governance for an uninitiated public sector worker. The "intangibles" measured by the surveys—that is, the attitudes, concerns, and lifestyle needs of CEOs—became rhetorical tools that could be used to transform the material reality of New York City and State into commodities, to turn places of diverse use values into a space of pure and abstract exchange. Here, New York City and State become the "product" to be sold, their "corporate reputation" the asset to be measured. The "affected publics" and "consumers" of New York who were surveyed, and those presumably of greatest import to its economic development, were limited to the tiny minority of tourists, travelers, and the "business community." Meanwhile, the voices of these key groups were articulated more powerfully than ever before, and given a new quasi-scientific legitimacy. Before, the business lobby had to stand outside the gates of government; now they had two of their own members at the helm of the DOC, actively soliciting their views on crucial questions of economic development, and elevating their voices above the din of competing interest groups—whether labor, small business, or the public sector.

Reading these reports as historical documents is also revelatory, as they indicate the growing influence of the private sector on government decision-making during this period of crisis. Through the reports, the only ones commissioned in the name of economic development, the business sectors received audience at the highest levels of New York State government, and played a significant role in shaping New York's economic development policy behind the scenes. According to the DOC's annual report for 1976, the CBI research ultimately "resulted in" the passage of the Omnibus Tourism Bill, appropriating $4.3 million for the department to undertake a "multi-media tourist advertising campaign" in June 1977.[32] As for the YSW study, according to annual reports and legislative reports from the offices of Governor Carey, we know that it was used successfully as a lobbying device to bring about many of the sweeping changes it recommended, particularly in the area of taxation and bureaucratic restructuring.[33] Thus, for example, the DOC annual report of 1978–1979 states that in 1977, "a well researched business plan [was put in place] for expenditure control and tax reductions that included tax cuts, incentives, and fiscal programs along with some 60 pro-business measures passed by the legislature and signed into law." The YSW recommendations also had an impact in terms of the DOC's marketing strategy. This is similarly true of the less well-known corporate retention campaign "New York State Votes 'Yes' for Business."[34]

Finally, the CBI and YSW reports should be analyzed intertextually. The fact that they were commissioned and ultimately read simultaneously says a great deal about the dual economic development agenda of the state, embracing Doyle's original vision of getting *both* middle managers *and* tourists to want to come to New York City. We saw this strategy appear in 1971, with ABNY's combination of populist PR and behind-the-scenes lobbying at VIP breakfasts. Now, five years later, the very public drive by city and state agencies to increase tourism and transform the image of New York City through a state-wide campaign was accompanied by even greater legislative efforts to alter budgetary and tax policy. The enactment of what YSW refers to euphemistically as "pro-business product modifications" was actually the result of hard-fought battles by realtors, hoteliers, and other pro-business forces to reshape such policy in favor of their agenda, and against that of organized labor and the welfare state.

The Art and Politics of City Marketing

Despite the larger size of the YSW report, and the broader impact of the pro-business legislation that resulted from it, Dyson and Doyle always made clear that tourism should be emphasized *above* business development, if only in official marketing campaigns. As revealed in a subsequent audit of the agency, the DOC made a particular case for the greater funding for tourism marketing than for business development, since tourism was seen as "a more visible and positive commodity than business development."[35] In other words, one of the most important uses of tourism marketing was as a public relations tool for both internal and external consumption, distracting public attention from the DOC's far more controversial pro-business agenda. Tourism marketing transcended conflict, presenting an inclusive face of New York City for everybody, rich and poor, citizen and visitor, to enjoy. The image of business development, on the other hand, was characterized by "liberal" New Yorkers as "exploitative" and "ruthless"— according to the CEOs cited in the YSW report—and in any case did not look so good politically in a time of crisis and austerity. In this arena, art and design were all-important. Now the task fell to WRG to come up with the most "visible and positive" campaign possible for the modified product that was New York City.

"Love" Saves the Day

Of all the radical, counter-cultural themes of the 1960s, the one that survived with its hipness intact into the individualistic backlash of the 1970s was "love." This form of love preserved its psychedelic, erotic, and libratory connotations, but dropped the more politicized "peace" that had once been attached to it at the hip. This free-floating love permeated 1970s pop culture, and it comes up repeatedly in Mary Wells Lawrence's autobiographical reminiscences of that period. She recalls, for instance, that though she had no time for decorating WRG's first modest office space on Madison Avenue in 1971, she did "plaster the walls with Love posters . . . [toss] psychedelic pillows around and . . . [allow] Mick Jagger to sing 'Have You Seen Your Mother, Baby?' in the waiting room."[36] And, in explaining the remarkable success of her upstart firm, she says simply: "[We were] idealistic in those days, all about hope and love, it helped paint us the way our clients wanted us to be, the way we were when we were young."[37]

And as WRG was well aware, the love signifier was also a highly effective marketing device—most of all when selling its services to "uncool," establishment clients who needed to appeal to the new "youth culture" or face extinction. Such firms were looking for an ad agency that itself embodied and could speak to this culture, and the love theme helped convince them WRG was such an agency. When WRG was hired by Menley

& James, "a company chockablock full of elegant WASPs," to help them "break into the steaming youth market with a cosmetics line designed specifically for younger women," the product line Wells Lawrence came up with was called, simply, "Love," and was packaged in a series of titillating, phallic-shaped bottles.[38] Similarly, when WRG landed its watershed "Rebel" contract with American Motors, the concept Wells Lawrence used to win over a boardroom full of skeptical executives was "Love," as she recounted:

> I talked about love in advertising, a word I always felt I had to decipher because businessmen acted as if love were an erotic Russian word they did not understand. (Love? What's love got to do with it?) I said that if we did not communicate that we loved our cars, nobody else would love them, either. I explained that love in advertising is an attitude toward the product and also toward the reader and the viewer. In some subtle way, every ad, every commercial should produce a feeling of love between the product and the potential buyer.[39]

The love theme, along with other strategies like the elimination of what Wells Lawrence called "old school logos," helped humanize and personalize the identity of both the company and the product they were selling. Without this, they were seen as nothing more than "a big corporation advertising, not just to you, but to a million other people, thereby killing much of the personal selling impact."[40] WRG staked its success on its ability to generate this "personal selling impact" through its ads, and to turn companies around in the process.

Thus, it was not surprising that love should have been the theme that both the WRG adman in charge of the account, Charlie Moss, and the Deputy Commissioner with a background in marketing, Bill Doyle, hit upon. The question of precisely who came up with the "I Love New York" slogan is a matter of debate, with everyone from the campaign's PR man Bobby Zarem to Governor Hugh Carey claiming credit. John Dyson's account seems credible. He remembers someone trying a different slogan, and then realizing it would not work without "love" in it. As he said,

> [Someone came up with] "New York, New York. It's a Heck of a State." Bill Doyle said, "That's so bad, I can't even show it to John" . . . I remember Bill Doyle saying that the words that matter in advertising are: "new," "free," "improved," and "love" . . . And he comes back the next day and says, "Well, 'I love New York' has 'love' and 'new' in it. So I got two of the four powerful words of advertising." So he says, "What do you think?" So I said, "That's terrific, let's do that."[41]

In any case, New York was a city that needed to reposition itself against the competition and appeal to a younger, hipper, more affluent crowd of middle managers and tourists, and the slogan "I Love New York" was quickly embraced by all involved. Nonetheless, a good slogan, even one filled with "love," would not be enough to turn around the image of a city in the depths of a fiscal crisis. Referring to the "height of horrors" that had been reached in the city with the "crime wave" and "garbage strikes" of 1976–1977, Wells Lawrence noted, "New York was a mess and in a lot more financial trouble than American Motors had been. I was never comfortable when clients were poor and New York was broke."[42] For any chance of success, the love slogan would have to be attached to a powerful visual logo that could be extended to print and television media; to an array of "collateral" products and souvenirs; and distributed through "package tours" and corporate partnerships with airlines, bus-lines, hotels, and restaurants. In short, New York would have to be marketed as aggressively and comprehensively as old-school cosmetics or American Motors automobiles.[43]

Milton Glaser and I♥NY

As Bill Doyle put it, what "I Love New York" needed now was a "visualization"—that is, a brand identity to visually unify the disparate elements of the campaign, and symbolically unify the diverse and even antagonistic elements of the "New York" commodity. Milton Glaser, who as we saw in Chapter 3 accomplished precisely this at *New York* magazine, the most influential urban lifestyle magazine of the day, was the natural choice for the job.[44] As artistic director of *New York* and co-founder of Pushpin Studios, Glaser developed the design aesthetic of the "new journalism."[45] Through his bold and playful innovations in typeface, layout, and illustration, he provided the graphic complement to the experimental editorial content in a way that seemed characteristically "New York." Much of this involved traveling visually between "high and low" cultural references, eschewing "beauty" for "clarity," via design dominated by his rich literary sensibility. While he emphasized the need for simplicity, and loved pop culture, he believed this should always be mixed with more sophisticated concepts. In this sense, the genius of Milton Glaser's graphic design was to be universally accessible and yet never to underestimate the intelligence of his audience. These tensions, he believed, mirrored the gritty yet smart "New York sensibility," and the best of city life. His minimalist yet complex invention for the DOC, "I♥NY," was very much in this spirit, and was quickly seen as somehow authentically "New York."

Glaser did not come up with the famous logo on his first try. Always a fast worker, he first did something simple and quick—two lozenges, with a strip of text in the top lozenge reading "I Love," and in the bottom lozenge "New

York." It was immediately accepted, but Glaser himself was unhappy with it. The next day, he was sitting in a taxi and had the realization "there's a better way to do it," so redid the logo on a piece of paper in his pocket. He then phoned Doyle and told him he had a better version, to which Doyle responded, "Oh, don't bother. I've gotten all these commissioners together and it's impossible to change it." But Glaser insisted, until finally Doyle consented to look at the new logo. Many, including some at WRG, thought it was "too cryptic."[46] To test the logo's readability, Doyle had I♥NY t-shirts printed and "test-marketed" them himself, by wearing them while he and his wife were vacationing in Barbados. After numerous tourists there stopped Doyle on the street to see where they could buy one of the t-shirts, he fully endorsed the new design upon his return.[47] "But, amazingly enough," Glaser reflected, with all the bureaucratic wrangling, "it almost didn't happen."[48]

Glaser himself, a designer steeped in the theory of graphic communication, always knew the logo was not too cryptic—rather just cryptic enough. He appreciated the degree to which people enjoy solving the right kind of "design puzzle." In this sense, I♥NY was one of Glaser's most successful puzzles. According to him, this was not only because of the iconography, but because of the different connotations generated by the visual symbolism of the logo as a whole:

> [It was a] funny little thing . . . a little complex because there's a puzzle in the iconography. "I" is a complete word, "♥" is a symbol for an emotion, and "NY" are initials for a place. So anybody who sees it has to do a little translating in order to get it . . . But part of it is also a purely visual phenomenon. It is the contrast of the black and the red, the softness of the heart, the voluptuous, feminine quality of the heart. And the angular, aggressive character of the typeface. Somehow it had an effect on people.[49]

However it worked, Glaser's design was remarkably effective, both semiotically and as a marketing tool. It communicated well when printed on official New York City and State tourist merchandise and, as we shall see, when integrated within print and television advertising campaigns. Meanwhile, due to the DOC's shrewd tactic of allowing people to reproduce it without enforcing copyright, the logo spread like wildfire.[50] In what may be one of the earliest cases of what is now known as "viral advertising," I♥NY was hawked on thousands of unofficial items at corner souvenir stands and in shops throughout the city and beyond. It soon became "the pace setter in tourism destination marketing" and "the most copied tourism logo in the world,"[51] with thousands of places, people, and product manufacturers around the world borrowing its structure and inserting their own name—from "I♥Harare" to "I♥Beagles"—in its script. As Glaser reflected:

> I thought we'd do a six-month campaign and it would be over . . . Why it became so identified with the city, so durable, I don't know. And it spread all over the world. You can't go anywhere without seeing it. It's just crazy. I've done a lot of work in my life, but this just had a profound effect. And after thirty years, it's still not dead.[52]

At a time of fiscal crisis, the personalized message and ingenious design of I♥NY served to remind people of a certain quality of urbanity that they still admired, even loved, in the midst of decline. And as part of a massive media campaign, the slogan and logo soon became globally associated with New York, and the closest thing the city ever had to an official brand.

From Crisis to Consensus: The Impact of I♥NY, 1977–1983

As the I♥NY campaign planning got under way, and as the legislature was preparing to spend unprecedented millions to fund this new breed of place marketing, the city was spiraling out of control. Residents were starting to feel the long-term impact of lay-offs and joblessness, of planned shrinkage and cutbacks in services, of the elimination of new low-income housing, of unchecked waves of arson and strings of garbage-collector strikes. This was the daily, grinding reality for the majority of New Yorkers, and it was wearing down the spirit of the city. Glaser remembered those fiscal crisis days: "You might say that the city was in a state of deep depression, not only financially, but psychically."[53]

I♥NY represented none of this messy, everyday reality that New Yorkers lived through at this time. Rather, the PR campaign sought to tap into people's collectively held mental representations of New York as a better place, and to communicate this through the use of media. In the process, it hoped to distract attention from, and make people forget, the material reality. Glaser wistfully recalled the uplifting effect of the campaign, not only on tourists, but on New York's beleaguered inhabitants. To him, New York was largely a state of mind, and a good marketing campaign was enough to change that state of mind:

> I think originally the I♥NY campaign was fundamentally driven by tourism and the loss of revenue because people weren't coming here. It was focused outwardly. But I think its most profound effect was inward, which is to say it reminded [New Yorkers themselves]

of their own commitment to life in the city. And I actually think that that's a much more powerful instrumentality . . . One thing we know is that reality is conditioned by belief . . . Whatever you believe turns out to be what you perceive as real . . . And when people felt "this is a horrible, desperate place to be," it was; and the day that they felt "this is a marvelous place and I want to live here," it became that.[54]

This inward effect was precisely what WRG was aiming for, hoping that throngs of New Yorkers wearing I♥NY t-shirts would replace the burned-out South Bronx on the nation's TV screens. This authentic enthusiasm of New Yorkers for their city would be set in contrast to representations of the city's decay.[55] Nevertheless, the strategy did meet with some skepticism. *Time* magazine, for instance, editorialized: "if New York's morale really is better these days, it may be because so many of those who hated the place left."[56] Nonetheless, Glaser's sense of New Yorkers' reaction to the campaign was valid. Many people were relieved and uplifted finally to see this show of support for their embattled city, and were happy to participate directly by wearing a t-shirt. The symbol of love signified empathy, even solidarity, among New Yorkers and between them and the rest of the world. It implicitly expressed the anxiety that New York, and all that it represented, might cease to exist, and at the same time voiced the hope that, through love, it could survive. In this sense, I♥NY tapped into what Frederic Jameson would call (just two years later) the underlying "utopian impulse in mass culture," an impulse easily exploited to legitimate political ends.[57]

And indeed, I♥NY did a masterful job of political legitimation. If you believed in the campaign, the fact that there were real crises out the window, down the street, or in an adjoining borough did not have to worry you. Wells Lawrence compared the campaign to the satirical film *Wag the Dog* in which "a fake war is created for political reasons and an anthem is created to move people and make them believe there really is a war." So too for WRG: "Charlie [Moss] was Dustin Hoffman and I was Robert De Niro and we had New Yorkers marching right past all the garbage singing 'I Love New York.'"[58] With the aid of such theater, Wells Lawrence suggested, pressure on the city to clean up its garbage was relieved, except in the Midtown theater district, where tourists and TV cameras might see it.

The Campaign

In the print and television campaign's advertisements, guides, and commercials, images of working-class communities north of 96th Street or across the East River in Brooklyn and Queens were largely omitted, while the city's "attractions" primarily focused on three Manhattan elements: Fifth

208 • Part II: The Battle to Brand New York

Avenue shopping, Broadway theater, and "the new downtown nightlife" around the World Trade Center. The media campaign combined, as Dyson had intended, a sense of New York as a great place to visit and a great place to make money.

WRG hired three people to work on the TV campaign: Charlie Moss, advertising director, Steve Karmen, pop-jazz musician and jingle writer, and TV cameraman and film director Stan Dragoti. The first two commercials they shot had to capture the two main aspects of the campaign that CBI had predicted people would respond to: Broadway shows in the city and the natural beauty of rural, upstate areas. The commercials were designed literally to "star Broadway," featuring performers from all the best shows of that year. And, fortunately for the campaign, this was not such a hard sell. 1977 turned out to be one of the best years on Broadway in terms of the quality and popularity of its first-run musicals, many of which went on to become contemporary classics—including *A Chorus Line*, *Annie*, and *The Wiz*. Yet, due to the decline in tourism, many of these shows were threatened with closure. As a result, even though the campaign had little money to pay large casts, the shows were so desperate to stay on Broadway, they were willing to work for free. As Moss recalled:

> We anticipated trouble with the Broadway show tourist spot. We wouldn't be able to get all the shows in. Since we ran out of money, we worked out a deal. Where people worked for the minimum scale that was possible. We paid them I think it was $357 dollars for their time. [The] mercenary reason [was] they all were in shows that needed business. During the course of the filming there was a snow storm, but they all came. And stayed for twenty-seven takes.[59]

The commercial was shot on a Broadway theater stage, using the New York City skyline as backdrop in most scenes. Thus, while the emphasis was on the talent and excitement of the theater, there was still clearly an effort to represent the office towers and skyscrapers beyond Broadway. This helped to personalize and draw the viewer into this larger vision of the city as a whole. This was reproduced by the cinematography, which, according to Wells Lawrence, broke conventions in the representation of theater on television:

> Traditionally, Broadway shows were advertised in a representational style as you would see them in a performance from somewhere in the audience. Stan [Dragoti] wanted to do something really new, and he thought of directing the stars of the shows in a presentational style, they would present themselves to you while singing the

Wells, Rich, Greene, Inc. 767 Fifth Avenue · New York, N.Y. 10022 · Plaza 8-4300

I LOVE NEW YORK
BROADWAY SHOW TOURS

New York State Department of Commerce

60-seconds

(MUSIC IN)

(MUSIC IN)

(MUSIC UNDER) VO:
There's only one Broadway
... It's in New York ...

(CAST OF "A CHORUS
LINE" SINGING I LOVE
N.Y.)

(CAST OF "THE WIZ"
SINGING I LOVE N.Y.)

(CAST OF "GREASE"
SINGING I LOVE N.Y.)

(CAST OF "THE KING AND
I" SINGING I LOVE N.Y.)

(CAST OF "ANNIE"
SINGING I LOVE N.Y.)

VO: Introducing "I Love
New York"

Broadway Show Tours
(CAST OF "CHAPTER TWO")

... 16 specially priced
packages of shows and
hotels.

For a free booklet, see your
travel agent or
(CAST OF "THE GIN GAME")

call toll free, 800 331-1000.
(CAST OF "THE MAGIC
SHOW")

DRACULA: I Love New York
... especially in the evening.

(MUSIC OUT)
(SUPER: I LOVE NEW YORK
BROADWAY SHOW TOURS)

Figure 7.1 I♥NY and Broadway.
In the first television commercial for the campaign, WRG used innovative cinematography to create a personal, emotional connection between viewers and Broadway performers, and by extension, with New York City.

Courtesy Empire State Development Corporation

"I Love New York" anthem. The presentational style would create an exultant connection between the Broadway stars and you, the TV viewer that would not only make you feel you absolutely had to see those shows but also remind you that you loved New York.[60]

"The Most Talked about and Successful Tourism Program in the Nation"

And so it was that in 1977, a year of blackouts, lay-offs, and the Summer of Sam, New York increased its tourism budget from $400,000 to $4.3 million and hired WRG, one of the hippest ad agencies in the country, to design an upbeat, Broadway-oriented campaign. Additional financial support was provided by ABNY, while the New York City CVB provided travel agents and new package deals for "theater weekends" and vacations linking the city and the state. Milton Glaser, still artistic director of *New York* magazine, applied techniques of the urban lifestyle genre to media spreads selling the city to a young, affluent consumer. *New York* also produced some of the campaign's first tourist maps and guides, which it provided as inserts as well as separate editions, and ran I♥NY ads prominently in its pages.

The campaign launch was accompanied by ingenious PR events, coordinated by two of the top PR agents in the city: Bobby Zarem and Howard Rubenstein (who also worked with ABNY). They worked alongside the DOC to ensure that constant press releases were going out for these events—and the media dutifully covered all of them. The first of these was the campaign's celebration of its launch on Valentine's Day, 1978. At a gala luncheon at the Tavern on the Green, Governor Hugh Carey unveiled the new Broadway-themed TV commercial with its cast in attendance, including the stars of *A Chorus Line*, *The Wiz*, *Annie*, *Grease*, and other current hits. There he announced that 32 million viewers would see the ad, which was being broadcast throughout the Northeast, and was the first of hundreds to be produced by the agency. Then the party moved to Studio 54 to dance to the new "disco version" of the "I Love New York" theme song, along with, according to the DOC's press release, "hundreds of colorful and interesting people who keep New York alive at night." These included many of the hottest local film, TV, and art stars, such as Carrie Fisher, Mariel Hemingway, Andy Warhol, and Gilda Radner, star of the new, hugely popular late night TV show *Saturday Night Live*, which was filmed in, and heavily featured, New York. For the grand finale, buildings across the city lit up to spell "I♥NY," most prominently the World Trade Center, thus making the logo visible on the skyline, and creating a widely circulated image used in later commercials and promotions.[61]

The state cited a follow-up psychographic study by CBI which showed that "the five week summer campaign alone" raised New York City's "aware-

The New York Times/Neal Boenzi

Singing "I Love New York" are, from left: Yul Brynner, Mayor Koch, Governor Carey, Diana Ross and Frank Langella. Entertainers and politicians gathered at The Tavern on the Green to promote theater-going on Broadway.

For Valentine's, It's 'I Love New York Day'

Figure 7.2 The Launch of I♥NY on Valentine's Day, 1978.
City and state officials now took part in New York City marketing, alongside New York's most critically acclaimed performers in theater, music, and dance.

New York Times

ness" level by 6 percent and its "appeal" factor by 10 percent. Furthermore, DATO had already selected the I♥NY campaign as "the Best State Travel Promotion Campaign of 1977."[62]

And indeed, the campaign proved to be an astonishing success, according to more follow-up studies by CBI. In one year, it stimulated an 11.8 percent increase in travel receipts in New York City. The $4.3 million tourist promotion effort reaped $14.3 million in tax revenues, which CBI calculated (by rounding upwards) as translating to $4 in tax revenue for every $1 spent on the campaign.[63] This statistic became one of the most circulated in the months following the launch, and seemed to contribute to the campaign's momentum.

The CVB was emboldened by the results. In the two weeks following the first TV advertisement, which aired on February 14, 1978 in New York and five surrounding states, the CVB received more than 17,000 requests for tour package brochures through the Commerce Department's toll-free number.

They averaged 1,500 inquiries a day, doubling the past record. Because of this, they demanded greater funding from the city, complaining that New York was still only seventeenth in the nation in tourism funding, yet was handling some of the greatest call volume, and was the hottest tourism market, of any city.[64] According to CVB numbers, released to the press: "New York City, where tourists are counted like money in the bank, attracted a record total of 16.75 million visitors who pumped an estimated $1.6 billion into the local economy"—which led Mayor Koch to decide to more than triple the city's contribution to the CVB's budget, to $2 million, the following year.[65]

It seemed New York was no longer dependent on one-time events. Even without a Democratic Convention, the city saw a major increase in tourist numbers and spending, and an unprecedented 840 conventions booked. The campaign even appeared to be putting New York State ahead of the rest of the country in tourism, according to the US Travel Data Center, which sampled six private state attractions, and found visitor volume increased 56.7 percent between 1976 and 1977—as compared to only 0.1 percent nationally.[66]

By July 1978, the DOC deemed the trial run of the I♥NY television campaign in the Northeastern United States to have been be so successful they made it nationwide.[67] Under a novel cost-sharing arrangement with four airlines—United, Eastern, Braniff, and North Central—commercials were "test marketed" in Houston, Miami, Nashville, Dallas, Chicago, and Milwaukee. The airlines agreed to set up one-stop ticket counters for hotel and theater reservations with airline tickets.[68] According to the marketing consultant who arranged the deal, the cost of air-time for the ads would be split fifty–fifty, and, to inaugurate the campaign, "New York celebrities will be flown to the various cities for promotional parties."[69]

By its second year, I♥NY had become "the most talked about and successful tourism program in the nation," according to the DOC.[70] It received "unprecedented media coverage" on local and national TV and in the press. It won all the awards for which it was eligible, including the DATO Marketing Award for two years running, a special Tony Award for its Broadway TV commercial, the Cue Golden Apple Award, the New York Hotel Association Award, the Ad Expo Award, and two national Clio Advertising Awards.[71] The glamorous Mary Wells Lawrence, head of WRG, was invited to speak all over the nation to represent both the campaign and the rejuvenated face of New York City.

Now the inspiring story being told was not simply about a miraculous little marketing campaign, but about the amazing success of the New York tourism industry, and the comeback that it signaled for the city. As the *Tribune* enthused on its front page:

> People have rediscovered New York. This is the greatest visitor area in the world. It's just a combination of factors. The theater is booming, restaurants are booming, the opera is booming, department store sales are up and the museums are crowded. There's an "up" feeling now despite all the problems we've had.[72]

And, indeed, a range of tourism-related industries *were* booming. The League of New York Theaters and Producers called 1978 "the busiest year" in the theater district's history.[73] Major tour operators said package tour sales to the city had increased an average of 246 percent over the previous year.[74] And though smaller hotels and rooming houses were closing, the city was "quietly giving birth to the biggest tourist hotel building boom in its history," with major investors competing to meet "the demand for deluxe accommodations."[75] Charles Gillett called tourism "now the city's leading growth industry." Hotelier and ABNY vice-president Preston Robert Tisch went a step further, arguing that tourism's growth was sparking a "resurgence" of New York City as a whole: "Today our industry is in a stronger position than at any time in history. Moreover our strength has become one of the major economic resources of the city. Our vitality has served as a sparkplug for the resurgence of our great city."[76] This sentiment was echoed by Mayor Ed Koch, who said he would rally the city to increase support for these efforts. He called for greater city spending for the CVB, and for the building of a new convention center on the West Side, arguing: "If New York City is to expand its economic base and flourish in the years ahead, a top priority must [be] not only [to] maintain its position as a center of tourism and commerce, but expand it." Immediately thereafter, Gillett trumpeted what he regarded as a "sea-change" in the public sector's attitude towards city marketing.[77]

Finally, the popular success of I♥NY had a lasting impact on the approach to business development undertaken by both New York City and State. From now on, what John Dyson identified as the "more positive commodity" of tourism marketing, and the newly minted I♥NY brand, would be used to promote the DOC's more controversial slate of economic reforms that were intended to entice corporations to stay in or move to New York. Thus, in late 1978, when the Broadway-based campaign was expanding its reach to a nationwide audience, WRG was commissioned to create a series of economic development spots to be aired in the tri-state area, and in other targeted parts of the country. One of the products of this was a 1979 commercial featuring corporate CEOs extolling the numerous tax breaks they had received from New York State as the reason why *they* loved New York, and then breaking into the catchy "I Love New York" jingle over the text: "New York is getting down to business, so business is starting to sing a different tune." WRG also combined the I♥NY logo with that of

Figure 7.3 I♥NY and "business development".
From the beginning of I♥NY, attracting businessmen with tax breaks was as important as attracting tourists with Broadway shows—though the former were targeted far more carefully so as not to detract from the "positive," populist image of the tourism side of the campaign.

Courtesy Empire State Development Corporation

the lesser-known "Made in New York" campaign. The latter, developed in the 1960s, had been created to promote the state's agriculture and industrial products, but was now focused on attracting corporate headquarters and high-end services to in New York City. Thus, WRG created commercials that sold the fact that, rather than California, Pennsylvania, or North Carolina, "the biggest tax cuts of any state were . . . Made in New York."[78]

Evaluating the Impact of I♥NY

Many things about tourism in New York City in the late 1970s are hard to dispute. Between 1976 and 1980, the years of the start of the I♥NY campaign, revenue generated by tourists increased by $1.7 billion, or 340 percent. The hotel occupancy rate reached an unprecedented 80.2 percent

Table 7.1 Changes in the New York City travel and tourism sector, 1976–1988.

Date	Hotel Occupancy Rate (%)	Conventions	Number of Visitors (million)	Visitor Spending ($ billion)
1976	73.0	—	16.5	0.5
1977	—	820	16.75	—
1978	—	840	16.9	1.6
1979	80.2	—	—	1.8
1980	78.4	—	17.1	2.2
1981	73.5	—	—	—
1982	—	933	16.9	2.0
1983	72.2	938	17.1	2.2
1988	76.7	—	19.8	2.65

Source: CVB figures as cited in articles in the *New York Times*, 1977–1984; Auletta, *Streets Were Paved with Gold*; Pannell Kerr Forster, *Trends in the Hotel Industry*, 1981–1983; Chipkin, "New York City's Campaign for Agency Business"; Sterne, "A Good Tourist Year Cited for New York."

and conventions were on the rise, prompting a wave of new hotel construction (see Table 7.1). Tourism appeared to be a relatively easy way for the city to get a quick infusion of cash into city coffers. And at a time of increasing global competition, it made sense to cultivate this place-based industry in combination with other pro-business incentives as a new source of economic leverage for New York.

But fundamental questions about the impact of this new economy remained, questions that were particularly important to raise in a time of crisis. First, how should claims about the crucial role of marketing in generating tourism and broader development be evaluated? Second, what was the impact of rising tourism on the overall economy, and who benefited most from this growth? And finally, should scarce public resources be expended on new economic development strategies whose wider social benefits remained unproven? With the exception of an audit by the New York State Comptroller, however, these questions seem to have been left unasked. It appears rather that most discussions driving the move to this new approach happened behind the closed doors of economic development agencies. I devote the remainder of this chapter to reopening the debate, and considering its wider implications.

The Impact of "Awareness" and "Image" on Tourism

As we have seen, beginning from fiscal year 1976–1977 through 1977–1978, the DOC undertook a radical new approach, devoting its entire budget of $400,000 to conduct market research. It then used its entire expanded budget of \$4.3 million to launch the I♥NY marketing campaign. Its task in 1978–1979 was to assess the effectiveness of the program and prove to the state that it had made a wise investment. As it turns out—and despite its own glowing reports—this was never accomplished. Instead, there was a highly unusual, combative exchange between the State Comptroller's office and the DOC Commissioner John Dyson. In one corner, the technocratic State Comptroller, Arthur Levitt, Sr., who had served in his post since 1955, believed in "standard, quantitative" indicators of economic growth—things like growth in sales, jobs, payroll, establishments, and revenue. In the other corner, the entrepreneurial Commissioner believed in new, "psychographic" methods to measure marketing impact called "advertising awareness studies"—correlating "awareness" of ads with "appeal" of the "product."[79] Based on these indicators—that is, a correlation between "strong unaided awareness" of I♥NY with an increase in "appeal" by "ten percent for upstate and thirteen percent for New York City"—Dyson predicted an *unspecified* "increase in tourism related expenditures and their concomitant yields of tax revenues and jobs."[80]

While audits are meant to be critical, this one was exceptionally harsh in both content and tone.[81] It essentially said that the DOC had completely failed to substantiate "any of its claims" about the benefits of this massive campaign, and indeed that it would be impossible to do so since the data provided had to do only with "awareness" and "image," items which in the Comptroller's view were not "hard data."[82] The audit stated flatly, "Overall, the marketing plans for tourism and business development were not sufficiently detailed or specific," either in terms of "the allocation of their budgets, or the measures of effectiveness of their programs,"[83] and thus it was impossible to "evaluate whether the State received a positive return on its sizeable investment." Ultimately, the Comptroller found that "without considering other factors that affect vacation habits," the DOC was incapable of proving any "causal relationship" between I♥NY and improvements in tourism, even on its own terms.[84]

In his equally terse, ten-page rebuttal, Dyson offered the DOC's "strenuous objections to the content, style, and conclusions" of the audit, calling it "unfair, unsubstantiated, and inaccurate in many respects."[85] According to Dyson, "every single one of [our] indicators went up overall since the onset of ILNY [and] given these facts, all made known in extensive detail to the auditors, we fail to comprehend their statement."[86] And in any case, he argued, all "experts" in market research know that media and advertising studies should not be expected to demonstrate causality, and if the auditors could not understand that, they were essentially behind the times.[87]

The DOC's accounting problems were by no means unique. How can anyone ever *prove* to a client the impact of a single advertisement, or for that matter an entire campaign?[88] Even after a carefully researched, test-marketed campaign has been released, targeting all the right psychographics, and profits have gone up or down dramatically, there is no way to prove that there is a direct, causal correlation between these two events. This is, of course, a fact that clients paying a lot of money to advertising agencies do not like to hear—particularly public sector clients who are answerable to the legislature in a period of fiscal crisis. In this case, it should be remembered that the rationale for the beneficial effect of such an inexact science was rejected by the State Comptroller, albeit with no evident effect on future spending for I❤NY by the DOC.

The Impact of Tourism on the Economy

By the end of the decade, it was becoming apparent that even with a dramatic upsurge in tourism, combined with the massive "stimulus" of hundreds of millions of dollars in tax cuts, the overall economy of New York City and State was still in steep decline. In fact, by 1980, both the city and the state found themselves entering another recession. While some of this was due to what the incoming Governor Mario Cuomo referred to as a "generally bleak national economic situation," New York's decline was far deeper and longer than that of the rest of the nation—and similar to other industrialized states in the Northeast and Midwest.[89] The trouble was most apparent in New York's escalating rates of unemployment, which rose sharply in 1979 to 7.1 percent, and to 7.5 percent in 1980—as compared to 5.8 percent nationally—and would top 9 percent by 1982, the highest the state had seen in the post-war era.[90] Meanwhile, business activity hit a "plateau," with only two of seven sectors in New York's economy advancing by 1980: FIRE and services. Because of this and the tax cuts that went into effect in 1979, the city and state's overall revenues went into steep decline, creating the conditions for another fiscal crisis only five years after the last one. Tourism, it seemed, was doing nothing to prevent this.

Part of the problem in assessing the impact of tourism on the overall economy was due to the data provided by tourism officials and the consultancy firms they hired: that is, tourism spending, hotel occupancy rates, and conventions booked. Unlike research on advertising effects, those studying tourism impact *could* have tracked hard numbers—like employment and number of establishments—which were considered standard measures of industrial strength by the US Census at the time. Had they done so, they might have seen a more troubling dynamic than that provided by their own indicators. Big players in tourism and marketing appeared to weather the storm of crisis and expand their profits as we saw in the previous chapter (see Table 6.2, above; see also Appendix, Table A.2). Between 1967 and 1977, hotels and motels, amusement and recreation, and advertising all saw "revenue" from consumption rise dramatically. This growth did have the effect of increasing tax revenues to the city, but this was offset by losses in other areas. Most strikingly, many jobs were lost in each of these sectors, particularly in hotels and motels, which lost close to half of their workforce in this period. In addition, with the exception of amusement and recreation, the number of establishments in these sectors shrank significantly—an indication of industry consolidation, as large corporate hotels and advertising firms came to dominate the market, and as smaller (and often older) establishments were put out of business.[91] Thus, although they contributed substantially to the city's coffers, the growing profits of tourism and marketing also served to exacerbate the adverse effects of the fiscal crisis, when measured in terms of jobs and income for average New Yorkers.

These contradictory dynamics became only more severe between 1980 and 1982, when the prolonged recession and strong dollar deterred foreign visitors, both nationwide and in New York. Despite a rise in conventions, the overall number of visitors fell from 17.1 million to 16.9 million, the lowest level since 1978. Visitor spending declined from $2.2 billion to an estimated $2 billion, and hotel occupancy from 78.4 to 73.5 percent over the same period.[92] While the number of jobs in certain significant sectors, like hotels, began to increase in this period, the tourism cluster overall lost an additional 16,000 jobs between 1977 and 1982. Tracked between 1967 and 1982, this meant that 87,200 jobs, or 45 percent of the entire tourism sector, were lost between 1967 and 1982 (see Figures 7.4 and 7.5).

Evaluated in terms of its impact on employment rather than tourism spending alone, and compared in these terms with other major economic sectors, tourism appeared more like a flat tire than a sparkplug. In fact, tourism was *number one* in the city in terms of the percentage of jobs lost over the course of the 1970s, and more similar to manufacturing—which lost 44 percent of its jobs over the same period—than with the sectors that it was meant to help promote—such as services and FIRE—which gained 34 percent and 14 percent, respectively. One could still argue that the improved city image provided by tourism marketing was beneficial for helping these two growing sectors. Nonetheless, these benefits did not make up for the net jobs lost city-wide between 1967 and 1982, which at over 356,000 represented a 10 percent decline. Ultimately, the city was becoming increasingly dependent on tourism and high-end services, and these industries were not sufficiently redressing the job loss associated with the crisis.[93]

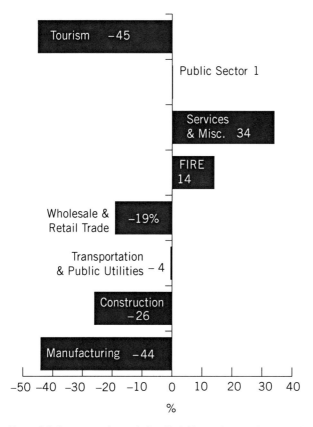

Figure 7.4 Percentage change in New York City employment by economic sector, 1967–1982.

Source: New York State Department of Labor and US Department of Commerce, Bureau of the Census, 1967, 1972, 1977, and 1982.

Note
"Tourism" category derived from a cluster analysis based on the Empire State Development Corporation's "New York State Industry Cluster Profiles" (Division of Policy and Research, May 1998).

Spending for Tourism and Marketing in Times of Austerity

In defense of tourism and marketing, the point can be made that New York City's economic prospects would have been even more bleak had it not been for the impact of tourism spending and increased tax revenue that came with it. Even if one showed negative impacts of growth in the industry—that is, a loss in employment despite rising revenues—it is conceivable that average New Yorkers benefited from enhanced social services paid for out of these tax dollars. And in any case, it would be hard to argue with the fact that overall spending on tourism was relatively small compared to other areas. This had always been one of the great attractions of tourism as an economic

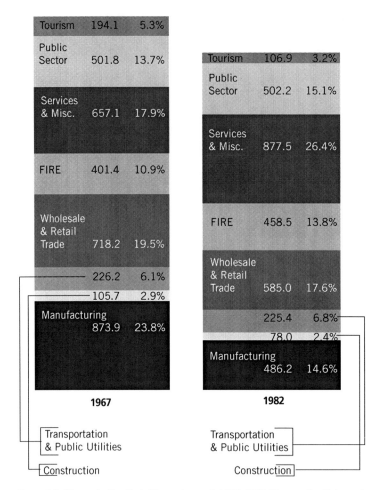

Figure 7.5 Change in New York City employment, 1967–1982 (thousands of jobs and percentage change).

Source: New York State Department of Labor and US Department of Commerce, Bureau of the Census, 1967, 1972, 1977, and 1982 .

development strategy: tourism and marketing were ways to make a "fast buck," requiring little expenditure, political debate, or legislation up front.

Yet, when one looks at tourism spending in the context of the overall restructuring of the city's budget, it is hard to understand how average New Yorkers came out ahead. On the one hand, one sees a marked increase in spending on tourism and marketing at both city and state levels between the late 1960s and early 1980s (see Figures 7.6 and 7.7). On the other hand, one sees that this increase in spending occurred alongside of a 20 percent cut in the city's total budget, which reduced overall spending in 1983 to a level not

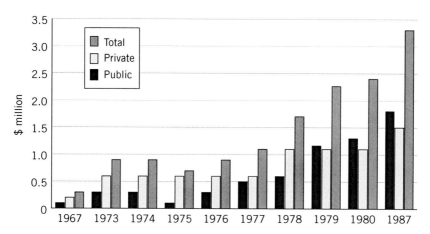

Figure 7.6 Tourism and marketing spending for New York City, 1967–1987.

Source: CVB figures as cited by: Michael Sterne, "A Good Tourist Year Cited for New York" and Rosemary Metler Lavan, "The Word on Apple Tourism? Lacking. Experts Fear a Long Lost Summer Will Visit upon Us," *Daily News*, April 30, 1991.

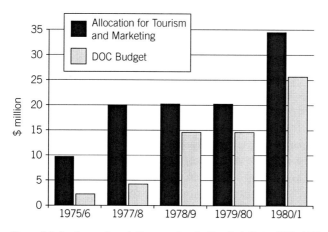

Figure 7.7 Tourism and marketing spending for New York State, 1975–1981.

Source: New York State Department of Commerce, *An Economic Strategy for the 1980s: A Report to the Council on State Priorities*, 1981; New York State Assembly Standing Committee on Commerce, Industry, and Economic Development, *Annual Report*, December 13, 1976; Paul Marinaccio, "State Officials Now Wonder if Tourists Will Still Love New York," *New York Newsday*, November 23, 1988.

seen since the late 1960s (see Figure 7.8). Virtually every area of the city budget was seriously affected by this retrenchment—with the exception of "housekeeping services" like parks and sanitation (see Appendix, Figures A.1 and A.2).[94] Most deeply cut were the city's largest budget categories: education and "redistributive" expenditures for a range of social welfare

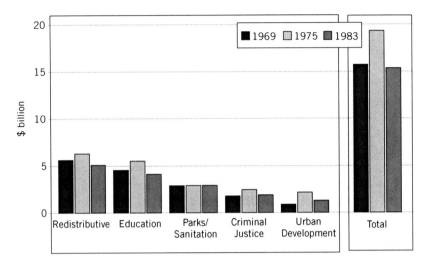

Figure 7.8 Relative public expenditures for New York City, 1969–1983.

Source: Brecher and Horton, "The Public Sector," 109–110. Figures adjusted for inflation based on the Consumer Price Index conversion for 1983.

programs, both of which were reduced to pre-1969 levels. Meanwhile, in the remaining categories of criminal justice and "urban development"—that is, transportation and infrastructure—cuts were significant, if not as severe.[95] Certainly no other area of public spending saw any major growth.

In this context, the dramatic increase in spending for tourism, marketing, and business development constituted a profound shift in public sector priorities. It sent a clear message that stimulating growth in these areas was a more urgent concern than maintaining social services, welfare, and infrastructure for the majority of residents at their current levels. It also left open the question: might more balanced spending have led to greater and more evenly distributed economic benefits in the long run?

Conclusion: Ladies and Gentlemen, the Bronx Is Burning

Some of the worst looting during the blackout of the summer of 1977 occurred in the devastated neighborhoods of the South Bronx, previously victim to the depredations of Robert Moses's urban planning and Roger Starr's planned shrinkage policies. Perhaps because of the particularly apocalyptic backdrop they provided, media attention continued to focus on the neighborhoods' bombed-out streets even after the long, hot summer had ended. In particular, there was international fascination in the story of the Bronx going up in flames at the hands of its own residents, as arson in the neighborhood continued unabated. Common to almost all of this coverage was its fixation on the visual tableau of devastation, and avoidance of any investigation into the social and historical causes for it.

By far the most infamous of these images was captured in October 1977, during the World Series match-up between the New York Yankees and the LA Dodgers at Yankee Stadium in the Bronx. It was a series already heavy with symbolism. The Bronx Bombers were up against the Dodgers, a team that only twenty years earlier had abandoned Brooklyn, and their adoring fan base, for the warmer, wealthier climes of Los Angeles. New York boosters were hoping the symbolically freighted series would provide some free publicity, and prove that the city, like its baseball team, could beat their Sunbelt arch-nemesis. But that hope was to be dashed by a brief cutaway during the second game of the series, when a cameraman happened to pan across the South Bronx neighborhood just beyond the stadium, and caught within the frame a building on fire less than a mile away. Upon seeing the image on his monitor, sports announcer Howard Cosell suddenly stopped his half-time banter and barked into the microphone: "There it is, ladies and gentlemen, the Bronx is burning!" When the camera then zoomed in on the building, it became clear no effort was being made to douse the flames. Cosell, now fuming, cried out, "What's wrong with these people? Don't these people have any self-respect?"[96]

These images and remarks were instantly broadcast to scores of millions of viewers watching the game. And over the following days, they were replayed for millions more on countless news shows and newspaper front pages—getting as much coverage as the apparently less interesting fact that the Yankees had won both the game and the World Series. Backed by spectacular imagery, the message sent to the world was clear: "these people," in other words those poor, mostly black and Latino New Yorkers still living in neighborhoods like the South Bronx, were responsible for the senseless, self-destructive ruin of their own city. Unlike the Civil Rights era of the 1960s, full of national soul-searching and federal commissions on urban unrest, by the late 1970s it was politically correct to blame those living in segregated and impoverished American ghettos for their terrible conditions.[97] For despite President Jimmy Carter's visit to the South Bronx the following month, replete with somber coverage and the promise of a plan to repair the inner cities of America, no significant steps were taken to address the problem at the local, state, or federal level. Rather, the image of urban ruin exemplified by the South Bronx was once again fodder for late night TV stand-up routines and B-movie thrillers.

I❤NY was a crowning achievement in the effort to "purge" the city of its liberal ways in the wake of the fiscal crisis, but did little to address the growing needs of the city's population. Rather, the campaign ushered in a new model of economic recovery that emphasized short-term strategies like city branding and incentives for business over and above long-term investments in public infrastructure, collective consumption, and the support of a mixed economic base. This constituted a massive, dual effort: to transform the image of New York City as a product in the minds of out-of-towners, while resisting demands for services, welfare, and working-class jobs coming from New York's own citizens. In so doing, I♥NY helped to create a deep and enduring divide between these two constituencies, and a stark contradiction between the image of recovery and the reality of growing poverty. In this sense, it also created the potential for never-ending image crises, justifying ever-greater expenditures on marketing. These features of life in New York City are among the most enduring legacies of this path-breaking campaign and of the fiscal crisis era as a whole.

The Legacy of the 1970s

CHAPTER 8

New York City as a Symbol
of Neoliberalism

There is a new spirit of individual initiative rising in our land, and
a good deal of the credit belongs to you and to your colleagues . . .
When New York was in trouble, groups which had quarreled for
years joined together to fight for the greater good of saving the city.
Labor, business, government, voluntary associations all pitched in
. . . In your beliefs, your efforts, and your accomplishments, you are
setting the course to progress and freedom that our nation must
follow. You are that tough little tug that can pull our ship of state
off the shoals and out into open water. You believe private initiative,
the private sector are essential to economic and social progress, and
so do all of us in our administration.

> President Ronald Reagan, speaking to the
> New York City Partnership, January 14, 1982[1]

If I can make it there
I'll make it anywhere . . .
It's up to you, New York, New York.

> Lyrics of "New York, New York"
> by Fred Ebb, 1977[2]

On January 14, 1982, the first anniversary of his inaugural address, President
Ronald Reagan visited the Grand Ballroom of the Waldorf Astoria Hotel in
New York City to give another highly symbolic address—this time before the

financial luminaries of the New York City Partnership. After a glowing introduction by David Rockefeller, chairman of the board of Chase Manhattan
Bank and founder of the Partnership, Reagan strode to the podium sporting
an I♥NY scarf just given to him by Mayor Ed Koch, setting off a flurry of
camera flashbulbs and a standing ovation from the New York City crowd.
Then he gave a rousing speech about "the spirit of shared sacrifice" that
allowed New York's financial and political leadership to overcome the city's
recent troubles by trading the welfare state for "private initiative." Thus New
York became a beacon for the Reagan administration's own plans for radical
political and economic reform—"a tough little tug that can pull our ship of
state off the shoals and into open water." It was an event imbued with paradox and political stagecraft, the crowning moment in the decade-long
transformation of New York City's image from "working-class city" to a symbol for the nation's new, pro-business economy and emerging right wing.

Reagan could not have chosen a better slogan to represent his free-market
mission than I♥NY. In the wake of the New York fiscal crisis of the mid-
1970s, people were beginning to hold up the city's marketing-led economic
"recovery" as a compelling model for an anxious nation in transition. Here
was a famously liberal city that epitomized just about everything the
conservative, anti-urban movement opposed—renowned for its union
activism, embrace of the welfare state, and racial and ethnic diversity. Yet
here also was a city that, in the throes of crisis, became a primary test site for
the neoliberal reforms preached by Milton Friedman in the 1970s, and
embraced by Reagan and Margaret Thatcher in the 1980s—involving the
radical reorientation of the role of government through privatization,
deregulation, and the devolution of government responsibility to the local
level. What's more, the city also held an enduring place in popular culture
as the nation's most important proving ground—as poignantly conveyed by
"New York, New York," Kander and Ebb's defiant paean to "old New York"
which came out in the depths of 1977. Thus, the Republican reasoning went,
if neoliberalism could make it in New York, it could make it anywhere. If
New York City could be disciplined and transformed into a model of fiscal
conservatism and neoliberal governance, it would only be a matter of time
before the rest of the nation fell into line. By 1985, when the Frank Sinatra
version of "New York, New York" hit the Top Ten, and Mayor Koch awarded
it the designation of "New York's Official Song," the anthem's poignancy had
been replaced with triumphalism, as the city's brand name became
synonymous with the indomitable spirit of the individual, and of the free
market itself.

New York's association with a *laissez-faire* approach was, of course, not
new. Throughout its 300-year history the city's image and class system had
been split between the elite realm of high finance and high culture and the

(a)

Figure 8.1 Reagan loves New York.
(a) President Ronald Reagan speaks before the New York City Partnership about the importance of private sector initiatives, on the first anniversary of his inauguration, January 14, 1981. (b) Reagan wears an I❤NY scarf, given to him by Mayor Ed Koch.

Courtesy Ronald Reagan Library

(b)

working-class world of blue-collar jobs and mass popular culture. Yet, given the size and strength of the city's working class, and its wealth of media and culture industries—from print and publishing to theater and television—representations of working-class New York circulated at least as widely as those of the elite city. Upper-crust periodicals had to compete with the penny press, city-view books with muck-raking journalism, Carnegie Hall with vaudeville, the Metropolitan with Coney Island, and even the city's booster literature trumpeted both "sunshine and shadow" to sell the city. Thus, the elite designation, while certainly influential, had never been coordinated or powerful enough to take the upper hand. Furthermore, though US elites were heavily tied to New York City through their relationship to Wall Street and the Manhattan corporate headquarters complex, culturally speaking they were historically at odds with the city—especially in the post-war period of McCarthyism and the so-called "urban crisis."

With the declining power of the city's working class in the wake of the fiscal crisis, however, New York's branding coalition could impose an image that allowed conservatives to identify with the city not only financially but culturally as well. Through the international I♥NY campaign, an increasingly corporatized *New York* magazine, as well as the broader economic recovery with which both were associated, New York's official brand became highly profitable and easily digestible. The image itself was an ingenious combination of high and low that centered on two iconic sites. First, there was the World Trade Center, symbolizing the city's resurgent financial power and embrace of pro-business political principles. Second, there was the hip yet family-friendly theater district in Times Square, cleaned up for middle-class consumption. This image was haunted by its "other"—the increasingly violent representations of New York in films that depicted the inhuman underbelly of the glittering metropolis. Meanwhile, complex, nuanced representations of New Yorkers—whether rich or poor, white collar or blue collar—grew increasingly rare in a mainstream context.

And so by the 1980s, with President Reagan himself setting the stage, New York's conversion story became a powerful *city-myth*, as Mike Davis has called such productive and ahistorical narratives.[3] Like Atlanta after the fires of the Civil War, pundits and politicians cast New York as a phoenix rising from the ashes, in this case symbolized by the glittering façade of the Twin Towers and the unblinkered lights of Broadway. In this version, the devastation that the city survived was caused not by war, but by the ravages of its own liberal politicians. For decades, the story went, the city's bloated and corrupt bureaucracy had been held hostage by labor unions and welfare rights groups. They had repeatedly acquiesced to demands for higher wages and more generous public services by raising taxes and borrowing from the federal government, while corporations and the middle class left town. And now, finally, as a result of suffering through the worst fiscal crisis in the nation's history, New York had been "purged" and forced to "change its ways"—as the CEOs quoted in the Yankelovich, Skelly, and White report had hoped, and as the no-nonsense Republicans in the White House had demanded. This mythic narrative was to produce a new, hegemonic common sense about the fiscal crisis, and the lessons that should be learned from it. The first lesson was about the causes of the crisis: powerful unions and the welfare state. The second was about the neoliberal "recovery" that followed: it was necessary, the right thing to do, and in any case, to paraphrase Margaret Thatcher, there was no alternative.

As we have seen in this book, however, the lessons of the fiscal crisis are far more complex. It was certainly true that popular demands on city funds increased in the 1960s and early 1970s at the same time that the city purse was shrinking. Yet it is easy to see the justification of these demands, made, as they were, in response to mounting economic pressures on average New Yorkers as a result of rising unemployment, stagflation, and the needs of new immigrants. Meanwhile, such popular demands were accompanied, if not overshadowed, by the demands of the finance and real estate lobby in the same period. With the aid of powerful advocacy groups like the Association for a Better New York (ABNY), such lobbying led to generous tax breaks as well as massive public borrowing to subsidize an unprecedented wave of private office and high-end residential real estate development in Manhattan in the late 1960s—development that the market could not bear, and that cost the city hundreds of millions of dollars of a time of already-escalating debt. Concomitantly, it was the avowed policy of the Nixon and Ford administrations to starve American cities of funds for social programs like public housing and job training, funds that had once been provided through the New Deal and Great Society programs, and of which New York City was a leading recipient. Thus, rather than simply placing blame for New York's fiscal crisis on the shoulders of the city's poor and working class, and on those politicians who acceded to some of their demands, it is important that we recognize the constellation of factors that created the conditions for crisis, including the causal role played by economic and political elites at the local, state, and federal levels.

Similarly, as we have learned, New York's "recovery" from crisis was far more complicated than the city-myth would have us believe. It was true, as Reagan contended, that unprecedented "partnerships" were forged between government, business, and labor at this crucial time, as a result of which a political and economic restructuring occurred that enabled the city to avoid bankruptcy and rebuild. It was also true that hundreds of millions of dollars entered the city's struggling economy in the form of tax revenues, tourist spending, and new investments. And, in certain ways, the city did benefit from its improved image in the eyes of the world. Nevertheless, the myriad benefits gained from the new partnerships, revenues, and image did not "trickle down"—to borrow the phrase Reagan favored—equally to all New Yorkers.

Such uneven benefits were apparent early on. They were seen in the profiting of local banks even at the height of the crisis, in the use of planned shrinkage policies to turn city land over to private developers, and in the remarkable growth in tourism revenues despite downsizing and lay-offs. But most importantly, these imbalanced benefits lived on through the more fundamental realignment of the public sector—or what the report by Yankelovich, Skelly, and White called "pro-business product modifications." These modifications involved rewriting the tax code to benefit business and real estate, undercutting the bargaining power of municipal unions by using their pensions to underwrite city bonds, weakening rent control and stabilization laws, imposing permanent austerity on social programs aimed at the poor, increasing policing and surveillance in the city center, and establishing unelected bodies like the Financial Control Board and the New York City Partnership to provide the private sector continued influence in public affairs for decades to come.

These modifications, combined with the expert marketing of the I♥NY campaign, did indeed create a hospitable environment for new investment and business development, particularly in the "new economy" sectors of business services, tourism, and media, which created new jobs and revenue streams for the city. But it should be remembered that these modifications also created a more hostile environment for organized labor, the working class, and the poor. As was to become increasingly apparent in the coming decades, the changes that resulted in what many on Wall Street, Main Street, and in the White House considered a total "recovery" also entailed a profound loss of power, status, and democratic access for many average New Yorkers.

In the end, the great accomplishment of the city-myth was to transform the pain and complexity of the fiscal crisis into a simple, uplifting lesson: the "New York model" of civic liberalism had died, and in its place a *New York model of neoliberalism* had rightfully arisen. Through a combination of marketing and pro-business restructuring, this model has been successfully branded, forever changing the image and material reality of New York City, and providing a powerful base from which the neoliberal ideology could spread its wings and rise nationally and internationally in the coming decades.

In the remainder of this chapter, I will critically assess some of the complex legacies of neoliberal New York. First, I will look at the rising fortunes of key members of the original branding coalition that formed in the 1970s and benefited from neoliberal restructuring, including financial and real estate elites, the media industry, and the new middle class. Following this, I will address the more pernicious effects of this restructuring—from rising poverty and income inequality to a decline in affordable housing—as well as emergent political strategies that are confronting these effects. Ultimately, I hope that this analysis will contribute to a more balanced understanding of New York City's recent history and of the ramifications of this history for New York and other cities in the present day.

Winning the New York City Power Game: The Branding Coalition in the 1980s

By the 1980s there was a new degree of coordination between the various groups that had come together in the 1970s to form New York's branding coalition. These included the finance, real estate, and tourism elites, the new middle class, the culture industries, and the entrepreneurial city and state governments. With the immediate crisis averted, the specter of Fear City no longer haunted the elites, and the urgency to mobilize behind all-encompassing marketing campaigns dissipated. Nonetheless, the strategies and alliances created in that period of rupture lived on, in combination with broader shifts in New York's class structure, and in the attitude of its elected officials.

Public–Private Partnership

The New York City Partnership (NYCP) was the ideal podium for President Reagan to use to proclaim the dawning of a new era. According to the NYCP's annual report of 1981, Reagan viewed the organization as "America's most influential private sector group concerned with improving economic and social conditions in urban America."[4] This was because NYCP represented, as David Rockefeller put it, "a new model for social problem-solving" in the 1980s. Public–private partnerships served as channels through which public funds and corporate donations could flow into urban economic development now that welfare state programs were discredited.[5]

This notion of "partnership," and the VIP breakfast at which it was unveiled to the nation, was clearly influenced by the pioneering work of ABNY.[6] Yet, unlike this earlier model, NYCP avoided PR stunts and marketing campaigns, focusing instead on behind-the-scenes lobbying to influence policy and budget decisions, and on securing financing for large-scale real estate development projects. This shift in focus reflected the fact that a good deal of marketing had now been taken over by city and state government, and was itself fully integrated within overall strategies of economic development. By 1986, the New York State Department of Commerce endorsed I♥NY as the official slogan for all of its operations, linking it to broader efforts like "Made in NY," and launching nationwide commercials showing the state's pro-business, low-tax credentials. At the New York City level, Ed Koch, the self-proclaimed "booster mayor," trumpeted his pro-business philosophy to the press at every opportunity, as in the following interview in *Business Week* in 1984: "The job of government is to provide a climate for jobs and business . . . You need business to feel that they are not the enemy."[7]

In the Koch and Cuomo era, marketing no longer led economic development, but became seamlessly integrated into a broader, unapologetically business-focused appeal. Moving beyond the populist strategy of the Big Apple and I♥NY campaigns, the city's new Office of Economic Development and the state's Department of Economic Development (formerly the Department of Commerce) used ever-greater financial incentives to promote the city's new "climate" for business and investment.[8] Significantly, the representational universe of the campaigns also shifted. In a survey of all Wells, Rich, Greene ads for I♥NY from the 1980s, the dominant iconography for New York City now was limited to the skyline and landmarks of Manhattan, the lights of Broadway, and glamorous dining and shopping, while ads featuring Broadway performers, Big Apple lapel pins, and other signs of solidarity with the city were abandoned. Such images now formed a generic backdrop to the city's star attraction: billions of dollars in tax breaks and subsidies for real estate development, tourism, and corporate retention, and by 1983, lavish new accommodations for meetings and conventions at the Javitz Center.[9]

Rapid real estate development, in turn, generated its own flurry of media attention. Former city councilman Franz Leichter remembered the attitude of city leaders at the time:

> Real estate provided a visible sign of development. You could see buildings go up, the ground-breaking ceremonies, the major press conferences broadcasting what was going on. Industrial parks, small business, economic development monies to deal with broader impediments to economic development like the need for transportation infrastructure and better education—these were more laborious and time-consuming solutions. There was no immediate gratification . . . The idea was let's get buildings up fast and let's spur development without regard to whether the subsidy was needed or could have been used in a more beneficial way.[10]

Leichter noted that the city and state governments' new priorities were part of a broader "current" first articulated by Housing Commissioner Roger

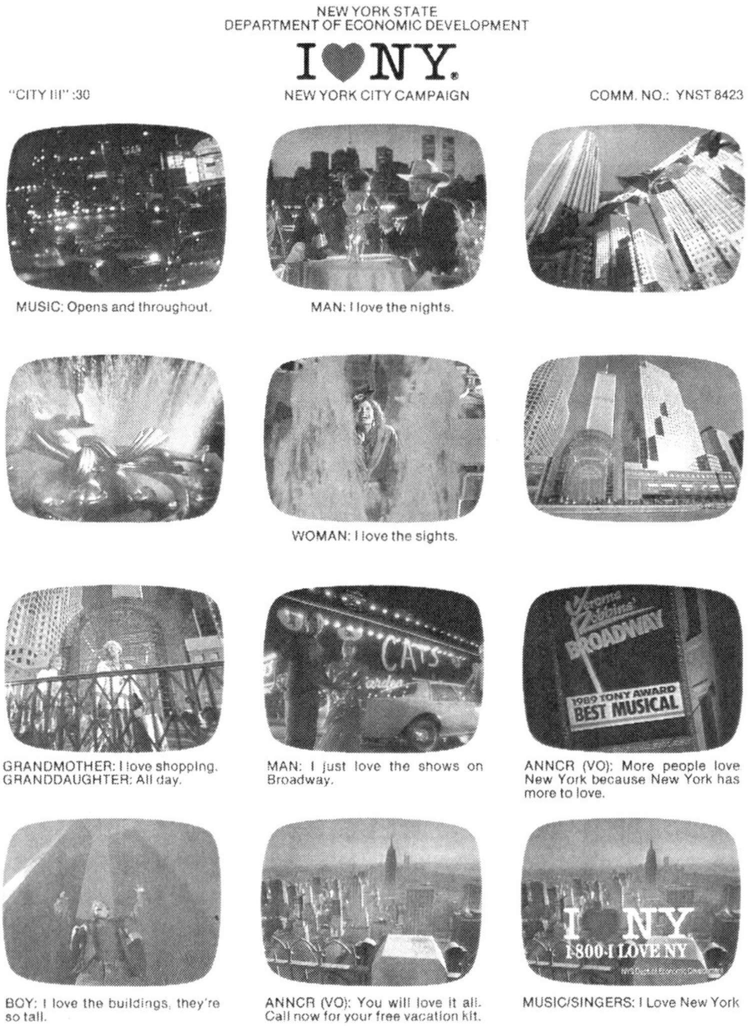
NEW YORK STATE
DEPARTMENT OF ECONOMIC DEVELOPMENT
I ♥ NY.
"CITY III" :30
NEW YORK CITY CAMPAIGN
COMM. NO.: YNST 8423
MUSIC: Opens and throughout.
MAN: I love the nights.
WOMAN: I love the sights.
GRANDMOTHER: I love shopping.
GRANDDAUGHTER: All day.
MAN: I just love the shows on Broadway.
CATS
BROADWAY
1989 TONY AWARD BEST MUSICAL
ANNCR (VO): More people love New York because New York has more to love.
BOY: I love the buildings, they're so tall.
ANNCR (VO): You will love it all. Call now for your free vacation kit.
I NY
1-800-I LOVE NY
MUSIC/SINGERS: I Love New York

Figure 8.2 The I♥NY campaign of the 1980s.
As the campaign evolved, the emphasis shifted from one of personal connection to New York, as inspired by Broadway stars, to one of sheer awe at the city's entertainment, shopping, and real estate, as inspired by tourists.
Courtesy Empire State Development Corporation

Starr—that "the city had to ignore poor and working-class people and attract more affluent people."[11] As Leichter observed, "It's not that subsidies didn't exist before; it's that they tended to go to the middle and working class," as in the famed Mitchell–Lama middle-income housing development program and tax abatements for industrial and commercial development. Now, through amendments to city and state housing and economic development law, public subsidies were redirected to developers building office towers, condominiums, and other "luxury buildings."[12] In opposition to this trend, Leichter and a "small band" of political critics fought for urban planning that would address the "overall economic conditions" affecting small business, the manufacturing sector, and access to quality education and housing for low- and middle-income New Yorkers, rather than "ad hoc development" that responded to the demands of particular corporations and developers.[13] But the status of middle- and working-class constituencies was no longer as powerful as it once had been, and not nearly as influential as the "voice of the business community" had become. So, beginning in the late 1970s and continuing through the 1980s, critics were sidelined, and gifts to the private sector mounted. These gifts, and the marketing packages in which they were wrapped, facilitated the rise of a spectacular new complex of corporate headquarters, hotels, restaurants, elite residences, luxury shops, and entertainment spaces serving the needs of out-of-towners and the wealthy, and enhancing the visibility and brand value of Manhattan-based global firms.

The Tourism, Finance, and Media Boom of the 1980s

As one local newspaper put it as early as 1978, the city was "quietly becoming [a] world tourist haven," and the trend increased over the course of the 1980s.[14] Business travelers, convention-goers, and international tourists— the three tourism segments that spent the most and stayed the longest— began arriving in ever-greater numbers during the 1980s.[15] And to greet them, the number of new luxury hotels and tourism facilities increased significantly during this period. The sudden glut of rooms meant that hotel occupancy rates grew only slightly, but visitor numbers and spending rose appreciably (see Table 7.1, p. 215 above).

Meanwhile, as John Dyson predicted in 1977, the "more visible and positive commodity" of tourism led the way to broader business development. The newly branded tourist image of New York City, combined with the enhanced business climate promoted by both city and state, banished the "asphalt jungle" stereotype and the city's reputation as a "working-class city." This enticed not only tourists but investors, CEOs, and the upper middle class to return to the city in climbing numbers.

Leading the way was New York's financial and banking sector, which saw unprecedented growth and profit in the wake of the fiscal crisis period.[16] Whereas in 1970 New York City had 47 banks with assets of $10 billion, by 1985 it had 191 banks with assets of $238 billion, employing 27,000 people.[17] Concomitantly, New York was able to maintain its total share of US banking assets, while steadily increasing its share of foreign deposits in US banks, and its number of branches for foreign banks. Most importantly for this sector, by the mid-1980s, New York City-based firms held a quarter of the assets of the world's 130 largest institutional investors, and the city became the headquarters for a quarter of all major US securities firms.[18]

The city's growing cluster of media and culture industries also benefited from this new climate.[19] In the same way that WRG and *New York* had exploited the institutional matrix of media and marketing in New York City in the previous decade, corporate media and advertising firms of the 1980s exploited their proximity to the growing finance, tourism, and real estate sectors. According to one study, New York City accounted for 20 percent of national employment in "information-intensive industries" in this period, and had a higher ratio of such employment than any other cities except for Washington and Boston.[20] As Saskia Sassen noted at the time, New York City's agglomeration of high-end services countered the conventional wisdom that with the rise of faster, global communication networks, and the off-shoring of production, corporations and services would not need to cluster, and would quickly flee the high rents, expenses, and congestion of big cities.[21] As it turned out, while this calculation still applied for the older manufacturing-based economy, it did not for the new "information economy." In the latter, highly specialized "producer services" became embedded in "value-added processes of production," and companies needed various specialists—such as those in high-technology and creative fields— to remain close at hand. Thus, the specialized knowledge and creativity necessary for innovation and coordination within the media industry "[heightened] the importance of traditional centers," and helped spur the growth of technically and socially networked "global cities."[22] New York City in the 1980s was a leader among global cities, becoming an international media and finance capital in a new, more integrated way.

Business services took advantage of media's growth, becoming deeply involved in film, TV, and new media activities at many levels. Banks began taking equity positions in media and entertainment ventures, accounting firms began creating entertainment or media divisions, and investment houses began handling media- and entertainment-related stocks and bond offerings on a far larger scale.[23] By the late 1980s, with the stock market crash and the onset of recession, media and entertainment caught up with business services to become New York's fastest-growing sector, and its firms some of the biggest political and economic actors in the city.

In addition to the merging of media with business services, this period was one of mergers between media and marketing firms. Advertisers and market researchers established a variety of strategic, financial, and creative linkages with the media corporations that their clients could access. This transformed the production of media, from broadcasting to publishing, and from news to entertainment, as new marketing techniques like product placement and branding increasingly blurred the line between original editorial/creative content and advertising. Media and marketing were now considered to be part of the same field, and came to influence all other cultural industries with which they interacted—in particular business services, tourism, and entertainment.

A prime example of this increased convergence was the rapid rise in the early 1980s of Bloomberg LP, a company at the vanguard of both information media and the use of branding and marketing to extend a name across media platforms. After being released from Solomon Brothers following a merger at that company, CEO Michael Bloomberg used his $10 million severance package, plus a $30 million investment from Merrill Lynch, to start his financial media company. This grew rapidly into a multifaceted enterprise providing real-time financial and business data, data analysis, as well as television and radio programs—understanding that global distribution networks were as important as content in this new age. Meanwhile, Bloomberg ensured that every component, interface, network, and media product would be proprietary and carry the Bloomberg brand name. The success of this strategy, in addition to the competitive pressure posed by transnational giants like Rupert Murdoch's News Corporation, inspired a new scale of media mergers in the late 1980s (for example, the Time–Warner and NBC–Cablevision mergers). This trend would dramatically accelerate in the 1990s, as deregulation and privatization of media became even more sweeping, and as New York City became the headquarters capital for global corporate media.

The Bloodless Revolution: the Triumph of the "New Middle Class"

The broader shift in New York City's economic mix in the late 1970s and early 1980s was reflected in its emerging social hierarchy, which now included the media and culture industries in its upper ranks, alongside the old guard of finance and real estate. The editors and journalists of New York, having chronicled the changing dynamics of the city's "power game" in the magazine's New Year issues since the late 1960s, noted this shift with great interest, especially since it signaled their own ascendancy and that of their aspiring, "new middle-class" readers.[24] At the same time, they noted how the shift entailed the city's increasing corporatization and its greater beholdence to bond-holders and bankers.

Ken Auletta captured this transformation in the last of the annual power-game cover stories published by New York in 1977. The cover headline read, "After the Bloodless Revolution: The New Power Game," and was personified by an enormous, angry, white, baby boy toppling skyscrapers like

Godzilla.[25] The thrust of Auletta's article was the unobstructed rise to dominance of a new class, and the city's radical shift in priorities to suit its needs. He observed: "The bloodless revolution . . . slipped in like the fog . . . New York City, which used to be preoccupied with helping the poor, is now preoccupied with winning investor confidence."[26] He then quoted a range of experts to make his point, including David Burke, secretary to Governor Carey, who admitted bluntly, "The people we've been appealing to throughout this crisis are not so much the voters as the investors." Labor mediator and "astute observer of power" Theodore Kheel summed up the situation as follows:

> What we have witnessed is fantastic . . . There was a period where what was done in the city was based on what was good for the blacks. Earlier, it was based on what was good for the immigrants. Now the question is what is good for the bond market. We have seen—in the welfare capital of the world—the bond market take control of the fiscal policies of the city with no opposition. During this period when the liberals' structure was being dismantled, liberals were silent because they did not know what to say.[27]

As the old guard slipped into the ether of back-room deals, and as the "liberals" remained silent or were marginalized, the "New Society" was finding footholds with which to climb. And climb they did. In the boom years between the late 1970s and mid-1980s, many of this new middle class entered the ranks of "upper professionals." Whereas salaried professionals and managers represented only 5 percent of New York's working population from the nineteenth to the mid-twentieth century, by the mid-1980s they represented an astonishing 30 percent of the labor force, and formed a new "dominant class."[28] This largely white, disproportionately male stratum benefited directly from the city's embrace of a neoliberal strategy of development. They filled the high-skilled jobs of the financial and information-based economy the city was courting. They received tax breaks for renovating lofts and starting new businesses. And they became the core constituency for the victorious electoral coalitions—in the Koch and Giuliani administrations—that were faithfully to reflect their interests.

The Uneven Landscape of "Recovery"

One of the most startling news stories about New York City to emerge in the early 1980s was one that many New Yorkers today might take for granted: the fact that 25 percent of the city's population now lived in poverty. Emmanuel Tobier, a researcher from New York University, first sparked public awareness of this phenomenon in a 1984 report commissioned by the non-partisan Community Service Society, and entitled "The Changing Face of Poverty." The report began, "For far too many people, the city has been transformed from a place of opportunity and hope to one of want and hopelessness. While New York remains a city of gold for those at the top of the economic ladder, it has become a city of despair for many elderly, for the homeless, for women and children barely subsisting on public welfare."[29] It went on to describe the conditions that led to its main finding: by 1982, one in four New Yorkers were living below the federally mandated poverty line (of $10,178 a year for a family of four).[30]

The report went to great lengths to frame the unprecedented nature of this statistic. While poverty had risen nationally since 1970, Tobier noted, in New York a "sharp rise" began in the early 1970s, continued through the decade, and spiked upwards between 1979 and 1984. This pushed the poverty rate in New York City for both individuals and families above that of the nation to a degree not seen since such statistics began to be kept in the post-war period (see Figure 8.3). It made New York's economy look more similar to other large, post-industrial cities like Detroit, Los Angeles, and Philadelphia than to the nation as a whole.[31] What's more, this occurred after a thirty-year national trend of steadily declining poverty rates, increased median incomes, and a growing middle class across all racial and ethnic groups—trends which had lifted the fortunes of New Yorkers, on average, more than Americans as a whole. These improvements were, by most accounts, the result of national factors and policies of which New York was a major beneficiary: a robust post-war economy, progressive taxes, and, by the 1960s, the targeted programs of the Johnson administration's War on Poverty. Thus, in the four decades following World War II, the city's poverty rate declined at a steady rate almost always ahead of the national average, reaching a historic low of 12.4 percent for individuals and 11.5 percent for families, down from an individual rate of 16 percent in 1959, and from an estimated 26 percent in 1947.

These gains were effectively erased in just over a decade. By 1984, the rate reached 25 percent—9 percent higher than the nation as a whole, and roughly equivalent to rates of half a century earlier.[32] This increase occurred, meanwhile, despite the simultaneous outmigration of 800,000 New Yorkers in the same period—indicating how entrenched this new poverty was becoming.[33] It occurred almost exclusively in black and Latino neighborhoods outside of increasingly wealthy, white enclaves of Midtown Manhattan and the Upper West and East sides, indicating the highly uneven social geography that was emerging.[34] And, in what was also a new trend, poverty was now concentrated among non-elderly New Yorkers—that is, working-age single adults, and female-headed households—indicating the extent to which factors like joblessness, family breakdown, and lack of childcare support were exacerbating the problem. This led to the "startling" statistic that approximately 50 percent of New York City children were poor in 1984, compared to 20 percent only a decade earlier.[35] "Without massive intervention," Tobier warned, "it is probable that this unfortunate trend will continue throughout the 1980s."[36]

And so it did. For the next two decades, in the absence of the "massive intervention" prescribed by Tobier, the poverty rate in New York City remained relatively constant, at between 20 and 25 percent of the population. This rate paralleled growth in poverty nationwide, though consistently at almost twice the national rate.[37] This illuminated the fact that the rise of the "new economy" in New York was accompanied not only by increasing and exceptional wealth but by increasing and exceptional poverty, and, thus, a dramatic widening of the class divide.

This dynamic first became apparent in the early 1980s, and was characterized by scholars at the time as the "dual city" phenomenon.[38] Since then, this thesis has been confirmed. Much like the extremes of wealth and poverty that occurred at the height of New York's "Gilded Age" in the late nineteenth century, sharp differentials in earnings coincided precisely with the "boom years" of 1977–1987. New York's wealthiest 10 percent saw their incomes grow over 20 percent, and accounted for a third of all income gains of that

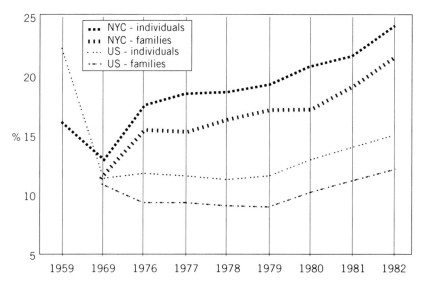

Figure 8.3 Percentage of individuals and families living in poverty in the United States and New York City, 1959, 1969, and 1976–1982.

Source: Tobier, "The Changing Face of Poverty"; Horton and Brecher, *Setting Municipal Priorities 1986*.

decade, while the top 20 percent accounted for half of such gains. Meanwhile, the poorest 20 percent saw their incomes decline by 17.5 percent over the same period, and found themselves worse off not only relative to wealthier people but even when compared to their own earnings a decade earlier.[39]

How can we explain growing poverty alongside New York's "recovery" and expanding wealth? To answer this question I will turn to three factors that I have touched on throughout this book, and that were central components of the economic restructuring that accompanied urban branding in the 1970s. The first was the reorientation of the public sector, and with it the cutbacks in services and subsidies aimed at low- and moderate-income New Yorkers. Related to this, the second factor involved the privatization and deregulation of the city's housing market, which, in combination with city marketing, led to rapidly escalating monopoly rents and a housing crisis for many New Yorkers. The third factor was an economic development strategy focused on attracting corporations and high-end services, rather than supporting a more mixed economic base, which led to declining incomes as well as rising unemployment for many working- and middle-class New Yorkers.

Reorienting the Public Sector

When New York's 24 percent poverty rate was first "brought to light" at a City Council hearing, with the publication of Tobier's report, the news immediately led to a rebuke by the Koch administration. According to the Office of Finance and Economic Development: "it did not represent the position of the administration, which has been emphasizing economic gains in recent months."[40] Some detractors echoed Roger Starr's critique of the mid-1970s: that the city was simply attracting too many poor people from other places in search of welfare. Taking something of a middle road, Mayor Koch acknowledged the problem uncovered by the report, but attributed it entirely to federal-level welfare cutbacks by the Reagan administration, stating, "I am happy that the city's economy is getting stronger, but we cannot make up on the local level for federal massive reductions."[41]

There was some truth to these contentions. The city was still grappling with the needs of new immigrants from the Caribbean, brought to New York through Operation Bootstrap in the 1960s to fill industrial-era jobs that were fast disappearing. And the federal government under Reagan was indeed tightening restrictions in the provision of core anti-poverty programs like Aid to Families with Dependent Children, Food Stamps, CETA, and Medicaid. But as was beginning to become apparent, the problem of growing poverty and inequality in New York City was not merely something imported from outside or imposed from above. Rather, it was a problem that this newly restructured city was itself producing. First and foremost, the city's new, market-oriented approach entailed a radical change in the function of the urban public sector—one similar to, and no less significant than, the change simultaneously occurring at the federal level. It is worth emphasizing that this approach did not necessarily involve "reductions" in public spending, as Koch said, but rather the *reorientation* of such spending in a new direction, and in the name of new priorities.[42] In the wake of the New York City fiscal crisis, government moved away from its traditional role as manager of public welfare and "collective consumption" resources like housing, recreation, and education. All of these were now subject to severe cutbacks in the name of austerity. At the same time, government focused considerable energy and resources in two main areas. First, spending was targeted at enhancing the city's "quality of life"—and the perception of quality of life—for the new middle class, corporations, and tourists. Such spending was increasingly supplemented and governed by the above-mentioned public-private partnerships formed in the 1970s, and entailed increased spending—particularly for the city center—on policing and security, parks and sanitation, graffiti removal, and marketing. Related to this, the city sought to stimulate private sector economic growth, particularly on behalf of high-end services and real estate, through deregulation, tax cuts, and privatization. As Susan Fainstein put it, under Mayor Koch, "The achievement of economic growth and fiscal solvency was substituted for service provision as the test of government legitimacy."[43]

Meanwhile, the mentality of crisis came to prevail in the social policy arena, even during boom times. In 1986, Eric Lichten labeled this phenomenon the "austerity state," in which class relations based on the "conditions of crisis, selective scarcity, and corporate domination" that prevailed in the mid-1970s were "institutionalized as austerity" for future generations.[44] Thus, city funds cut from social programs and public housing during the fiscal crisis were never fully restored, even when growing tax revenues from tourism and real estate led to budget surpluses, leading government to cede its role in whole or in part as a provider of such services. This shift created a special burden for lower-income New Yorkers, who could not so easily switch over to services provided by the private sector, as many wealthier New Yorkers did, once their classrooms became overcrowded, their housing deteriorated, or their neighborhood pools and recreation centers shut down.[45] Over time, this increasing public divestment and privatization undermined the city's culture of civic liberalism and chipped away at what were previously considered "public goods" and "entitlements."

Housing, Homelessness, and Monopoly Rents

Housing is another area in which neoliberal restructuring has adversely affected the working and middle classes in New York City. Sky-rocketing rents have been one of the most spectacular indicators of "economic growth" over the past three decades, with median gross rents shooting up 700 percent between 1970 and 1999.[46] During the same period, similar increases have occurred in the value of New York City commercial and residential real estate overall. One leading factor is the growth of what David Harvey has called "monopoly rents"—the amount of rent that can be earned based on claims to the distinctiveness of a location.[47] The increase in public and private sector investments in central city infrastructure, policing and security, and tourism marketing has contributed to the rise in such monopoly claims. This has occurred alongside a constant campaign of rent deregulation and the rezoning of poor and working-class neighborhoods to stimulate gentrification and new investment.

Meanwhile, since the early 1970s, little significant investment has been made in public or affordable housing at the city, state, or federal level. Predictably, the city's existing stock of affordable housing has been seriously eroded. Whereas in 1970 there was a *surplus* of 270,000 units of affordable housing, by 1999 there was a *shortage* of some 390,000 apartments.[48] This has lead to chronic overcrowding in what remains of the city's affordable housing, as well as a rise in the phenomenon now known as "modern homelessness." Much like the initial reactions to Emmanuel Tobier's findings on the sudden appearance of widespread poverty in the early 1980s, the

Figure 8.4 Homeless people sleep beneath the shelter of the Visitors Information Center, 1991.

New York Daily News

recent origins of the seemingly eternal problem of homelessness may be surprising to some. This was noted in a 2002 report by New York's Coalition of the Homeless:

> An old saying tells us that "the poor are always with us." However, regardless of the wisdom of that time-worn phrase, it is decidedly untrue about the homeless poor. While homelessness is certainly not a new phenomenon in the United States or in New York City, where it dates back to at least the colonial era, there is no question that *modern homelessness* is a unique historical occurrence. Indeed, one must go back to the Great Depression to find another period in New York history when homelessness was such a routine, persistent, visible feature of urban life . . . From the end of World War II until the late 1970s it was a rare sight, outside of familiar "skid row" precincts like the Bowery, to see New Yorkers sleeping in the streets and other public spaces, or to witness tens of thousands of children and their families cycling each year through emergency shelters and welfare hotels.[49]

The crucial turning point in the rise of homelessness in New York City occurred in 1979, ironically at the beginning of the city's so-called "economic recovery." Since that year, when an unprecedented 2,000 people were tallied in New York City shelters, the scale of homelessness has increased dramatically.[50] In 2004, the average number of homeless New Yorkers living in shelters each night reached 36,930, the highest figure in the city's history.[51] In the intervening years, figures trended upwards, with spikes occurring during the "boom times" of the late 1980s and late 1990s.[52] In addition to falling real incomes for the poor, this reflected the escalating cost of buying and renting living space that occurred during these flush times, combined with the seemingly permanent state of austerity imposed on the city's spending for homeless services and affordable housing. In this sense, homeless figures were the tip of the iceberg, an extreme indicator of a much broader housing crisis in the city. Rising numbers of low- and moderate-income New Yorkers began spending increasing portions of their incomes on rent and mortgage payments, and were pushed ever further away from the city center or forced to leave the city altogether.

Restructuring the Economic Base

Another way in which New York City's chosen path of economic development exacerbated poverty and inequality was through the active restructuring of the city's job market. As New York's economy became increasingly dependent upon white-collar services, it shifted away from the city's traditional mix of industrial, commercial, public, and service sector jobs. While broader national and global forces undoubtedly contributed to this transformation, these forces were carefully "propagated" and directed by local politics.[53] For instance, eminent domain and blight laws were used to turn still-thriving downtown industrial zones into luxury housing, loft developments, and financial districts—eliminating tens of thousands of manufacturing jobs that otherwise might have remained. At the same time, the formidable tactics of the crisis regime were brought to bear on the once influential public sector unions, further undercutting their political power and wages.

The white-collar, service sector jobs that were created, meanwhile, were insufficient to replace the hundreds of thousands of relatively well-paid, mostly unionized, blue-collar jobs lost over the previous decade. In what may be considered an early instance of the "jobless recovery" phenomenon noted in subsequent decades, few jobs were created by the city's vaunted "economic growth," which was measured in terms of profits earned, rather than levels of employment and income. A dramatic example of this was the tourism sector, in which healthy job growth would have been expected given the consistent growth in visitor spending. Yet the trend identified in Chapters 6 and 7, in which rising revenues were accompanied by lay-offs and consolidation, continued through this period. Meanwhile, the new service jobs that were created were increasingly polarized—concentrated at the very high and the very low ends of the skill and income spectrums—while entry-level jobs required training that had not been necessary in the industrial era. As a result, Tobier noted in 1984, "in the last two years the city has gained 141,000 jobs, but mostly in businesses that require white collar skills that many poor do not have."[54]

Jobs in these image-sensitive service industries were also highly susceptible to the volatility of global markets and consumer taste, and more prone to downturns and lay-offs. This meant that New York's economy, with its growing dependence on these industries, also became more unstable, suffering greater and longer-term damage during downturns and recessions than did the nation as a whole. Those laid off from low-end service jobs, with less of a financial cushion, suffered most from these downturns.

And so, with a bifurcated service economy, and with the decline in unionized blue-collar and public sector jobs, the city saw its middle and working classes shrink and extreme wealth and poverty grow. This polarizing trend was only to intensify over the coming decades.

Opportunities in the New Economy

New York's job picture for the working and middle classes has not been entirely bleak since the fiscal crisis. Given the reorientation of the public sector noted above, funding for municipal employment did not actually shrink in the long run, but rather was redeployed functionally and geographically. For instance, while jobs in recreation, job training centers, and higher education were cut, particularly in the outer boroughs, ranks have continued to swell in criminal justice, economic development, and the Port Authority, particularly in Manhattan. And despite considerable losses to privatization, as well as the ever-present threat of New York's Taylor Law, which makes it illegal for public sector workers to strike, a number of municipal unions have successfully fought to maintain positions, wages, and benefits.

Meanwhile, important new opportunities arose to organize workers in the private sector—particularly in heavily branded, globally networked service sector industries like tourism, healthcare, communications, security, and real estate. As some unions understood, these industries were heavily invested in their presence in New York City, and could not simply move offshore once labor demands increased. In addition, the concentration of ownership in ever-fewer hands, combined with the concentration of workers in larger and more global companies, was a boon for labor unions as it increased the potential scale of organizing campaigns, and the degree of leverage which such coordinated campaigns could wield over employers.

Thus, in the decades of restructuring following the New York fiscal crisis, visionary unions seized opportunities to organize workers, particularly in core public sector areas and in the service industries. Yet it remains the case overall that New York City labor, and the working class more broadly, has a long way to go to regain the political, economic, and cultural power it wielded during the heyday of the immediate post-war era.

Who Has the Right to the City?

Alongside the rise in monopoly rents and the widening class divide, New York City has become an unparalleled site of urban commodification. Beginning in the 1980s, traditionally bohemian and working-class neighborhoods in the Lower East Side, SoHo, and Brooklyn began to be gentrified, pricing out the artists and long-time residents who had made these neighborhoods distinct, hip, and desirable for investors. By the 1990s, New York's most famous public spaces—from Times Square to Fifth Avenue to Central Park—had grown increasingly privatized, corporatized, and surveilled. As "quality-of-life" policing increased throughout the city, and as the value of New York City real estate sky-rocketed, so too did penalties for certain forms of artistic and political expression—from parades and protests to street art and graffiti.[55] Meanwhile, policies governing the public display of advertising and other forms of commercial expression were loosened considerably. The city's contradictory stance only intensified the struggles over public space and representational power that we first saw emerge in the 1970s.

We are reminded that the branding of New York in this earlier era, and its legacy over the proceeding decades, was not simply a process of symbolic commodification. Rather, it entailed a two-pronged effort to transform New York's image as a product in the minds of its targeted consumers, while pursuing economic development strategies that prioritized the interests of business, real estate, bond-holders, tourists, the new middle class, and elites over those of low- and moderate-income New Yorkers and the working class.

New York's public and private sector leadership claimed that the rapid growth and good publicity generated from this dual strategy would act like a giant "sparkplug," improving the lot of the city as a whole. And in some ways it did—generating certain types of jobs, boosting morale for many, and improving security. These benefits may be measured in the rising value of New York City bonds and real estate, the growth of the corporate head-quarters complex and service sector, the declining crime rate, and the rebound of the tax base.

Yet as poverty rose, the middle class shrank, and the city became a prohibitively expensive place in which to live, it also became clear that this sparkplug was incapable of generating the kind of broad-based urban development that would benefit all or even most New Yorkers. In the meantime, a rift developed between the interests of residents and "out-of-towners," one that mapped onto and intensified existing class tensions. At best, city branding papered over this rift; at worst, it exacerbated it, projecting a dominant image of New York from which far too many actual New Yorkers felt excluded—in cultural, political, and economic terms.

Some may justify these problems as a price worth paying for the city's remarkable comeback. Yet such rationales avoid important questions about the path not taken. Would New York City have rebounded from the fiscal crisis for other reasons associated with its global city status? And, in any case, could its rebound have been even greater, more evenly distributed, and more sustainable had the city chosen a different strategy of recovery? What might New York City look like today, for instance, if a democratic process rather than business-led crisis regime had governed its redevelopment? If the bene-fits had been spread more evenly across the five boroughs, and targeted the neediest communities, rather than concentrated at the center and focused on those already well-off? If a mixed economy had been safeguarded, rather than jettisoned for one dependent upon finance, real estate, and tourism? And if, over the last thirty years, the city had prioritized investments in social services, public infrastructure, and affordable housing, rather than corporate subsidies, "quality-of-life" enhancement, and city marketing?

We will, of course, never know the answers to these hypothetical questions, or resolve these counterfactual histories. But the alternative possibilities to which they point are very much worth considering as we continue to grapple with the legacies of an urban development path laid out in the 1970s, and with the broader national and global influence of the New York City model of neoliberalism.

As a range of urbanists and activists now argue, it is possible to pursue more just and equitable paths of urban development in which the use versus exchange value of cities is prioritized, and in which the interests and needs of all "city users" more fully coincide.[56] To this end, urban citizens in New York City and beyond are proposing new approaches that give local communities and workers a greater voice in the running of their city, a greater share of its economic benefits, and a greater role in the shaping of its dominant cultural representations. What's more, they are finding opportunities and developing new tactics for organizing in this context. So, in closing, I will briefly discuss some arenas in which people are taking on the contradictions of the branded metropolis, and in so doing asserting what Henri Lefebvre famously called the "right to the city."[57] These arenas include: the struggle for affordable housing; new approaches to labor organizing; worker- and resident-centered tourism strategies; and equitable forms of arts and cultural development.

Since the 1980s, local groups in cities from Philadelphia to New Orleans to New York, faced with similar housing crises, have mobilized in creative ways to address the need for affordable housing. Much of this work has taken a preservationist form—protecting existing stocks of public and subsidized housing created in the era of the welfare state—or has gone in more collectivist directions—as in the case of housing cooperatives and reclamations of vacant or abandoned land and housing.[58] Alongside such neighborhood- and policy-specific efforts, some have attempted to address the issue on a wider scale, pushing for increased public investment in the preservation and new development of housing, the elimination of subsidies to luxury development, and the shoring up and expansion of rent regulations.[59] Most recently, advocates have fought for "inclusionary zoning" provisions in municipal charters, which ask developers to set aside a certain percentage of new development for affordable housing in exchange for bonuses.[60] Such zoning ordinances are still voluntary and narrow, and many argue that until they are mandatory and wide they will not be effective at developing a critical base of new housing.[61] Nonetheless, the move to a city-wide scale of organizing in recent years is an important direction for advancing housing rights.

In the realm of labor, as noted above, innovative service-sector unions based in branded global cities have found new opportunities for organizing workers, gaining leverage at the bargaining table, and launching broader economic justice campaigns. One union that adapted well to this situation was the Service Employees International Union (SEIU), which has grown most powerfully in global cities like New York, Los Angeles, and Houston. For instance, SEIU's Property Services Division, representing security guards and cleaners in large office and residential buildings, grasped early on that the same major real estate owners and service contractors have a presence in a variety of global cities., and so developed national and even international campaigns to pressure these employers to improve standards for workers in their various properties. And in New York, SEIU has taken advantage of the city's effort to brand itself and its buildings as safe post 9/11, launching "New York Safe and Secure," a successful campaign for better training, wages, and working conditions for security guards in these buildings.

Similarly, the ever-growing urban tourist industry—quintessentially place-based and image-sensitive—has provided new opportunities for organized labor and local residents. HERE, the union representing hotel and restaurant employees, has launched and won simultaneous organizing and living-wage campaigns in numerous cities, and recently created a powerful national agency, Inmex, to help plan big meetings that support unionized hotels.[62] Meanwhile, in an effort to gain more control over tourism jobs and dollars in post-hurricane New Orleans, local communities have developed grassroots strategies of "tourism from below" that rival tourism strategies generated by elite growth coalitions who concentrate their efforts and profits at the city center.[63] With such examples in mind, scholars of tourism argue that both urban "citizens and visitors" may benefit from the growth of this outwardly focused industry.[64] In the best-case scenario, local citizens can benefit from the quality-of-life improvements, cultural amenities, and jobs that are created to attract global visitors. Visitors, meanwhile, can benefit from high-quality public services like transportation, education, and parks; and from the knowledge that their dollars are helping to support living wages, benefits, and cultural continuity for workers and residents.

A final arena of organizing and scholarship concerns locally based arts and cultural development. As we have seen, these creative forces are now typically used by real estate developers to stimulate gentrification and raise monopoly rents, thus displacing the diverse communities that revalorized their neighborhoods in the first place. With this in mind, the most successful and sustainable forms of arts and cultural development are ones integrally tied to the creation of permanent, affordable housing for artists and other residents, as well as of semi-autonomous public spaces like community centers, galleries, and schools. And so a new wave of urban planners now argues against "export-oriented" models of cultural development—those targeting tourists through official, centralized "arts districts"—showing the greater benefits of "consumption-based" strategies that foster cultural districts throughout the city run by and for local artists and audiences, and that include subsidized artist housing and neighborhood-based art centers.[65] The latter produce dollars that circulate in the local economy as well as locally rooted cultural forms and scenes (which also, unsurprisingly, become a significant draw for tourists).[66]

These emerging approaches to urban sociology, planning and activism highlight the need to expand our conception of urban citizenship, and to link it to real campaigns on the ground. While of limited power on their own, a combination of such approaches is needed if we are to make sense of and confront the effects of the branded city. This is a city that has created new jobs, globalized its influence, and increased the potential profits that can be made through association with the urban image. Yet it is also a city that poses profound challenges to free expression and access to public space; to the availability of living-wage jobs and affordable housing; and to the power of everyday people to shape the direction and priorities of urban development. With its stark contradictions and sparkling façades, the branded metropolis provokes us to return to Lefebvre's question: "Who has the right to the city?" And it pushes us to ask a new question: "Who has a right to the image of the city, and, with it, to a shared vision of the city's future?"

Re-branding the Wounded City

The catastrophic events of September 11, 2001 had a profound impact on the branded image of New York City. No one was more aware of this than Milton Glaser, the graphic designer who created the original I♥NY logo in 1977, at the nadir of the New York fiscal crisis. As Glaser recounts, "I woke up a couple days after 9/11 and said, 'You know, I♥NY just doesn't mean the same thing anymore after that.' And that's something that has to be understood." So he set to work to create a new logo and slogan for the city, one that could capture something of the feelings of those New Yorkers who lived through this tragedy. He came up with "I♥NY More Than Ever," which incorporated the logo from the original campaign but now with a small black mark on the bottom left side of the heart that approximated the site on the island of Manhattan where the attacks took place. He explained how the idea came to him:

> Because that was the effect it produced on me. The idea that suddenly this could happen to this giant of a city. A powerful giant is one thing. A vulnerable giant is much more loveable. Once we realized how vulnerable we were, all these people's hearts just opened. They said, "I love this place. This can't happen to us. We have to do something." So I did this thing.[1]

Glaser initially reached out to the Empire State Development Corporation (ESDC, formerly the Department of Commerce), which began the

Figure E.1 Milton Glaser's response to 9/11.

Courtesy Milton Glaser Studio

I♥NY campaign, to see if they would like to use his new design, but after two weeks he had still not heard back from them. So he took matters into his own hands and created his own pro-bono campaign. First, he took the design to the School of Visual Arts, where he teaches. He immediately received support from the school's director, located a printer to make 5,000 copies, and found a group of students to put them up in store windows all over the city. He then sent a copy to two colleagues from his *New York* magazine days, who were now on staff at the *Daily News*: journalist Pete Hammill and editor Ed Kosner. The very next day, they used the poster as the back page of the Sunday edition, for people to tear off and post themselves, thus instantly putting millions of copies on the streets. Glaser then donated copies to numerous charities and benefits, where the image was used as an effective fundraising device at a crucial time.[2] As with the original I♥NY of 1977, Glaser managed to create a design that channeled people's individual and collective feelings for their city in its hour of need. As he understood it: "Everybody felt the same way. Everybody felt hurt and the nature of that hurt was to make us feel more devoted to the city."[3]

The one group with whom Glaser's new design did not resonate, however, was its copyright holder, the ESDC. Unlike the early days of I♥NY, when the logo was purposely allowed to circulate to broaden its exposure, since the 1990s a new breed of brand management had chosen to take a different tack: copyrighting the image, standardizing its use, and vigilantly pursuing trademark-infringement cases.[4] This included a pro-bono campaign to raise money for the victims of 9/11 that was created by the original designer of I♥NY. Once the new logo was in wide circulation, as Glaser recalled, "a bureaucrat" from the ESDC called him up:

> He said, "We'd like to use your I♥NY More Than Ever. And I said, "Great, no charge." And he said, "The only thing is we'd like to take the black mark off the heart." I said, "No, no, you don't understand, that's the whole idea for the poster—we've been hurt." And he said, "No, we won't put a black mark on the heart." And I said, "Well, then, you can't use it" . . . [Two weeks later] I get a letter from the guy who was monitoring the appropriate use of I♥NY, a threatening letter saying that they're going to put me in jail if I don't show them all the receipts and how much money I made from this. This is illegal use of their logo, and so on. I couldn't believe it.[5]

Glaser then wrote a letter to Governor George Pataki and to the *New York Times* complaining about the matter. The ESDC dropped its charges, and Glaser dropped the campaign. The next week, David Catalfamo, ESDC's senior deputy commissioner, explained the position of his agency: "We think the heart of New York is bigger and stronger than ever. We don't want to show a damaged heart."[6] Instead ESDC launched two new campaigns: a 25th anniversary version of I♥NY, emphasizing Manhattan shopping and entertainment, and "New York Stronger Than Ever," accompanied by a red, white, and blue infinity symbol. As Glaser noted, "There's not a lot of poetry in politics or marketing."[7]

Debating the City Image

As I have documented in this book, it was in the 1970s that New York's immense representational power was first harnessed to project a standardized set of images of the city around the world, with repercussions far exceeding image makers' expectations or intentions. "Asphalt jungle" representations sparked political recrimination and exacerbated the city's fiscal crisis. Savvy lifestyle magazines and marketing campaigns reminded out-of-towners why they loved New York, and helped promote the city's broader "recovery." Graffiti that ran counter to such marketing came to have enormous influence on art scenes around the world, while at home it was criminalized to a degree not seen in other cities.

In the wake of the World Trade Center attacks, during New York's worst crisis since the 1970s, with the attention of the world again focused on the city, debates over the appropriate use of the city image grew similarly heated—as the above example makes clear. Many New Yorkers were concerned that these tragic events would be symbolically exploited for inappropriate political and/or economic ends. This concern was voiced only days after 9/11, when thousands of pro-peace New Yorkers put orange stickers in windows and on cars that read "Our Grief Is Not a Cry for War," in anticipation of the city's loss being used to justify a military response. The debate reached a new scale during the 2004 Republican National Convention, when the massive "counter-convention" protested and satirized the party's appropriation of New York City and 9/11 in myriad demonstrations throughout the city.[8] And the debate continues to this day over the design for a memorial at Ground Zero, and the appropriate mix of commercial real estate on the footprints of the former towers.

On the other hand, as in the 1970s, local political and economic elites were mainly concerned with restoring the city's "climate" for business and tourism. Only days after 9/11, Mayor Rudolph Giuliani and Governor Pataki called on all Americans to come to New York and spend money as a way of "restoring the symbol of the city." Once again, powerful public–private partnerships came together to guide the city's recovery efforts in a pro-business, marketing-led direction. In this case the goal was to "re-brand" the post-9/11 city, and to offer economic incentives to shoppers, tourists, and corporations tied in to September 11. The groups involved included: NYC&Co. (formerly the Convention and Visitors Bureau), ESDC, the New York City Partnership, the Association for a Better New York as well as the newly formed Lower Manhattan Development Corporation. With the assistance of major media and marketing firms, they convened new branding coalitions such as New York Rising and the Crisis Communications Committee. As reported in the *Wall Street Journal*, "for the city's official marketers New York isn't just a wounded city, but a challenged brand [and] like all challenged brands, it needs . . . an overarching scheme to reposition itself in the American popular consciousness."[9]

These "official marketers" debated how the re-branding of the World Trade Center site itself should be handled in these sensitive times. *Wall Street Journal* reporter Ruth Shalit divided these positions into two camps, the "pile fetishizers" and the "pile minimizers," with the former seeking to market quasi-spiritual pilgrimages to Ground Zero and the latter seeking to downplay the tragedy and focus on New York's victorious spirit.[10] A balance was tentatively struck, with efforts to emphasize the city's unflagging strength and patriotism in the face of tragedy, while also capitalizing on the flood of sympathy evoked by the attack. But ultimately the balance shifted towards the pile minimizers. ESDC did help fund a multi-million-dollar "Ground Zero Viewing Platform" on Church Street to accommodate the thousands of visitors and locals that traveled there to see the site, but it also carefully steered clear of any overt reference to the events of 9/11 in its marketing of the city.

The Bloomberg Era

New York's re-branding was catalyzed by Mayor Michael Bloomberg, a former media mogul and masterful brand marketer. As we saw in Chapter 8, Bloomberg was founder and CEO of Bloomberg LP, one of New York's biggest global financial media corporations. He is also a billionaire without any prior political experience who participated in no mayoral debates, but won office in 2001 largely by spending $75 million of his own money on marketing (at the time, the most spent on any non-presidential political race in US history). As a business strategy, Bloomberg has long understood the value of extending a brand, naming his company, the terminals it produces, and the content it distributes via web, radio, and TV after himself. And in the aftermath of 9/11, his marketing approach was put into effect on behalf of the city. As he said in his State of the City Address after taking office:

> We're going to imaginatively, aggressively, and relentlessly market our cultural attractions and all our competitive advantages . . . We're confident [this] will win us attention from businesses around the world that are looking for new markets and opportunities for growth. And we'll take advantage of our brand. New York is the best-known city on the planet. Our skyline is recognized world-wide. News from our streets reaches homes around the globe. At last count, more than 340 songs have been written about New York. Yet, as a city we've never taken direct coordinated custody of our image. By changing that, we can realize additional city revenues immediately.[11]

Echoing financiers' response in 1975, Bloomberg sought to combine intensive marketing with tax breaks for businesses to address the current crisis. In collaboration with reinvigorated CEOs of the NYCP, he accelerated the corporate retention strategy of the Office of Economic Development under Mayors Beame and Koch, and the Economic Development Corporation under Mayor Giuliani, allowing $5.5 billion of the $20 billion in federal aid to go to corporate tax breaks, regardless of whether companies actually stayed in the city, or had ever intended to leave in the first place.[12] He established a position of "chief marketing officer" in 2003 to oversee all promotion and marketing efforts, and in 2006 consolidated all such efforts—from big events to sponsorships to tourism—under the roof of an expanded, better-funded, professionalized NYC&Co. Since then the agency has placed ten new international offices throughout Europe and Asia, hired global brand managers from corporate hotel chains to its staff, and boasted the largest growth in tourism for any city in the nation.[13]

The response of the Bloomberg administration was understandable. In purely economic terms, it was the city's symbolic loss that reached out beyond the sixteen-acre site in Lower Manhattan and shook the confidence of investors, tourists, and citizens in New York and around the world. It sent deep and enduring shock waves throughout global stock markets far surpassing the cost of replacing the office space, jobs, or even gold bullion stored within the buildings. And it helped to send the city itself into a dive rivaling its 1975 fiscal crisis, costing some 150,000 jobs and between $83 billion and $100 billion in overall projected economic impact in the year following the attacks. This was due to a combination of factors, but high among them was the damage to the city's long-cultivated commercial image—or *brand*—as inviolate global finance center and tourist destination. New York's situation was far from unique, as many other "tourist cities" saw their economies crash in the months following the attack. However, while the others soon began to rebound, New York's combined infrastructural devastation and dependence on the financial, real estate, and tourism sectors cost jobs and income for a far longer period.[14]

The attacks of 9/11 revealed the huge amount of financial and political power branded images now wield over New York, and the immense, unseen work involved in maintaining them. In the weeks following the atrocity, thousands of movies, commercials, business logos, postcards, and tourist guides that pictured the Twin Towers suddenly found their message radically revised and either had to edit out this newly tragic symbol or leave it in and allow for the new association. Beyond the shocking hole in the skyline, people suddenly became aware of the ubiquity of the towers in the commercial media. While polls revealed that most New Yorkers had never even visited the WTC, the image of the towers had become interchangeable with that of the city as a whole in marketing and media consumed by people around the world. The city's branding coalition wanted to ensure that now the city as a whole—and in particular the tourism and real estate industries—did not suffer from the damage to their most valuable icon.

The upbeat, pile-minimizing approach was successful in many ways. The city attracted a growing wave of "patriotic tourism," channeling two dozen meetings to New York at least in part because of 9/11, including the two biggest and most coveted tourist industry conventions.[16] According to the Downtown Alliance, the WTC observation deck attracted an average of 1.8 million visitors a year. By 2003, its ruins had attracted double that number. As a *New York Times* article in 2002 noted: "the fallen trade center site has done what it could not do when standing: turn the financial district into one of the city's top attractions."[16]

Yet the city's immediate turn to marketing, tourism, and business development was also problematic—and not only because the tragedy precipitating it led so many New Yorkers to urge the city not to commercialize their grief. For while it was true that marketing had attracted tourist and investment capital back to the city over the last thirty years, it was also the case that these sectors were among the most image sensitive and volatile, with the potential to cause economic damage vastly disproportionate to their size. This, combined with retrenchment by a recession-laden federal government, led to increasing debt, pressure on social services, and double-digit unemployment—in other words, a replay of many of the fiscal crisis conditions of the mid-1970s. Thus, this was also a time to critically reexamine brand marketing as a central mode of urban economic development.

Yet, rather than diversifying the regional economy, expanding social services, or scaling back the commercialization of the WTC site, the current development approach has also been similar to that of the 1970s: using public funds for integrated brand marketing campaigns. Indeed, the Bloomberg administration seems largely to have copied the "recovery" model of the late 1970s: imposing austerity measures and extracting concessions from unions, while cutting business taxes, offering incentives, and marketing the dream of a pleasurable and profitable city to an affluent global audience.[17]

While brand marketing has shown its power to attract tourism and investment for New York City over the last thirty years, it has also shown its limits. In the same way that the WTC could successfully market its façade while its interior remained under-utilized, so too the re-branded city may continue to attract tourists without adequately addressing or ameliorating underlying economic disparities. We are reminded that while branded logos may be effective marketing tools for cities, they purposely reveal precious little about the material reality behind the commodity that they promote. Now, as New Yorkers—and urban citizens around the world—struggle through recurring periods of crisis, the contradictions of branding must be appreciated for a more just and representative process of urban redevelopment to be won.

Appendix

Table A.1 New York City employment by economic sector, 1967–1982 (thousands).

Year	Total	Manufac- turing	Construc- tion	Transport & Public Utilities	Wholesale & Retail Trade	FIRE	Services & Miscellaneous	Public Sector	Tourism
1967	3,675.4	873.9	105.7	226.2	718.2	401.4	657.1	501.8	194.1
1972	3,567.0	688.3	101.6	205.0	670.3	447.8	707.2	568.6	176.8
1977	2,762.1	545.6	66.9	213.4	600.6	417.3	738.0	519.3	113.0
1982	3,318.8	486.2	78.0	225.4	585.0	458.5	877.5	502.2	106.9
# change 1967–1982	–356.6	–387.7	–27.7	–0.8	–133.2	+57.1	+220.3	+0.4	–87.2
% change 1967–1982	–10.0	–44.0	–26.0	–0.4	–19.0	+14.0	+34.0	+0.1	–45.0
Rank 1967		1	8	6	2	5	3	4	7
Rank 1982		4	8	6	2	5	1	3	7

Source: New York State Department of Labor and US Department of Commerce, Bureau of the Census, 1967, 1972, 1977, and 1982.

Note

"Tourism" category is derived from a cluster analysis based on the Empire State Development Corporation's "New York State Industry Cluster Profiles" (Division of Policy and Research, May 1998).

Table A.2 Tourism, media, and marketing (select services) in New York City, establishments and employment, 1967–1982.

Industry	1963		1967		1972		1977		1982	
	Establish-ments	Employed	Establish-ments	Employed	Establish-ments	Employed	Establish-ments	Employed	Establish-ments	Employed
Total NYC Private Sector	N/A	N/A	201,486	3,225,740	173,470	3,141,599	139,082	2,714,385	161,236	2,896,979
Hotels & Motels	654	N/A	1,029	43,341	787	37,345	549	22,984	442	29,902
Amusement & Recreation	4,045	N/A	1,676	25,751	1,540	21,539	1,786	21,943	1,965	27,380
Printing & Publishing	N/A	141,200	4,117	123,711	3,607	105,430	3,398	99,255	3,090	103,997
Radio, TV, News	N/A	N/A	59	15,643	83	19,372	210	15,252	175	24,914
Motion Pictures	1,285	N/A	1,036	22,357	1,104	21,946	1,313	18,283	1,320	19,101
Advertising Consulting	4,231	N/A	1,341	44,649	1,278	34,264	1,237	33,258	1,326	38,600
& PR		N/A	2,155	27,647	2,498	33,427	2,096	23,528	2,375	36,307

Source: US Department of Commerce, Bureau of the Census, Census for Business, 1963, 1967, 1972, 1977, and 1982.

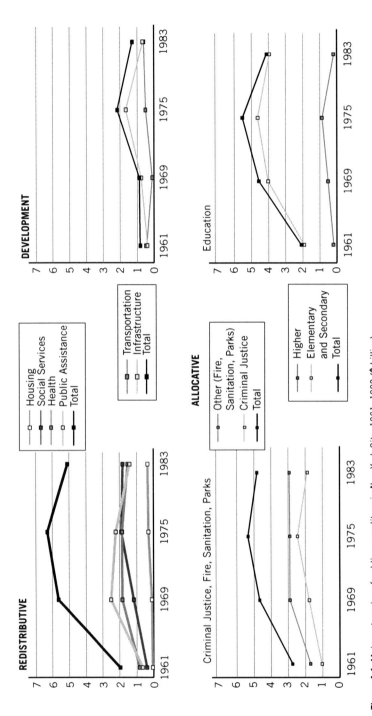

Figure A.1 Major categories of public expenditure in New York City, 1961–1983 ($ billion).

Source: Adapted from Brecher and Horton, "The Public Sector."

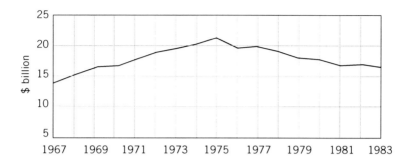

Figure A.2 Total spending by New York City, 1967–1983.

Source: Adapted from Brecher and Horton, "The Public Sector."

Notes

Prologue

1 Donald Flynn, "As City Sinks into Sea, the Visitors Bureau Churns," *Sunday News*, April 11, 1971. *Planet of the Apes*, directed by Franklin Schaffner, came out in 1968 and became a major box-office success. It told the story of an astronaut crew led by George Taylor (Charlton Heston) that crash-landed on a planet in the distant future on which apes were the dominant species and had enslaved human beings. The famous final scene shows Heston and Linda Harrison escaping on horseback down a beach and discovering the Statue of Liberty sunk in the sand—thus realizing that they are actually on earth, and that humans (presumably those in New York City) had brought an end to their civilization millennia before, enabling apes to evolve to take over the planet.

2 *Ibid.*

3 Preston Robert Tisch, President, and Charles Gillett, Executive Vice-President, New York Convention and Visitors Bureau, Inc., to Guido Vittori, General Manager, Alitalia, March 25, 1971. In "Convention and Visitors Bureau" file, at the New York City Municipal Archives.

4 On the response from Alitalia, and need for higher-powered lobbying, see, "Memorandum from Manuel Carballo, Assistant to the Mayor, n.d. In "Convention and Visitors Bureau" file, at the New York City Municipal Archives. For Aurelio's letter, see Richard Aurelio, Deputy Mayor, City of New York, to Guido Vittori, General Manager, Alitalia, April 14, 1971. In "Convention and Visitors Bureau" file, at the New York City Municipal Archives. Aurelio's letter read in part: "I am writing to you to express my strong objection to the recent series of misleading and distasteful advertisements by Alitalia Airlines. . . . New York City has long been a major gateway for Italians entering this country. Giovanni Di Verazzano discovered New York Harbor in 1524, eighty-five years before Henry Hudson reached these shores. We will in fact be celebrating this important event on Friday, April 16th. Since that famous discovery, New York has become the home of Italians coming to this country to seek a new life."

5 As cited in Flynn, "As City Sinks into Sea."

6 *Ibid.*

7 *Ibid.*

8 Robert E. Dallos, "NY Comeback: The Big Apple Taking Bigger Tourism Bite." *Los Angeles Times*, July 14, 1978.

9   On the cultural impact of 1970s New York on a national and global scale, see, for example: John Allen Farmer, ed., *Urban Mythologies: The Bronx Remembered since the 1960s* (New York: The Bronx Museum of the Arts, 1999); Henry Chalfant's documentary *From Mambo to Hip Hop* (City Lore, 2005); Jeff Chang, *Can't Stop, Won't Stop: A History of the Hip-Hop Generation* (New York: St. Martin's Press, 2005); Tim Lawrence, *Love Saves the Day: A History of American Dance Music Culture, 1970–1979* (Durham, NC: Duke University Press, 2003); Marvin J. Taylor, ed., *The Downtown Book: The New York Art Scene, 1974–1984* (Princeton, NJ: Princeton University Press, 2006).
10 On New York's exceptionalism as a capital of "civic liberalism" in the US, see: Jewel Bellush and Dick Netzer, eds., *Urban Politics: New York Style* (Armonk, NY and London: M. E. Sharpe, 1990).
11 On the symbolic economy, see, in particular, Scott Lash and John Urry, *Economies of Signs and Space* (London: Sage, 1994).
12 See, for example, John R. Logan and Harvey L. Molotch, *Urban Fortunes: The Political Economy of Place* (Berkeley: University of California Press, 1987).
13 On branding as part of a larger strategy of restructuring, see: Susanna Hart and John Murphy, eds., *Brands: The New Wealth Creators* (New York: New York University Press, 1998); and Naomi Klein, *No Logo: Taking Aim at the Brand Bullies* (London: Picador, 2000). On rise of place marketing, see: Briavel Holcomb, "Marketing Cities for Tourism" in *The Tourist City*, ed. Dennis Judd and Susan S. Fainstein (New Haven, CT: Yale University Press, 1999) and Neil Morgan, Annette Pritchard, and Roger Pride, eds., *Destination Branding: Creating the Unique Destination Proposition* (London: Butterworth-Heinemann, 2002).
14 Mary Holloway, author interview, March 30, 2003.
15 Yankelovich, Skelly, and White, Inc., *Research to Support New York State's Economic Development Activities: Discovery Phase: Qualitative Hypotheses.* Prepared for State of New York Department of Commerce, March 1977.

Chapter 1

1   Walter Benjamin, *The Arcades Project* (Cambridge, MA: Harvard/Bellknap, 1999), 392. While economistic Marxists argued that the base "produced" the cultural and ideological superstructure, Benjamin argued for a dialectical relationship between the two. Further, he associated the category of collective "dream" with the realm of ideology. As he says: "The superstructure is the expression of the infrastructure [i.e., base]. The economic conditions under which society exists are *expressed* in the superstructure—precisely as, with the sleeper, an overfull stomach finds not its reflection, but its expression in the content of dreams, which from a causal point of view, it may be said to 'condition.' The collective, from the first, expresses the conditions of its life. These find their expression in the dream and their interpretation in the awakening."
2   Henri Lefebvre, *Production of Space* (Cambridge, MA: Blackwell, 1991), 33, 39. By "representational space," Lefebvre refers to the associated images and symbols through which space is perceived. This concept is part of a larger project to create a unifying theory of the production of space in urban life, showing the ways in which space is both a social product and "serves as a tool of thought and action . . . [and as] a means of control and hence of domination, of power."
3   See David Harvey, *The Condition of Post-Modernity* (Oxford: Blackwell, 1989); Michael Sorkin, ed., *Variations on a Theme Park: Scenes from the New American City and the End of Public Space* (New York: Hill and Wang, 1992). On the term "new urban sociology," see Sharon Zukin, "A Decade of New Urban Sociology," *Theory and Society* 9 (1980) and John Walton, "Urban Sociology: The Contributions and Limits of Political Economy," *Annual Review of Sociology* 19 (1993).
4   Sharon Zukin, "Space and Symbols in an Age of Decline," in *Urban Cultures Reader*, ed. Malcolm Miles, Tim Hall, and Iain Borden (London: Routledge, 2000).
5   The most influential of these in the 1960s was the Fantus Company. By 1975 it began to produce its annual "State Rankings of Business Climate," which became the industry standard. For a history of these firms, see Bernard L. Weinstein and Robert E. Firestine, *Regional Growth in the United States* (New York: Praeger, 1978).

6   On institutional matrix, see Janice Radway, *Reading the Romance: Women, Patriarchy, and Popular Literature* (Chapel Hill: University of North Carolina Press, 1984), ch. 2. According to this idea, successful media forms emerge within a matrix of new technologies, skillful entrepreneurs, a shifting management structure, and a demanding audience. For earlier work on the relationship between the changing institutional matrix and representational power, see Miriam Greenberg, "Branding Cities: A Social History of the Urban Lifestyle Magazine," *Urban Affairs Review* 36:2 (November 2000).

7   Cities like Atlanta, for example, had been "competing to attract economic growth almost from the time they were established," when the Atlanta Chamber of Commerce launched a successful promotional campaign in the 1850s to attract the first rail lines to pass through the Southeast, the construction of which was followed by a massive wave of investment and migration into the city. See Christopher Law, *Urban Tourism: The Visitor Economy and the Growth of Large Cities* (London: Continuum, 2002), 35–6. To a lesser, though still significant, degree, forward-thinking European cities also competed with each other, and boosted themselves, when they built new town halls, organized large exhibitions, and opened new museums and holiday resorts.

8   On critical infrastructure see: Sharon Zukin, *Landscapes of Power: From Detroit to Disney World* (Berkeley: University of California Press, 1991), 258–259; Charles Rutheiser, *Imagineering Atlanta: Making Place in a Non-Place Urban Realm* (London: Verso, 1996). These spaces included a range of new urban entertainments and spectacles—from amusement parks and department stores in New York and London to the perpetual sunshine of urban beaches and boulevards in Los Angeles—as well as new models of urban housing, planning, and design. See Mike Davis, *City of Quartz: Excavating the Future in Los Angeles* (London: Verso, 1990), ch. 2, for his discussion of the dialectic between "Sunshine and Noir."

9   See Raymond Williams, *The Country and the City* (New York: Oxford University Press, 1973); Phillip Kasinitz, Robert Jackall, and Arthur Vidich, *Metropolis: Center and Symbol of Our Times* (New York: New York University Press, 1995); Peter Stallybrass and Alon White, *The Politics and Poetics of Transgression* (Ithaca, NY: Cornell University Press, 1986); Peter Hall, *Cities of Tomorrow: An Intellectual History of Urban Planning and Design in the Twentieth Century* (Oxford: Blackwell, 1988), ch. 1. Some critics were fueled by a romantic longing for a simpler and more community-oriented rural life in the face of what they perceived as the alienation and crass materialism of the capitalist city. Others, more concerned with the issue of law and order, were terrified by what they saw as the breakdown of social mores and hierarchies brought about by rapid urbanization and the mixing of class and race. Still others, in particular social reformers and socialist city planners, were horrified by the inhumane living and working conditions endured by the urban poor in overcrowded neighborhoods and factories, which were seen as endemic to the large industrial city.

10   On city view books see P. B. Hales, *Silver Cities: The Photography of American Urbanization, 1839–1915* (Philadelphia, PA: Temple University Press, 1984); on panoramas see Christine Boyer, *The City of Collective Memory: Its Historical Imagery and Architectural Entertainments* (Cambridge, MA: MIT Press, 1994).

11   Hales, *Silver Cities.*

12   Vanessa Schwartz, *Spectacular Realities: Early Mass Culture in Fin-de-Siècle Paris* (Berkeley: University of California Press, 1998).

13   Luc Sante, *Low Life: Lures and Snares of Old New York* (New York: Vintage, 1992); Chris Mele, *Selling the Lower East Side: Culture, Real Estate, and Resistance in New York City* (Minneapolis: University of Minnesota Press, 2001). Stallybrass and White, *The Politics and Poetics of Transgression*, 137, apply Bahktinian theories of the carnival to textual representations of the nineteenth-century urban slum, and show how through all manner of writing, from sanitary reports, to reformer tracts, potboilers, and novellas, the bourgeoisie "made the grotesque *visible* whilst keeping it at an *untouchable* distance," allowing "the slum [dwellers] . . . into the bourgeois study and drawing room, to be read as objects of horror, contempt, pity, and fascination."

14   Graeme Gillough, *Myth and Metropolis: Walter Benjamin and the City* (Cambridge: Polity Press, 1996).

15   On newspapers and the *faits divers* press, see Schwartz, *Spectacular Realities*; David Henkin, *City Reading: Written Words and Public Spaces in Antebellum New York* (New York: Columbia University Press, 1999); Peter Fritsche, *Reading Berlin, 1900* (Cambridge, MA: Harvard

University Press, 1996). On the modern novel and Victorian slum literature, see Stallybrass and White, *The Politics and Poetics of Transgression*. On cinema, see Miriam Hansen, *Babel and Babylon: Spectatorship in American Silent Film* (Cambridge, MA: Harvard University Press, 1991); James Donald, *Imagining the Modern City* (London: Athlone, 1999), ch. 3.

16   Fritsche, *Reading Berlin*, 3.

17   On the rise of Convention and Visitor Bureaus during the Depression, see Law, *Urban Tourism*.

18   Good examples of this are Atlanta and New Orleans. See, for example, Rutheiser, *Imagineering Atlanta*, and Kevin Fox Gotham, *Authentic New Orleans: Race and Culture in Urban Tourism* (New York: New York University Press, forthcoming).

19   See United States Travel Service, *Promoting Travel to the United States* (Washington, DC: United States Travel Service, US Department of Commerce, 1962).

20   *Ibid.*

21   On the growth machine, see Logan and Molotch, *Urban Fortunes*.

22   Dennis R. Judd, ed., *The Infrastructure of Play: Building the Tourist City* (Armonk, NY: M. E. Sharpe, 2003), 4.

23   NATO was established as an unincorporated non-profit association with no paid staff. See Travel Industry Association of America, *Travel Industry Association of America: 60 Years of Service and Achievement, 1941–2001* (Washington, DC: Travel Industry Association of America, 2001), 1.

24   *Ibid.*

25   See, for example, John B. Lansing and Ernest Lilienstein, *The Travel Market 1955: A Report to the Travel Research Association* (Ann Arbor: Survey Research Center, Institute for Social Research, University of Michigan, 1955). Lansing conducted the same nationwide travel market survey with a variety of co-authors every year between 1955 and 1965. See also John B. Lansing and Dwight Blood, *The Changing Travel Market* (Ann Arbor: Survey Research Center, Institute for Social Research, University of Michigan, 1964). These extremely broad studies focused on the "demand side" of the equation, which was what Katona's classic consumer research model was geared to measure. In the early 1960s, the Travel Research Association began working with the Business Research Division of the University of Colorado in an apparent shift towards studies of the "supply" side of the question, also at a very macro level. See L. J. Crampon, *Characteristics of Successful Tourist Destination Areas in the United States* (Boulder: Business Research Division, University of Colorado, 1964) and *Characteristics of the Tourist or Travel Market of a Given Destination Area* (Boulder: Business Research Division, University of Colorado, 1964).

26   US Department of Commerce, Bureau of the Census, *Tourism as a Job Creator* (Washington, DC: Area Redevelopment Administration, US Department of Commerce, June 1962); *Tourist Industry and Redeveloped Areas* (Washington, DC: Area Redevelopment Administration, US Department of Commerce, July 1964); *Tourism and Recreation* (Washington, DC: Office of Regional Economic Development, US Department of Commerce, March 1967).

27   For compendia of these numerous studies, see C. R. Goeldner and Gerald L. Allen, *Bibliography of Tourism and Travel: Research Studies, Reports, and Articles* (Boulder: Business Research Division, University of Colorado, in Cooperation with Western Council for Travel Research, and Travel Research Association, 1967); C. R. Goeldner and Karen Dicke, *Bibliography of Tourism and Travel: Research Studies, Reports, and Articles* (Boulder: Business Research Division, University of Colorado 1971), Volumes I–III.

28   The most influential of these in the 1960s was the Fantus Company, *The Manhattan Outlook: A Projection to 1985 of Operating Conditions in New York City for Office Employers* (New York: The Fantus Company, 1975). By 1975 it began to produce its annual "State Rankings of Business Climate," which became the industry standard. For a history of these firms, see Weinstein and Firestine, *Regional Growth in the United States*.

29   Kevin Lynch, *The Image of the City* (Cambridge, MA: MIT Press, 1960).

30   On Fordism, see Harvey, *The Condition of Postmodernity*, ch. 9, and Ash Amin, ed., *Post Fordism: A Reader* (Oxford: Blackwell, 1995).

31   Manuel Castells, *The City and the Grassroots: A Cross-cultural Theory of Urban Social Movements* (Berkeley: University of California Press, 1985). As Castells argues, many of these new social movements can be defined by a common demand for equal access to "collective consumption" goods like housing, healthcare, and education. A range of urban social

movements innovated strategies of civil disobedience in urban neighborhoods, welfare offices, and college campuses that pressured the state for reforms. These can be distinguished from race riots, or what many called "rebellions," which were provoked by similarly endemic inequities, yet were largely unorganized outbursts taking the form of looting, destruction of property, and the further decimation of the poorest urban neighborhoods.

32 Ibid. For many historians of the 1960s, a unifying thread between disparate and often antagonistic social movements was their desire to "take it to the streets," and make public their demands for social justice through the appropriation of public space. See Alexander Bloom and Wini Breines, "Takin' It to the Streets": A Sixties Reader (New York: Oxford University Press, 2003).

33 New York City began to lose the bulk of its port industry, which had driven the regional economy since the nineteenth century, while Los Angeles and Atlanta saw major lay-offs in the aerospace industries that had moved there during World War II. New York and Los Angeles also saw increasingly militant strike activity, and all three saw protests in response to poor living conditions in the inner cities, as well as a general rise in crime. See Janet Abu Lughod, New York, Chicago, Los Angeles: America's Global Cities (Minneapolis: University of Minnesota Press, 1999). In the United States, this tension was exacerbated by class divisions on the left between identity-based social movements, the anti-war movement, and organized labor, which was also becoming more militant at this time. See Bloom and Breines, "Takin' It to the Streets," 164–189.

34 Such confrontations are often epitomized by the "race riots" in the streets of cities throughout the US between 1964 and 1968—culminating with Newark in 1967. But the political dimension of many of these battles becomes apparent when one considers the massacre of unarmed political protesters in the Plaza de Tlatelolco in Mexico City in 1968, which took place in advance of the 1968 Olympics in that city, and was carried out by the military. Similarly, the famous "hard-hat riot," in which scores of construction workers attacked a peaceful march of anti-Vietnam protesters in Wall Street in 1971 has been found to have been largely instigated by the New York City police. See Joshua Freeman, Working Class New York: Life and Labor since WWII (New York: New Press, 2000).

35 Robert Beauregard, Voices of Decline: The Postwar Fate of US Cities (London: Blackwell, 1993).

36 On racist tropes in TV news of this era, see Stuart Hall, "Racist Ideologies and the Media," in Media Studies: A Reader, ed. Paul Marris and Sue Thornham (New York: New York University Press, 2000). And as Beauregard shows, a number of ideological tropes came together through anti-urban discourse: the fear of mass urban populations (geselschaft) destroying the civility and familiarity of premodern village life (gemeinshaft); the image of "slum" neighborhoods as cesspools breeding degradation and immorality; and depictions of the residents of these neighborhoods—the poor, the foreign born, and people of color—as animalistic and inherently violent.

37 Alvin Toffler, Future Shock (New York: Bantam, 1970).

38 For structural causes of long-term urban decline in New York City from the 1960s on, and earlier in other US cities, including Detroit, see Thomas Sugrue, The Origins of the Urban Crisis: Race and Inequality in Postwar Detroit (Princeton, NJ: Princeton University Press, 1996). Some, like Douglas Rae, in CITY, trace the origins of the crisis in New Haven all the way back to 1915.

39 Many supply-side economists attribute the original cause of inflation to the 1971 signing of the Bretton Woods Agreement, which detached the US dollar from the international gold standard, and deprived monetary policy of a specific price reference.

40 See, for example, Amin, Post-Fordism and Harvey, The Condition of Post-Modernity.

41 Barry Bluestone and Bennett Harrison, The Great U-Turn: Corporate Restructuring and the Polarizing of America (New York: Basic Books, 1988).

42 Harkening back to the free market, "liberal" political economy of thinkers like Adam Smith, neoliberal philosophy was promulgated by mid-century theorists like Friedrich Von Hayek, and popularized and institutionalized in the 1970s by economists like Milton Friedman and others at the University of Chicago, often under the rubric of "supply-side" economics. On supply-side theory see Jude Wanniski, The Way the World Works (New York: Regnery Publishing, 1998). On the broader political and economic philosophy of neoliberalism, see Milton Friedman, Free to Choose: A Personal Statement (New York: Harcourt Brace Jovanovich, 1980). As an indication of the popular influence of this view at this time, this book was also made into a ten-part television series on PBS.

43 For analyses of the "neoliberal turn" by the state in the US and globally in the 1970s, see David Harvey, *A Brief History of Neoliberalism* (Oxford: Oxford University Press, 2005) and Neil Brenner, "New State Spaces: Urban Governance and the Rescaling of Statehood" in *Global Cities: A Reader*, ed. Neil Brenner and Roger Keil (New York: Routledge, 2006). For a synthesis of literature on the role of neoliberalism in urban restructuring in the US in particular, see Jason Hackworth, *The Neoliberal City: Governance, Ideology, and Development in American Urbanism* (Ithaca, NY: Cornell University Press, 2007).

44 See Hall, *Cities of Tomorrow*, ch. 11; David Harvey, "From Managerialism to Entrepreneurialism: The Transformation of Urban Governance in Late Capitalism," in *Spaces of Capital: Towards a Critical Geography* (Oxford: Blackwell, 2001).

45 Logan and Molotch, *Urban Fortunes.*

46 While these arrangements began in the 1960s and 1970s, and were called civic associations and local development corporations, they became known primarily as public–private partnerships in the 1980s. David Rockefeller, CEO of Chase Manhattan, claimed this was based on the success of the New York City Partnership, which he founded in 1979, and which he said was the first to use the title. David Rockefeller, "Ingredients for Successful Partnerships: The New York City Case," in *Public–Private Partnerships: Improving Urban Life*, ed. Perry Davis (New York: Academy of Political Science/New York City Partnership, 1986).

47 Gregory Squires, *Unequal Partnerships: The Political Economy of Urban Redevelopment in Postwar America* (New Brunswick, NJ: Rutgers University Press, 1989), 3. The final quote comes from Bluestone and Harrison, as cited in *ibid.*, 1. The full quote reads: "Leaders may call these deals 'public private partnerships' and attempt to fold them under the ideological umbrella of *laissez faire*. But they must be seen for what they are: the reallocation of public resources to fit a new agenda. That agenda is no longer redistribution, or even economic growth as conventionally defined. Rather, that agenda entails nothing less than the restructuring of the relations of production and the balance of power in the American economy. In the pursuit of these dubious goals, the public sector continues to play a crucial role."

48 See, for example, David Osborne and Ted Gaebler, *Reinventing Government: How the Entrepreneurial Spirit Is Transforming the Public Sector* (New York: Penguin, 1992).

49 See Neil Smith, *Uneven Development* (New York: Routledge, 1984).

50 See Neil Smith, "Gentrification, the Frontier and the Restructuring of Urban Space," in *Gentrification of the City*, ed. Neil Smith and Peter Williams (Boston: Allen and Unwin, 1986)

51 On creative means of luring real estate development in the 1980s, see Susan S. Fainstein, *City Builders: Property Development in New York and London, 1980–2000* (Lawrence: University of Kansas Press, 2001). On loft living, see Sharon Zukin, *Loft Living: Culture and Capital in Urban Change* (New Brunswick, NJ: Rutgers University Press, 1989).

52 See, for example, Jason Hackworth on the "reinvested urban core" in *The Neoliberal City: Governance, Ideology, and Development in American Urbanism* (Ithaca, NY: Cornell University Press, 2007), ch. 6.

53 Harvey, *Spaces of Capital*. This is true whether the city functions as a center of production, consumption, or public or private service provision.

54 *Ibid.*, 398.

55 Dennis Judd and Susan S. Fainstein, eds., *The Tourist City* (New Haven, CT: Yale University Press, 1999); John Hannigan, *Fantasy City: Pleasure and Profit in the Postmodern Metropolis* (New York: Routledge, 1999).

56 On "theming" see Michael Sorkin, ed., *Variations on a Theme Park: Scenes from the New American City and the End of Public Space* (New York: Hill and Wang, 1992); Jerry Kearns and Chris Philo, *Selling Places: The City as Cultural Capital Past and Present* (New York: Pergamon Press, 1993); Mike Featherstone, "City Cultures and Post-Modern Lifestyles," in *Post Fordism*, ed. Ash Amin; Rutheiser, *Imagineering Atlanta*; and Mark Gottdiener, *The Theming of America: Dreams, Media Fantasies, and Themed Environments* (Boulder, CO: Westview Press, 2001). On the increased control over urban space this involves, including the building of prisons and the use of surveillance and policing, see Mike Davis, *City of Quartz: Excavating the Future in Los Angeles* (London: Verso, 1990) and Don Mitchell and Lynn A. Staheli, "Clean and Safe? Property Redevelopment, Public Space, and Homelessness in Downtown San Diego," in *The Politics of Public Space*, ed. Setha Low and Neil Smith (New York: Routledge, 2006).

57 As Harvey states in his essay "The Art of Rent: Globalization and the Commodification of Culture," in *Spaces of Capital*, 405, "The collective symbolic capital which attaches to names

and places like Paris, Athens, New York, Rio de Janeiro, Berlin and Rome is of great import and gives such places great economic advantages relative to say, Baltimore, Liverpool, Essen, Lille and Glasgow. The problem for these latter places is to raise their quotient of symbolic capital and to increase their marks of distinction to better ground their claims to the uniqueness that yields monopoly rent. Given the general loss of other monopoly powers through easier transport and communications and the reduction of other barriers to trade, the struggle for collective symbolic capital becomes even more important as a basis for monopoly rents."

58 A seminal moment in this regard was the gentrification of the New York's Lower East Side in the 1980s. As Neil Smith and Christopher Mele have shown, this traditionally working-class, counter-cultural neighborhood was famously resistant to gentrification until developers, aided by local government incentives, struck on the strategy of marketing the area's unique cultural qualities to young, upwardly mobile professionals—selling it as the city's bohemian, risqué, "urban frontier." See Neil Smith, "The Lower East Side as Wild, Wild West," in *Variations on a Theme Park*, ed. Sorkin, and Christopher Mele, *Selling the Lower East Side*.

59 Lorenzo Vicario and P. Manuel Martinez Monje, "Another 'Guggenheim Effect'? Central City Projects and Gentrification in Bilbao," in *Gentrification in a Global Context: The New Urban Colonialism*, ed. Rowland Atkinson and Gary Bridge (London: Routledge, 2005).

60 Judd and Fainstein, *The Tourist City*.

61 As Neil Morgan and Annette Pritchard, *Tourism, Promotion, and Power: Creating Images, Creating Identities* (New York: John Wiley and Sons, 1998), 63, put it, "Image emerges as a key marketing tool in an industry where potential consumers must base buying decisions upon mental images of product offerings rather than being able to physically sample alternatives." This becomes the theme of their next book on "destination branding": see Neil Morgan, Annette Pritchard, and Roger Pride, eds., *Destination Branding: Creating the Unique Destination Proposition* (London: Butterworth-Heinemann, 2002).

62 See Motivational Programmers, Inc., "The Creative Consumer," *Holiday*, February 1969. This is the earliest study I have yet found correlating lifestyle research and marketing to the tourism industry. As described by Goeldner and Dicke, *Bibliography of Tourism and Travel*, 19, "This study discusses a new type of data in marketing research. The new technique, called 'life style' information by some, and named 'psychographics' by others, describes people not only by how much they make, and how much education they have, but also by their individual styles of life which make more probable the purchase of some products and services, and reduce the changes of buying others. The study presents many interesting marketing delineations and illustrates the use of new market research techniques."

63 See Weinstein and Firestine, *Regional Growth in the United States*, and Gregory John Ashworth and Henk Voogd, "Marketing and Place Promotion," in *Place Promotion: The Use of Publicity and Marketing to Sell Towns and Regions*, ed. John Robert Gold and Stephen Ward (Chichester: Wiley, 1994).

64 As Law, *Urban Tourism*, 5, points out, this common estimate is quite conservative, as it only measures the number of people crossing borders, rather than those traveling domestically and regionally. As a result it ignores the increase in "day-trippers" and those in large countries like the US who are traveling within their own borders.

65 Morgan and Pritchard, *Tourism, Promotion, and Power*, 140. On integration of urban tourism campaigns in general, see Law, *Urban Tourism*. As Law, 72, describes: "Over the past 20 years, the strategy of urban tourism has moved from the very simple idea of advertising a few attractions to a much more comprehensive approach which seeks to develop a product, understand the visitor markets for the product, make the city user-friendly for tourists (consumers), and create organizations which can promote and sell the city."

66 On the role of lifestyle for the new middle class, see Arthur Vidich, *The New Middle Classes: Life-Styles, Status Claims, and Political Orientations* (New York: New York University Press, 1995). On urban lifestyles in particular, see Greenberg, "Branding Cities."

67 Morgan and Pritchard, *Tourism, Promotion, and Power*, 73. In this sense, location marketing has fed off the increasingly powerful product placement sub-industry, which has arisen "as Hollywood producers have sought additional sources of income to offset rising production costs, and as advertisers have searched the media horizons for underused and less resisted venues for their promotions."

68   Other researchers have dubbed such direct versus indirect exposure as "projected" and "organic" media images, i.e. those that stem from attempts to influence consumer images of destinations through target marketing, as opposed to those from a "lifetime of socialization" to popular culture, literature, and education. See *ibid.*, 65.

69   See Susan Strasser, *Satisfaction Guaranteed: The Making of the American Mass Market* (New York: Pantheon, 1989) and Klein, *No Logo*.

70   Marx, *Capital*, I, ch. 1, section 4.

71   Randy Martin, *On Your Marx: Relinking Socialism and the Left* (Minneapolis: University of Minnesota Press, 2002). Martin makes the important point that Marx's discussion of the "commodity fetish" at the start of *Capital* is fundamentally about the danger of such disarticulation—and not, as is often assumed, about the "false consciousness" of the masses who bow down before the commodity like a fetish.

72   Guy Debord, *The Society of the Spectacle* (New York: Zone Books, 1999). As Debord, 12, says: "The whole life of those societies in which modern conditions of production prevail presents itself as an immense accumulation of spectacles. All that once was directly lived has become mere representation. Images detached from every aspect of life merge into a common stream, and the former unity of life is lost forever. Apprehended in a partial way, reality unfolds in a new generality as a pseudo world apart, solely as an object of contemplation. The tendency toward the specialization of images-of-the-world finds its highest expression in the world of the autonomous image, where deceit deceives itself. The spectacle in its generality is a concrete inversion of life, and, as such, the autonomous movement of non-life."

73   On "psychographics," its relation to changing lifestyle trends in the post-war period, and its application to advertising and marketing, see William D. Wells, ed., *Life Style and Psychographics* (Chicago: American Marketing Association, 1974). On measures of "corporate reputation" in the minds of consumers, as developed by the firm Yankelovich, Skelly, and White, see Brooke W. Mahoney, *Business and Society: A Thirty Year Perspective* (New York: Volunteer Consulting Group, Inc., 2000). On measures of "consumer attitudes," see Sidney J. Levy, "Roots of Marketing and Consumer Research at the University of Chicago," *Consumption, Markets and Culture* 6:2 (June 2003). As Levy points out, new private sector market research firms were influenced by academic centers of market research, in particular the University of Chicago-based Committee for Research on Consumer Attitudes and Behavior in the 1950s, which pioneered the application of behavioral psychology to the problems of business.

74   For standard branding textbooks see, for example, Hart and Murphy, *Brands*. Regarding conferences and conventions devoted to the topic, Stuart Elliot, "The Importance of Famous Brand Names is Stressed by Executives at an Ad Conference," *New York Times*, October 12, 1999, C8, noted how the ninetieth annual gathering of the Association of National Advertisers, the trade organization representing the nation's largest marketers, was devoted entirely to the theme "Brand Building for the 21st Century."

75   See Jean Noel Kapferer, *Strategic Brand Management: New Approaches to Creating and Evaluating Brand Equity* (New York: Addison Wesley, 1996).

76   Klein, *No Logo*. This coincided with new "cultural strategies" of controlling the corporate workforce. For headquarters and service-oriented firms, a new corporate culture glorified senior managers and CEOs while emphasizing worker performance and excellence, creating incentives and regulations to condition and control workers, and discourage unionization. See Paul Du Gay and Stuart Hall, eds., *Production of Culture/Cultures of Production* (London: Sage, 1997), ch. 5.

77   Klein, *No Logo*, ch. 9.

78   Donald Katz, *Just Do It: The Nike Spirit in the Corporate World* (Holbrook: Adams Media Corporation, 1994).

79   On the evolution of the concept of value under capitalism see Karl Marx, *Capital*, Vol. I (London: Penguin, 1990), chs. 1–4. An interesting contrast between brand value and notions of "use value" is offered by Richard Tedlow, a Harvard Business School professor and veteran marketing researcher: "Branding is a way of creating *the idea* of value in a product . . . [It] is about reassurance, about consistency, about loyalty, about repurchase behavior," regardless of the inherent usefulness of the product itself. See Peggy Caylor, "What's in a Name!" *National Real Estate Investor*, May 1999, 4–5.

80 While branding obscures conditions at the point of production, this does not fully explain the resurgence of sweatshop labor at the end of the twentieth century. To understand this, it is necessary to trace the rise of "free trade zones," and the desperate economic conditions of countries that accept them on their territory. This in turn requires a larger discussion of neoliberal forces of globalization, and in particular the role of the International Monetary Fund, World Bank, and World Trade Organization. On this cluster of issues see, for example, Richard Peet, *Unholy Trinity: The IMF, World Bank and WTO* (London: Zed Books, 2003).

81 Klein, *No Logo*, 195–196.

82 *Ibid.*, 195. Quoting Walter Landor, CEO of Landor Brand Management, taken from the Landor website. A similar comment is made by Peter Schweitzer, president of advertising giant J. Walter Thompson, who says: "The difference between products and brands is fundamental. A product is something that is made in a factory. A brand is something that is bought by a customer." See *ibid.*

83 Leon Shiffman and Leslie Lazar Kanuk, *Consumer Behavior* (Englewood Cliffs, NJ: Prentice Hall, 2001).

84 In setting stock price "brand net value" is considered essential—i.e., how many consumers recognize the brand, and its average appeal among these consumers. On this, see David Aacker, *Managing Brand Equity: Capitalizing on the Value of a Brand Name* (New York: Maxwell Macmillan International, 1991).

85 Morgan and Pritchard, *Tourism, Promotion, and Power*, 140. According to a 1997 study, the Nike and Coca-Cola logos, along with those of Shell and McDonald's, are recognized by almost 90 percent of the global population—placing the brand value of commercial logos well above religious symbols like the Christian cross, which is reportedly recognized by only 50 percent of the global population. Their brand recognition score is exceeded only by the five rings of the Olympic symbol.

86 An interesting example of this was the firm Landor Associates, which was one of the leading firms in "corporate reputation" studies in the 1960s and 1970s, and today has moved on to become a leader in "corporate branding," changing its name to Landor Brand Management. For current work on the role of reputational capital in the valuation of stock, as well as new approaches for measuring and branding this "intangible asset," see e.g.: B&Q, *Unlocking the Hidden Wealth of Organizations: The Development and Communication of Intangible Assets* (London: Cass Business School, 2003); Kevin T. Jackson, *Building Reputational Capital: Strategies for Integrity and Fair Play That Improve the Bottom Line* (Oxford: Oxford University Press, 2004), and "What Price Reputation?," *Business Week*, July 9, 2007 (no author).

87 Stuart Hall, "Encoding/Decoding," in *Media Studies: A Reader*, ed. Paul Marris and Sue Thornham (New York: New York University Press, 2000), 51–61.

88 This practice has been referred to as "culture jamming." See, for example, Kalle Lasn, *Culture Jam: The Uncooling of America* (New York: Eagle Brook, 1999); and Klein, *No Logo*, Part III.

89 I have been influenced here by Naomi Klein's discussion of the "brand boomerang" that threatens the reputations of disreputable corporations, and specifically the tactics of "anti-advertising" and "culture jamming." See *ibid.*, section 4. But while culture jammers are organized in their efforts, my use of counter-branding extends to unforeseen one-time events that may also damage the brand.

90 On "*detournement*," see Guy Debord and Gil J. Wolman, "Methods of Détournement," in *Situationist International Anthology*, ed. Ken Knabb (Berkeley, CA: Bureau of Public Secrets, 1981).

91 It should be noted that these rates are constantly ratcheting up due to the intensely competitive nature of the market, the demand from public officials to show results, and the need for aggressive legal protection of the trademarked brand image.

92 For a powerful historical account of how New York City was situated as a "center of difference" that was both vital to US democracy and a lightning-rod for the nation's anti-urban tendencies, see Thomas Bender, *The Unfinished City: New York and the Metropolitan Idea* (New York: New Press, 2002).

Chapter 2

1 Paul Goldberger, "Moses, Master Builder, Dead at 92," *New York Times*, July 30, 1981, 1. As Goldberger put it in Moses's obituary: "The urban renewal scandals [of the late 1950s] were perhaps the most serious setbacks [in Moses's career], and in 1959 an opportunity arose for a graceful exit: the presidency of the 1964–65 New York World's Fair was offered to him."

2 "TV to Cover Fair with 75 Cameras: Braces for Opening, Johns Talk and Demonstrations," *New York Times*, April 22, 1964, 95; "Satellite to Carry Fair's First Day," *New York Times*, April 12, 1964, 84; "Fair Has Color TV Just for Visitors: Gives Shows 12 Hours a Day over 'Closed Circuit,'" *New York Times*, May 4, 1964, 34; Val Adams, "TV Going to Fair for Opening Day: WABC and CBS Schedule Programs," *New York Times*, April 7, 1965, 95. Here Adams noted that the twenty-six-minute color film, "To the Fair," by Frederic Thompson and Alexander Hammid, which had already been shown in theaters nationwide, would now be broadcast on a hundred stations throughout the country between April and the opening day of the Fair.

3 Immediately after the close of the Fair, this pavilion moved to Epcot Center in Florida, becoming one of the most popular and familiar Disney attractions of all time.

4 One of the major critics of the city spending on the Fair was James Farmer of CORE, who advocated using the money instead to rehabilitate slum housing, saying it was a far better risk: "The World's Fair loan was more than $40 million. That was a risk loan without lasting benefit. The city lost money on such a loan in 1939–40. So what are the priorities? Finance or human health?" Charles Bennet, "City's Slum Plan Defended by CORE," *New York Times*, February 13, 1964, 20.

5 "City Expecting Spending Spree of Billions in Next Two Years," *New York Times*, April 22, 1964, 22.

6 Richard J. H. Johnston, "Shouts Mar Johnson's Talk at Pavilion," *New York Times*, April 23, 1964, 26.

7 Johnny Carson's one-liner summed up the sentiment of many, "They've got a belly dancer at the Moroccan Pavilion now, but she has a cobweb in her navel." See "The Great Carsoni," *Time*, May 28, 1965. See also Richard Shepherd, "Show Biz and Big Biz are Offering Entertainment," *New York Times*, April 22, 1964, 22.

8 There is no better example of this disconnect than the comments made by Robert Moses on the Harlem and Brooklyn riots during an event honoring Utah Day, held in front of the massive reproduction of the Mormon Temple in Salt Lake City at the main entrance to the Fair. Seeking to dispel talk of the negative effect the riots would have on Fair attendance, Moses denounced the "articulate observers" who "magnify urban disorder, resentments and frustrations," and the "ugly, noisy hoodlums" who cause them. He then went on to criticize New Yorkers who are sympathetic to such politics, in favor of the quiet, rural heartland: "The truth is we have too many smarties around New York. People from the vast hinterland of our country have more detachment, tolerance and forbearance." Walter Carlson, "Moses Says that 'Observers' Magnify Reports on 'Disorders,'" *New York Times*, July 25, 1964, 48.

9 "To the Bitter End," *Time*, October 29, 1965.

10 It allowed most presenters to break even or at least enhance their "prestige," providing a dramatic break from the twenty-year decline of the local tourism industry, and lending legitimacy to ongoing efforts to institutionalize summer cultural offerings. See "City to Be a Summer Festival Again for Visitors," *New York Times*, April 22, 1964, 26.

11 Moses's dream of converting the Flushing Meadows site into an elaborate permanent park had to be scaled down considerably.

12 Robert Alden, "Fair Moves to Counter Bad Publicity," *New York Times*, June 27, 1964, 16.

13 *Ibid.*

14 Edwin G. Burrows and Mike Wallace, *Gotham: A History of New York City to 1898* (New York: Oxford University Press, 1999), 153–155, 509–528.

15 *Ibid.*, 674–679.

16 David Henkin, *City Reading: Written Words and Public Spaces in Antebellum New York* (New York: Columbia University Press, 1999).

17 For example, Roger Whitehouse, *New York: Sunshine and Shadow: A Photographic Record of the City and Its People from 1850 to 1915* (New York: Harper & Row, 1974).

18 This followed two decades of seeking profits through the global expansion of short-wave radio, with limited success.

19   Robert McChesney and Edward Herman, *The Global Media: The New Missionaries of Global Capitalism* (London: Cassell, 1997).
20   This was further ensured when Hollywood movie studios, the only potential competitors at this point, initially refused to let their sound stages be used for television. In addition, due to time-zone differences and inadequate recording equipment, it was far easier for other cities to receive live broadcasts from New York than to produce their own.
21   Chancey Olinger, "Advertising," in *The Encyclopedia of New York City*, ed. Kenneth T. Jackson (New York: New York Historical Society, 1995).
22   *Time* was headquartered in Chicago, but its major news division and editors were based in New York City.
23   Eric W. Gustafson, "Printing and Publishing," in *Made in New York: Case Studies in Metropolitan Manufacture*, ed. Max Hall (Cambridge, MA: Harvard University Press, 1959). While there was an increase in commercial publishing and the use of the new linotype press by smaller magazines, by the early 1970s the industry had contracted to roughly half the size it was at its height in the 1920s.
24   McChesney and Herman, *The Global Media*, 19. This was also due to geopolitical shifts, with the AP and UP benefiting from the dominant global role of the US after World War II. The German Wolf had declined as a result of the demise of the Nazi regime in Germany. Meanwhile, the Russian Tass was growing at this point. Note: Agence France Press was formerly Havas. United Press would become United Press International in 1958.
25   John L. Hess, "Foreign Correspondents Find New York the World's Hottest Beat," *New York Times*, November 22, 1972, 37. The article notes that some 680 foreign reporters had been posted in New York City, "to cover the city and, from this vantage point, the United States and the Western Hemisphere." This number of foreign reporters was three times the number of US correspondents in all other countries. And according to a survey conducted for the article, foreign correspondents picked New York over Washington by three to one, largely due to their preference for the cultural life of the city.
26   James L. Baughman, "Television," in *The Encyclopedia of New York City*.
27   Michael Denning, *The Cultural Front: The Laboring of American Culture in the Twentieth Century* (New York: Verso, 1996); Paul Buhle and Dave Wagner, *Hide in Plain Sight: The Hollywood Blacklistees in Film and Television, 1950–2002* (New York: Palgrave, 2003); Baughman, "Television."
28   Freeman, *Working Class New York*, 7. As Freeman says, "Everywhere Americans looked—in newspapers and magazines, on billboards, television, and at the movies—blue collar workers were heroically portrayed. The sense that they had come into their own was not just the product of official and unofficial opinion makers; as the war ended manual workers had tremendous élan, a self-confidence growing out of the successful unionization campaigns before the war and their strategic position, steady work, and rising income during it."
29   Mark Jacobson, "New York, You Oughta Be in Pictures," *New York*, December 30, 1975, 40. The blacklist targeted a disproportionate number of New Yorkers working in Hollywood, and in particular Jewish and black New Yorkers, and banished the "New York sensibility" from Hollywood films, and with it "the hopes of the New York crowd for a cinema of ideas in this country." This led many to believe further that "the blacklist was aimed as much at New York as at the Communists." Prominent New York artists, writers, and filmmakers called before the HUAC included: Elia Kazan, Edward G. Robinson, Clifford Odets, Lillian Hellman, Dashiell Hammett, and Lee J. Cobb. Those who were blacklisted included: Dalton Trumbo, John Howard Lawson, Langston Hughs, Abraham Polonsky, Walter Bernstein, Arnold Manoff, and Zero Mostel, Ring Larndner Jr., Martin Ritt, and Herschell Bernardi.
30   Buhle and Wagner, *Hide in Plain Sight*, 16.
31   Notable in this genre are also Rod Serling's initial shorts for *Playhouse 90* in the early 1960s.
32   This scene was supported by institutions like the Film Arts Society and the Anthology Film Forum, and provided fertile ground for early experimenters like Maya Deren and Hans Richter, realists like Robert Drew and Richard Leacock, and art stars like Andy Warhol.
33   For an evocative description of New York City soundstages in Hollywood, see James Sanders, *Celluloid Skyline: New York and the Movies* (New York: Alfred A. Knopf, 2001).
34   See Ellen Stern, "How to Make a Movie in New York," *New York*, December 30, 1975, 55–60. The one-stop system was officially known as "Executive Order No. 10," signed in June 1966.

According to Stern, the first director of the office was Walter Wood, "who tells you that he has been a newspaper man, a PR man, an advertising man, and especially a movie man— having produced *The Hoodlum Priest, Escape from East Berlin,* and *The Todd Killings.*" The real brains behind the operation was a "bespectacled gingersnap" named Mary Imperato, who had worked for the old agency since 1956 and was an expert at how to navigate the relevant city agencies for permits.

35 As Imperato remembered in *ibid.*, 56, "If you needed a street, you came to me. Before you filmed, a messenger had to go around and get permission from Water, Gas, and Electric; from the Department of Highways and the Department of Buildings. I was the one who did the running. I'd take the train down to the Municipal Building to get the signatures from these guys. Meantime, the production people were complaining because the signing took time. The chief inspector of the Police Department had to sign, and he'd be out, and we'd have to wait for him to get back."

36 When asked about the impact of this shift, Lumet, then in the midst of shooting *Dog Day Afternoon,* responded: "[Before] we used to budget for [bribes]. You'd start shooting at 7:30 in the morning and have to take care of all three shifts: the sergeant who'd stop by in his car, and the cops on the street. Nobody's on the take anymore. Now you have to force a cop to take a cup of coffee on a cold day." *Ibid.*

37 See, for example, Vincent J. Cannato, *The Ungovernable City: John Lindsay and His Struggle to Save New York* (New York: Basic Books, 2001), 560; Sanders, *Celluloid Skyline,* ch. 7.

38 Stern, "How to Make a Movie in New York."

39 Franklin Whitehouse, "Hotel Business Improving Here," *New York Times,* February 12, 1967, 288. The article notes that twenty-one venerable hotels—including the Savoy Plaza and the Astor—were either demolished or converted to apartments between 1965 and 1967. This was twice the number between 1945 and 1964.

40 On the role of business travel, see *ibid.* On international travel, see "Fair Biggest Draw for Visitors to US," *New York Times,* April 27, 1964, 20. On growth of international tourism in US, see, for example, John Hamilton, *et al., International Tourism* (New York: The Economist Intelligence Unit, 1970). This primer on the international tourism industry states that in the previous decade, tourism had come to involve the movement of 200 million people annually with expenditures of $15 billion. It demonstrates the general increase of travel outside national borders, particularly from the US to abroad. On the latter issue, see also Etienne Miller, "US Spending for Foreign Travel Totaled $4 3/4 Billion in 1967," in *Survey of Current Business* 48:6 (Washington, DC: Office of Business Economics, US Department of Commerce, June 1968). Miller reports that US tourists spent $4.75 billion in 1967, an increase of 17 percent over the previous year. Meanwhile, spending by foreigners traveling in the US increased 6 percent to a record $1.9 billion.

41 City and County Data Book for 1967 (Bureau of the Census, 1967).

42 Clarence Francis, President, Economic Development Council of New York City, Inc., to the Honorable John V. Lindsay, Mayor, September 20, 1966. In "Convention and Visitors Bureau" file, New York City Municipal Archives. This letter was attached to the document by the Convention and Visitors Bureau: "A Report on the City's Interest in the NY Convention and Visitors Bureau, Inc." September 19, 1966. For additional data on state of the tourism industry in the 1960s—from the perspective of the CVB—see the following CVB annual reports: New York City Convention and Visitors Bureau, *A Story of Salesmanship: 1967 Annual Report; Selling New York: 1968 Annual Report; Success Story: Annual Report, 1969;* and *Annual Report, 1970* (all New York: New York City Convention and Visitors Bureau, 1967–1970). The reports are kept at the New York City Municipal Library, and are the only publicly accessible reports issued by the Convention and Visitors Bureau to this date.

43 On the effort by the CVB to receive greater support from the Lindsay administration, see: Clarence Francis, President, Economic Development Council of New York City, Inc., attachment to "A Report on the City's Interest in the NY Convention and Visitors Bureau, Inc." September 19, 1966; and Preston Robert Tisch to Mayor John V. Lindsay, October 20, 1970, attachment to the CVB's annual report. All documents kept in the "Convention and Visitors Bureau" file, New York City Municipal Archives. On internal lobbying and PR efforts, see the glossy annual reports mentioned in n.42.

44 See, for example, Joyce Purnick's review of Vincent Cannato's book *The Ungovernable City* in "The Last Mayor of Fun City," *New York Times,* July 15, 2001.

45   Dick Schaap, "What's New in Fun City?," *New York World Journal-Tribune*, January 7, 1966, 13.

46   *Time*, November 14, 1969.

47   As cited in Beauregard, *Voices of Decline*.

48   See, for example, the following *Time* editorials: "Crime and the Great Society," March 24, 1967; "Violence in America," July 28, 1967; "The Fear Campaign," October 4, 1968; and "What Makes a City Great?," November 14, 1969.

49   For example, Alvin Toffler, *Future Shock* (New York: Bantam, 1970).

50   This argument is made powerfully by Beauregard in *Voices of Decline*.

51   Buhle and Wagner, *Hide in Plain Sight*.

52   As Buhle and Wagner, *ibid.*, 23, ask: "What was 'normal'? In this view, the habits of the middle class, naturally; the suburbs, increasingly; and, for men, employment in some sort of service sector or corporate structure rather than the blue-collar production of goods. As television producers and directors soon learned, this meant few treatments of racial minorities except in some servile roles, and very few inner-city slum dramas . . . (except as locations for one-shot dramas)."

53   Olinger, "Advertising."

54   Clay Felker, author interview, August 27, 2003.

55   Beauregard, *Voices of Decline*.

56   These include *Saturday Night at Fort Apache*, a documentary profile on the 41st Precinct in the South Bronx, produced by New York Illustrated, aired on WNBC-TV in 1973; and *Savage Street*, which also appeared on WNBC in 1973. For more examples the best source is Vanderbilt University's Television News Archives.

57   This refers to the televised prison riot of 1971 that focused national attention on the abuses of the prison system.

58   On such references, see, for example, Lydia Yee, "Photographic Approaches to the Discourse on the South Bronx," in *Urban Mythologies: The Bronx Remembered since the 1960s*.

59   As depicted in many films about Vietnam veterans recently returned home—from *Taxi Driver* to *Coming Home*. These fictionalized veterans often responded to deteriorating conditions they found in urban neighborhoods as if they were still in combat, showing symptoms of post-traumatic stress disorder.

60   Beauregard, *Voices of Decline*.

61   The "Harlem Riot" of 1964 should be considered one of, if not the first, in the wave of "race riots" that occurred in northern US cities between 1964 and 1971. Nonetheless, it is not considered "major" either in scale or in damage caused by comparison to the "Watts Rebellion" of 1965, or to those in Newark and Detroit in 1967, Chicago in 1968, or Washington in 1969. See, for example, Terry Anderson, *The Sixties* (New York: Longman, 1999), ch. 3.

62   Joe Austin, *Taking the Train: How Grafitti Art Became an Urban Crisis in New York City* (New York: Columbia, 2001); Beauregard, *Voices of Decline*; Pauline Kael, *For Keeps* (New York: Dutton, 1994); Sanders, *Celluloid Skyline*.

63   For an excellent appraisal of the complex and contradictory cultural forces of Times Square, see William R. Taylor, *Inventing Times Square: Commerce and Culture at the Crossroads of the World* (New York: Russell Sage, 1991).

64   See Lynne Sagalyn, *Times Square Roulette: Remaking the City Icon* (Cambridge, MA: MIT Press, 2001).

65   Murray Schumach, "Tourism Business in Slump Here," *New York Times*, August 2, 1971, 29. Shumach notes: "To a lesser extent, the growth of prostitution and pornography establishments in Midtown has also kept tourists away, though there are some tourists who are drawn by pornography."

66   *Midnight Cowboy* was directed by John Schlesinger. It won Academy Awards in 1969 for Best Picture, Best Screenplay, and Best Director. It was the first X-rated film to be nominated for an Academy Award.

67   On the "New Hollywood" directors, see Peter Bikind, *Easy Riders, Raging Bulls: How the Sex-Drugs-and-Rock'n'Roll Generation Saved Hollywood* (New York: Simon and Schuster, 1998) and Robert Phillip Kolker, *A Cinema of Loneliness: Penn, Kubrick, Scorsese, Spielberg, Altman* (New York: Oxford University Press, 1988).

68   On the political backdrop and content of American films of the 1970s, see Michael Ryan and

Douglas Kellner, *Camera Politica: The Politics and Ideology of Contemporary Hollywood Film* (Bloomington: Indiana University Press, 1988) and David A. Cook, *American Cinema in the Shadow of Watergate and Vietnam, 1970–1979* (Berkelely: University of California Press, 2002). On the role of these films in generating a new, counter-cultural youth market for Hollywood, see especially Aniko Bodroghkozy, "Reel Revolutionaries: An Examination of Hollywood's Cycle of 1960s Youth Rebellion Films," *Cinema Journal* 41 (Spring 2002).

69　This history is related at the website <www.at149st.com>, which calls itself "New York City's Cyber Bench." Run by two of the major writers who got their start in New York City in the 1970s, the site is devoted to preserving the history of the artform and to celebrating its roots in New York. It is open to critique from other writers and is regularly updated. Therefore, it constitutes one of the more reliable historical sources on New York City graffiti from the perspective of its participants.

70　Author interview with Little Soul, "Old Timers' Day," at 5 Pointz, August 25, 2006.

71　Austin, *Taking the Train.*

72　See Norman Mailer, Mervyn Kurlansky, and John Narr, eds., *The Faith of Graffiti* (Washington, DC: Library of Congress, 1974); Jack Stewart, "Subway Graffiti: An Aesthetic Study of Graffiti on the Subway System of New York City, 1970–1978," Ph.D. dissertation, New York University, 1989, 163–166.

73　Mailer, Kurlansky, and Narr, eds., *The Faith of Graffiti.*

74　On this point, see Stewart, "Subway Graffiti."

75　@149st., <www.at149st.com>.

76　Austin, *Taking the Train.*

77　Author interview with Flint Gennari, July 17, 2007.

78　See Craig Castleman, *Getting Up: Subway Graffiti in New York* (Boston: MIT Press, 1982), 79–81; Stewart, "Subway Graffiti," 232–235.

79　Austin, *Taking the Train*, 50. In this context, Austin also mentions Guy Debord, who, in *The Society of the Spectacle*, had made this point earlier concerning the French Situationists. As Austin notes, the Situationists saw, and sought to reveal through their "interventions," the extent to which, in the modern era, "shared urban public space is always a mass commercial spectacle, always watched by the mass media, always under surveillance in one form or another."

80　Austin, *Taking the Train.*

81　Tania Long, "Moses Says Press Harmed the Fair: 'Tricks' of Journalism Are Blamed for Cut in Crowds," *New York Times*, October 15, 1964, 1.

Chapter 3

1　Antonio Gramsci, *Selections from Cultural Writings* (Cambridge, MA: Harvard University Press, 1991), 421.

2　Felker, author interview. This concept is so central to Felker's thinking that he uses this quote to introduce his annual introductory lecture to students at UC Berkeley's Magazine Studies masters' program, where he is now director.

3　Gramsci, *Selections from Cultural Writings*, 389.

4　*Ibid.*, 419–421.

5　One significant exception is Tom Wolfe, inventor of the term "radical chic," who was from an affluent and conservative background.

6　Jim Bellows, "Who Says Newspapers Have to Be Dull? Jim Bellows Takes Over *New York Herald Tribune*," *WorldNetDaily*, April 30, 2002. Michael Barone, the editor of the *Almanac of American Politics*, coined the term "*Herald Tribune* Republicanism" to refer to the old guard culture and politics of the East Side's "Silk Stocking District."

7　Jim Bellows, *The Last Editor: How I Helped Save the* New York Times, *the* Washington Post, *and the* Los Angeles Times *from Dullness and Complacency* (Kansas City, MO: Andrews McMeel Publishing, 2002).

8　Felker, author interview.

9　Felker understood the rise in lifestyle titles to be a result of the post-war shift in consumer spending power and taste. As he put it in his interview with the author: "Up until the war, conventional wisdom was reflected in publications like *Life, Saturday Evening Post, Colliers*, etc. After the war everyone came home, and suddenly there were ten glorious years of the economy. People had everything, while the rest of the world was in tatters. Americans all went in different directions . . . Now we had a five-day, forty-hour work-week. People had time and money to do what they wanted. Leisure time. So that made for diverse interests."

10   See Hugh Hardy, ed., *The Politz Papers: Science and Truth in Marketing Research* (Chicago: The American Marketing Association, 1990), 280–290. Felker was probably one of the first to use Politz surveys when he was one of five consultants chosen by *Time/Life* in 1954 to help create what was to become *Sports Illustrated*.

11   Felker, author interview. Most likely, Felker was referring to the following study: Alfred Politz Research, Inc., *A Study of the Household Accumulative Audience of LIFE. Conducted for LIFE by Alfred Politz Research Inc.* (New York: Time, Inc., 1950 and 1952).

12   As Felker explained: "*Life* understood the idea of the 'moneyed middle class.' But they didn't understand the huge effect it would have on [the magazine]. We [at *New York*] understood this instinctively. If someone told us they we were picking up all these trends, we would have said they didn't know what they were talking about. We were like the sunflower gradually turning toward the sun. That's just what young people do." Felker, author interview.

13   As Felker pointed out repeatedly in his interview with the author, too many magazine editors and publishers from the 1980s until today have forgotten the importance of such principles as passion and taking the reader's side, and are instead completely dominated by market research studies, focus group findings, and copying the style but not the substance of earlier, successful prototypes.

14   Milton Glaser, author interview, August 30, 2003.

15   As Bellows, "Who Says Newspapers Have to Be Dull?," described Wolfe, he was as stylish as he was talented: "His prose rollicked along with unexpected words embedded in pages that were covered with a confetti of punctuation marks. If his prose was eye-catching, so was he— his trademark was a gleaming white suit. It didn't take editorial brilliance to put Tom Wolfe to work writing features for *New York*."

16   For the original formulation of this definition, see Tom Wolfe's cover story: "The Birth of 'The New Journalism': Eyewitness Report by Tom Wolfe," *New York*, February 14, 1972. See also Tom Wolfe and E. W. Johnson, eds., *The New Journalism* (New York: Harper & Row, 1973) and John Hollowell, *Fact and Fiction: The New Journalism and the Nonfiction Novel* (Chapel Hill: University of North Carolina Press, 1977).

17   Glaser, author interview.

18   See Thomas Frank, *The Conquest of Cool* (Chicago: University of Chicago Press, 1997).

19   Indeed, Glaser was known as "president" and "design director" from *New York*'s founding in 1968 until its sale to Rupert Murdoch in 1977. As Pete Hamill, in "Pete Hamill on Milton Glaser," <www.petehamill.com>, June 26, 1999, remembers of their early collaboration: "I'd often find myself in the cubicle next to Felker's office, parked behind a typewriter, watching both men in action. Felker would arrive each morning, brimming with ideas he had absorbed the evening before while doing his rounds of cocktail parties, openings, dinner parties. Over coffee, he would unload his notions to an audience of one: Milton Glaser. 'What we should do is . . .' Felker would begin, and ideas for articles would pour from him in an excited rush. Glaser, from his totally focused silence, would fix him with those penetrating eyes and say: 'That's fine, Clay, but what's the headline?' Or 'I think I know what you mean, Clay, but how do I illustrate that concept?' And I realized that although Felker edited the magazine, Glaser edited Felker."

20   As Milton Glaser remembered in his interview with the author: "It was an interesting combination of personalities. Clay was an out-of-town guy who was constantly in awe and astonished by New York, and anxious to find out where the bones were buried and who was around and what was happening. And I was born and bred in New York, in the Bronx, and so I knew New York from the point of view of an insider, never astonished about anything. And we had different strengths. I had talent at translating ideas into images and Clay had marvelous editorial ideas. And we were just a very good team . . . Of course Clay and I represented very different points of view about what things should look like—I mean Clay's taste and my taste had very little in common. We were always fighting, always at each other's throats. (Let's just say his general recommendation would be 'make it big and make it red'). But what Clay did is that he gave me autonomy, which is not true for most art directors. I actually had a position equivalent to Clay. And so when it came to the final judgment about what was possible, I had power."

21 *Ibid.*

22 Journalist Marshall Loeb saw this as an early indication of Felker's "fearlessness" as an editor. As Loeb says in "The Ten Qualities of Successful Editors," *Columbia Journalism Review* (January/ February 2000), "After the *New York Herald Tribune* folded in 1966, he simply went out among the venture capitalists and raised millions to buy the rights to the paper's Sunday supplement, *New York* magazine, which he led to glory. Felker had never done anything like this before, but associates say that the idea of failure never entered his mind." <http://backissues.cjarchives.org/year00/1/loeb.asp>.

23 "New Owners Will Publish New York Magazine," *New York Times*, November 7, 1967, 37.

24 Standard Rate and Data Service, *Standard Rate and Data Service Consumer Magazine Advertising Source* 79:10 (Des Plaines, IL: SRDS, 1997).

25 Clay Felker was one of five editors selected as the first recipients of the Editors Hall of Fame Awards created by the American Society of Magazine Editors. According to a notice distributed by the society, Felker "broke new ground in fearlessly encouraging writers to find their own voice, and, in doing so, he reinvented and set a new standard for the city magazine. Gutsy, charming and brashly original, Felker's *New York* magazine became the indispensable handbook to the city that bears it name." See "Awards," *Berkeley Gazette*, May 1, 1996.

26 Miriam Greenberg, "Branding Cities: A Social History of the Urban Lifestyle Magazine," *Urban Affairs Review* 36:2 (November 2000), 228–263.

27 In this *New York* magazine was influenced by Susan Sontag's "Notes on Camp." For this essay, see Susan Sontag, *Against Interpretation and Other Essays* (New York: Picador, 2001). In his posthumous homage to Sontag, "Bright Lives, Big City," *New York Times*, January 2, 2005, *New York* writer Pete Hamill wrote: "In the early 1960s . . . I first read Susan Sontag's 'Notes on Camp.' Suddenly, I knew that it was all right to be thrilled by Beckett and Ionesco and Joyce, while also loving Dean Martin. I was starting then to see the city in the same way that Sontag saw our culture. I could love the brownstones of Gramercy Park and embrace Times Square, too. I could, on the same day, travel from the Metropolitan Museum to Hubert's Flea Circus on 42nd Street."

28 Glaser, author interview.

29 I chose to focus on the January and June editions because they are often "special issues" devoted to articulating an urban lifestyle in a new way. In January this often involves defining the most important lifestyle trends—issues, attitudes, leisure activities, hot neighborhoods, hip restaurants, "people to watch," etc.—for the year ahead. In June, it involves identifying the most important lifestyle trends for the summer.

30 *New York*, April 8, 1968, 1. It is also significant that the skyline pictured is of the West Side of Manhattan. It was at this time that the West Side, and particularly the Upper West Side, was beginning to gentrify despite, or because of, its designation as a site of major urban renewal which forcibly moved poor and working-class residents.

31 *Ibid.*, 59–61.

32 *Ibid.*, 87–89.

33 *Ibid.*, 53–57.

34 *Ibid.*, 57.

35 Letter to the Editor, *ibid.*, 1.

36 Tom Wolfe, "Radical Chic: That Party at Lenny's," *New York*, June 8, 1970, 26–56. This essay has been reprinted in Tom Wolfe, *Radical Chic and Mau-Mauing the Flak Catchers* (New York: Bantam, 1999).

37 *Ibid.*, 27. "*Nostalgie de la boue*" translates as "nostalgia for the mud."

38 *Ibid.*, 5.

39 *Ibid.*, 39.

40 "The Odd Couple," *Time*, June 17, 1974.

41 "Between the Lines," *New York*, April 4, 1974, 4.

42 Advertising insert, January 3, 1972.

43 *New York*, December 21, 1970.

44 *Ibid.*, 3.

45 *Ibid.*, 32–33.

46 *Ibid.*, 51–55.

47 *Ibid.*, 3, 39.

48 Sharon Zukin, *Point of Purchase: How Shopping Changed American Culture* (New York: Routledge, 2004), 183–186.

49 Gael Greene, "The Menu Rap and How to Beat It," *New York*, April 8, 1968, 60–61.

50 The feature lasted no more than a few months, ending in June 1970. Ultimately, the consumer handbook concept was extended into popular *New York* guidebooks.

51 John Bradshaw and Richard Neville. "Killer Bee Reaches New York," *More*, February 1977, 13–23.

52 Promotional insert, January 1, 1973

53 John Peter, "*New York*'s Evolutionary Design," *Folio*, June 1986, 121–122.

54 "Playing *New York*'s Power Game," *Time*, January 10, 1977, 49.

55 David Shaw, "City Magazines," in *Journalism Today: A Changing Press for a Changing America* (New York: Harper's College Press, 1977), 184–185. The earliest Diner's Club and American Express credit card ads appeared in the pages of *New York*.

56 Clay Felker, *The Power Game: From the Pages of New York Magazine* (New York: Simon and Schuster, 1969).

57 *Ibid.*

58 Wolfe, "Radical Chic," 38.

59 Richard Reeves, "The Boss of New York and Other Powerful People," *New York*, January 1, 1973, 26. The articles in this issue included a number of variations on the theme. For instance, Michael Kramer, 30–31, wrote about "The Ten Most Powerful Labor Leaders"; Pileggi, 32–33, about "Criminal Power"; Tobias, 33–34, about "Money Power"; Diamond, 42–43, about "Media Power"; Rich, 44–45, about "Power in the Arts"; and Schaap, 46–48, about "The Ten Most Indispensable People in Town."

60 Reeves, "The Boss of New York." Written in 1973, this is an explanation of Rockefeller's dominance of the previous year's list.

61 Cover, *New York*, January 5, 1970.

62 Cover, *New York*, January 4, 1971.

63 Cover, *New York*, January 3, 1972.

64 Cover, *New York*, January 1, 1973.

65 Cover, *New York*, January 14, 1974. Milton Glaser's illustration is entitled "Locking Horns over Power."

66 Robert Daley, "The Struggle for Control in the City: Winners and Losers," *New York*, January 14, 1974, 29.

67 Daley, a former police officer, offers only complaints and questions about the shift, rather than analysis. For instance, on "big oil" he says: "The president of the United States ought to swat them down, or someone should. Is there no one strong enough in this shaky world? Where has all the power gone?" In his final words he seems totally mystified: "How few *names* there are. One looks around to see who wields vast power, and for the moment one sees only the struggle for it." Related articles include the piece by Michael Korda, "Time Is Power, Money, Sex," *New York*, January 14, 1974, 29–30, and Richard Reeves, "Powerful Ideas—Has Their Time Come?," *ibid.*, 39.

68 Nicholas Pileggi, "The Power Game, 1975: Visible and Invisible Men," *New York*, January 13, 1975, 30–35. As Pileggi put it: "Today, with the city firing school teachers and closing firehouses, survival seems to be on the minds of most New Yorkers. It is in the nature of these times that much of the city's power shifts into the hands of any power broker, visible, invisible, or fake. Some day, when the economy is no longer a matter of primary concern the predatory underwriters, political manipulators, and mob loan sharks will no longer dominate New York so completely. But the speed with which the city recovers its economic and philanthropic balance will depend upon the shape in which it is left by the invisible men with power who are now riding high."

69 *Ibid.* The photo is entitled, "There's more to the city's invisible movers and shakers than meets the eye." A related essay, Michael Korda, "Office Power—You Are Where You Sit" appeared in Korda's book, *Power! How to Get It, How to Use It* (New York: Ballantine, 1975). As editor-in-chief at Simon and Schuster, Korda was clearly aware that the topic had a wide readership. His book was reissued multiple times between 1975 and 1985.

70 Stuart Little, "How to Start a Magazine," *Saturday Review*, June 14, 1969, 63; Ronald Marmarelli, "*New York* Magazine," in *Regional Interest Magazines of the United States*, ed. Sam G. Riley and Gary Selnow (Westport, CT: Greenwood Press, 1991).

71 *Ibid.*, 213.
72 Quoted in "Notes on People," *New York Times*, July 14, 1971, 41.
73 Mary Thom, *Inside Ms.: 25 Years of the Magazine and the Feminist Movement* (New York: Henry Holt, 1997).
74 *Ibid.*
75 The other "seven sisters" included: *McCall's, Redbook, Cosmopolitan, Good Housekeeping, Family Circle,* and *Woman's Day.*
76 Glaser, author interview.
77 Felker, author interview.
78 Wolfe, *Radical Chic,* 79.
79 This new era in urban lifestyle magazines was exemplified by *Los Angeles Magazine.* See Greenberg, "Branding Cities."

Chapter 4

1 Wolfgang Quante, *The Exodus of Corporate Headquarters from New York City* (New York: Praeger, 1976), 76–77.
2 ABNY's web-history, <www.ABNY.com>, 2002.
3 While the rating categories across these three agencies were different, their meaning was roughly equivalent—i.e., the value of New York City's bonds was moved from secure "investment grade" into "high-risk" or "speculative" territory. It is also significant that these agencies appeared to downgrade their ratings in concert with one another. In July 1965, Dun and Bradstreet downgraded the city's bonds from "good" to "better medium grade." Two days later, Moody's Investors Service lowered its rating from "A" to "Baa." A year later Standard and Poor's Corporation dropped the city rating from "A" to "BBB."
4 For example, Standard and Poor's rating for the UDC was "AA," and that for the state was "AAA."
5 For broader analysis of how bond-rating agencies disciplined cities like New York in this period, see Jason Hackworth, "Local Autonomy, Bond-Rating Agencies and Neoliberal Urbanism in the United States," *International Journal of Urban and Regional Research* 26:4 (December 2002), 707–725.
6 Edward Ranzal, "Publicity Is Said to Bar Better Credit for City," *New York Times*, February 10, 1971, 86.
7 *Ibid.* Indeed, it is notable that Standard and Poor's ratings for New York State and the UDC held from 1966 through 1971, even as the UDC, a massive state agency, repeatedly failed to balance its books, a development that many read subsequently as a harbinger of the city's own fiscal crisis. Yet, it was only once the UDC entered technical bankruptcy that the agency downgraded its rating for both the agency and the state. This seems to underscore Brenton's point that what distinguished New York City was not so much its fiscal profligacy as the size of its budget combined with the terrible publicity it constantly received.
8 Richard Reeves, "Civic Group Is Formed," *New York Times*, February 10, 1971, 1. The article notes: "The association's primary goal is to establish a positive image for New York, the importance of which was pointed up yesterday by the Standard & Poor's Corporation, the investment rating service."
9 *Ibid.* For the first article on the association, see David K. Shipler, "New Group Seeks to Keep Business: Association Wants to Halt Exodus from the City," *New York Times*, January 3, 1971, 34. Other prominent members from the tourism and real estate industries included Robert Tisch, president of Loew's Corporation, owner of hotels and theaters; Alan V. Tishman of Tishman Realty; and Irving Schneider, executive vice-president of Helmsely-Spear, Inc. Those representing mercantile and banking interests included Bruce Gimbel of Gimbel's, Robin L. Farkas of Alexander's, and Raymond O'Keefe, senior vice-president of Chase Manhattan.
10 Reeves, "Civic Group Is Formed."
11 *Ibid.*
12 Quante, *The Exodus of Corporate Headquarters,* 42, describes a decline from a high in 1956 of 140 firms to a low in 1974 of 64. The Department of Commerce's Office of Metropolitan Area Operations, on the other hand, estimated in 1972 that 200 of the nation's 750 largest corporations had their headquarters in New York City. In 1973, the number had dropped to

112 out of 500. See *Annual Reports* for 1972 (16) and 1973 (16). The New York State Comptroller's Office, "Audit Report on Financial and Operating Practices: New York State Department of Commerce" (Albany, NY: Office of the State Comptroller, Division of Audits and Accounts, December 31, 1974), 3, estimated that thirty corporate headquarters had left the city between 1970 and 1974, but did not specify size.

13   Quante, *The Exodus of Corporate Headquarters*, 62–63. New York was certainly not alone in losing out to this Sunbelt shift. In a comparison with ten other Eastern and Midwestern cities, New York City lost the most of its corporate headquarters overall. But as a percentage of the total, Detroit, Pittsburg, Philadelphia, and St. Louis lost more, since they were more dependent on single industries. And New York almost tied with Chicago and Boston, cities of comparable economic diversity, if not the same stature as capitals of corporate headquarters.

14   See Le Corbusier. "New York Is Not a Completed City," in *Metropolis: Center and Symbol of Our Times*, ed. Philip Kasinitz, Robert Jackall, and Arthur Vidich (New York: New York University Press, 1995).

15   Quante, *The Exodus of Corporate Headquarters*, 57, notes that these advantages often brought the fleeing firms back to New York soon afterwards.

16   As cited by William H. Whyte, "End of the Exodus: The Logic of the Headquarters City," *New York*, September 20, 1976, 88.

17   David Perry and Alfred J. Watkins, eds., "The Rise of the Sunbelt Cities," *Urban Affairs Review* 14 (1977). As Ann Markusen, "The Economics of Postwar Regional Disparity," in *Readings in Urban Theory*, ed. Susan Fainstein and Scott Campbell (London: Blackwell, 1997), 102–131, notes, the combination of a non-union locale and a conservative local political climate has long been the preference, if not the requirement, of US military contractors, who were some of the biggest investors in post-war Sunbelt development.

18   See Karen Gerard and Richard G. Birchall, *Corporate Relocation—the Impact on the Chase Manhattan Bank and the City of New York* (New York: Chase Manhattan Bank, Economic Research Division, July 1971).

19   Quante, *The Exodus of Corporate Headquarters*, 77.

20   See description in Whyte, "End of the Exodus."

21   *Ibid.*, 90.

22   By Richard Severo and Bill Carter, "Johnny Carson, Low-Key King of Late-Night TV, Dies at 79," *New York Times*, January 24, 2005.

23   James F. Reilly, "The Financial Feasibility of the Convention Center, Report for the New York City Committee of Urban Priorities," *New York Times*, 1972, III-2, discussed New York's slipping bond rate, and its relationship to media coverage.

24   Some of the most famous, pioneering artists in this development included PHASE 2, BLADE ONE, and TRACY 168. As Henry Chalfant and Peter Silver illustrate in their landmark documentary *Style Wars*, which appeared in 1981, the mural movement, which emphasized skill and time taken to do a piece, was opposed by the "taggers," who would do quick "throw ups" over these masterpieces. In general, taggers were concerned only with the quantity of their coverage, leading to rivalries between them and representatives of the mural movement.

25   New York City Convention and Visitors Bureau, *New York City Visitors Industry* (New York: CVB, June 1977).

26   Yankelovich, Skelly, and White, Inc., *Research to Support New York State's Economic Development Activities.*

27   See Fantus Company, *The Manhattan Outlook.*

28   Stuart Hall, "Encoding/Decoding," in *Media Studies: A Reader*, ed. Paul Marris and Sue Thornham (New York: New York University Press, 2000).

29   It should be noted that the same was not true of other tourist cities, particularly in the Sunbelt. See New York City Convention and Visitors Bureau, *New York City Visitors Industry.*

30   Travel Research Association, *Proceedings of the Annual Conference*, Vol. I (Salt Lake City: Bureau of Economic and Business Research, College of Business, University of Utah, 1970).

31   Quante, *The Exodus of Corporate Headquarters.*

32   New York State Department of Commerce, *Annual Report* (Albany, NY: New York State Department of Commerce, 1971), 1.

33   *Ibid.*, 2. As a State Comptroller's audit of the agency complained in 1974, New York State Comptroller's Office, *Audit Report on Financial and Operating Practices: New York State Department of Commerce* (Albany, NY: Office of the State Comptroller, Division of Audits and

Accounts, December 31, 1974), since 1970 the state had fallen far behind in its competitive position vis-à-vis other states: "New York State at one time was the industrial hub of the Nation. Notwithstanding the Department's efforts, recent economic indicators show that the State's position of leadership is being challenged or has been surpassed in some economic sectors by other states. The State's population has stopped growing. The State's share of personal and per capital income has fallen as compared to the Nation, [and] growth in nonagricultural employment, particularly in manufacturing, has lagged behind the nation." *Ibid.* The audit cites US Census Bureau statistics to back up these claims, e.g., between 1958 and 1972, the state lost 224,500 manufacturing jobs, with the greatest loss occurring in the New York City area, where most of the manufacturing establishments were located. New York City also had the slowest growth rate among all the economic regions in the state.

34 New York State Department of Commerce, *Annual Report* (Albany, NY: New York State Department of Commerce, 1972); *Annual Report* (Albany, NY: New York State Department of Commerce, 1973).

35 Generally speaking, there was a feeling in Albany that New York City, a.k.a. the "downstate" political and economic machine, had an inordinate amount of power, which it used to support a population—made up mostly of working-class Italians, Jews, Irish, blacks and Latinos—that did not reflect the rest of the population of the state. Meanwhile, New York City officials were angered by the imbalance in the amount of assistance it received from the state government—25 percent of the overall budget—versus the amount the city paid Albany in the form of taxes—over 40 percent of the total tax receipts, reflecting both its greater economic activity as well as a population that constituted over 30 percent of the state's total population.

36 Mary Holloway, author interview. Mary Holloway was executive director of ABNY for thirty years, retiring in 2002.

37 *Ibid.*

38 *Ibid.*

39 ABNY's web-history.

40 Alton Marshall, interview conducted for *The Lew Rudin Way*, 2006.

41 As Alton Marshall said, *ibid.*: "[There was] a recognition that we were not just about trying to convince the government to do everything . . . the public sector could work with the private sector and the private sector had equal responsibility. As a matter of fact, I think you'll find that in the thrust of ABNY, what developed was a sense that, if anything, the private sector had to take on more and more responsibility—sometimes more than the public sector was able to take on."

42 Alton Marshall, *ibid.*, brought up this point when discussing ABNY's approach to devising "quality-of-life" policy for the city. He contrasted this private sector-led approach in the early 1970s to that of the Giuliani administration in the 1990s: "Mayor Giuliani grabbed onto those quality-of-life things, and he did it from a public sector approach. What we were doing was primarily a private sector approach with the assistance of the government. And we started with John Lindsay when he was Mayor. And we were an important adjunct to his administering the city." This contrast will be discussed in the next chapter.

43 "Letter to the Editor," *New York Times*, March 18, 1973.

44 Franklin Vitullo, "High Rent Apartments Are Making a Comeback," *New York Times*, June 6, 1971, R1.

45 "Hearing Divided on Zoning 'Bonus': High-Density Housing Plan for East Side Debated," *New York Times*, May 19, 1972, 41. "Private Sector Steps up Construction of Apartments," *New York Times*, January 21, 1973.

46 John Darnton, "City Granting Reductions in Realty Tax at a Fast Rate," *New York Times*, August 24, 1975, P1.

47 *Ibid.*

48 *Ibid.*

49 Alton Marshall and Mary Holloway are two important exceptions. It is interesting that they were chosen to be the public faces of ABNY, accompanying Rudin to all major events, meeting the press, etc.

50 Marshall, interview for *The Lew Rudin Way*, recalls: "I remember one time, [Rudin] and I and Rex Tompkins—and both Rex and I are gentiles—went down to see the heads of thirteen commercial banks at J. P. Morgan's headquarters. And we went in and made our pitch that they should join ABNY. That they should get into this program of doing what we could do

about things that ought to be corrected. And telling everybody about the wonderful things that New York City still had that nobody else in the world had. And we got a very cool reception. And the next day I called Lew, and I said, 'Lew, what happened?' And Lew said, 'Oh, we were too Jewish.' I said, 'It was two to one.' And he said, 'Well, they thought we were too Jewish.'"

51 Mary Holloway, author interview, recalled how "Rudin, along with Alan V. Tishman and Irving Schnieder, initially approached the old Chamber of Commerce, the old organization founded downtown by Alexander Hamilton. They wanted to create a movement against rent control on commercial real estate [which was then being proposed by the state legislature]. But they found that the leadership [of the Chamber of Commerce] was made up of the same guys who were leaving," and they were not interested.

52 Alton Marshall described the approach as "two-pronged" in his interview for *The Lew Rudin Way*.

53 While this was the standard membership paid, Mary Holloway noted that there was a sliding scale for "a few members," such as public universities, that paid $2,500.

54 ABNY's web-history.

55 *Ibid.*

56 Holloway, author interview.

57 ABNY's web-history.

58 Val Adams, "Boom Year for Tourism," *New York Times*, April 6, 1969. Adams's article describes the annual luncheon of the CVB board at the New York Hilton. Preston Robert Tisch, CVB president, president of Loew's Theaters, Inc., and owner of the New York Hilton, spoke first, commenting: "More people visit New York than any other city in the world. This explains why tourism is second only to the garment/fashion industry as an income producer." The next speaker was Mayor Lindsay, who said that "tourism is of prime importance to us" and urged business concerns to support the CVB as "a terribly good investment."

59 Office of John V. Lindsay, Press Release 114–71, March 1, 1971.

60 *Ibid.*

61 Barry Popik, "The Big Apple," <www.barrypopik.com>, 2004. Popik is the self-proclaimed authority on the history of the "Big Apple" moniker. His website details historical usage in popular culture. He credits John J. FitzGerald, a sports columnist for the *New York Morning Telegraph*, with having first put the New York nickname into print on January 15, 1920, 3.

62 Joseph Nathan Kane and Gerard L. Alexander, *Nicknames and Sobriquets of US Cities and States*, 3rd edn (Metuchen, NJ: Scarecrow Press 1979).

63 Marshall, interview for *The Lew Rudin Way*.

64 Holloway, author interview.

65 Marshall, interview for *The Lew Rudin Way*.

66 Holloway, author interview.

67 Victor Gotbaum, interview conducted for *The Lew Rudin Way*, 2006.

68 Holloway, author interview. Holloway noted that the sanitation campaigns were linked to efforts to rehabilitate alchoholic homeless men in the area.

69 John Darnton, "Crime-Monitoring TV Goes on in Times Sq.," *New York Times*, September 26, 1973, 86.

70 *New York Times*, March 27, 1975, 65.

71 Holloway, author interview.

72 Marshall, interview for *The Lew Rudin Way*.

73 Holloway, author interview.

74 The Office of Television, Broadcasting, and Film was officially created in 1966.

75 Holloway, author interview. According to Holloway, Rudin's wife at the time had previously been married to a movie producer, so he knew a lot of other TV and movie producers through her. As a result, many producers would try to use Rudin to "get to the mayor" in order to get the clearance and security assistance they needed to use prominent locations for shoots—a process that could otherwise be fraught with corruption, require bribes, etc. The Office of Television, Broadcasting, and Film was created to help streamline this process and eliminate corruption.

76 *Ibid.*

77 Marshall, interview for *The Lew Rudin Way*.

78 *Ibid.*

79   "A Gain in Tourism Predicted by City—1974 Seen as 'Better Year' than 'Good Year' of 1973," *New York Times*, April 19, 1974.

80   James O'Connor, *The Fiscal Crisis of the State* (New York: St. Martin's Press, 1973); Giovanni Arrighi in Samir Amin *et al.*, *Dynamics of Global Crisis* (New York: Monthly Press, 1982), 55. For them, the chaos that accompanied crisis obscured the deeper logic of creative destruction, an essential dynamic of capitalism, through which old institutional arrangements that hampered capital accumulation had to be destroyed in order for new ones to be created that allowed for greater profitability. Eric Lichten, *Class, Power, Austerity: The New York City Fiscal Crisis* (Amherst, MA: Greenwood Press, Bergin and Garvey Publishers, 1986), 3, expresses this position well: fiscal crisis should be viewed not simply as "a result of badly mismanaged macroeconomic policy" nor "a momentary aberration which can be set right by balancing budgets according to business rationality," but instead as "part of and the consequence of a class-based struggle over wealth, income, and economic security."

81   See Beauregard, *Voices of Decline.*

82   See, for example, Charles W. Morris, *The Cost of Good Intentions* (New York: W. W. Norton, 1980).

83   Raymond Horton, *Municipal Labor Relations in New York City* (New York: Praeger, 1973); Ken Auletta, *The Streets Were Paved with Gold: The Decline of New York: An American Tragedy* (New York: Random House, 1979); Morris, *The Cost of Good Intentions.*

84   Joshua Freeman, *Working Class New York: Life and Labour since WWII* (New York: New Press, 2002), 7–8: "At the end of WWII, roughly half of New York's wage workers made, moved, or maintained physical objects for a living, everything from corsets to skyscrapers to aircraft carriers. In 1946, 41% of the employed labor force consisted of craftsmen, operatives, laborers, foremen, and kindred workers, the occupational groupings usually considered blue collar. Another 12 percent were service workers, many of whom performed manual labor: domestic servants, firemen, janitors, elevator operators, and the like . . . Similarly commercial workers were manual, working class positions." In 1950, seven of the nation's ten largest cities had a higher percentage of their workforces engaged in manufacturing than New York did. Nonetheless, in absolute terms, "New York City had a goods-producing economy unprecedented in size, output, and complexity. In 1947, NY had more man jobs than Philadelphia, Detroit, Los Angeles, and Boston put together."

85   Between 1960 and 1970, under mounting pressure from the welfare rights movement, the city used Great Society and Model City programs to expand welfare rolls and extend services more widely to its poorest residents. For more on the welfare rights movement, see Frances Fox Piven and Richard A. Cloward, *Regulating the Poor: The Functions of Public Welfare* (New York: Pantheon Books, 1971). As Bellush and Netzer, *Urban Politics*, write, by 1965, an unprecedented 500,000 New Yorkers were receiving welfare. The years between 1960 and 1973 saw a dramatic increase in labor activism and militancy, particularly among public sector unions. See Mark Maier, *City Unions: Managing Discontent in New York City* (New Brunswick, NJ: Rutgers University Press, 1987) and Freeman, *Working Class New York.* As Maier, 137, 154–5, documents, city workers participated in some thirty strikes, and numerous other job actions, between 1960 and 1975. Most of these occurred during Lindsay's two terms in office, and were some of the bitterest strikes in the city's history, including: transit (1966), teachers (1967 and 1968), sanitation (1968), drawbridge and sewage treatment plant operators (1971), police (1971), and firefighters (1973).

86   See Nancy Foner, *From Ellis Island to JFK: New York's Two Great Waves of Immigration* (New Haven, CT: Yale University Press, 2000) and Tricia Rose, *Black Noise: Rap Music and Black Culture in Contemporary America* (Hanover, NH: Wesleyan University Press, 1994).

87   For critics on the left see Kim Moody, *From Welfare State to Real Estate: Regime Change in New York City, 1974 to the Present* (New York: New Press, 2007) Lichten, *Class, Power, Austerity*, and Robert Fitch, *The Assassination of New York* (New York: Verso, 1993). As Fitch points out, while other cities across the country were facing mounting deficits as a result of shrinking revenue and increasing need for spending on social welfare, what made New York's crisis *sui generis*, and far more serious, was its "debt-propelled housing program to support the elites."

88   Much of this pressure was exerted by the state's own governor, Nelson Rockefeller, whose family was one of the largest landowners in Manhattan's downtown and Midtown financial districts, and whose brother David was the CEO of the family's Chase Manhattan Bank.

89 The largest and most disastrous of these was the Urban Development Corporation, created by Rockefeller in 1967. It went bankrupt in 1973, losing the state hundreds of millions of dollars, and leading to a federal-level investigation of its practices. Tens of other, smaller LDCs were created in the mid- to late 1960s, and met similar fates in the real estate recession of the early 1970s.

90 See "Manhattan New Office Building Construction (1960–1992)," in Fitch, *The Assassination of New York*, 280. Fisk draws on data from the Real Estate Board of New York Research Department. Totals do not include additions, reconstructions, or mixed-use buildings.

91 The greatest example of the use of rent to subsidize private real estate is the World Trade Center. When it was unable to rent its ten million square feet of office space, the city and state governments, along with the New York and New Jersey Port Authority, stepped in to rent over half of the space.

92 Fitch, *The Assassination of New York*, ix.

93 Moody, *From Welfare State to Real Estate*, 58–59; Graduate School of Public Affairs, *Real Property Tax Policy for New York City* (New York: New York University, 1980).

94 For good example of this, see Fred Ferretti, *The Year the Big Apple Went Bust* (New York: Putnam, 1976).

95 See Lichten, *Class, Power, Austerity*, 95–126; William K. Tabb, *The Long Default: New York City and the Urban Fiscal Crisis* (New York: Monthly Review Press, 1982), 22–25; Jack Newfield and Paul Du Brul, *The Abuse of Power: The Permanent Government and the Fall of New York* (New York: Viking, 1977); Roger E. Alcaly and David Mermelstien, eds., *The Fiscal Crisis of American Cities* (New York: Vintage, 1977).

96 "Fighting the Unthinkable," *Time*, September 8, 1975, 9.

97 Freeman, *Working Class New York*.

98 The most prominent of Carey's consultants was Felix Rohatyn of Lazard Freres. In addition, Carey consulted with Simon H. Rifkind, former federal judge, Richard Shinn, president of Metropolitan Life Insurance Corporation, and Donald B. Smiley, CEO of R. H. Macy. As Freeman, *Working Class New York*, 260, observes: "In [consulting with these men], he was asking leaders of large capital, who had a national and international orientation that left them normally oblivious to day-to-day city affairs, to shape a solution to the fiscal crunch."

99 Newfield and Du Brul, *The Abuse of Power*, 178–182; Robert W. Bailey, *The Crisis Regime: The MAC, the EFCB, and the Political Impact of the New York City Financial Crisis* (Albany: State University of New York Press, 1984), 27–29; Lichten, *Class, Power, Austerity*, 129–134.

100 Ferretti, *The Year the Big Apple Went Bust*. Specifically, the city called on workers to forgo a 6 percent pay increase scheduled for July 7 or accept, with proportional pay reductions, a four-day work-week. After the unions rejected the proposal, Beame called for a huge reduction in CUNY admissions, closing library branches and health facilities, and the immediate elimination of 38,000 city jobs.

101 On the split between union leaders and their rank-and-file membership on concessions during the fiscal crisis, see Maier, *City Unions*.

102 Freeman, *Working Class New York*.

103 As Freeman points out, *ibid.*, 265, while the MAC had succeeded in selling two $1 billion bond issues, there was little interest in subsequent offerings. This is why Carey and his advisors, Rohatyn, Simon Rifkind, and William Ellinghouse (NY Telephone president), drafted an omnibus bill for the Emergency Financial Control Board (EFCB)—in "another effort to reopen private capital markets."

104 See Maier, *City Unions*. DC 37's Gotbaum led other leaders in supporting the EFCB bill in exchange for two concessions: collective bargaining would continue, and attrition would be used before lay-offs in workforce reduction. While Gotbaum and his allies won the first concession, they lost the second, and the city laid off eight thousand teachers and para-professionals at the end of summer 1975. Critics at the time, like Maier, argued that the emphasis on collective bargaining, in the midst of downsizing and increasingly common "no-strike pledges," stifled union militancy and elevated union leadership and bureaucracy. Stanley Aronowitz made a similar argument, on a broader scale, in *False Promises: The Shaping of American Working Class Consciousness* (New York: McGraw-Hill, 1973).

105 This event is recounted by Ed Koch in his interview for *The Lew Rudin Way* documentary, 2006. It was during this trip that Rudin came up with the novel strategy of having corporate

tenants pre-pay their real estate taxes, thus making tens of millions of dollars available to the city.

106   Charles J. Orlebecke, "Saving New York: The Ford Administration and the New York City Fiscal Crisis," in *Gerald Ford and the Politics of Post-Watergate America*, Vol. II, ed. Bernard J. Firestone and Alexej J. Ugrinsky (Westport, CT: Greenwood Press, 1993), 321. Referring to William Simon's memoir, *A Time for Truth* (New York: Reader's Digest Press, 1978), Orlebecke states Simon's sole concerns in allowing the city to go into bankruptcy were: "avoiding civil unrest, and preserving confidence in the financial structure, particularly the banking system." *Ibid.*

107   "Seasonal loans" were Rohatyn's idea. New York City borrowed pieces of the loan from the federal government at the beginning of the fiscal year, and paid it back at the end, when a new piece of the loan would be made available. Gerald Ford recalled this settlement in his interview with Robert Rudin for *The Lew Rudin Way*, 2006, giving some indication of his attitude towards the city unions, and the city itself, at the time: "The Mayor and the council were much too generous in pay increases for city employees, with all the retirement benefits. The Mayor and Governor came down to see if Uncle Sam could bail them out. Simon had [been] tough on those New York people. We came to a responsible conclusion where the federal government would, at the beginning of the New York fiscal period, loan them money, and in the end they would pay us back."

108   As Freeman, *Working Class New York*, 268, writes, down the line, this position would "would irrevocably link the unions to the cause of city solvency, no matter what the social cost."

109   *Ibid.*, 269. The new bail-out package (following Simon) involved raising taxes by $200 million, placing a moratorium on repayment of $2.6 billion in debt, and a shift from short-term to long-term bonds (a year later found unconstitutional in state court). In addition, some cost of future pension fund contributions shifted from city to employee.

110   Newfield and Du Brul, *The Abuse of Power*. Preston Robert Tisch, interview conducted for *The Lew Rudin Way*, 2006. Tisch first introduces himself by saying: "I've been [working] in New York forty-two years now. We've been successful. We've been developers of some small degree of office buildings, housing, and particularly hotels. And we got to know a lot of people about the city, because they've been involved in city politics. We used to [be called] the 'permanent government' over the years." Later, in response to the question "Do you believe Lew's vision for New York was the same as yours?," Tisch responds: "Most definitely . . . And I'm going back over twenty-five years . . . from 1975, 1976 to when he unfortunately passed away in 2001. There's no question that we both believed in helping whoever was the Mayor at the time . . . I used a phrase, 'permanent government.' I remember Jack Newfield wrote it in the *Village Voice* at that time . . . and I said, 'What does he mean? Is he taking a shot at us?' [But] basically he was right, because we all, many of us, stayed with it over the years."

111   See, for example, Lichten, *Class, Power, Austerity*; Felix Rohatyn, "New York and the Nation," *New York Review of Books* 28, January 21, 1982; Tabb, *The Long Default*.

Chapter 5

1   Committee for Public Safety, "Welcome to Fear City—A Survival Guide for Visitors to the City of New York." A copy of the pamphlet is located in the Jack Bigel Archive on Municipal Finance and Leadership at Baruch College, New York City.
2   *Ibid*, emphasis in original.
3   *Ibid.*
4   *Ibid.*, author's emphasis.
5   "Unions vs. New York," *New York Times*, June 12, 1975, 36.
6   Glenn Fowler, "Union 'Guide' to Fear City Is Banned by a Court Order," *New York Times*, June 13, 1975, 1. Mr. Beame concluded, "I wish to reassure every citizen and every visitor . . . that their safety and welfare are a paramount priority and will remain so regardless of temporary economic setbacks."
7   Glenn Fowler, "Unions Put off to Monday Giving out 'Fear' Leaflets," *New York Times*, June 14, 1975, 1.
8   Fowler, "Union 'Guide' to Fear City."
9   Tom Goldstein, "Leaflet Ban Is Called Unconstitutional: News Analysis," *New York Times*,

June 14, 1975. The doctrine is named after Supreme Court Justice Oliver Wendell Holmes, who first presented it in 1919.

10   *Ibid.*

11   Fowler, "Unions Put off to Monday." Meanwhile, the Transit Authority got a separate restraining order, based on the grounds that specific warnings in the pamphlets—for example, that visitors should "never ride the subway for any reason whatsoever," and that buses in Midtown Manhattan can be ridden during daylight hours "at only slight risk"— would mean that "its efforts to maintain ridership would be irreparably damaged . . . leading to heavy operating deficits." See Glenn Fowler, "City Officers Win Right to Go Ahead with 'Fear' Drive: But They Decide to Hold off for a Few Days—Tax Collections Are Cut," *New York Times*, June 17, 1975.

12   Fowler, "Unions Put off to Monday."

13   Goldstein, "Leaflet Ban." Abrams had led the successful defense of the *New York Times* against the federal government's efforts to stop publication of the Pentagon Papers just one year previously. He was thus also perplexed by the staunch, pro-censorship position taken by the editorial board of the *Times* in this case.

14   Glenn Fowler, "'Fear City' Booklet Rights Again Upheld," *New York Times*, June 18, 1975, 19.

15   Fowler, "Unions Put off to Monday." As Fowler reported, almost incredulously, "From all outward appearances, the unions participating in the campaign were not encountering broad opposition from rank and file or from delegate assemblies."

16   Leonard Buder, "20,000 City Teachers Press Demands; Fact-Finding Panel Is Called into Talks," *New York Times*, September 5, 1975, 20. Indeed, the sanitation workers tied the slogan to a city-wide garbage strike in August, the hottest month of the year, when piled-up garbage smelled worst, an action that caused additional damage to the city's image, to say nothing of its quality of life.

17   Fowler, "'Fear City' Booklet."

18   *Ibid.*

19   *Ibid.*

20   *Ibid.* This first point was underscored by Rudin: "We have strongly suggested a number of means of cutting expenditures to Mayor Beame. But the final determination of where the cuts are applied must be left to the city administration, which is in possession of all the facts about the city's fiscal condition." The second point was emphasized in the lead paragraph of the *Times'* coverage: the CPS "received a sharp setback when a prominent businessmen's organization likened the council's 'Fear City' campaign to 'burning down the factory in a labor dispute.'"

21   *Ibid.*

22   Leslie Maitland, "Tourists Flocking to City Despite Its Fiscal Woes," *New York Times*, July 31, 1975.

23   Glenn Fowler, "City Countering 'Fear' Campaign: Heads of Visitors Bureau to Tour 4 Cities Abroad," *New York Times*, June 21, 1975, 14. The USTS gave a special grant to the CVB for this purpose.

24   *Ibid.*

25   The "planned shrinkage" concept was first made known in January 1976 in a speech to a gathering of the Real Estate Board of New York and subsequent interviews with the trade publication *Real Estate Weekly*, and only made known to the wider public in February 1976 in a short *New York Times* article.

26   Andrew Ross, *The Chicago Gangster Theory of Life: Nature's Debt to Society* (New York: Verso, 1994), ch. 2.

27   Roger Starr, "Making New York Smaller," *New York Times Magazine*, November 14, 1976.

28   This is despite the fact that Starr was both well aware of these costs and, initially, willing to acknowledge them. Unlike other leading officials of the crisis regime, Starr publicly detailed the detrimental role of the city's borrowing via quasi-public authorities to fund private sector real estate development, once private mortgage markets had dried up. As he said towards the beginning of his famous *New York Times Magazine* article, *ibid.*, 1–2, "[The money of the city's creditors], entrusted to life-insurance companies and major banks, was loaned by those institutions to finance the construction of office buildings, hotels, motels, and luxury apartments houses in New York. Only lately have some of the sophisticated managers of foreign money realized that they misperceived New York City's future. Some major new

mortgages have been foreclosed; other projects were put into the deep freeze even before they were finished. When mortgages from commercial sources began to slow down, the [city's private sector] turned to government sources. More billions of dollars, corralled from less sophisticated savers all over the nation, flowed into municipal notes and bonds that paid for revenue-producing projects developed by the Port Authority, the New York State Housing Finance Agency, the Urban Development Corporation, and the New York State Dormitory Authority. To the extent that they were based on gross underestimates of future revenues, they have increased the burdens of the [city government]." However, this does not mean Starr saw the perpetrators of this practice as responsible for their actions. In convoluted fashion, he argued that the lesson the city should learn from such over-borrowing was to make its public sector smaller, and less responsible for social welfare, rather than hold any private sector actors accountable for problems they helped cause. It should also be noted that in Starr's retrospective on the fiscal crisis, *The Rise and Fall of New York* (New York: Basic Books, 1989), the above analysis was completely absent. While still placing blame for the city's deficit of the early 1970s on its borrowing to make mortgage payments, Starr now focused on mortgages of public housing projects for low- and middle-income New Yorkers, and no longer on those of "office buildings, hotels, motels, and luxury apartments houses."

29 "Rohatyn Urges a City Plan for Industry," *New York Times*, March 16, 1976.

30 Freeman, *Working Class New York*, 275, cites one example from 1975, in which the Dollar Savings Bank, then the largest mortgage lender in the city, and the fifth largest in the country, issued only thirty-two mortgages in the entire borough of the Bronx.

31 See, for example, David Harvey, *The Limits to Capital* (New York: Verso, 1999).

32 For editorials that later outlined much of the critique, see Anna Quindlen, "Must the City Sacrifice the Poor to Lure Back the Middle Class? Fantasyland," *New York Times*, August 12, 1979; Fergus Bordewich, "The Future of New York: A Tale of Two Cities," *New York Times*, July 23, 1979; and "Clearance Work Stirs Objections," *New York Times*, February 10, 1980.

33 Glenn Fowler, "Starr's 'Shrinkage' Plan for City Slums Is Denounced," *New York Times*, February 11, 1976, 49.

34 Joseph Fried, "Housing," in Francis X. Clines, "Carey Urges Neighbors Not to Downgrade New York," *New York Times*, March 3, 1976, 31.

35 "Minority Caucus Bids Starr Quit: Calls Housing Chief's Plan for Poor Areas 'Racist,'" *New York Times*, March 5, 1976, 13.

36 Thomas A. Johnson, "Rohatyn Scored by Congressmen: Badillo and Rangel Critical of Blighted-Areas Plan," *New York Times*, March 17, 1976.

37 There was debate over whether Starr voluntarily resigned or was asked to step down by the Beame administration. In any case, his departure was a protracted process, making it seem involuntary. His possible resignation was first announced in May and confirmed in July 1976. See Joseph Fried, "Starr, New York City Housing Chief, Will Leave Post by Fall," *New York Times*, May 22, 1976, 24, and "Starr Resigning as Chief of New York City Housing," *New York Times*, July 9, 1976, 30. Starr ultimately stepped down in September.

38 In terms of halting the construction of new housing, New York was participating in what was a nationwide phenomenon in the 1970s, after federal funding for construction of public housing was ended by the Nixon administration in 1972.

39 Deborah Wallace and Roderick Wallace, *A Plague on Both Your Houses* (New York: Verso, 1998).

40 *Ibid.* The health and safety experts Deborah and Roderick Wallace conducted the most extensive study of the history, scope, and distribution of the city's cuts in fire service, and the relationship this had to the increase in fires in particular neighborhoods. In their study, they found that social engineers, some of them from the Rand Corporation Fire Project, supervised the deliberate degradation of fire control resources in areas the engineers of shrinkage had slated for clearance. Ultimately, over the course of two years about 10 percent of New York's fire companies were eliminated, 20 percent of manpower cut, and emergency response systems whittled down. This occurred primarily in ten of the city's poorest neighborhoods, located mainly in the Bronx and Brooklyn. As response time fell in these still heavily populated neighborhoods by between five and ten minutes (a deadly amount in fire terms), an "inevitable fire epidemic" resulted. This then exacerbated the problem of housing abandonment by landlords. When the dust settled, the Wallaces calculated that about two million poor people had been uprooted by the end of the decade.

41 Michael Daly, *Daily News* crime reporter in the 1970s, speaking on the panel, "New York City in the 1970s: The Pre-Gentrification Years," Gotham Center for New York City History, May 18, 2005.

42 According to the City and County Data Book for 1983 (Bureau of the Census, 1983) between 1970 and 1980 New York City lost 825,000 residents, while the New York metropolitan area lost 915,000, or 20 percent of its population.

43 Dennis Judd, "Constructing the Tourist Bubble," in *The Tourist City*, ed. Dennis Judd and Susan S. Fainstein (New Haven, CT: Yale University Press, 1999), 35–53.

44 For a powerful articulation of this new realization among residents in neighborhoods cut off by planned shrinkage, see Marshall Berman, "Views from the Burning Bridge," in *Urban Mythologies: The Bronx Remembered since the 1960s*.

45 "Glory Days," *New York Times*, January 2, 2005. As John Leguizamo said in response to the question of which era in New York was his favorite: "My favorite era [was] the 70s. New York was funky and gritty and showed the world how a metropolis could be dark and apocalyptic and yet fecund. The death of disco and the birth of hip-hop all happened in our cradle of civilization, as if the Tigris and Euphrates Rivers, or rather the Hudson and East Rivers, were hugging the new Mesopotamia of funk. In the Bronx, my black and Latin brothers and sisters created break dancing and rapping."

46 *Ibid*. These included Laurie Anderson and John Leguiziamo, as well as Mary Ellen Mark and Fran Lebowitz.

47 *Ibid*.

48 From the Gotham Center panel, "New York in the 1970s," ibid.

49 For histories of the extreme nature of the abandonment of the Bronx in the 1960s, see in particular: Robert Caro, *The Power Broker: Robert Moses and the Fall of New York* (New York: Knopf, 1974) and Evelyn Gonzalez, *The Bronx* (New York: Columbia University Press, 2004).

50 *Ibid*.

51 On the broader cultural renaissance in the Bronx in the 1970s, see Chang, *Can't Stop, Won't Stop*; Farmer, *Urban Mythologies: The Bronx Remembered since the 1960s*, and the documentary by Henry Chalfant, *From Mambo to Hip Hop: A Bronx Tale* (New York: City Lore, Inc., 2006).

52 The question of what constitutes the fifth element of hip hop is open to debate and interpretation. Jessica Green, for instance, has called "the neighborhood" the fifth element, as this is the space through which all the elements come together. As cited by Austin, *Taking the Train*, 50. For more on founding forces in hip hop like Bambaataa and DJ Kool Herc, see Rose, *Black Noise* and Chang, *Can't Stop, Won't Stop*.

53 Johannes Fabian, as cited by Juan Flores, *From Bomba to Hip-Hop: Puerto Rican Culture and Latino Identity* (New York: Columbia University Press, 2000), 20.

54 On intersections between African American and Latino cultures in neighborhoods in the Bronx, Harlem, and Brooklyn in this period, see *ibid*. and Raquel Z. Rivera, *New York Ricans from the Hip Hop Zone* (New York: Palgrave, 2002). On Jamaican influence via MCs like Kool Herc, see Chang, *Can't Stop, Won't Stop*.

55 Rose, *Black Noise*.

56 *Ibid*.

57 *Ibid*.

58 This scenario was famously captured in the movie *Wild Style* (1981), in which a downtown producer, played by Debbie Harry, ventures up to the wilds of the Bronx to witness the artistry of such early giants as Fab Five Freddy and the Cold Crush Brothers. Rap music's lack of media exposure was to change somewhat by the 1980s with the rise of the music video and the proliferation of films like *Wild Style* and *Breakin'* (1984) that portrayed break dancing, mc'ing, and dj'ing. But its image was still associated with the outer boroughs, rather than the heart of Manhattan, thus not impacting the "image crisis" directly.

59 @149st., <www.at149st.com>.

60 *Ibid*.

61 Castleman, *Getting Up*.

62 Berman, "Views from the Burning Bridge," 73.

63 *Ibid*.

64 *Ibid*.

65 Lady Pink in an interview with the author, emphasis in the original.

66 International exhibits include: "The Aesthetics of Graffiti," April 28–July 2, 1978, San
    Francisco Museum of Modern Art; "*Les murs murmurent, ils crient, ils chantent*" Centre
    Georges Pompidou, Paris, 1982; "Arte di Frontiera: New York Graffiti," Palazzo delle
    Esposizioni, Rome, September 11–October 21, 1984; "Graffiti," Museum Boymans-Van
    Beuningen, Rotterdam, October 22–December 4, 1983; "Classical American Graffiti Writers
    and High Graffiti Artists," Galerie Thomas, Munich, April 5–June 2, 1984.
67 A small number of exhibits in New York City included graffiti, including a group show at the
    Whitney in 1975, the Mud Club in 1977, and the "New York/New Wave" at P.S.1 Institute
    for Art in 1981.
68 The first great framing of this debate was in Tony Silver and Henry Chalfant's *Style Wars*
    (1982). For a historical overview of the war on graffiti through the 1980s, see Austin, *Taking
    the Train.*
69 See the interview with Ed Koch in *Style Wars* in which he defines "lifestyle crimes" in relation
    to graffiti.
70 Stern, "How to Make a Movie in New York," 55.
71 *Ibid.,* 60.
72 *Ibid.* Examples included getting the Department of Highways to repave Orchard Street from
    Houston to Delancey so that the camera would not shake during a crucial chase scene in
    Thieves, having the Parks Department remove graffiti for the period drama *Hester Street,* and
    frequently sending the Sanitation Department out ahead of a film crew to clean the streets, or
    hose them down to create the impression of rain-slicked concrete.
73 *Ibid.,* 56. As evidence of the concern, the article goes on to cite protests from the Port
    Authority over use of a subway car for a hijacking in *The Taking of Pelham One Two Three*
    and from the Port Authority and JFK Airport over the hijacking of a plane in the final scene
    of *Dog Day Afternoon.* In both cases, the city agencies were concerned about the image that
    would be presented, as well as safety hazards. The MOFTB was responsive to the agencies,
    promising that they would cover costs and ensure the propriety of the scene.
74 Austin, *Taking the Train.*
75 Vincent Canby, "New York's Woes Are Good Box Office," *New York Times,* November 10,
    1974. See also Robert Stern, Thomas Mellins, and David Fishman, *New York 1960:
    Architecture and Urbanism between the Second World War and the Bicentennial* (New York:
    Monacelli Press, 1995), 1174–1196.
76 Mark Jacobson, "New York, You Oughta Be in Pictures," *New York,* December 30, 1975, 42.
    Jacobson was willing to acknowledge grudgingly that there were "some great New York
    moments" in the spate of recent films like *Where's Poppa?, The Taking of Pelham One Two
    Three, John and Mary, Born to Win, Midnight Cowboy,* and *The French Connection.* But he also
    felt "something was missing" in all these movies. For instance, though *The French Connection*
    used "impeccable locations" to create "an aura of potential violence," and had great
    pyrotechnics, editing, character studies by Gene Hackman, and direction by William
    Friedkin, it still lacked authenticity, and the true New York sensibility. "There's still the feeling
    that this picture knows its way around town like an attuned and venturesome tourist. But
    don't ask it what school it went to."
77 *Ibid.*
78 *Ibid.,* 43.
79 Independent film took off in New York City much more so than in Los Angeles during the
    1960s.
80 Jacobson, "New York, You Oughta Be in Pictures," 44.
81 Woody Allen's romantic comedies *Annie Hall* (1977) and *Manhattan* (1979) were two of very
    few films of the period that significantly challenged the New York exploitation genre—and
    did so with his typically neurotic, self-depreciating humor. *Annie Hall,* starring Diane Keaton
    as the beautiful, scatter-brained love interest of anxiety-ridden Allen, won numerous
    Academy Awards and remains one of the most influential American films—in part because
    of its ability to embody a distinctive New York sensibility so sorely lacking by the late 1970s.
    Indeed, its famous conclusion in which Keaton leaves Allen for the shallow, New Age scene
    in Los Angeles can be read as a swipe at the rising Sunbelt. Meanwhile, *Manhattan*—with its
    lush black-and-white cinematography and the lead character's endlessly reiterated love of his
    city despite his failed love-life—was seen at the time as unabashedly boosterish, a kind of
    nostalgic reply to the contemporary *Death Wish* universe. This view, of course, had its own
    narrowness—i.e., characters limited to slices of pavement on the Upper West and Upper East

Sides. Nonetheless, it must be said that Allen was one of very few filmmakers capable of countering the hegemony of a dystopic New York in this period.

82 According to the Internet Movie Database, *Death Wish* grossed $22 million, making it one of the top grossing films of the 1970s.

83 Roger Ebert, "Death Wish," *Chicago Sun-Times*, January 1, 1974.

84 *Ibid.*

85 A direct quote from *Taxi Driver*, 1976.

86 On the iconic role of Travis Bickle, see, for example, Kolker, *A Cinema of Loneliness.*

87 Yee, "Photographic Approaches to the Discourse on the South Bronx." Nowhere was this more true than in films shot amid the rubble-strewn lots of the South Bronx. As Bronx Museum curator Lydia Yee noted: "The image of the burnt-out Bronx provided a blank slate on which any number of myths could be overlaid . . . As a mythical signifier, the streets of the South Bronx loose their unique history, their particular character. And consequently, the Hollywood screenwriter is able to fill the neighborhood with a fantastic cast of characters."

88 Jacobson, "New York, You Oughta Be in Pictures," 44.

89 Freeman, *Working Class New York*, 281.

Chapter 6

1 See David Harvey, "From Managerialism to Entrepreneurialism: The Transformation of Urban Governance in Late Capitalism."

2 Rudin's son Robert, who conducted the interview with Ford for *The Lew Rudin Way*, 2006, made a laughing reference to the *Daily News* headline "Ford to City: Drop Dead": "A lot of people were upset initially [with your position towards New York]. But my father knew how important it was, how much you helped the city. When you came to New York, to Federal Hall [to speak to ABNY], he was very proud."

3 It should be noted that while their relationship was solidified in this period, they in fact first met in "the late 60s or early 70s playing golf," and were to continue to golf at the same club, and participate in Ford's "invitational" celebrity tournaments, for the next twenty-five years until soon before Rudin's death in 2001. This is according to Ford in his interview for *The Lew Rudin Way.*

4 David Rockefeller, "Ingredients for Successful Partnerships: The New York City Case," in *Public–Private Partnerships: Improving Urban Life*, ed. Perry Davis (New York: Academy of Political Science/New York City Partnership, 1986), 122–123. It is interesting to note that the NYCP both learned and sought to differentiate itself from ABNY.

5 This turnaround, it should be noted, was not universal. More conventional merchant bankers, like the MAC chairman Felix Rohatyn, were more leery of marketing-led strategies than those in real estate and tourism. And even among the latter there was disagreement, with the older generation arguing against working with government and adopting untested PR methods. Lew Rudin, for instance, debated with his own father, company founder Sam Rudin, about involving the family firm in politics and city marketing. Holloway, author interview.

6 New York City Department of City Planning, *Economic Recovery: New York City's Program for 1977–1981* (New York: New York City Department of City Planning, 1976).

7 *Ibid.* See sections on "Tax Program," 21–27, and "Office of Economic Development," 28–33.

8 *Ibid.*, "Marketing the City," 34–37.

9 *Ibid.*, 34.

10 *Ibid.*

11 *Ibid.*

12 Michael Sterne, "A Good Tourist Year Cited for New York: Convention and Visitors Bureau Reports its Records Show that 1976 Was One of City's Best," *New York Times*, January 4, 1977.

13 For accounts of the excited preparations in New York City and cities nationwide in anticipation of the Bicentennial, see the clippings file in the archived boxes of the New York City Bicentennial Corporation at the New York City Municipal Library.

14 It is known that the police took pictures of the train, but none of these has ever been released to the public.

15 Austin, *Taking the Train*, 1.

16 Michael Sterne, "Visitors Bureau Reports Boom in Tourism," *New York Times*, October 16, 1976.

17 Edward Sorel, "Preview of Coming Attractions," *New York*, December 30, 1975, 69.
18 *Ibid.*
19 Owen Moritz, "The Towering Question: Whose Top is Tops?," *Daily News*, January 12, 1976, 4.
20 Fred Ferretti, "Sky-High Dining in 'Windows,'" *New York Times*, July 16, 1976, 63.
21 *Ibid.*
22 *Ibid.*
23 Gael Greene, "The Most Spectacular Restaurant in the World," *New York Times*, May 31, 1976, 42–52.
24 *Ibid.*
25 New York City Convention and Visitors Bureau, "Advertisement" (New York: New York City Convention and Visitors Bureau, 1976).
26 Sterne, "Visitors Bureau Reports Boom in Tourism."
27 Abraham Beame, Mayor of New York, and Victor Marrero, Chairman of City Planning Commission, *New York's Visitors Industry* (New York: New York City Department of City Planning, #77-15, June 1977), 1. In order to make this claim, this new industry cluster had first to be measured and defined. This, the report acknowledged, was not an easy task, since "visitor activities are tightly interwoven with other services, and, consequently, difficult to identify." Nonetheless, the report identified the "major components of the complex of activities labeled the 'visitors industry' in New York City," including: 400 hotels, 17,000 eating and drinking establishments, 12,000 taxis, 400 motion picture theaters, and 60 department stores.
28 Sterne, "Visitors Bureau Reports Boom in Tourism."
29 *Ibid.*
30 See US Department of Commerce, Bureau of the Census, 1977.
31 Municipal Assistance Corporation, *Annual Report: 1976* (New York: Municipal Assistance Corporation, 1976).
32 *Ibid.*, 23.
33 Sterne, "A Good Tourist Year Cited for New York."
34 *Ibid.*
35 Beame and Marrero, *New York's Visitors Industry*, 1.
36 *Ibid.*
37 *Ibid.*, 28.
38 *Ibid.*, 26. This assessment was based on the findings of a "1975 City Planning Dept Survey" of visitors' bureaus in seven cities. From this it was found that while private subscription was higher in New York's CVB, the bureau's budget was smaller relative to total city visitors, and it received less from the city. The survey further compared New York to other cities in terms of the "quality of promotional literature," the number and use of "package tour brokers," and the media placement of advertisements. It was found that New York was at a disadvantage, since it did not advertise in trade publications, magazines, or newspapers, but rather "concentrates instead on enhancing the city's image through press releases in out-of-town publications." Meanwhile, other cities were "attempting to attract foreign visitors [by] placing ads in foreign press, via the Department of Commerce Travel Service, and promotional program and tour of the city for foreign and domestic agents during 'familiarization tours' organized by airlines."
39 Sterne, "Visitors Bureau Reports Boom in Tourism."
40 *Ibid.*
41 Stuart Hall, "Encoding/Decoding," 51–61.
42 This according to a special A&E documentary, *Biography: David Berkowitz: Son of Sam* (1999).
43 The name was even more deeply embedded in popular culture in 1999, with the release of the Spike Lee movie *Summer of Sam.*
44 According to the *Time* article, "Night of Terror," July 25, 1977, 21, the vast majority of this $1 billion loss was a result of the looting. Losses directly incurred by the city include $4 million in lost tax revenue and $5 million in overtime to police and firemen. Estimates of business losses—beyond the looting—included up to $15 million in lost brokerage commissions for Wall Street and $20 million for retail stores.
45 For example, one of the most devastated areas was in Bushwick and Bedford Stuyvesant, Brooklyn, where a 1.5-mile section of Broadway, the main business thoroughfare, was

completely gutted by looting and fires. To this day, many of the storefronts on that section of Broadway, and surrounding housing units, remain abandoned.

46 "Night of Terror," 21.
47 George Will, "Shock of Recognition," *Newsweek*, July 25, 1977, 80.
48 Tom Nicholson, "The Impact," *Newsweek*, July 25, 1977, 17. In an aside, "Night of Terror," 21, reported that five hundred Windows on the World diners finished their meals by candlelight and rode to the ground on a service elevator powered by generator.
49 *Ibid.*, 17.
50 Nicholson, "The Impact," 23.
51 In *ibid.*, the word "plague" is used twice, on 19 and 26. "Fever" and "orgy of looting" both appear in "Night of Terror," 16.
52 *Ibid.*, 21 and 16. The full quote reads: "At Hearn's department store in Brooklyn, youths stripped clothing from window mannequins, broke their limbs and scattered them on the floor. Said Miguel Ten, a Viet Nam veteran who stood guarding Arnet's Children's Wear store: 'This reminds me of Pleiku in 1966. There was a war out here. And the mannequins remind me of the dead people I saw in Nam without legs and arms.'"
53 Nicholson, "The Impact," 18.
54 *Ibid.*
55 *Ibid.*,17.
56 *Ibid.*, 30.
57 *Ibid.*
58 *Ibid.*
59 *Ibid.*
60 *Ibid.*
61 *Ibid.*, 21.
62 *New York* cover for January 1, 1978.
63 Ernest Dickinson, "Tourists Hotels Languish as Mecca Loses Its Magic," *New York Times*, February 22, 1976.

Chapter 7

1 Yankelovich, Skelly, and White, Inc., *Research to Support New York State's Economic Development Activities*, 21, 23.
2 Harvey Chipkin, *New York City's Campaign for Agency Business* (New York: American Society of Travel Agents (ASTA) Management, 1988), C1. Chipkin is citing CVB numbers.
3 *Ibid.*
4 Mary Wells Lawrence, "Baby Boom, Creative Boom," *Advertising Age*, June 18, 1990, 66.
5 Neil Smith, "Geography, Difference and the Politics of Scale," in *Postmodernism and the Social Sciences*, ed. Joe Doherty, Elspeth Graham, and Mo Malek (London: Macmillan, 1992), 57–79. As Smith has argued, in periods of global economic restructuring and crisis, such as New York faced in the 1970s, localities often attempt to reorganize their political and economic resources on a larger regional scale in order to withstand the forces of global capital and the global market.
6 This point was emphasized by my fellow panelists on the "Government–Business Relations" panel at Researching New York 2004, SUNY Albany's annual New York State history conference. All noted the tendency among New York State governors, from Al Smith through Herbert Lehman, and even including Rockefeller, to play a Fordist role, seeking to regulate the relationship between organized labor, the private sector, and a large, strong government sector. This changed under Carey, New York's first post-Fordist governor.
7 Beame and Marrero, *New York's Visitors Industry*.
8 The OED divisions included: Division of Industrial and Corporate Development; Ombudsmen and Small Business Services Division; Division of Foreign International Commerce; and Division of Science and Technology.
9 The divisions within the Office of Economic Planning, Administration, and Marketing included: Administrative and Legal Services; Division of Marketing and Advertising; Division of Tourism; and Division of Economic Research and Statistics. See New York State Assembly, *Report of the Subcommittee on Tourism* (Albany: Assembly Standing Committee on Commerce, Industry and Economic Development, May 1, 1976).

10 For a fascinating account of the thinking of the Department of Commerce at this time—including why they had never before launched a tourism marketing campaign, and their unprecedented decision to commit the entire economic development budget to market research—see the transcript of the lecture given by former Department of Commerce director John Dyson at Cornell University Department of Applied Economics and Management, <http://eclips.cornell.edu>.

11 Wells, ed., *Life Style and Psycho-graphics.*

12 Levy, "Roots of Marketing and Consumer Research at the University of Chicago."

13 Adam Arvidsson, "On the 'Pre-History of the Panoptic Sort': Mobility in Market Research," *Surveillance and Society* 1:4 (2004).

14 This quote was found at YSW's current website, <http://www.dyg.com/dygscan.htm>. It continues: "Shifts in social values—people's hopes, dreams, fears, ideas about right and wrong—have proven to be reliable leading indicators of future changes in consumer behavior, public policy and the overall social structure. Thus, understanding trends in social values has always been a logical foundation for building sound business strategies. In today's turbulent consumer environment, basing business strategies on leading edge consumer information is not only logical; it is critical for success. Business must look to the future—to the evolving social structure—to the consumer of tomorrow."

15 YSW's other, equally influential invention, born in 1971, was the *Yankelovich Monitor.* This was an annual national survey that correlated consumption habits to US lifestyle trends and attitudes on diverse social issues. The key psychographic measured in the *Monitor*, and the reason why so many established companies were buying it, was the "new youth," now defined in terms of their lifestyles, attitudes, and buying habits. In their dash to reach this market, advertisers made the *Yankelovich Monitor* the industry standard. It occupied this position until the early 1980s, when it was surpassed by the VALS studies put out by SRI.

16 Mahoney, "Business and Society: A Thirty Year Perspective." This survey has been the longest lived of YSW's products, as YSW joined with *Fortune* magazine to develop the Corporate Reputation Index that is still used to this day.

17 Mary Wells Lawrence, *A Big Life in Advertising* (New York: Alfred A. Knopf, 2002), 88.

18 Hazel Warlaumont, *Advertising in the 60s: Turncoats, Traditionalists, and Waste Makers in America's Turbulent Decade* (London: Praeger, 2001), 175. Advertising historian Warlaumont documents that "as advertising clients scrambled to modernize their image from bureaucrat to hipster, an all-too-familiar request to their ad agencies was 'I want an ad like Bernbach's,' or 'I want the Wells look,' 'the Burnett look,' or the 'new look' in advertising."

19 Empire State Development Corporation, "John Dyson 25th Anniversary Tribute," videotape, 2002.

20 New York State Department of Commerce, *Annual Report* (Albany: New York State Department of Commerce, 1976). As the report, n.p., states: "[CBI conduced this survey] because of a longstanding dearth of adequate data regarding the State's tourist industry and because of the drastic reduction in the budget during the past six years. This provided the facts and figures to prove the vital importance of the tourist industry to the economy of New York State . . . [as well as] a wealth of demographic and psychographic data which will permit the development of highly sophisticated advertising and marketing campaigns."

21 Consumer Behavior, Inc., *A Study of the New York State Vacation Market.* Prepared for the New York State Department of Commerce, August 1977.

22 Yankelovich, Skelly, and White, Inc., *Research to Support New York State's Economic Development Activities.*

23 According to my analysis, 85 percent of the "experts" included along with CEOs for extensive interviews were from the business community. The others were public officials. The outside data included articles in *US News and World Report*, *New York* magazine, and from location consulting firms.

24 Yankelovich, Skelly, and White, Inc., *Research to Support New York State's Economic Development Activities*, 2–6.

25 *Ibid.*, 7–9.

26 *Ibid.*, 22.

27 *Ibid.*, 7–9.

28 *Ibid.*, 23.

29 *Ibid.*, 24.

30 *Ibid.*, 95
31 *Ibid.*, 96.
32 New York State Department of Commerce, *Annual Report*, 1976.
33 *Ibid.* In the year following this report, New York's tax law was indeed dramatically altered. These changes included repealing both the bond and stock transfer tax, providing tax exemption for business expansion (with particular focus on New York City), extending the Job Incentive tax credit to the entire state, and seriously reducing the personal income tax. Information provided by the YSW report was also referred to as justification for the restructuring of the DOC. As to the question of labor and welfare laws, while these did undergo significant change in the years following the report, I am still researching the extent to which this report may have had an impact.
34 New York State Department of Commerce, *Annual Report* (Albany: New York State Department of Commerce, 1978–1979). This campaign was geared towards informing businesspeople of all these new pro-business measures, illustrated with glossy photos of suburban industrial parks and high-tech production facilities, and was circulated mainly at conventions and through industry publications. This campaign was short-lived, becoming, in 1980, the powerful "Made in New York" campaign, which is still operating today.
35 New York State Comptroller's Office, *Financial and Operating Practices of the Department of Commerce* (Albany: Office of the State Comptroller, Division of Audits and Accounts, December 31, 1978), 2.
36 Wells Lawrence, *A Big Life in Advertising*, 51.
37 *Ibid.*, 51–52.
38 *Ibid.*, 52–53. Her description of her clients goes further in emphasizing their prurience: "everyone of them had pink cheeks in winter and a perfect Massachusetts tan in summer, they were the only clients I ever had that blushed, but maybe it was something about us. They were very correct, from Philadelphia."
39 *Ibid.*, 85.
40 *Ibid.*, 88.
41 Empire State Development Corporation, "John Dyson 25th Anniversary Tribute."
42 Wells Lawrence, *A Big Life in Advertising*, 137–138.
43 Ironically, despite its efforts to re-brand itself, American Motors continued to suffer financially and was eventually taken over.
44 Glaser, author interview.
45 For a historical overview of Glaser's early and influential career, first with Pushpin Studios and then at *New York*, see Milton Glaser, *Graphic Design* (New York: Overlook TP, 1983) and Seymour Chwast, *The Push Pin Graphic: A Quarter Century of Innovative Design and Illustration* (San Francisco: Chronicle Books, 2004).
46 Glaser, author interview.
47 Empire State Development Corporation, "John Dyson 25th Anniversary Tribute."
48 Glaser, author interview.
49 *Ibid.*
50 Holloway, author interview, said that it was DOC marketing official Natel Matulatt who was responsible for the ingenious strategy of not enforcing the I♥NY copyright. This approach changed in the 1990s, and today the state is extremely vigilant in policing the use of I♥NY, as will be discussed in the Epilogue. See: Kirsten Dorsch, "Brand Battles: New York Loves Its Trademark," *Business Week*, July 18, 2005.
51 I♥NY and New York State Department of Economic Development, *5 Year Tourism Master Plan, 1994–98* (New York: New York State Department of Economic Development, 1993).
52 Glaser, author interview.
53 *Ibid.*
54 *Ibid.*
55 On the importance of getting locals to buy into tourism campaigns, see Christopher Law, *Urban Tourism: The Visitor Economy and the Growth of Large Cities* (London: Continuum, 2002), ch. 1. This may also be seen as an instance from the 1970s of what Thomas Frank saw as "new advertising's" success in offering "the public authenticity, individuality, difference, and rebellion" that was demanded by the counter-culture generation of the 1960s. Thomas Frank, *The Conquest of Cool* (Chicago: University of Chicago Press, 1997), 9.

56 As cited in Austin, *Taking the Train*, 142.
57 Frederic Jameson, "Reification and Utopia in Mass Culture," in *Signatures of the Visible* (New York: Routledge, 1992).
58 Wells Lawrence, *A Big Life in Advertising*, 140–141.
59 Charlie Moss, interviewed for Empire State Development Corporation, "John Dyson 25th Anniversary Tribute."
60 Wells Lawrence, *A Big Life in Advertising*, 141–142.
61 New York State Department of Commerce, Press Release, "Valentine's Day to be 'I Love New York' Celebration" (Albany: New York State Department of Commerce, February 14, 1978). See also, Press Release, "Thousands Proclaim 'I Love New York' in Valentine's Day Celebration" (Albany: New York State Department of Commerce, February 16, 1978).
62 New York State Department of Commerce, *Annual Report*, 1977–1978, 19.
63 Consumer Behavior, Inc., *Study of Effectiveness of the New York State Department of Commerce "I Love New York Theater Weekends" Campaign*. Prepared for the New York State Department of Commerce, May 1978.
64 James Sterba, "New York Sees Record Tourism," *New York Times*, May 12, 1978.
65 Robert McFadden, "16.7 Million Visitors in 1977 Set Record for New York City," *New York Times*, December 24, 1977.
66 Consumer Behavior, Inc., *Study of Effectiveness of the New York State Department of Commerce "I Love New York Theater Weekends."*
67 James Sterba, "I♥New York Campaign Going National," *New York Times*, July 7, 1978.
68 Negotiations were under way with other foreign carriers serving Europe and South America. New York State Department of Commerce, Press Release, "Legislature Gives Commerce Department $10.5 million for 'I Love New York' Promotion's Second Year" (Albany: New York State Department of Commerce, April 10, 1977).
69 Sterba, "I♥New York Campaign Going National."
70 New York State Department of Commerce, *Annual Report*, 15.
71 *Ibid.*, 16.
72 Vito Turso, "Tourism Boom Sparking City's Resurgence," *Tribune*, March 1, 1978, 1.
73 *Ibid.* As Turso notes, *Variety* also reported an increase in theater attendance of 20 percent in the first eight weeks of the campaign, and of 14 percent fifteen weeks later. According to a local survey, theater was now the city's biggest tourist draw, four times more popular than the Empire State Building.
74 New York State Department of Commerce, *Annual Report*, 1978–1979.
75 "City Quietly Becoming World Tourist Haven," *City News*, August 29, 1978, 33. As the article explained: "When Harry Helmsley announced plans in 1976 to build the Palace Hotel, eyebrows raised—but his $25 million investment triggered a rush of activity."
76 Sterba, "New York Sees Record Tourism." It should be noted that Tisch, perhaps being loyal to his ABNY colleagues, gave thanks to the Big Apple campaign created seven years earlier for the reason that "New Yorkers have a new image of themselves and their city."
77 *Ibid.*
78 Wells, Rich, Greene storyboards for "business development" commercials were found at the Duke University marketing and advertising archives. The first is dated January 12, 1979. The second is from the early 1980s.
79 This emerging tool of consumer researchers made use of survey, interview, and focus-group data to ascertain the degree to which consumers were "aware of" advertising campaigns. This question was further narrowed down according to respondents' "aided" versus "un-aided" recall of a particular campaign, and then according to the influence this campaign had on their desire to purchase the product, or on their decision not to do so.
80 New York State Department of Commerce and John S. Dyson, Commissioner, *Response to Comptroller's Office Final Draft Audit AL-St-11-79* (Albany: New York State Department of Commerce, July 2, 1979).
81 I looked at over twenty years of audits to make this comparison.
82 New York State Comptroller's Office, *Financial and Operating Practices of the Department of Commerce*, 3. As the audit states, with italics in the original: "The plan for business development listed improvements in the State's image and increased awareness of programs as its goals. *We believe [on the other hand] that quantifiable, marketing objectives are essential to measure overall effectiveness.*"

83   The Comptroller's report went on to make allegations of potential "conflicts of interest" since some employees of WRG were paid on two lines, and "ended up evaluating their own work." This, however, was not the main line of critique, so I did not discuss it.

84   New York State Comptroller's Office, *Financial and Operating Practices of the Department of Commerce.*

85   New York State Department of Commerce and John S. Dyson, Commissioner, *Response to Comptroller's Office Final Draft Audit.*

86   *Ibid.,* 3. As Dyson states: "First, 70% of people surveyed had an extraordinarily high unaided recall of the ILNY tourism ads. Secondly, awareness and appeal of State tourism resources were up when measured. We continue to increase our share of the tourism market at the same time as awareness and appeal and the market share of our competitive states is down. We believe that any rational judge would conclude that the two are inextricably, if not causally, related."

87   *Ibid.* As Dyson states: "It is impossible for anyone to precisely demonstrate causality between mass media advertising and 'sales.' We can provide the auditors with expert testimony on this subject if they so desire. It is equally impossible to precisely define a causal relationship between advertising and awareness and appeal for commonly understood reasons of social science and market research methodology."

88   This point was made effectively in the recent Frontline documentary on advertising and marketing called *The Persuaders* (PBS, 2004). As the PBS host, Douglas Rushkoff, noted, by the 1990s, the way around this conundrum was "saturation"—i.e., to create the most all-encompassing marketing environment possible, in which there is no space outside advertising, so that the risk of ads having no influence is eliminated. This will be very relevant in terms of what happens to the physical and symbolic space of New York City in the 1990s.

89   New York State Department of Commerce, "Economic Review: Prolonged Recession Dampens State's Growth," in *Annual Report* (Albany: New York State Department of Commerce, 1981–1982). As this review, 1, states: "New York State's economy appeared to be continuing its expansion resulting from the impetus of recent tax cuts and improved business incentives. Since that time, however, a faltering national economy has taken a severe toll everywhere and, although New York has fared better than most other states, our upward progress has been seriously slowed. Nationally the recovery from the brief 1980 recession was the shortest and weakest in the post-war period, and the economy fell into a uniquely far-reaching and widespread downturn in the mid-summer of 1981. This persisted in 82, and although NY fared better in this period than many other industrial states, the recession, nevertheless, took its toll."

90   US Department of Commerce, Bureau of the Census, 1985.

91   This loss of establishments, it will be recalled from Chapter 2, began in the early 1960s, with the demolition of many of New York's oldest hotels and their conversion into residential and office real estate. Then as now, high labor costs were cited as a reason for their closing. The larger corporate hotels that took their place were far more efficient and profitable, largely by keeping labor costs down, and by attracting higher-spending business travelers and foreign tourists.

92   Pannell Kerr Forster, *Trends in the Hotel Industry: New York City* (New York: Pannell Kerr Forster, 1981–1983).

93   "Foreign Tourism off as the Dollar Gains," *New York Times,* June 29, 1981; Joyce Purnick, "New York City Suffers First Drop in Tourism in Five Years," *New York Times,* August 16, 1981; "Tourism Dips in City in 1981," *New York Times,* December 29, 1981.

94   See Charles Brecher and Raymond Horton, "The Public Sector," in *Dual City: Restructuring New York,* ed. John H. Mollenkopf and Manuel Castells (New York: Russell Sage Foundation, 1991), 109–110.

95   It should be added that these cuts were not evenly distributed. As we saw earlier with the city's policies of planned shrinkage and blight clearance, the center of the city, i.e., wealthier neighborhoods in Manhattan and those closest to the city's command and control functions, received a disproportionate amount of uniformed services, infrastructural development, and housekeeping in the immediate aftermath of the crisis, as compared to the outer boroughs and poorer neighborhoods of Manhattan.

96   Berman, "Views from the Burning Bridge," 72 ff., notes that this was part of a broader phenomenon that occurred when national TV came to the Bronx for the World Series. "The Yankees played in the World Series for three of the Bronx's most disastrous years, 1976–1978

(they won the last two). Every year the national television producers managed to find burning buildings, and every time the announcers spoke in Cosell's 'shocked, shocked' voice. By 1978, cynics wondered if the arson wasn't specially made for TV."

97 *Ibid.* Marshall Berman remembers the effect of this attitude on many Bronx arson victims caught in the harsh spotlight of the local TV news: "What a relief it must have been to think of the fires as something 'these people' were *doing to themselves*: then you wouldn't have to worry about whether the Bronx's troubles were somehow your troubles . . . One of the things that gave the situation a particularly sinister twist is how many Bronx people came to see themselves as 'these people,' how many victims of suspicious fires came to think of themselves as prime suspects. On the local news, you could see families weeping in front of their smoking buildings, and asking, 'What did we do?' There were plenty of journalists and pseudo-social scientists (often subsidized by right wing foundations) only too glad to tell them their character flaws."

Chapter 8

1 New York City Partnership, *Annual Report* (New York: The Partnership, 1981–1982).
2 "New York, New York," by composer John Kander and lyricist Fred Ebb, was written for the 1977 Martin Scorsese film *New York* starring Robert De Niro and Liza Minnelli (who sang the song). A Frank Sinatra recording of "New York, New York" brought the song much wider fame.
3 Mike Davis, *City of Quartz.*
4 New York City Partnership, *Annual Report*, 1981–1982.
5 According to David Rockefeller's chapter, "Ingredients for Successful Partnerships: The New York City Case," in *Public–Private Partnerships: Improving Urban Life*, ed. Perry Davis, NYCP invented the notion of "partnership." As he says: "When we began the NYCP in 1979, we selected partnership from a list of a dozen or so names to signify a new and greater unity among the many components of New York's private sector. While we had government and organized labor very much in mind, the word partnership had not been conceived as a new model for social problem-solving through joint public–private ventures . . . [Before] many people thought of partnerships only in terms of law firms, tax shelters, or perhaps living arrangements."
6 As Rudin and Alton Marshall implied, the Rockefellers and their old-money, WASP cohort had never been interested in joining ABNY—which was in many ways a social-climbing vehicle for a new generation of non-WASP elites in finance, real estate, advertising, and tourism.
7 *Business Week*, July 23, 1984, 99.
8 Another dynamic that occurred was the DOC's marketing and spending on I♥NY in this period became skewed towards upstate. According to my own count of Wells, Rich, Greene print ads from the Duke University Advertising and Marketing Archives, only 30 percent of ads focused on New York City in the 1980s, as compared with 80 percent in the 1970s. Nonetheless, according to market research, "top of the mind" awareness of the campaign, nationally and globally, was still associated with New York City, as opposed to upstate. See Davidson Peterson Associates, Inc., *A Study of the Effectiveness of the New York State Tourism Promotion Program.* Prepared for the New York State Department of Commerce, January 1984.
9 On the range of such subsidies, see Susan Fainstein, *City Builders*, 55–62.
10 Author interview with Franz Leichter, 2006.
11 *Ibid.*
12 *Ibid.* The most famous piece of legislation here was the city's 421-a Property Tax Exemption, which provided ten to twenty years of tax exemption to real estate developers under very loose guidelines. Created in 1975 to spur development at the height of crisis, the program continued to the time of writing, despite the complete turnaround of the real estate market. Mayor Koch created a set-aside of 20 percent affordable housing in the 1980s for those developers building within an "exclusion zone" of Manhattan between 14th and 96th streets. But this has proved to be largely ineffectual at producing affordable housing, and the program as a whole has cost the city billions of dollars in forgone taxes. See Pratt Center for Community Development and Habitat for Humanity, *Reforming New York City's 421-a Property Tax Exemption: Subsidize Affordable Homes Not Luxury Development*, April 2006.
13 *Ibid.* This band included then city councilwoman Ruth Messinger and Alexander Grannis in

the state assembly, as well as former head of the Urban Development Corporation William Stein.

14　"City Quietly Becoming World Tourist Haven," 33.

15　New York Convention and Visitors Bureau, *Domestic Leisure Travel to New York City* (New York: Convention and Visitors Bureau, 1992). As the report noted, by 1987, one in three New York tourists was from abroad.

16　Martin Shefter, *Political Crisis/Fiscal Crisis: The Collapse and Revival of New York City* (New York: Columbia University Press, 1992), 153; Julian Brash, "Invoking Fiscal Crisis: Moral Discourse and Politics in New York City," *Social Text* 21 (2003). In addition to the city's enhanced climate for business, other political and economic factors lay behind this remarkable, post-fiscal crisis growth. The scarcity of capital for New York City during the crisis and the collapse of the city's bond market—which some of these same banks helped to cause—allowed the banks to receive high interest rates for the money they eventually loaned the city through the Municipal Assistance Corporation and Emergency Financial Control Board. This new institutional power also provided leaders in banking and finance with control over the city's budget and spending priorities, political leverage that ultimately benefited their own industries.

17　Mollenkopf and Castells, eds., *Dual City*, 7.

18　*Ibid.*

19　Public and private groups issued a range of reports analyzing the cluster's growing influence. Some focused on New York's "media and communications sector," a combination of old media—motion pictures, advertising, and book publishing—and new media based in web design. On this, see Citizens Budget Committee, *Media and Communications Industries in New York City* (New York: Citizens Budget Committee, December 8, 1998). Others emphasized the "entertainment arts complex," or the burgeoning economy based in theater, film, restaurants, and support services. See Exploring the Metropolis, Inc., *The Entertainment Arts Industry in New York City, Part 3: The Film and Video Industry—A Profile* (New York: Exploring the Metropolis, Inc., December 1997). Still others saw the nexus in "cultural tourism" and the "media and culture sector," i.e., businesses from media and advertising to popular entertainment and museums, linked to expanding waves of leisure and business travel. See Port Authority of New York and New Jersey, *Destination New York–New Jersey: Tourism and Travel to the Metropolitan Region, Pt. 2 of Tourism and the Arts in the New York–New Jersey Region* (New York: Port Authority of New York and New Jersey, December 1994); New York City Comptrollers' Office, *Wish You Were Here*, February 1993, 17. Yet all agreed that some integrated form of media and cultural production was becoming as powerful as the once-dominant financial services sector.

20　Matthew Drennan, "Information Intensive Industries in Metropolitan Areas of the United States," *Environment and Planning A* 21 (1989), Tables 6 and 7.

21　Saskia Sassen, *Cities in a World Economy* (Thousand Oaks, CA: Pine Forge Press, 1994); Saskia Sassen and Frank Roost, "The City: Strategic Site for the Global Entertainment Industry," in *The Tourist City*, ed. Dennis R. Judd and Susan S. Fainstein (New Haven, CT: Yale University Press, 1999), 143–154.

22　Sassen, *Cities in a World Economy*, 66. Thus the need for spatial proximity was not only about face-to-face interaction, but reflected the fact that "economies occur in such specialized firms when they locate close to others that produce key inputs or whose proximity makes possible joint production of certain service offerings."

23　Exploring the Metropolis, Inc., *The Entertainment Arts Industry in New York City, Part 3.*

24　On "new middle class," see Vidich, *The New Middle Classes.*

25　*New York*, January 10, 1977. Melinda Bordelon's illustration is entitled "A new power game is born, and it is no bundle of joy."

26　*Ibid.*, 32–33.

27　*Ibid.*

28　See Steven Brint, "Upper Professionals: A High Command of Commerce, Culture, and Civic Regulation," in *Dual City*, 155.

29　Emmanuel Tobier, "The Changing Face of Poverty: Trends in New York City's Population in Poverty, 1960–1990," 1984. The report was financed by New York University, and prepared for the Community Service Society. On the study, see Joyce Purnick, "Poverty Worsens in City, Study Finds," *New York Times*, December 12, 1984, 42.

30   The study reported almost identical findings to another large-scale survey conducted by the Human Resources Administration between 1979 and 1984. See Joyce Purnick, "HRA Sees 25% of People in City Below Poverty Line," *New York Times*, December 12, 1984, B3.

31   At this time, the poverty rates for others cities included Detroit at 30 percent, Philadelphia at 22 percent, and Los Angeles at 19 percent.

32   Tobier, "The Changing Face of Poverty." As Tobier, 47, notes: "For minority families the decline was much worse. During the 1970s the real income of an average black family fell by ten percent. In the preceding decade, it had risen by 26 percent."

33   *Ibid.*, 58–59. Thus Tobie, 58, notes that while there 800,000 fewer people in 1982 than there had been in 1970, there were 227,000 more poor people.

34   *Ibid*, 53–57.

35   *Ibid.* 52–53.

36   As cited by Joyce Purnick, "Poverty Worsens in City, Study Finds."

37   See the Community Service Society report, based on census data, Mark Levitan, "Poverty in New York, 2002: One-Fifth of the City Lives Below the Federal Poverty Line," September 30, 2003. The report shows that since the early 1970s, New York's poverty rate has averaged 1.7 times the nation's rate. In 2003, one in five New Yorkers (20.5 percent) lived in poverty, as compared to one out of eight Americans (12.1 percent) nationwide. The total number of New York City residents in poverty was a little under 1.7 million, an "enormous" figure. As Levitan, 3, notes, if New York's poor resided in their own municipality, "[they] would constitute the fifth largest city in the United States; only Houston, Chicago, Los Angeles, and the rest of New York would have a larger population."

38   Mollenkopf and Castells, eds., *Dual City.*

39   *Ibid.*, 11. "Extreme poverty" means those earning less than 75 percent of the poverty level.

40   Purnick, "Poverty Worsens in City, Study Finds." As the article noted, the critique was made by an aide to Kenneth Lipper, Deputy Mayor for Finance and Economic Development.

41   *Ibid.*

42   See in particular the special issue by Neil Brenner and Nik Theodore, "Neoliberalism and the Urban Condition," *City* 9: 1 (April 2005) and Brash, "Invoking Fiscal Crisis."

43   Fainstein, *City Builders*, 95.

44   Lichten, *Class, Power, Austerity*, viii.

45   For a recent example of this phenomenon, see Timothy Williams, "Difficult Choices for the Old Rec Center," *New York Times*, July 9, 2007. Williams shows how the severe budget cuts made to parks and recreation in 1970s were never restored, leading government to cede its role as the provider of such services, particularly in poor and working-class neighborhoods.

46   According to Patrick Markee, *Housing a Growing City: New York's Bust in Boom Times* (New York: Coalition for the Homeless, July 2002), 1, median gross rents (including rent and utilities) increased from $509 to $700 in 2002 dollars between 1991 and 1999. During the same period, similar increases occurred in the value of New York City commercial and residential real estate overall.

47   David Harvey, "The Art of Rent: Globalization and the Commodification of Culture," in *Spaces of Capital.*

48   Markee, *Housing a Growing City*, states that 517,345 low-cost units were lost out of a total of 1,008,114 between 1990 and 2000. Between 1990 and 2000 alone, New York City had lost over 50 percent of its stock of apartments affordable to low-income renters.

49   *Ibid.*

50   *Ibid.*

51   *Ibid.*

52   For instance, in 1998 at the height of the 1990s boom, the number of homeless in New York spiked 58 percent to 21,000.

53   As Mollenkopf and Castells, eds., *Dual City*, 7, note: "No other city has done more to propagate the forces of global economic change and none has felt their impact more strongly."

54   As quoted in Purnick, "Poverty Worsens in City, Study Finds." For his analysis of the data, see Tobier, "The Changing Face of Poverty," 71–93.

55   The increase in the penalty for graffiti writing from a misdemeanor to a felony offense between the 1970s and 1990s is an important example of this new climate.

56   On the competition between classes of "city users" in the contemporary global city, see in particular Guido Martinotti, "A City for Whom? Transients and Public Life in the Second-Generation Metropolis," in *The Urban Moment*, ed. Robert Beauregard and Sophie Body-Gendrot (London: Sage, 2002), 155–184. On the essential role of urban citizenry in the cultural life of the city, see Thomas Bender, "Cities, Intellectuals, and Citizenship," *Citizenship Studies* 3 (1999), 203–220. On balancing the needs of citizens and visitors, particularly tourists, see Lily M. Hoffman, Susan S. Fainstein, and Dennis R. Judd, *Cities and Visitors: Regulating People, Markets, and City Space* (Oxford: Blackwell, 2004).

57   See Henri Lefebvre, *Writings on Cities* (London: Blackwell, 1996), 179 and 194–196.

58   See Hackworth, *The Neoliberal City*, 191–193.

59   Prominent groups in New York City involved in this work include Housing First and the Association of Neighborhood Housing Developers.

60   Tom Angotti, "Inclusionary Zoning," *Gotham Gazette*, September 2006.

61   See Brad Lander and Laura Wolff Powers, "New York City: The Case for Inclusionary Zoning," Pratt Institute Center for Community and Environmental Development and PolicyLink, 2004.

62   On the role of tourism in the living-wage campaign in Los Angeles, see Andy Merrifield, *Dialectical Urbanism: Social Struggles in the Capitalist City* (New York: Monthly Review Press, 2002). On Inmex, see <www.inmex.org>. Inmex's mission: "to maximize the impact [of] meetings and conventions dollars . . . on the lives of hotel workers and the communities they live in." For a trade article on such socially conscious meeting planning, see Brendan M. Lynch, "The Good Event: An Enlightening Look at the Many Ways Your Meeting Can Benefit Others," *Meetings and Conventions*, March 2007.

63   Gotham, *Authentic New Orleans*.

64   Hoffman, Fainstein, and Judd, *Cities and Visitors*.

65   See Ann Markusen, "An Application to the Rural Cultural Economy," forthcoming in *Agricultural and Resource Economics Review* 36 (2007).

66   See the special issue on "Arts, Culture, and Community" in *Progressive Planning*, Fall 2005. One oft-cited example of such work that is mentioned here is Project Row Houses in Houston, in which local, mainly African-American artists revitalized a dilapidated, historic district in the city's 3rd Ward to create a vibrant, low-income, arts-oriented community. Challenges persist, particularly with the push of gentrification in adjoining neighborhoods, but the internationally recognized experiment and others like it in cities around the world provide important models of equitable, culturally based urban development.

Epilogue

1   Glaser, author interview.

2   For instance, the design was used in a fundraiser for the local public radio station, WNYC, to help rebuild its FM transmitter, which had been atop the north tower of the World Trade Center and was completely destroyed by the attacks of 9/11. They sold individual, silk-screened posters for $100 a piece and signed copies for $1,000 a piece. According to Glaser, they "raised $190,000 to put their antenna back in shape." Kirsten Dorsch, "Brand Battles: New York Loves Its Trademark," *Business Week*, July 18, 2005. Dorsch notes, "As others tried to tap the design over the years, state legal eagles have filed close to 3,000 trademark objections" with the US Trademark and Patent Office. The issue of protecting the integrity and value of the brand appears to be the paramount concern, as opposed to getting more from licensing fees, which totaled only $900,000 from 2000 to 2005.

3   Glaser, author interview.

4   Dorsch, "Brand Battles."

5   Glaser, author interview.

6   Joyce Purnick, "Metro Matters: New Yorkers, Walking a Line to Keep Going," *New York Times*, October 15, 2001, B1.

7   *Ibid.*

8   On the symbolic tactics employed by both the convention and the counter-convention, see Miriam Greenberg, "Marketing the City in Crisis: Branding and Restructuring New York City in the Post 9/11 Era," in *Consuming the Entrepreneurial City*, ed. Anne Cronin and Kevin Hetherington, (New York: Routledge, forthcoming).

9   Ruth Shalit, "Brand New: How Do You Sell New York Now? Great Minds Are Working on It," *Wall Street Journal*, November 9, 2001, W17.

10 *Ibid.*

11 Mayor Michael Bloomberg, State of the City Address, 2003. For discussion of a pioneering approach to branding at Bloomberg LP, see "Case Study: Bloomberg," in B&Q, *Unlocking the Hidden Wealth of Organizations*, 33–40. For an article linking Michael Bloomberg's approach to branding and corporate governance at Bloomberg LP and in City Hall, see Tom Lowry, "Bloomberg: The CEO Mayor," *Business Week*, June 14, 2007.

12 See Jonathan Bowles, *Payoffs for Layoffs*, Center for an Urban Future, February 10, 2001; Charles Bagli, "Staying or Not Wall Street Giants Could Reap Aid," *New York Times*, March 21, 2002; J. Fitzgerald, *Retention Deficit Disorder*, NYC Inc./Center for an Urban Future, March 2002.

13 Press Release, "NYC Leads USA in Tourism Growth," NYC & Co., July 31, 2007. This has also benefited the real estate and hotel industries enormously. As the press release notes: "New hotel development throughout the City's five boroughs is expected to help meet increased visitor demand, with nearly 13,000 new or renovated hotel rooms being added to hotel room supply by 2010, expanding the total of 72,150 rooms to 85,000. Manhattan alone will gain 50-plus hotels and 8,000 rooms over the next three years, representing the largest increase ever."

14 Leslie Eaton, "City Is Still Losing Jobs Despite Signs of a Rebound on the National Level," *New York Times*, March 22, 2002, B1, B3.

15 Janny Scott, "Tourists to the Rescue of a Wounded City: New York Finds Sympathy a Powerful Draw," *New York Times*, March 24, 2002, B1, 47.

16 Jayson Blair, "Here Dignity Rubs Elbows with Demand: Ground Zero Crowds Don't Please Everyone," *New York Times*, June 26, 2002, B1, B4.

17 Budgetary spending has increased under Bloomberg, but this is mostly to enhance "quality of life," and reflects "his desire to make New York attractive to people and businesses." See "spending on select departments" in Diane Cardwell, "Under Bloomberg, Budget and Revenues Swell." *New York Times*, September 17, 2007, B1.

Selected Bibliography

Aacker, David A. *Managing Brand Equity: Capitalizing on the Value of a Brand Name.* New York: Maxwell Macmillan International, 1991.

Abu-Lughod, Janet L. *New York, Chicago, Los Angeles: America's Global Cities.* Minneapolis: University of Minnesota Press, 1999

Alcaly, Roger E., and David Mermelstien, eds. *The Fiscal Crisis of American Cities.* New York: Vintage, 1977.

Amin, Ash, ed. *Post Fordism: A Reader.* Oxford: Blackwell, 1995.

Amin, Samir, *et al.*, eds. *Dynamics of Global Crisis.* New York: Monthly Press, 1982.

Anderson, Arvid, and Marjorie A. London. "Collective Bargaining and the Fiscal Crisis in New York City: Cooperation for Survival." *Fordham Law Journal* 10 (1983).

Anderson, Terry H. *The Sixties.* New York: Longman, 1999.

Aronowitz, Stanley. *False Promises: The Shaping of American Working Class Consciousness.* New York: McGraw-Hill, 1973.

Arvidsson, Adam. "On the 'Pre-History of the Panoptic Sort': Mobility in Market Research." *Surveillance and Society* 1:4 (2004).

Ashworth, Gregory John, and Henk Voogd. "Marketing and Place Promotion." In *Place Promotion: The Use of Publicity and Marketing to Sell Towns and Regions*, edited by John Robert Gold and Stephen Ward. Chichester: Wiley, 1994.

Atlas, James. "Beyond Demographics." *Atlantic*, October 1984.

Auletta, Ken. "After the Bloodless Revolution: The New Power Game." *New York*, January 12, 1976.

—— "The Power Game: This Year They're Doing It With Mirrors." *New York*, January 10, 1977.

—— *The Streets Were Paved with Gold: The Decline of New York, an American Tragedy.* New York: Random House, 1979.

Austin, Joe. *Taking the Train: How Graffiti Art Became an Urban Crisis in New York City.* New York: Columbia University Press, 2001.

Baer, William. "On the Death of Cities." *The Public Interest* 45 (Fall 1976).

Bagli, Charles. "Staying or Not, Wall Street Giants Could Reap Aid." *New York Times*, March 21, 2002.

Bailey, Robert W. *The Crisis Regime: The MAC, the EFCB, and the Political Impact of the New York City Financial Crisis.* Albany: State University of New York Press, 1984.

Baker, Russell. "The City in the Hair Shirt." *New York Times*, June 28, 1975.

Baran, Paul A., and Paul M. Sweezy. *Monopoly Capital: An Essay on the American Economic and Social Order*. New York: Monthly Review Press, 1966.

Barnouw, Erik. *The Golden Web: A History of Broadcasting in the United States, 1933–1953*. New York: Oxford University Press, 1968.

Barthes, Roland. *Mythologies*. New York: Hill and Wang, 1972.

Baughman, James L. "Television." In *The Encyclopedia of New York City*, edited by Kenneth T. Jackson. New York: New York Historical Society, 1995.

Beame, Abraham D. "Cities Here to Stay, with Business Help." *The American City* 91 (July 1976).

—— and Victor Marrero. *New York's Visitors Industry*. New York: New York City Department of City Planning, #77-15, June 1977.

Beauregard, Robert. *Voices of Decline: The Postwar Fate of US Cities*. London: Blackwell, 1993.

Bellush, Jewel, and Dick Netzer, eds. *Urban Politics: New York Style*. Armonk, NY, and London: M. E. Sharpe, 1990.

Benjamin, Walter. *Illuminations*. New York: Schocken, 1996.

—— *The Arcades Project*. Cambridge, MA: Harvard/Bellknap, 1999.

Berman, Marshall. *All That Is Solid Melts into Air: The Experience of Modernity*. New York: Penguin, 1988.

—— "Views from the Burning Bridge." In *Urban Mythologies: The Bronx Remembered since the 1960s*, edited by John Allen Farmer. New York: The Bronx Museum of the Arts, 1999.

Beschloss, Steven. "Button-Downs and Fat Lapels." *Crain's New York Business*, March 13, 1989.

Bloom, Alexander, and Wini Breines. *"Takin' It to the Streets": A Sixties Reader*. New York: Oxford University Press, 2003.

Bloomberg, Michael, *Bloomberg by Bloomberg*. New York: Wiley, 2001.

Bluestone, Barry, and Bennett Harrison. *The Great U-Turn: Corporate Restructuring and the Polarizing of America*. New York: Basic Books, 1988.

Bogart, Michele H. *Advertising, Artists, and the Borders of Art*. Chicago: University of Chicago Press, 1995.

Booker, Christopher. *The Seventies: The Decade that Changed the Future of London*. New York: Stein and Day, 1980.

Bordewich, Fergus M. "The Future of New York: A Tale of Two Cities." *New York Times*, July 23, 1979.

Bourdieu, Pierre. *Distinction: A Social Critique of the Judgment of Taste*. Cambridge, MA: Harvard University Press, 1984.

—— *Language and Symbolic Power*. Cambridge, MA: Harvard University Press, 1991.

Boushey, Heather. "The Needs of the Working Poor." Testimony before the US Senate, Committee on Health, Education, Labor, and Pensions, February 14, 2002.

Bowles, Jonathan. "Payoffs for Layoffs." New York: Center for an Urban Future, Report, February 10, 2001.

Brash, Julian. "Invoking Fiscal Crisis: Moral Discourse and Politics in New York City." *Social Text* 21 (2003).

Brenner, Neil. "New State Spaces: Urban Governance and the Rescaling of Statehood." In *Global Cities: A Reader*, edited by Neil Brenner and Roger Keil. New York: Routledge, 2006.

Brenner, Neil, and Nik Theodore. "Neoliberalism and the Urban Condition." *City* 9:1 (April 2005).

Brecher, Charles, and Raymond Horton. "The Public Sector." In *Dual City: Restructuring New York*, edited by John H. Mollenkopf and Manuel Castells. New York: Russell Sage Foundation, 1991.

Breslin, Jimmy. "And Proud of It." *New York Times*, August 20, 1975.

Brint, Steven. "Upper Professionals: A High Command of Commerce, Culture, and Civic Regulation." In *Dual City: Restructuring New York*, edited by John H. Mollenkopf and Manuel Castells. New York: Russell Sage Foundation, 1991.

Buhle, Paul, and Dave Wagner. *Hide in Plain Sight: The Hollywood Blacklistees in Film and Television, 1950–2002*. New York: Palgrave, 2003.

Burd, Gene. "The Selling of the Sunbelt: Civic Boosterism in the Media." In *The Rise of Sunbelt Cities, Urban Affairs Annual Reviews* 14, edited by David Perry and Alfred Watkins. London: Sage Publications, 1977.

Burrows, Edwin G., and Mike Wallace. *Gotham: A History of New York City to 1898*. New York: Oxford University Press, 1999.

Business/Labor Working Group, *Summary Report of the Business/Labor Working Group on Jobs and Economic Regeneration in New York City*. New York: Business/Labor Working Group, January 1977.

Canby, Vincent. "New York's Woes Are Good Box Office." *New York Times*, November 10, 1974.

Cannato, Vincent J. *The Ungovernable City: John Lindsay and His Struggle to Save New York*. New York: Basic Books, 2001.

Caro, Robert A. *The Power Broker: Robert Moses and the Fall of New York*. New York: Alfred A. Knopf, 1974.

Castells, Manuel. *The Urban Question: A Marxist Approach*. Cambridge, MA: MIT Press, 1979.

—— *The City and the Grassroots: A Cross-cultural Theory of Urban Social Movements*. Berkeley: University of California Press, 1985.

Castleman, Craig. *Getting Up: Subway Graffiti in New York*. Boston: MIT Press, 1982.

Caylor, Peggy. "What's in a Name!" *National Real Estate Investor* (May 1999).

Chang, Jeff. *Can't Stop, Won't Stop: A History of the Hip-Hop Generation*. New York: St. Martin's Press, 2005.

Chipkin, Harvey. "New York City's Campaign for Agency Business." New York: American Society of Travel Agents (ASTA) Management, 1988.

Chwast, Seymour. *The Push Pin Graphic: A Quarter Century of Innovative Design and Illustration*. San Francisco: Chronicle Books, 2004.

Citizens Budget Committee. *Media and Communications Industries in New York City*. New York: Citizens Budget Committee, December 8, 1998.

Coalition for the Homeless. "A History of Modern Homelessness in New York City." New York: Coalition for the Homeless, November 2004.

Cocks, Catherine. *Doing the Town: The Rise of Urban Tourism in the United States, 1850–1915*. Berkeley: University of California Press, 2001.

Consumer Behavior, Inc. *A Study of the New York State Vacation Market*. Prepared for the New York State Department of Commerce; John Dyson, Commissioner, August 1977.

—— *Study of Effectiveness of the New York State Department of Commerce "I Love New York Theater Weekends" Campaign*. Prepared for the New York State Department of Commerce; John Dyson, Commissioner, May 1978.

Cook, David A. *American Cinema in the Shadow of Watergate and Vietnam, 1970–1979*. Berkeley: University of California Press, 2002.

Costikyan, Edward. "The Ten Most Powerful Men in New York." *New York*, January 5, 1970.

Crampon, L. J. *Characteristics of Successful Tourist Destination Areas in the United States*. Boulder: Business Research Division, University of Colorado, 1964.

D. K. Shifflet & Associates, Ltd. *USA Travel Recovery/Monitor: A Blueprint for Rebuilding Travel*. New York: D. K. Shifflet & Associates, Ltd, December 3, 2001–February 15, 2002.

Daley, Robert. "The Struggle for Control in the City: Winners and Losers." *New York*, January 14, 1974.

Dallos, Robert E. "NY Comeback: The Big Apple Taking Bigger Tourism Bite." *Los Angeles Times*, July 14, 1978.

Darton, Eric. *Divided We Stand: A Biography of New York's World Trade Center*. New York: Basic Books, 1999.

Davidson Peterson Associates, Inc. *A Study of the Effectiveness of the New York State Tourism Promotion Program*. Prepared for the New York State Department of Commerce, January 1984.

Davis, Mike. *City of Quartz: Excavating the Future in Los Angeles*. London: Verso, 1990.

De Certeau, Michel. *Culture in the Plural*. Minneapolis: University of Minnesota Press, 1997.

Debord, Guy. *The Society of the Spectacle*. New York: Zone Books, 1999.

Denning, Michael. *The Cultural Front: The Laboring of American Culture in the Twentieth Century*. New York: Verso, 1996.

Donald, James. *Imagining the Modern City*. London: Athlone, 1999.

Dorsch, Kirsten. "Brand Battles: New York Loves Its Trademark." *Business Week*, July 18, 2005.

Drennan, Mathew. "Information Intensive Industries in Metropolitan Areas of the United States." *Environment and Planning A* 21 (1989).

Du Gay, Paul, and Stuart Hall, eds. *Production of Culture/Cultures of Production*. London: Sage, 1997.

Eaton, Leslie. "City Is Still Losing Jobs Despite Signs of a Rebound on the National Level." *New York Times*, March 22, 2002.

Elliot, Stuart. "The Importance of Famous Brand Names Is Stressed by Executives at an Ad Conference." *New York Times*, October 12, 1999.

Empire State Development Corporation. "John Dyson 25th Anniversary Tribute." Videotape, 2002.

Engels, Friedrich. *The Condition of the Working Class in England.* London: Penguin, 1990.

Epstein, Jason. "The Last Days of New York." *New York Times Book Review* 23:2, February 19, 1976.

Ewen, Stuart. *Captains of Consciousness: Advertising and the Social Roots of Consumer Culture.* New York: McGraw-Hill, 1976.

Exploring the Metropolis, Inc. *The Entertainment Arts Industry in New York City, Part 3: The Film and Video Industry—A Profile.* New York: Exploring the Metropolis, Inc., December 1997.

Fainstein, Susan S. *City Builders: Property Development in New York and London, 1980–2000.* Lawrence: University of Kansas Press, 2001.

Fantus Company. *The Manhattan Outlook: A Projection to 1985 of Operating Conditions in New York City for Office Employers.* New York: The Fantus Company, 1975.

Featherstone, Mike. "City Cultures and Post-Modern Lifestyles." In *Post Fordism: A Reader*, edited by Ash Amin. Oxford: Blackwell, 1995.

Felker, Clay. "Life Cycles of Magazines." *Antioch Review* (Spring 1968).

—— *The Power Game: From the Pages of* New York *Magazine.* New York: Simon and Schuster, 1969.

Ferretti, Fred. *The Year the Big Apple Went Bust.* New York: Putnam, 1976.

Fiscal Policy Institute. *The State of Working New York, 2001: Working Harder, Growing Apart.* New York: Fiscal Policy Institute, 2001.

—— *Pulling Apart in New York: An Analysis of Income Trends in New York State.* New York: Fiscal Policy Institute, 2002.

—— *The State of Working New York, 2003: Unbalanced Regional Economies through Expansion and Recession.* New York: Fiscal Policy Institute, 2003.

—— *New York's Job Shift from Higher-Paying to Lower-Paying Industries.* New York: Fiscal Policy Institute, 2004.

Fitch, Robert. *The Assassination of New York.* New York: Verso, 1993.

Fitzgerald, J. *Retention Deficit Disorder.* New York: NYC Inc./Center for an Urban Future, 2002.

Flores, Juan. *From Bomba to Hip-Hop: Puerto Rican Culture and Latino Identity.* New York: Columbia University Press, 2000.

Foner, Nancy. *From Ellis Island to JFK: New York's Two Great Waves of Immigration.* New Haven, CT: Yale University Press, 2000.

"Foreign Tourism off as the Dollar Gains." *New York Times*, June 29, 1981.

Fox, Stephen. *The Mirror Makers: A History of American Advertising and Its Creators.* New York: Morrow, 1984.

Frank, Thomas. *The Conquest of Cool.* Chicago: University of Chicago Press, 1997.

Freeman, Joshua. *Working Class New York: Life and Labor since WWII.* New York: New Press, 2000.

Frieden, Bernard J. and Lynne B. Sagalyn. *Downtown, Inc.: How America Rebuilds Cities.* Cambridge, MA: MIT Press, 1991.

Friedman, Milton. *Free to Choose: A Personal Statement.* New York: Harcourt Brace Jovanovich, 1980.

Fritsche, Peter. *Reading Berlin, 1900.* Cambridge, MA: Harvard University Press, 1996.

Gardyn, Rebecca. "Packaging Cities." *American Demographics* (January 2002).

Gerard, Karen, and Richard G. Birchall. "Corporate Relocation—The Impact on the Chase Manhattan Bank and the City of New York." New York: Chase Manhattan Bank, Economic Research Division, July 1971.

Gillough, Graeme. *Myth and Metropolis: Walter Benjamin and the City.* Cambridge: Polity Press, 1996.

Glaser, Milton. *Graphic Design.* New York: Overlook TP, 1983.

Goeldner, C. R., and Gerald L. Allen. *Bibliography of Tourism and Travel: Research Studies, Reports, and Articles.* Boulder: Business Research Division, University of Colorado, in Cooperation with Western Council for Travel Research, and Travel Research Association, 1967.

Goeldner, C. R., and Karen Dicke. *Bibliography of Tourism and Travel: Research Studies, Reports, and Articles.* Boulder: Business Research Division, University of Colorado, 1971, Volumes I–III.

Goodwin, Mark. "The City as Commodity: The Contested Spaces of Urban Development." In

Selling Places: The City as Cultural Capital Past and Present, edited by Jerry Kearns and Chris Philo. New York: Pergamon Press, 1993.

Gotham, Kevin Fox. *Authentic New Orleans: Race and Culture in Urban Tourism.* New York: New York University Press, forthcoming.

Gottdiener, Mark. *The Theming of America: Dreams, Media Fantasies, and Themed Environments.* Boulder, CO: Westview Press, 2001.

Gramsci, Antonio. *The Prison Notebooks.* New York: Columbia University Press, 1991.

—— *Selections from Cultural Writings.* Cambridge, MA: Harvard University Press, 1991.

Greenberg, Miriam. "Branding Cities: A Social History of the Urban Lifestyle Magazine." *Urban Affairs Review* 36:2 (November 2000).

—— "The Limits of Branding: The World Trade Center, Fiscal Crisis and the Marketing of Recovery." *International Journal of Urban and Regional Research* 27:2 (June 2003).

Gupte, Pranay. "Integrity, Not Image Fixing, Is 'Real' Public Relations: Lunch at the Four Seasons with Howard Rubenstein." *New York Sun*, February 8, 2005.

Gustafson, Eric W. "Printing and Publishing." In *Made in New York: Case Studies in Metropolitan Manufacture*, edited by Max Hall. Cambridge, MA: Harvard University Press, 1959.

Hackworth, Jason. "Local Autonomy, Bond-Rating Agencies and Neoliberal Urbanism in the United States." *International Journal of Urban and Regional Research* 26:4 (December 2002).

—— *The Neoliberal City: Governance, Ideology, and Development in American Urbanism.* Ithaca, NY: Cornell University Press, 2007.

Hales, P. B. *Silver Cities: The Photography of American Urbanization, 1839–1915.* Philadelphia, PA: Temple University Press, 1984.

Hall, Peter. *Cities of Tomorrow: An Intellectual History of Urban Planning and Design in the Twentieth Century.* Oxford: Blackwell, 1988.

Hall, Stuart. "Encoding/Decoding." In *Media Studies: A Reader*, edited by Paul Marris and Sue Thornham. New York: New York University Press, 2000.

—— "Racist Ideologies and the Media." In *Media Studies: A Reader*, edited by Paul Marris and Sue Thornham. New York: New York University Press, 2000.

Hamilton, John G., *et al. International Tourism.* New York: The Economist Intelligence Unit, Ltd., 1970.

Hannigan, John. *Fantasy City: Pleasure and Profit in the Postmodern Metropolis.* New York: Routledge, 1999.

Hansen, Miriam. *Babel and Babylon: Spectatorship in American Silent Film.* Cambridge, MA: Harvard University Press, 1991.

Hardy, Hugh S., ed. *The Politz Papers: Science and Truth in Marketing Research.* Chicago: The American Marketing Association, 1990.

Harvey, David. *The Condition of Post-Modernity.* Oxford: Blackwell, 1989.

—— *The Limits to Capital.* New York: Verso, 1999.

—— *Spaces of Capital: Towards a Critical Geography.* Oxford: Blackwell, 2001.

Hart, Susanna, and John Murphy, eds. *Brands: The New Wealth Creators.* New York: New York University Press, 1998.

Hebdige, Dick. *Subculture: The Meaning of Style.* London: Penguin, 1979.

Henkin, David M. *City Reading: Written Words and Public Spaces in Antebellum New York.* New York: Columbia University Press, 1999.

Herman, Edward, and Robert McChesney. *The Global Media: The New Missionaries of Global Capitalism.* London: Cassell, 1997.

"Hip Consumers Stir up Adfolk, Fisher Tells Houston Forum." *Advertising Age*, March 1968.

Hoffman, David. Transcripts of interviews conducted for *The Lew Rudin Way* documentary, 2006.

Hoffman, Lily M., Susan S. Fainstein, and Dennis R. Judd. *Cities and Visitors: Regulating People, Markets, and City Space.* Oxford: Blackwell, 2004.

Holcomb, Briavel. "Marketing Cities for Tourism." In *The Tourist City*, edited by Dennis R. Judd and Susan S. Fainstein. New Haven, CT: Yale University Press, 1999.

Hollowell, John. *Fact & Fiction: The New Journalism and the Nonfiction Novel.* Chapel Hill: University of North Carolina Press, 1977.

Horton, Raymond D. *Municipal Labor Relations in New York City.* New York: Praeger, 1973.

—— and Charles Brecher, eds. *Setting Muncipal Priorities 1986.* New York: New York University Press, 1985.

"How New York Lurched to the Brink." *Time*, May 16, 1975.

Hudson, Edward. "Ken McFeeley, Union Leader." *New York Times*, October 20, 1986.

Israel, Paul. "Telegraphy." In *The Encyclopedia of New York City*, edited by Kenneth T. Jackson. New York: New York Historical Society, 1995.

Jackson, Kenneth T., ed. *The Encyclopedia of New York City*. New York: New York Historical Society, 1995.

Jacobson, Mark. "New York, You Oughta Be in Pictures." *New York*, December 30, 1975.

Jameson, Frederic. *Signatures of the Visual*. New York: Routledge, 1992.

Johnson, Thomas A. "Rohatyn Scored by Congressmen: Badillo and Rangel Critical of Blighted-Areas Plan." *New York Times*, March 17, 1976.

Judd, Dennis R., ed. *The Infrastructure of Play: Building the Tourist City*. Armonk, NY: M. E. Sharpe, 2003.

—— and Susan S. Fainstein, eds. *The Tourist City*. New Haven, CT: Yale University Press, 1999.

Kael, Pauline. *For Keeps*. New York: Dutton, 1994.

Kane, Joseph Nathan, and Gerard L. Alexander. *Nicknames and Sobriquets of US Cities and States*, 3rd edn. Metuchen, NJ: Scarecrow Press, 1979.

Kapferer, Jean Noel. *Strategic Brand Management: New Approaches to Creating and Evaluating Brand Equity*. New York: Addison Wesley, 1996.

Kasinitz, Philip, Robert Jackall, and Arthur Vidich. *Metropolis: Center and Symbol of Our Times*. New York: New York University Press, 1995.

Kearns, Jerry, and Chris Philo. *Selling Places: The City as Cultural Capital Past and Present*. New York: Pergamon Press, 1993.

Kelling, George L., and Catherine M. Coles. *Fixing Broken Windows: Restoring Order and Reducing Crime in Our Communities*. New York: Martin Kessler Books, 1996.

Klein, Naomi. *No Logo: Taking Aim at the Brand Bullies*. London: Picador, 2000.

Koch, Ed. *Mayor: An Autobiography*. New York: Simon and Schuster, 1984.

Kotler, Philip, *et al*. *Marketing Places*. New York: Free Press, 1994.

Korda, Michael. *Power! How to Get It, How to Use It*. New York: Ballantine, 1975.

Labor Community Advocacy Network to Rebuild New York. *Revitalize New York by Putting People to Work: A Jobs-Based Strategy for Economic Diversification and High-Road Growth*, March 13, 2003.

Lash, Scott, and John Urry. *The End of Organized Capitalism*. Cambridge: Polity Press, 1987.

—— *Economies of Signs and Space*. London: Sage, 1994.

Lasn, Kalle. *Culture Jam: The Uncooling of America*. New York: Eagle Brook, 1999.

Law, Christopher. *Urban Tourism: The Visitor Economy and the Growth of Large Cities*. London: Continuum, 2002.

Le Corbusier. "New York Is Not a Completed City." In *Metropolis: Center and Symbol of Our Times*, edited by Philip Kasinitz, Robert Jackall, and Arthur Vidich. New York: New York University Press, 1995.

Lefebvre, Henri. *Production of Space*. Cambridge, MA: Blackwell, 1991.

—— *The Urban Revolution*. Minneapolis: University of Minnesota Press, 2001.

Levy, Sidney J. "Roots of Marketing and Consumer Research at the University of Chicago." *Consumption, Markets and Culture* 6:2 (June 2003).

Lichten, Eric. *Class, Power, Austerity: The New York City Fiscal Crisis*. Amherst, MA: Greenwood Press, and Garvey Publishers, 1986.

Logan, John R. and Harvey L. Molotch. *Urban Fortunes: The Political Economy of Place*. Berkeley: University of California Press, 1987.

Lynch, Kevin. *The Image of the City*. Cambridge, MA: MIT Press, 1960.

McChesney, Robert. *Telecommunications, Mass Media, and Democracy: The Battle for the Control of US Broadcasting, 1925–1935*. New York: Oxford University Press, 1993.

Mahoney, Brooke W. "Business and Society: A Thirty Year Perspective." New York: Volunteer Consulting Group, Inc., 2000.

Maier, Mark. *City Unions: Managing Discontent in New York City*. New Brunswick, NJ: Rutgers University Press, 1987.

Mailer, Norman, Mervyn Kurlansky, and John Narr, eds. *The Faith of Graffiti*. Washington, DC: Library of Congress, 1974.

Markee, Patrick. *Housing a Growing City: New York's Bust in Boom Times*. New York: Coalition for the Homeless, July 2002.

Markusen, Ann R. "The Economics of Postwar Regional Disparity." In *Readings in Urban Theory*, edited by Susan Fainstein and Scott Campbell. London: Blackwell, 1997.

Marmarelli, Ronald S. "*New York* Magazine." In *Regional Interest Magazines of the United States*, edited by Sam G. Riley and Gary Selnow. Westport, CT: Greenwood Press, 1991.

Martin, Randy. *On Your Marx: Relinking Socialism and the Left.* Minneapolis: University of Minnesota Press, 2002.

Marx, Karl. *Capital*, Volume I. London: Penguin, 1990.

Mattelart, Armand. *Mapping World Communication: War, Progress, Culture.* Minneapolis: University of Minnesota Press, 1994.

Mele, Chris. *Selling the Lower East Side: Culture, Real Estate, and Resistance in New York City.* Minneapolis: University of Minnesota Press, 2001.

Mollenkopf, John H. and Manuel Castells, eds. *Dual City: Restructuring New York.* New York: Russell Sage Foundation, 1991.

Moody, Kim. *From Welfare State to Real Estate: Regime Change in New York City, 1974 to the Present.* New York: New Press, 2007.

Morgan, Neil, and Annette Pritchard. *Tourism, Promotion, and Power: Creating Images, Creating Identities.* New York: John Wiley and Sons, 1998.

—— Annette Pritchard, and Roger Pride, eds. *Destination Branding, Creating the Unique Destination Proposition.* London: Butterworth-Heinemann, 2002.

Morris, Charles W. *The Cost of Good Intentions.* New York: W. W. Norton, 1980.

Morris, Richard, and C. Davis Palmer. *New York City Fiscal Crisis: Villains and Victims.* New York: Metropolitan Applied Research, 1976.

Moss, Linda. "New York Media Survey." *Crain's New York Business*, September 11, 1989.

Motivational Programmers, Inc., "The Creative Consumer." *Holiday*, February 1969.

Muller, Peter O. "Are Cities Obsolete?" *The Sciences* 26 (March/April 1986).

Municipal Assistance Corporation. *Annual Report: 1976.* New York: Municipal Assistance Corporation of the City of New York, June 30, 1976.

Musser, Charles. "Filmmaking." In *The Encyclopedia of New York City*, edited by Kenneth T. Jackson. New York: New York Historical Society, 1995.

Newfield, Jack and Paul Du Brul. *The Abuse of Power: The Permanent Government and the Fall of New York.* New York: Viking, 1977.

New York City Commission on the Year 2000. *New York Ascendant*, June 1987.

New York City Comptrollers' Office. *Wish You Were Here*, February 1993.

New York City Department of City Planning. *Economic Recovery: New York City's Program for 1977–1981*, 1976.

New York City Partnership. *Annual Report*, 1981/1982.

New York State Assembly Standing Committee on Commerce, Industry, and Economic Development. *Report of the Subcommittee on Tourism*, May 1, 1976.

New York State Comptroller's Office. "Audit Report on Financial and Operating Practices: New York State Department of Commerce." Albany, NY: Office of the State Comptroller, Division of Audits and Accounts, December 31, 1974.

—— "Financial and Operating Practices of the Department of Commerce." Albany, NY: Office of the State Comptroller, Division of Audits and Accounts, December 31, 1978.

—— "Managerial Summary." Albany, NY: Office of the State Comptroller, Division of Audits and Accounts, 1979.

New York State Department of Commerce. *Annual Report.* Albany, NY: New York State Department of Commerce, 1971.

—— "An Economic Strategy for the 1980s: A Report to the Council on State Priorities." Albany, NY: New York State Department of Commerce, 1981.

—— "Economic Review: Prolonged Recession Dampens State's Growth." In *Annual Report.* Albany, NY: New York State Department of Commerce, 1981–1982.

—— and John S. Dyson, Commissioner. "Response to Comptroller's Office Final Draft Audit AL-St-11-79." Albany, NY: New York State Department of Commerce, July 2, 1979.

"Night of Terror." *Time*, July 25, 1977.

O'Connor, James. *The Fiscal Crisis of the State.* New York: St. Martin's Press, 1973.

Olinger, Chancey. "Advertising." In *The Encyclopedia of New York City*, edited by Kenneth T. Jackson. New York: New York Historical Society, 1995.

Orlebecke, Charles J. "Saving New York: The Ford Administration and the New York City Fiscal

Crisis." In *Gerald Ford and the Politics of Post-Watergate America*, Volume II, edited by Bernard J. Firestone and Alexej J. Ugrinsky. Westport, CT: Greenwood Press, 1993.

Pannell Kerr Forster. *Trends in the Hotel Industry: New York City*. New York: Pannell Kerr Forster, 1981–1983.

Patterson, Jack. "The Prospect of a Nation with No Important Cities." *Business Week*, February 2, 1976.

Patterson, Michael. "Cops and Fire to 'Warn' Tourists: Will Stress 'Fear City' at Terminals." *Daily News*, June 10, 1975.

Parrott, James, and Oliver Cooke. *Tale of Two Recessions: The Current Slowdown in New York City Compared to the Early 1990s*. New York: Fiscal Policy Institute, December 3, 2002.

Perry, David C. and Alfred J. Watkins, eds. "The Rise of the Sunbelt Cities." *Urban Affairs Review* 14 (1977).

Pick, Daniel. *Faces of Degeneration: A European Disorder, 1848–1918*. New York: Cambridge University Press, 1989.

Pileggi, Nicholas. "The Power Game, 1975: Visible and Invisible Men." *New York*, January 13, 1975.

Piven, Frances Fox, and Richard A. Cloward. *Regulating the Poor: The Functions of Public Welfare*. New York: Pantheon Books, 1971.

Popik, Barry. "The Big Apple." Available at <www.barrypopik.com, 2004>.

Port Authority of New York and New Jersey. "The Arts as an Industry: Their Economic Importance to the New York–New Jersey Metropolitan Region." New York: Port Authority of New York and New Jersey, February 1983.

Quante, Wolfgang. *The Exodus of Corporate Headquarters from New York City*. New York: Praeger, 1976.

Quindlen, Anna. "Must the City Sacrifice the Poor to Lure Back the Middle Class? Fantasyland." *New York Times*, August 12, 1979.

Radway, Janice A. *Reading the Romance: Women, Patriarchy, and Popular Literature*. Chapel Hill: University of North Carolina Press, 1984.

Rae, Douglas W. *City: Urbanism and Its End*. New Haven, CT: Yale University Press, 2003.

Ranzal, Edward. "Publicity Is Said to Bar Better Credit for City." *New York Times*, February 10, 1971.

Reagan, Ronald. "Remarks at the Annual Meeting of the National Alliance of Business." *The Public Papers of Ronald Reagan*, October 5, 1981.

—— "Remarks at the New York City Partnership Luncheon in New York." *The Public Papers of Ronald Reagan*, January 14, 1982.

Riis, Jacob. *How the Other Half Lives: Studies among the Tenements of New York*. Cambridge, MA: Harvard University Press, 1970.

Rivera, Raquel Z. *New York Ricans from the Hip Hop Zone*. New York: Palgrave, 2002.

Rockefeller, David. "Ingredients for Successful Partnerships: The New York City Case." *Public–Private Partnerships: Improving Urban Life*, edited by Perry Davis. New York: Academy of Political Science/New York City Partnership, 1986.

Rohatyn, Felix. "New York and the Nation." *New York Review of Books* 28, January 21, 1982.

Rose, Tricia. *Black Noise: Rap Music and Black Culture in Contemporary America*. Hanover, NH: Wesleyan University Press, 1994.

Rosenblum, Naomi. "Photography." In *The Encyclopedia of New York City*, edited by Kenneth T. Jackson. New York: New York Historical Society, 1995.

Ross, Andrew. *The Chicago Gangster Theory of Life: Nature's Debt to Society*. London and New York: Verso, 1994.

—— *Low Pay, High Profile: The Global Push for Fair Labor*. New York: New Press, 2004.

Rutheiser, Charles. *Imagineering Atlanta: Making Place in a Non-Place Urban Realm*. London: Verso, 1996.

Ryan, Michael, and Douglas Kellner. *Camera Politica: The Politics and Ideology of Contemporary Hollywood Film*. Bloomington: Indiana University Press, 1988.

Sagalyn, Lynne B. *Times Square Roulette: Remaking the City Icon*. Cambridge, MA: MIT Press, 2001.

Sanders, James. *Celluloid Skyline: New York and the Movies*. New York: Alfred A. Knopf, 2001.

Sante, Luc. *Low Life: Lures and Snares of Old New York*. New York: Vintage, 1992.

Sassen, Saskia. *Cities in a World Economy*. Thousand Oaks, CA: Pine Forge Press, 1994.

—— *The Global City: New York, London, Tokyo*. Princeton, NJ: Princeton University Press, 2001.

Sassen, Saskia and Frank Roost. "The City: Strategic Site for the Global Entertainment Industry."

In *The Tourist City*, edited by Dennis R. Judd and Susan S. Fainstein. New Haven, CT: Yale University Press, 1999.

Schaap, Dick. "The Ten Most Indispensable People in Town." *New York*, January 1, 1970.

Schiller, Herbert I. *Communication and Cultural Domination*. White Plains, NY: International Arts and Sciences Press, 1976.

Scott, Allen and Edward Soja, eds. *The City: Los Angeles and Urban Theory at the End of the Twentieth Century*. Berkeley: University of California Press, 1996.

Scott, Janny. "Tourists to the Rescue of a Wounded City: New York Finds Sympathy a Powerful Draw." *New York Times*, March 24, 2002.

Shalit, Ruth. "Brand New: How Do You Sell New York Now? Great Minds Are Working on It." *Wall Street Journal*, November 9, 2001.

Sheehy, Gail. "Fistful of Dollars: Featuring the Good, the Bad, and the Ugly: The Struggle for New York: Rupert Murdoch vs. Clay Felker, a Spaghetti Western." *Rolling Stone*, July 14, 1977.

Shefter, Martin. *Political Crisis/Fiscal Crisis: The Collapse and Revival of New York City*. New York: Columbia University Press, 1992.

Shiffman, Leon G., and Leslie Lazar Kanuk. *Consumer Behavior*. Englewood Cliffs, NJ: Prentice Hall, 2001.

Shorto, Russell. *The Island at the Center of the World: The Epic Story of Dutch Manhattan, the Forgotten Colony that Shaped America*. New York: Random House, 2004.

Simon, William E. *A Time for Truth*. New York: Reader's Digest Press, 1978.

Smith, Neil. *Uneven Development*. New York: Routledge, 1984.

—— "Gentrification, the Frontier and the Restructuring of Urban Space." In *Gentrification of the City*, edited by Neil Smith and Peter Williams. Boston: Allen and Unwin, 1986.

—— "Geography, Difference and the Politics of Scale." In *Postmodernism and the Social Sciences*, edited by Joe Doherty, Elspeth Graham, and Mo Malek. London: Macmillan, 1992.

—— *The New Urban Frontier: Gentrification and the Revanchist City*. New York: Routledge, 1996.

Sontag, Susan. "Notes on Camp." In *Against Interpretation and Other Essays*. New York: Picador, 2001.

Sorel, Edward. "Preview of Coming Attractions." *New York*, December 30, 1975.

Sorkin, Michael, ed. *Variations on a Theme Park: Scenes from the New American City and the End of Public Space*. New York: Hill and Wang, 1992.

—— and Sharon Zukin, eds. *After the World Trade Center: Rethinking New York City*. New York: Routledge, 2002.

Squires, Gregory. *Unequal Partnerships: The Political Economy of Urban Redevelopment in Postwar America*. New Brunswick, NJ: Rutgers University Press, 1989.

Stallybrass, Peter, and Alon White. *The Politics and Poetics of Transgression*. Ithaca, NY: Cornell University Press, 1986.

Starr, Roger. "Making New York Smaller." *New York Times Magazine*, November 14, 1976.

—— *The Rise and Fall of New York*. New York: Basic Books, 1989.

Stern, Ellen. "How to Make a Movie in New York." *New York*, December 30, 1975.

Stern, Robert A. M., Thomas Mellins, and David Fishman. *New York 1960: Architecture and Urbanism between the Second World War and the Bicentennial*. New York: Monacelli Press, 1995.

Sterne, Michael, "A Good Tourist Year Cited for New York: Convention and Visitors Bureau Reports Its Records Show 1976 was One of the City's Best," *New York Times*, January 4, 1977.

Stewart, Jack. "Subway Graffiti: An Aesthetic Study of Graffiti on the Subway System of New York City, 1970–1978." Ph.D. Dissertation, New York University, 1989.

Stohr, Kate. "I Sell New York." *Gotham Gazette*, March 2003.

Stone, Marvin. "Let Big Cities Die." *US News & World Report*, August 8, 1977.

Strasser, Susan. *Satisfaction Guaranteed: The Making of the American Mass Market*. New York: Pantheon, 1989.

Sugrue, Thomas J. *The Origins of the Urban Crisis: Race and Inequality in Postwar Detroit*. Princeton, NJ: Princeton University Press, 1996.

Tabb, William K. *The Long Default: New York City and the Urban Fiscal Crisis*. New York: Monthly Review Press, 1982.

Thompson, William C. *One Year Later: The Fiscal Impact of 9/11 on New York City*. New York: City of New York Office of the Comptroller, September 4, 2002.

Tobier, Emmanuel. "The Changing Face of Poverty: Trends in New York's Population in Poverty, 1960–1990." New York: Community Service Society, 1984.

Travel Industry Association of America. *Travel Industry Association of America: 60 Years of Service and Achievement, 1941–2001.* Washington, DC: Travel Industry Association of America, 2001.

"Unions vs. New York." *New York Times,* June 12, 1975.

US Department of Commerce, Bureau of the Census. *Tourism as a Job Creator.* Washington, DC: Area Redevelopment Administration, US Department of Commerce, June 1962.

—— *Tourist Industry and Redeveloped Areas.* Washington, DC: Area Redevelopment Administration, US Department of Commerce, July 1964.

Veblen, Thorstein. *The Theory of the Leisure Class.* New York: Modern Library, 1994.

Vicario, Lorenzo, and P. Manuel Martinez Monje. "Another 'Guggenheim Effect'? Central City Projects and Gentrification in Bilbao." In *Gentrification in a Global Context: The New Urban Colonialism,* edited by Rowland Atkinson and Gary Bridge. London: Routledge, 2005.

Vidich, Arthur. *The New Middle Classes: Life-Styles, Status Claims, and Political Orientations.* New York: New York University Press, 1995.

Waldinger, Roger. *Still the Promised City?: African-Americans and New Immigrants in Postindustrial New York.* Cambridge, MA: Harvard University Press, 1996.

Wallace, Deborah, and Roderick Wallace. *A Plague on Both Your Houses.* New York: Verso, 1998.

Walton, John. "Urban Sociology: The Contributions and Limits of Political Economy." *Annual Review of Sociology* 19 (1993).

Ward, Stephen V. *Selling Places: The Marketing and Promotion of Towns and Cities, 1850–2000.* New York: Routledge, 2000.

Warlaumont, Hazel G. *Advertising in the 60s: Turncoats, Traditionalists, and Waste Makers in America's Turbulent Decade.* London: Praeger, 2001.

Weinstein, Bernard L. and Robert E. Firestine. *Regional Growth in the United States.* New York: Praeger, 1978.

Weitzman, Joan. *City Workers and Fiscal Crisis: Cutbacks, Givebacks, and Survival.* New Brunswick, NJ: Rutgers University Press, 1979.

Wells Lawrence, Mary. "Baby Boom, Creative Boom." *Advertising Age,* June 18, 1990.

—— *A Big Life in Advertising.* New York: Alfred A. Knopf, 2002.

Whyte, William H. "End of the Exodus: The Logic of the Headquarters City." *New York,* September 20, 1976.

Williams, Raymond. *The Country and the City.* New York: Oxford University Press, 1973.

Wolfe, Tom. "Radical Chic: That Party at Lenny's." *New York,* June 8, 1970.

—— "The Birth of 'The New Journalism': Eyewitness Report by Tom Wolfe." *New York,* February 14, 1972.

Wolff, Michael. "35 Years: The Story of *New York.*" *New York,* April 7, 2003.

Working for America Institute. "US Hotels and Their Workers: Room for Improvement." Washington, DC: AFL-CIO, 2002.

Yankelovich, Daniel. "New Criteria for Market Segmentation." *Harvard Business Review* Spring (1964).

Yankelovich, Skelly, and White, Inc. *Research to Support New York State's Economic Development Activities: Discovery Phase: Qualitative Hypotheses.* Prepared for State of New York Department of Commerce, March 1977.

Yee, Lydia. "Photographic Approaches to the Discourse on the South Bronx." In *Urban Mythologies: The Bronx Remembered since the 1960s,* edited by John Allen Farmer. New York: The Bronx Museum of the Arts, 1999.

Zukin, Sharon. "A Decade of New Urban Sociology." *Theory and Society* 9 (1980).

—— *Loft Living: Culture and Capital in Urban Change.* New Brunswick, NJ: Rutgers University Press, 1989.

—— *Landscapes of Power: From Detroit to Disney World.* Berkeley: University of California Press, 1991.

—— "Space and Symbols in an Age of Decline." In *Urban Cultures Reader,* edited by Malcolm Miles, Tim Hall, and Iain Borden. London: Routledge, 2000.

—— *Point of Purchase: How Shopping Changed American Culture.* New York: Routledge, 2004.

—— *et al.* "From Coney Island to Las Vegas in the Urban Imaginary: Discursive Practices of Growth and Decline." *Urban Affairs Review* 33:5 (1998).

Index

@149st. 148
9/11 253–5, 256–7, 258–9, 305n2
21 Club 123
Abzug, Bella 174
advertising 59, 64, 298n18, 299n33, 300n78, n79; effect of psychographics on 196–8; effect on tourism 211–12; teaser ads 3, 5
Aid to Families with Dependent Children 242
Albany 109, 286n35
Alfred Politz Research 73
Alitalia 3, 5, 6, 267n4
Allen, Woody 151, 294–5n81
American Broadcasting Company (ABC) 51
American Manufacturing Company 197
Annie Hall (film, 1977) 294–5n81
Annie (musical) 208, 210
anti-urbanism 21–2, 25, 59, 269n9, 271n36
Apple Polishing Corps 118
Aronowitz, Stanley 289n104
arts/cultural development 51, 250–1, 305n66

asphalt jungle image 58–64, 66, 98, 100, 152–3, 164, 170, 236, 256
Associated Press 52
Association for a Better New York (ABNY) 15, 28, 99, 135, 161–2, 165, 167, 173–4, 176, 177, 201, 231, 233, 237, 256, 284n8, n9, 302n6; and the "Big Apple" campaign 115–16, 118–20; creation of 110–13, 286n41, n42, 286–7n50; and Fear City campaign 138, 139; legacies of 122–3; membership dues 113, 287n53; and the power breakfast 113–15; and putting pressure on television companies 120–2, 287n75; two-pronged approach 113–15, 287n52
Auletta, Ken 238–9
Aurelio, Richard 5
austerity policies 15–16, 219–22, 301n95
Austin, Joe 66

Badillo, Herman 143
Bambaataa, MC Africa 146
Baum, Joe 171, 173, 175
Baumgold, Julie 94